Adventurers All

There is a special aura of adventu...
You may begin in a one-room office and bra...
world . . . yet stay more-or-less in on...

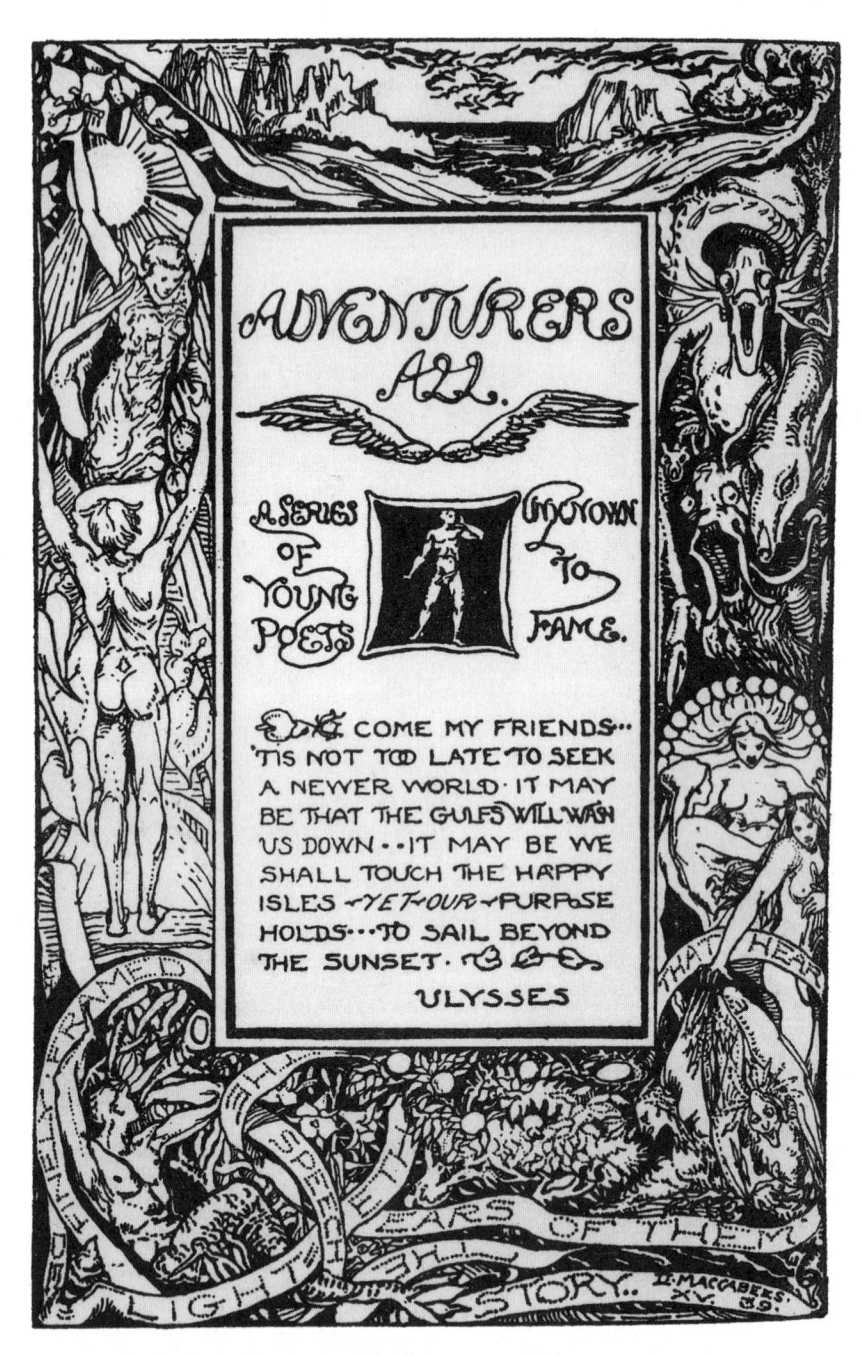

Frontispiece The first *Adventurers All*: title page opening.

LYRICAL POEMS

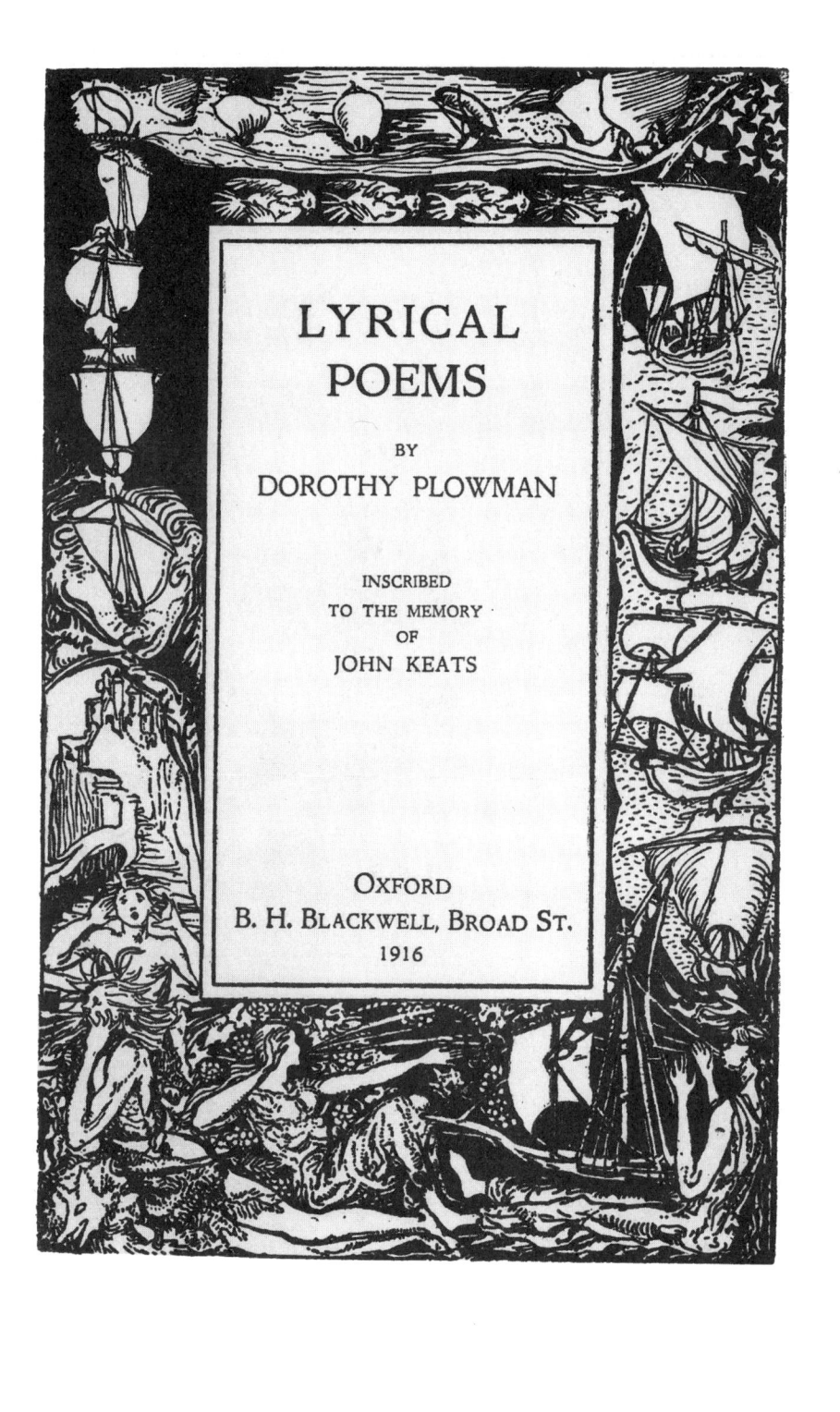

BY
DOROTHY PLOWMAN

INSCRIBED
TO THE MEMORY
OF
JOHN KEATS

OXFORD
B. H. BLACKWELL, BROAD ST.
1916

*To the memory of
Sir Basil Blackwell,
his fellow Blackwellians and
future generations of
booklovers*

Adventurers All

TALES OF BLACKWELLIANS
OF BOOKS, BOOKMEN, AND
READING AND WRITING FOLK

Sumite Castalios Nigris de fontibus haustus
From the Black Wells
draw ye the Muses draughts

COMPILED AND RE-TOLD BY

RITA RICKETTS

FOREWORD BY
JESSICA RAWSON
Warden of Merton College, Oxford

BLACKWELL'S · OXFORD

© 2002 by Blackwell's,
48–51 Broad Street, Oxford OX1 3BQ

The right of the Author to be identified as
the Author of this Work has been asserted
in accordance with the
Copyright, Designs and Patents Act 1988.

All rights reserved. No part of this publication
may be reproduced, stored in a retrieval system,
or transmitted, in any form
or by any means, electronic, mechanical, photocopying,
recording or otherwise, except as permitted by the
UK Copyright, Designs and Patents Act 1988,
without the prior permission of the publisher.

First published 2002 by Blackwell's

ISBN 0-946 344-35-3 (paperback)
ISBN 0-946 344-36-1 (hardback)

A catalogue record for this title is
available from the British Library

Set by Graphicraft Ltd, Hong Kong
Printed and bound in
Great Britain by
The Alden Press, Oxford

Contents

List of Illustrations, ix

Foreword, xi
JESSICA RAWSON

For Julian Blackwell, xiv

Acknowledgements, xvi

1 Introduction, 1
Setting out, 1
A fabulous wheel, 7
Of books and bookmen, 14
The literary man's house of call, 20
Grace before ploughing, 22
Beset by contradictions, 30
A venial fault, 33

2 Partners in Trade, 37
The 'First' Blackwells: Benjamin Harris and Nancy Blackwell, 37
Beginning in bookselling, 37
Mr Greatheart, 44
Anne Nancy Stirling Blackwell 1823–1887, 50

3 Merchant Scholar, 55
Benjamin Henry: the second B H Blackwell 1849–1924, 55
Growing pains, 55
An apprenticeship as lengthy as Jacob's was to Laban, 57
The name over the door, 61
Food for the soul, 79
Adventurers All, 82
Toiling in the vineyard, 88
A great and lone achievement, 101
Lydia (Lilla) Taylor Blackwell 1850–1927, 116

4 Play Days with Pegasus: Father and Son, 123
   Seven years of holiday!, 123
   Salad days, 128
   'An insight into publishing', 141
   Prompted to adventure, 147

5 The Gaffer, 179
   Basil Henry: the third B H Blackwell, 179
   A Jupiter of booksellers, 203
   Private pleasure: Marion Christine (Soans) Blackwell 1888–1977, 213
   Public duty, 225
   Knight of the Ring, 231
   Naturaliter Oxoniensis, 235
   Sir Gaffer, 247
   An independent spirit, 249
   News from everywhere, 252
   'The best read man in Britain', 258
   The Gypsy Scholar, 265
   Quiet, beneficent things, 269
   The final chapter, 272

Epilogue, 276
JOHN THWAITES

Postscript, 280
JULIAN BLACKWELL

Appendices, 283
1 Chronology, 283
2 The Gaffer's room, 288
3 Selected sources from the Blackwell archive and from Basil Blackwell's private papers, 292
4 Dramatis personae, 296
5 Gifts and bequests, 299
6 Play hours with Pegasus, 300

References, 302

Index, 315

List of Illustrations

Frontispiece The first *Adventurers All*: title page opening.		ii–iii
1	Julian Blackwell.	xiv
2	The cover of Wheels, published in 1916 and edited by Edith Sitwell: 'I sometimes think that all our thoughts are wheels'.	9
3	An upside down view of the Norrington Room.	28
4	Magdalen Bridge in 1814.	41
5	Benjamin Harris's gravestone in Holywell cemetery.	49
6	The exterior of the Broad Street shop in the early 1900s.	61
7	An internal view of the shop in the early 1900s.	62
8	The exterior of the shop in 2000.	63
9	The cover of catalogue No 1.	69
10	The participants in the Ripon Hall Conference in 1906.	74
11	Lilla Blackwell in 1906.	91
12	No 1 Linton Road from the garden.	93
13	Basil Henry Blackwell.	99
14	Basil Henry Blackwell and C Parker.	107
15	The Blackwell family and staff at Osse Field for Fred Hanks' jubilee celebrations, 29 June 1933.	110
16	Illustrations used for stationery and publicity between 1900 and 1950.	113
17	Basil Blackwell's room at Merton College.	127
18	Old Merton buildings: 'An Oxford which had hardly ceased from whispering from her towers the last enchantments of the Middle Age'.	129
19	Basil Blackwell and fellow students at the OUOTC Signal Section camp on Salisbury Plain in 1908: 'We felt that there was something extraordinary though indefinable in this quiet, shy little man, later known to history as Lawrence of Arabia'— he is seated, cross-legged, second from the right in front of Basil.	130
20	A parade at the OUOTC camp on Salisbury Plain in 1908.	131
21	A day on the river.	133

List of Illustrations

22 Basil (on the right) as an undergraduate, on the Merton barge. 134
23 The Merton eight with Austin Longland at the rear. 135
24 Sir Basil with the Blackwell coat of arms in Merton. 137
25 J M Dent in 1906. The Dent Memorial Lectures were founded in his memory. Sir Basil's was the first lecture of the series. 139
26 The cover of *Joy Street*. 146
27 The clerk of Oxenford from the Prologue of the Shakespeare Head *Chaucer*. 156
28 The opening page of the Prologue from the Shakespeare Head *Chaucer*. 158
29 The Gaffer in his Broad Street office, *c.* 1935. 164
30 The Gaffer and his secretary, Eleanor Halliday. 196
31 Angela Melvin with her son and Sir Basil—the oldest and the youngest of Blackwellians. 198
32 The Gaffer alongside the Muirhead Bone picture of the Broad Street interior. 204
33 Christine Blackwell—our lady of the daffodils—taking time out from taming her husband in the early 1970s. 215
34 Basil on holiday. 219
35 Basil with his family. 220
36 The Freedom of the City. 245
37 Basil at Osse Field. 254
38 John Thwaites, the manager of the Broad Street shop: 'Booksellers are a rare breed'. 277
Tailpiece The 1920 *Adventurers All*: title page opening. 318–319

Foreword

Basil Blackwell had regularly assured his friends, including my predecessor as Warden of Merton, that he intended to write his own 'history'. But he ran out of time. Shortly before his ninetieth birthday, he commissioned Sir Arthur Norrington to compile a book to mark the firm's centenary, in 1979. Time was of the essence, and using extensive taped interviews with Basil Blackwell, and subject drafts provided by the Blackwell family and employees, Sir Arthur Norrington duly wrote his account. His principal focus was on the commercial development of the Blackwell group of companies.

This present study by Rita Ricketts draws on a wider range of Sir Basil Blackwell's papers, collected together after his death. It describes the background of the Blackwells, and of those associated with them, in the context of Oxford and of a time in bookselling and publishing that is all but past. As her account reveals, the success of B H Blackwell's was, from its beginnings in 1846, inseparable from the people, time and place, that made it.

Sir Basil Blackwell is undoubtedly this study's central character; yet while his was the inspiration for the development of the firm in the twentieth century, he was fully aware of his dependence on all those who contributed to Blackwell's success over a century and a half of service to books and bookmen. In preserving, and recording their tales Sir Basil has provided much of the raw material for this latest study. It offers future generations a tantalisingly brief look at the lives of a cast of diverse people: from young boy-apprentices, to the grandees of politics and academia. Generations of writers, poets, academics and students habitually went to Blackwell's, not only for help with their research, but also to get their 'results' published. Within a year of the opening of the familiar Broad Street shop, in 1879, the imprint, B H Blackwell was launched. Later, at the instigation of Basil Blackwell, Blackwell's pioneered school textbooks and was in the forefront of scientific publishing, supporting the broadening of the traditional academic curriculum. At the same time, affordable editions of the classics were produced alongside finely printed collections of belles-lettres. In this way, Basil Blackwell expanded the work, and dreams, of his father.

Although the Blackwell's story begins before Queen Victoria came to the throne, it touches on social, political, economic and literary issues still relevant, contentious even, today. As Chairman and Chief Executive of the family business, Basil Blackwell had sought to extract a liberal synthesis from the competing political ideologies of capitalism and socialism, which would enable him to run a business where the individual benefited from both systems. The early B H Blackwells, Benjamin Harris and his son Benjamin Henry, and the subsequent Blackwell apprentices, were self-made men. But in turn they played their own part in the public crusade to secure wider, and continuing, access to education.

Concerned as he was with the education of others, Basil Blackwell's father was equally determined that his own son should have the access he himself had been denied as a youth. Showing some aptitude for classics, a trait both his father and grandfather had exhibited, Basil was offered a postmastership at Merton in 1907. He was the first person to go to university in his family, and, initially, he was daunted by the prospect. But he soon found kindred spirits among those 'who had been early imbued with the untroubled faith and the moral discipline which was in the best tradition of devout Victorian churchmanship'. And Chapel was indeed a daily feature of life at Merton at the turn of the century. Yet, for all his high-mindedness, Basil Blackwell was no ascetic; his studies often took second place to rowing, and tutorials meant more than 'just being taught'. 'Talking, walking and playing' was how he described his intercourse with his Merton tutors, in those 'last golden days' before the Great War. Subsequently, he wrote, 'I seldom enter my beloved College without a pang, for the names of so many of my contemporaries are engraved on the memorial to those killed'.

In his sixties, Sir Basil Blackwell was elected an Honorary Fellow of Merton College. Recalling Horace's words: '*Hoc erat in votes . . . nil amplius oro*', he insisted that 'unlike Virgil's husbandman, he did know his good fortune'. Merton had given him so much already: friendships from undergraduate days, a partner Adrian Mott (whom he called 'the keeper of his conscience'), the companionship of successive generations of young Fellows, and the continuous hospitality of the Common Room. As a measure of his esteem, he assembled a collection of the printed books of Aldus Manutius, the late fifteenth century Venetian friend of scholars, printer, publisher, and bookseller—'the man who cut the folio down to pocket size—the Dolphin which preceded the Penguin'. These volumes are much treasured by the College and have added immeasurably to the ancient Library.

Foreword xiii

The current President of Blackwell's, Sir Basil Blackwell's son Julian, has arranged for the Blackwell's archive to be lodged permanently in Merton College Library, and it will be openly available for research. As part of the proposed changes in Fellow's Quad, a room will be dedicated to the name of Sir Basil Blackwell, in his memory and also in recognition of the years of service given to the College, and the University, by Blackwell's.

Oxford, too, both as a city and a University, plays an important role in the story; all of the characters in the book have a connection with Oxford. And Blackwell's is an Oxford institution through and through. The first Blackwell bookseller, Benjamin Harris, had chosen to settle in Oxford, opening a small shop just over Magdalen Bridge, in 1846, and he was Oxford's first City Librarian. And here, in Oxford, the Blackwell's have remained, into the fifth generation, eschewing the temptations of the London commercial scene. Blackwell's, in conjunction with the Colleges of the University, has also helped to forge links with students, teachers and researchers from around the world.

Nonetheless, the University remained, and still remains, at the heart of Blackwell's work. This present study explains how a small bookshop, started in a room barely twelve feet square, became a legend in the academic bookselling world. The Blackwell family and its aspirations to support and advance education and learning have provided an essential part of the fabric of the University and the City.

JESSICA RAWSON
Oxford 2001

For Julian Blackwell

Writing at the time of his retirement in 1954, Sir Adrian Mott had these words to say about 'the latest family recruit': Julian Blackwell. 'He is a brilliant rowing man. From what I have seen of him, in his early days, I am sure he has a quiet reserve of character which means that he is a person to be reckoned with, who will soon take his place in the hierarchy of the firm'.

1 Julian Blackwell.

Julian became a prime mover in the firm and served his term as Chairman. He is now President of Blackwell's, and is still 'a force to be reckoned with'. It was Julian Blackwell who made possible the research, compilation and publication of these Blackwellian Tales. Without his doggedness, enthusiasm, encouragement and inspiration, they would not have been told.

Acknowledgements

First, my very special thanks to Julian Blackwell for all his support; his enthusiasm started and sustained the project, and to his sister, Corinna Wiltshire, and two former Blackwellians, whose dedicated work made it possible to resurrect the archives. To Dudley Lincoln, who encouraged and reassured 'the worker', while he was advising on the physical restoration of the room where the Blackwells, Benjamin Henry, and his son, Basil, had worked. Without the backing of Blackwell Publishing the book could not have been produced; John Robson edited and designed the book and was ever on the end of the telephone with firm reassurance. Other Blackwellians, too, were instrumental: Phil Browne, Angela Melvin, Ken New, Peter Berry (Blackwell's Tours) and many other 'academic advisors' on the shop floor, across many departments, as well as Philip Carpenter, Editor Blackwell Publishing. The patience of John Thwaites, the Manager of Blackwell's, stands out. John, who was Blackwell's Manager of the Year in 2000, had a start and a consequent success in bookselling somewhat reminiscent of Benjamin Henry's; like Basil Blackwell, John grew up 'over' a shop. In his office, busy Seniors: Alison, Tony, Ross and Owen, were great providers of calm, tea, sympathy and chocolate biscuits, and the night porter, John, a student worker, stayed on several occasions, keeping the shop open beyond the call of duty.

Sir Basil Blackwell's old College turned up trumps: I would like to thank the Warden of Merton, the librarians: Steven Gunn (Fellow in History) and Julia Walworth, and the archivist Michael Stansfield, and both Merton and St John's for their hospitality and for giving me a respite in which I could both begin and finish the work. The Blackwell archives will now be put into Merton's scholarly, and safe, hands; a move which would have gladdened the heart of Sir Basil Blackwell. The work was made easier when I was able to see, at will, all the old Blackwell imprints; thanks to the help, and time, of Steven Tomlinson of 'Western Manuscripts' in the Bodleian. A scholar-worker, Steven unravelled the mysteries of the catalogue system and found 'lost poems'. Staff at the new, Old Bank, and former students Lara Feigel and Jessica Mautner, and colleagues provided a captive audience for the litmus

Acknowledgements

test of a story's appeal. Tommy Ricketts and Charlie Swing, the younger generation of computer-literates, were ever at hand to guide the incompetent. Charlie was dedicated, in words and deed, to the finishing of the manuscript. As soon as her term finished, Charlie swung into action correcting material and preparing inventories. She was a paragon!

The Ricketts ménage and Matt Devine deserve special mention; they played their part, especially, says Jessie, 'making lots of cups of tea and going food shopping': they tolerated their mother, who, quite lost in the stories of the Victorian Blackwell's, often forgot her duties and was not as receptive as she should have been to the 'looting' tendencies of her two-year-old grandson, Nicolas. Colleagues at City of Westminster College picked up tedious administration, which the author also neglected, and former colleagues at South Hampstead High School and Tormead gave powerful doses of support, in a variety of ways. I am also very grateful for the support, the 'smooth running of things', occasioned by University College School, especially Bill Jones, Stuart Fitzgerald and Simon Bloomfield, with their timely 'blessing' of the Barbados cricket tour! This, together with the institution of 'the gap year' reprieved me from 'teen-care' long enough to finish the book. Various friends played a part in helping me to complete the whole task, research and writing, in less than a year: Clare and Jonathan Graffi, Christie and Anthamos Georgeades, Diana and Charles Goodhart, David Larman, Frank Schwalba-Hoth, Jackie Williams, Rose Beauchamp, Jean Watson, Judy and Mark Lane, Hilary King, Maggie and Bob, Paul and Alison Snow, Jenny and Phil Mitchell and conspirators, Amena, Trish, Kirsty and Judy S.

Finally, I had to come up to the mark for my friends Christine Castle and Peta Georgeades. Peta, especially, was amused, comforted and reassured by my renderings of early drafts of stories of Blackwell's goings-on, in her last cheerful months before she succumbed to cancer, a scourge which had claimed the lives of many in this book. Her verdict on the Blackwells men and women, stands: 'good, modest, well-mannered people who set an example. They worked hard, they loved books and valued the pursuit of knowledge for its own sake. Judging by their stories, they had no side and knew how to treat people from all walks of life. The Blackwells were storytellers, and I only wish I had been able to hear more of them'. I only hope I have done them, and her, justice.

Chapter 1
Introduction

Setting out

Shall it be my lot to go that way again,
I may give those that desire my account[2]

By the close of the good old, bad old, 'swinging' sixties, almost nothing would have been familiar to the early Blackwells; except, of course, for the timeless Classics, sitting, still, on the shelves of the Broad Street shop. The new literature broke the old rules, and put words, and ideas, into common usage that had previously been censored, hidden behind metaphor, allusion or brown paper covers. Philip Larkin had discovered, in his library perhaps:

> Sexual intercourse began
> In nineteen sixty-three
> (Which was rather late for me)—
> Between the end of the Chatterley ban
> And the Beatles first LP.[3]

Impervious to censorship, he had taught us neophytes that parents 'f . . . you up'. Parents, on the other hand, found their children profoundly troubling, with their unkempt long hair and 'unsuitable flowing, and flowery, kaftans', seen even on their sons! They didn't understand their offspring's music, wishing that Lucy would go into the bank, 'you must have a proper job dear', and stop dreaming of diamonds in the sky; going to the moon, however, was a realistic option. Technology had not yet made the jump that would have enabled us to watch England's legendary World Cup win, in 'glorious Technicolor'. Worse, our money was under threat: the government wanted to do away with pounds, shillings and pence, and, so that we wouldn't notice any ill effects, they first devalued the pound. To mark its passing, the Blackwell's flag was flown at half-mast. Picture yourself, then, having been on a boat on the river arriving at Blackwell's turnstile only to bump into its sprightly eighty-year-old Gaffer, a man with a kaleidoscope mind.

That is how I met Sir Basil Blackwell. Unlike 'your mum and dad', he admired the hippy garb: a faded, but embroidered, purple robe, untidy

('Can't you tie it back!') long hair, and shaggy sheepskin. Seeing me hesitating in the doorway—I was afraid I had bumbled into an exclusive club—he smiled winningly. 'Something very reminiscent of Morris', he muttered as he steered me into 'Literature'. 'Who?' I asked, not understanding. 'You', he said teasingly. Gaining interest I turned on him: hadn't I tried to emulate Morris with my own hand-printed tie and dye? What did the older generation know of one of my anti-capitalist heroes, I wondered? Quite a lot, as I soon found out. By now we had arrived on the first floor and I was being escorted into his inner sanctum. There, on the wall, was an original, hand-printed William Morris wallpaper, appositely named 'Powdered', circa 1874. 'Ever thought of a career in bookselling?' he asked me, pulling down volumes of books from his shelves. I must have looked horrified, for he didn't wait for an answer; instead, he tucked a copy of a book, *Beginning in Bookselling*, under my arm and showed me around the 'estate'. We went upstairs to where he had been born, a digression of some thirty minutes or more, and ended up in the lavatory, to view an ancient, but very finely tiled, water closet. 'What do you like to read?' he asked, gesturing at his own selection, lining the walls. 'Keats', I replied. 'Do you', he noted. 'I prefer Milton', he suggested, after a pause. 'Yes, I like him too', I quickly added. No longer apprehensive, I joined in his game: we capped each other's quotes, mostly from the well-known sonnets, and I was forced to retire, gratefully, long before he did. Thus began a beautiful friendship, on my part that is; he would not have remembered what must have been for him a regular kind of exchange. I never forgot his kindness to a total stranger off the street, and listened out for news of him. His death, in 1984, was reported in the New Zealand Press, where I was lecturing at the time.

For many years, after Sir Basil's death, Julian Blackwell had talked about his father's papers; but Julian was too busy, immersed in the daily running of Blackwell's, to do anything with them. When he retired as Blackwell's chairman, he had many projects in mind, one of which was a permanent memorial to his father, and the founders of Blackwell's: his grandfather, Benjamin Henry, and great-grandfather, Benjamin Harris. But what form should this take? Finishing another year of teaching, now in England, and able to find some quiet time at St John's, I suggested that we look at his father's personal papers and see what they were saying. As we read through the papers, five related projects, already half in bud in Julian's mind, crystallized. First, there was more than enough material in the archive to reconstruct his father's and grandfather's old office at Broad Street, a room that had been his country grandmother's sitting room and where his father had played as a child.

Secondly, after finding and restoring to its owner, the Library at St John's, a fragment that related to the Housman collection, the entire archive of papers seemed to beg a permanent home; lest, as Goethe said, 'We lay them aside never to read them again, and at last we destroy them out of discretion, and so disappears the most beautiful, the most immediate breath of life, irrecoverable for ourselves and for others'. Thus, thirdly, after some discussion with the Warden and Librarians of Merton, it was agreed that the Blackwell's archive should have a final, and safe, resting place, joining the collection of rare books that Sir Basil Blackwell had amassed for his old College during his lifetime. Fourthly, the Warden, Professor Jessica Rawson, in discussion with Julian, agreed that a seminar room, in the old quad, would be named in his father's honour.

Lastly, there remained the question of what to do with all the information in the papers. It just couldn't be put back into the boxes, to await a future chronicler; these tales of Blackwellians, many of which had been collected, and then penned, by Sir Basil, seemed resolute, they had to make an appearance. I was, willy-nilly, to be the their medium—their ghost writer. However daunting a task, I would be employed by very agreeable ghosts, who wouldn't lie down until their adventures, many of which had been passed on orally, were written down. Many of their stories were, of course, written down, and were in front of me, contained in the copious—and very diverse—writings, drafts, letters, articles, speeches and musings of Sir Basil. Basil Blackwell had always intended to write his own account, even though he wasn't sure if it would be of interest to others[4]. In the address to the congregation of the University of Oxford, on the occasion of Sir Basil Blackwell's admission as a Doctor of Civil Law, 27 June 1979, the Public Orator referred to the idea, 'put forward by that true Blackwellian, William (Rex) King', for a 'Boswell' to 'come forth and undertake the pleasing task of doing justice to the life and character of Benjamin Henry Blackwell'[5]. The earliest recorded call for a written record of the Blackwells had come earlier from the famous author, Dorothy L Sayers, who had cut her own literary teeth in the Blackwell's workrooms. But Sir Basil's sister Dorothy, writing in the mid-twentieth century, had doubted that the spirited tales of Blackwell's, mostly passed on by word of mouth, could be re-captured in writing. Fortunately this did not deter her. She left behind notes on the lives of her father and mother that recreated the sense of her gently austere father, the second B H Blackwell, and his independent and vivacious school teacher wife, Lilla. Benjamin Henry Blackwell, who had re-founded the Oxford firm, had been a man of few words and had not thought to provide an account of his life. For him the physical products of his labours, and the labours of his children, had provided record and legacy enough.

Sadly, none of the papers, and the love-letters Sir Basil Blackwell referred to, of the first B H Blackwell have survived, save for a scrap or two of invoices and a cutting reporting his untimely death, but Dorothy, listening to her father, recorded his accounts of Benjamin Harris's beginnings. A few of the second B H Blackwell's, Benjamin Henry's own scribblings have survived, on old scraps of minute book—he would never have wasted paper; he was a conservationist of Ruskin proportions. (Such was his interest in the preservation of the countryside, and the environment, that he might well have been a Green today; he was the first Liberal on Oxford City Council). Some selected material had already been put together for the study undertaken by Sir Arthur Norrington, commissioned to commemorate the Blackwell's Centenary. Sir Arthur Norrington, who worked for Oxford University Press and was a President of Trinity, Oxford, and Vice-Chancellor to the University of Oxford from 1960–62, tells the story of B H Blackwell Ltd, the two publishing firms—Basil Blackwell Publisher and Blackwell Scientific Publications—and that of many associated enterprises such as Munksgaard in Denmark and Blackwell North America. His order was much appreciated by this, present, cutter and paster. However, much material remained undusted, some was lost and some has yet to be discovered.

If Benjamin Henry was spare in his writing habits, his son, Basil was not. Shortly before Basil Blackwell died, in 1984, the *Oxford Times* declared that 'The man can almost be heard in the printed record, as can Lord Melbourne and the Duke of Wellington, both of whom died only a few years before the Gaffer's grandfather'. As I read Basil Blackwell's papers, they led me to investigate the books put out under the B H Blackwell imprint. Leafing through the early poetry series, I came across the title *Adventurers All: A Series of Young Poets Unknown to Fame*. The Blackwells played Ulysses: they were brave enough to take the risk of launching poets, at their own expense: 'Come my friends, tis not too late, to seek a newer world. It may be that the gulfs will wash us down. It may be we shall touch the happy isles. Yet our purpose holds: to sail beyond the sunset'. Unable to resist this call, I, too, set out. At first I thought my travels would take me no further than my desk. Given the quality of Sir Basil's accounts, there was no need for a Boswell, and I had all of the equipment necessary: a pair of scissors and a pot of glue; more accurately a word processor that did a very good cut and paste job. But it wasn't really that simple. I soon realized, what every professional biographer already knows, that the scribe gets in the way of material, and the material gets in the way of the scribe. In John Worthen's preface to *The Gang: Coleridge, the Hutchinsons and the Wordsworths*, he warns of the difficulties of the job: 'We write biographies of individuals as islands; we live as part of the mainland' and we cannot possibly tell the whole truth about individuals. In her recent book, *My East End*, Gilda O'Neill tells us that 'much of what we call history . . . the factual representation of the past, is as much to do with opinion, faith, dogma as any philosophical or religious system of belief'. This history, like hers, is interspersed with written and oral accounts where the participants, the characters in the book, have 'explained the meaning of the past . . . and thus the meaning of the present' for themselves.

Guided by the experts, I have tried to play it straight: concentrating on the main characters, and the interpretation of events from their point of view. But the stories, too, had their way; they set me off on adventures to times, and to places, that I didn't know, and I had to learn more about. Just finding my way through the minefield of Sir Basil's allusions and other people's epigrams, which he promiscuously coined, would have been journey enough for the faint-hearted. His 'selections' spoke for themselves: they put their part of the story better than I ever could have done. (I have included a selection of these quotes, many of which were family favourites at the time, and I have tried faithfully to source their origins). And I was hooked. Reading through the papers, I became a time-traveller, I ricocheted between Georgian England and the late twentieth century. My Odyssey started outside a small room in St Clements, Oxford, and took me to another tiny room, in Broad Street, from where I set sail beyond the shores of England. My adventures were not just restricted to the physical world: I was in training as an intellectual mountaineer; as Sir Basil would have said, one:

> Who turned at will, and with the same delight
> From Alpine Summits to the steeper height
> Of the mind's mountains.

I scaled the heights of little known Victorian and Edwardian poets, overhearing their wrangling and left guessing at the rivalry and in-fighting that must have gone on. I discovered their ageless origins in Horace, and in fragments of Housman:

> Into my heart an air that kills
> From yon far country blows:
> What are those blue remembered hills,
> What spires, what farms are those?

> That is the land of lost content,
> I see it shining plain
> And happy highway where I went
> And cannot come again[6].

I learned of the antics of the Blackwell apprentices, in the attics at Broad Street; I was brought down to earth in the lodgings, down by the canal, of a single mother, struggling to raise her three children. Here, beneath the iron girders and the broken glass:

> A savage woman screamed at me from a barge: little children began to cry;
> The untidy landscape rose to life; a sawmill started;
> A cart rattled down to the wharf, and workmen clanged over the iron footbridge;
> A beautiful old man nodded from the first storey window of a square red house,
> And a pretty girl came out to hang up clothes in a small delightful garden.
> O strange motion in the suburb of a country town: slow regular movements of the dance of death!
> Men and not phantoms are these that move in light
> Forgotten they live . . . [7]

Escaping the City, the stench of the canal was buried in the scent of old roses, and an Oxfordshire country garden, in Appleton, 'swept me back to those dusky mysterious hours in an Oriental storehouse when the rugs and carpets of Isfahan and Bokara and Samarkand were unrolled in their clothing and richness of texture . . . Rich they were, rich as a fig broken open, soft as a ripened peach, freckled as an apricot, coral as a pomegranite'[8]. Leaving their profligacy, I was transported down river to Kelmscott Manor, glimpsing Dante Rosetti's misty characters, which I hardly recognized as Morris's at this stage. Lurking in the muddy waters was 'The Ring', not the Tolkein one; it was found out about, a Knight won his spurs, and it was, more-or-less, vanquished. Other dangers threatened: the curses of pornography and crime. All was seen to be done on the Royal Bench of British justice, and Sir Basil dispensed his own qualities of mercy, as a Magistrate in the Juvenile Courts. Reading on, I encountered characters, major and minor, such as now rest in George Eliot's unvisited tombs, and the books they haled from. Unlike the days of the first B H Blackwell's, these classics are now widely available in easily affordable editions; and the Blackwells had played more than a modest role in this revolution. This revolution in publishing introduced me to a new language, not Anglo-Saxon, or Middle English, but the 9 pt Plantin of these affordable classics, with its neatly letter-spaced small capitals, cropped ascenders and descenders and Bullen's Caslon setting. Where, I wondered, would this take me?

Among the Blackwells' papers, I seemed beset by revolutions in every field, not just in publishing, and their history seemed in so many ways to chart our own: the ascendancy of a new educated class, the growth of the new universities, the development of a mass culture and mass consumerism, Britain's changing place in the world and the changing status of women and the family, the growth of a differentiated children's market and the revolution in information technology. Writing in 1976, Richard Blackwell had asked that the history of the firm should reflect this matrix: 'the context (of Blackwell's) has grown from local to national to international, and has been social, economic and political'[9]. And the Blackwells, like it or not, were going round on this big wheel.

A fabulous wheel

I sometimes think that all our thoughts are wheels

One of Basil Blackwell's earliest adventures in publishing poetry, in 1916, was a series called 'Wheels'. It was edited by Edith Sitwell, and the title poem was by Nancy Cunard:

> I sometimes think that all our thoughts are wheels
> Rolling forever through the painted world,
> Moved by the cunning of a thousand clowns
> Dressed paper-wise, with blatant rounded masks,
> That take their multi-coloured caravans
> From place to place, and act and leap and sing,
> Catching the spinning hoops when cymbals clash.
> And one is dressed as Fate, and one as Death,
> The rest that represent Love, Joy and Sin,
> Join hands in solemn stage-learnt ecstasy,
> While Folly beats a drum with golden pegs,
> And mocks that shrouded Jester called Despair.
> The dwarves and other curious satellites,
> Voluptuous-mouthed, with slyly-pointed steps,
> Strut in the circles while the people stare—
> And some have sober faces white with chalk,
> And roll the heavy wheels all through the streets

> Of sleeping hearts, with ponderance and noise
> Like weary armies on a solemn march—
> Now in the scented gardens of the night,
> Where we are scattered like a pack of cards,
> Our words are turned to spokes that thoughts may roll
> And form a jangling chain around the world,
> (Itself a fabulous wheel controlled by Time
> Over the slow incline of centuries.)
> So dreams and prayers and feelings born of sleep
> As well as all the sun-gilt pageantry
> Made out of summer breezes and hot noons,
> Are in the great revolving of the spheres
> Under the trampling of their chariot wheels.

What caught my particular attention was the way the Blackwells had tried to 'get off the wheel'; they were not to be constrained simply by their place in time and in society; they had wanted 'to relate the new order to the one dying or dead': to help scholars with their task of showing 'the continuity of the spirit of mankind in their assessment and understanding of the human predicament'[10]. Chiefly of interest to me, were the political paradoxes: the Blackwells were entrepreneurs, and committed to private enterprise, but they were passionately dedicated to improving the lot of the individual, and promoting the general good: 'we are bold to demand a standing among the most important societies for the improvement of man, physically, socially, morally and intellectually'. The Blackwells were, however, anything but prosaic, or paternalistic for that matter, in their practices. Theirs was the age of the worker-owner, rather than the tycoon; and Julian Blackwell remembered this being instilled into him as a raw recruit. Sir Basil, writing of the death of his own father, had chosen the lines: 'Now he his worldly task has done, home has gone and ta'en his wages'. Benjamin Henry was always grateful for the wages he earned. He and his wife Lilla had both known, as children, what it was to be poor. Given his parents' experiences, it was so easy for Basil to imagine situations, brought about by family circumstances and/or outside economic forces, where a livelihood, and thence security, could be removed. It was not surprising to find that the Blackwells were liberals, but that they were also sympathetic to the tenets of the Guild, and the later, Fabian Socialism.

The Blackwells trained craftsmen as individuals, not workers; introduced above average levels of wages; agitated for a shorter working week, at a time when the working week, and the working day, allowed no time for leisure; and encouraged and paid for their employees to 'better' themselves, enabling

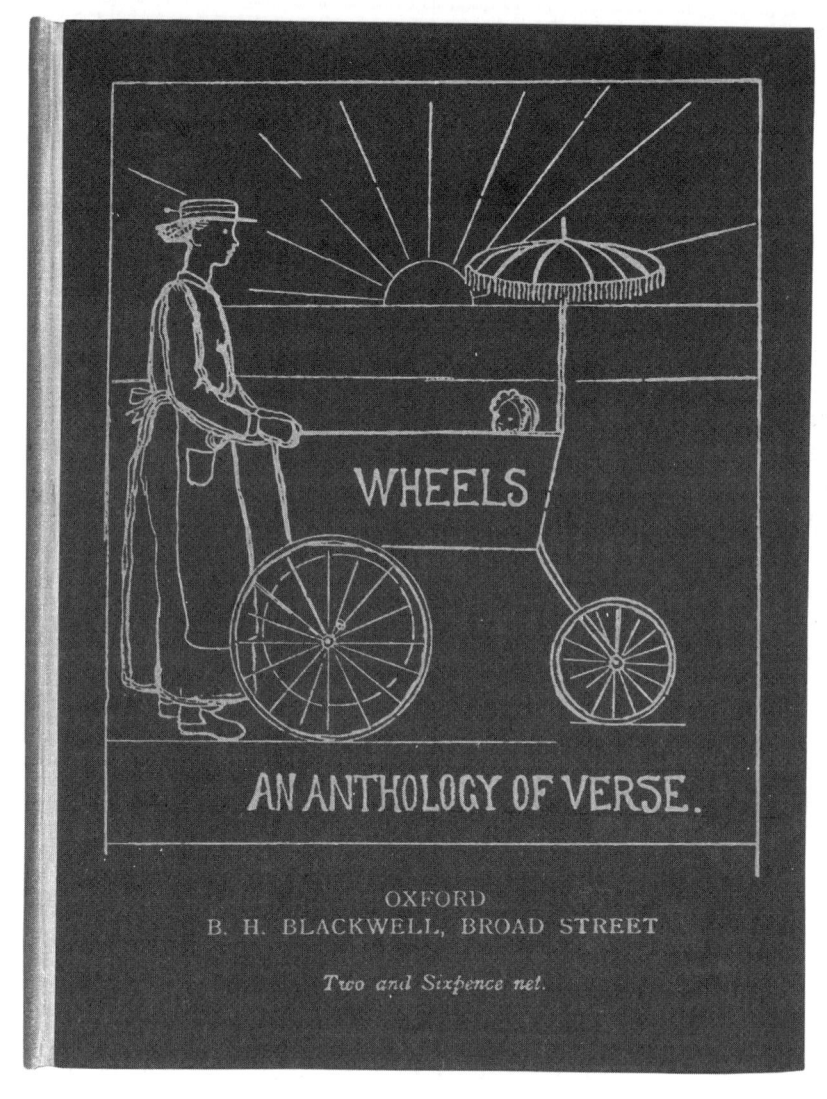

2 The cover of *Wheels*, published in 1916 and edited by Edith Sitwell: 'I sometimes think that all our thoughts are wheels'.

them to go to evening classes and, later, to study for extra-mural degrees. Before there was statutory regulation, and equal opportunity policies, the Blackwells had devised schemes that gave their staff share holdings, annual paid holidays, and life retirement pensions. Above all, the staff were part of the family community; they were given 'ownership' in the business, and the chance to go from the bottom to the top rung of the ladder. Sir Basil Blackwell had always wanted to reconcile the contradictions of capitalism and socialism, at least in his own workplace: for if the 'living intellect be corrupt or mischievous, what potency there for evil'. 'The truth', Sir Basil had written, 'is that all power is two-edged. The knife can kill or cure, gas may be a minister of mercy or torture'. 'Aristotle', Sir Basil's writings reminded me, 'built his theory of ethics on this *potentiality of contraries* in all the faculties of the soul of man.' Squaring this circle was a dilemma for the Blackwells. The Greek mythologists divined it before them:

O father of all of us, Paian Apollo,
Destroyer and healer, hear!

The Blackwells, father and son, had wrestled with the text 'what doth it profit a man if he should gain the whole world and lose his own soul?', a sentiment of which I continually, monotonously, remind my own children when they hassle me for 'state-of-the-art' trainers or Sky TV. Materialism, something the post Thatcher generation have again begun to question, was profoundly worrying for the Blackwells. Sir Basil continually referred to its contradictions in his writing: the issues surrounding the money changers in the temple, the rich man denied the Kingdom of Heaven, the temptations of the physical world, and the concerns of C S Lewis's *Screwtape*, together with the problem of pain, were puzzles he never solved. The Blackwells found some comfort, and they appealed to their more Victorian bent, in the austere sentiments of Milton (the poet I had learned to love when I was 'force-fed' him as part of the old 'O Level' Literature paper). Sober and steadfast, they took comfort from his advice that 'who best bear his mild yolk he serves him best'; and their simple, religious faith sustained them. I could relate to this: as a child I had dreamed away my life on the wooden pews of the local church, and in my head I could hear the hymns so familiar to the Victorian Blackwells. They were all pillars of 'The Church's One Foundation'.

Sheaving through Sir Basil's papers, in his spidery, but beautifully formed, hand, or on tissue-thin carbon copies, products of the good old-fashioned typewriter, I found stories of Sir Basil's own boyhood trials. He had been tempted by the flesh; marched to church in his Sunday best, he found himself wishing for a finer outfit. Arriving at church, his eyes were riveted on the splendidly attired Mr Vincent, the People's Warden. Basil should, of course, have been listening to the sermon, and if he had listened, he should have felt ashamed. As it was, the words of the sermon were lost on him as he examined the finery of Mr Vincent's silk hat and frock coat. But, as Basil's father must have pointed out, appearances weren't everything, even in those days, and more usually, Mr Vincent could be found in a journeyman's apron and old cloth cap in charge of the compositors in the family's printing firm. I reflected on the Blackwells' accounts of their church-going, which suggested an amendment to conventional wisdom: the Church of England was not only the place where the middle classes could be found at prayer, but, more commonly perhaps, the haven, and starting point, for the self-educated, as keen to make their way in the spiritual world as in the temporal. Education, in earlier times, for those without private means, was, mostly, only to be had at the hands of the churches. But these venerable institutions were not, on their own, able to provide universal education.

The liberal Blackwells saw an important role for the State, in education, as well as in the provision of other goods. As luck would have it, the progress of the Blackwells mirrored the changes in public education, and their work gave impetus to the changes; they paraded new subjects on their shelves, and published books in the technical fields of chemical engineering, medicine and social science. Education of the public, and individual self-betterment, had featured in almost everything they had done, either as individuals or Masters of Blackwell's. Before the family name was known, the earlier Blackwells had pioneered a branch of the teetotal movement in Oxford, providing a library and a tearoom, as an alternative to the public house. Benjamin Harris had helped to start the first public library, working until late to keep the doors open for working people so that they, too, could find Paradise in the world of books. His son, Benjamin Henry, of necessity a self-made man, had taught himself, learning poetry on his morning runs in Christ Church meadow, and Latin and Greek in his 'spare time'—what 'spare time'? Most Blackwellians who later played key roles in the management of the firm, some becoming Directors and 'Vice-Presidents' even, had come via the self-made route. Blackwellians were scholars of the world university, and 'of one of the better colleges—the one of Blackwell's', wrote Hugh Dyson, Fellow of Merton; where students 'did not live in a world where the young are paid and begged to read and think and talk and study, but in a world in which you had to pay for, and earn, all your privileges'.

Privilege was not a word that would ever have sprung to mind when I thought of the workload of the Blackwellian booksellers. They were in the business of 'service' from noon to night, for the best part of six days a week. To Basil's way of thinking, their lot could be summed up by Chaucer:

> For whan thy labour doon al is,
> And hast y-made thy rekeninges,
> Thou gost hoom to thy hoos anoon
> And also domb as any stoon,
> Thou sittest at another boke,
> Til fully clasived is thy loke.

And this wasn't just the staff; the first Blackwell had worked himself to death, the second customarily worked until he dropped, each night; and his son, Basil, I am told, was usually first over the threshold of the shop every morning. When, on the other hand, the earlier Blackwellians had had a moment of free time, there were fewer distractions: reading, rather than television, or fiddling with text messaging or e-mails, played a dominant role in their non-working lives. Skilled craftsmen were, in every way, as scholarly as their more fortunate contemporaries, as Sir Basil pointed out, when he said he preferred school-leavers to university graduates. The former were, in his opinion, 'in the best Victorian, and Edwardian, tradition of those with a love of learning and scholarship for its own sake'.

Although the Blackwells became famous for their legendary knowledge of books and their consummate service, obsequious they were not; they never could abide the divide between Town and Gown. And they had their share of little difficulties with both. It was in their character to inveigh against injustice, especially when perpetrated by governments and bureaucracies; for Basil Blackwell 'bureaucracy was next only in evil to dictatorship'. In fact, anything that harmed the individual was anathema to them, especially seeing generations of cannon-fodder dragged into war, by the authorities. Sir Basil had lost old friends that way; he had been tortured by the tales of the First World War Poets, and had published some of Wilfred Owen's poetry, to provide 'passing-bells for these who die as cattle'. But governments didn't learn; less than thirty years later, they were manufacturing nuclear weapons. Basil Blackwell, in his far off Garsington days, before the Great War, had sat at the feet of Bertrand Russell, and heard his gloomy prognostications. Later, when an aged Russell was in full flood in his 'ban the bomb', CND, mode, Sir Basil had written dismally of the 'potentiality of contraries' in the physical world that had 'reached its apogee in the atomic bomb'. All the Blackwells had witnessed the ill effects of man's inhumanity to man, from Balaclava to the Somme, from Dunkirk to Hiroshima, and, later, in the killing fields of Vietnam. What would they have felt, I wondered, about the new, nationalistic, European wars? Sir Basil had supported European political and economic co-operation, as an insurance against this worse kind of narrow nationalism.

Yet, the Blackwells were fiercely patriotic and personified the English way of life of the last two centuries; a way of life that is now a chimera much sought after by tourists to Oxford.

Against the social, political and economic backdrop, which was the commercial life of the Blackwells, was their literary life, both outward and inward. Through them I was reunited with the lines of writers and poets that had been buried in the maelstrom of my daily life; they made me stand and wait. Tiring of Milton's command, although his advice helped me to let everything sink in, I sought further adventures. I stalked the local repositories of knowledge, the City and County libraries, and discovered the underworld of the Bodleian. Here I was given generous helpings of advice and the sight of yet more material: threads of the Blackwell story in the published work of writers and journalists, not just from Oxford, but from around the world. Other professionals in the book trade added to the store. Staff at Blackwell's, retailing and publishing, and in the antiquarian department, took me under their wing and put me right. Seeking respite, 'tell me not here it needs not saying', I escaped into other 'Blackwell' country, 'in valleys green and still'. Not being a native, I discovered the meadows the Blackwells had roamed, watched the oarsmen, timelessly intent on the river, and lifted my eyes to Matthew Arnold's Cumnor Hill, much beloved by Benjamin Henry Blackwell, and then back to the old churchyards where the earlier Blackwells now lie. Back in Broad Street, there was more treasure to plunder, particularly an archive which had been efficiently, and lovingly assembled by Julian's sister, Corinna Wiltshire, and, consequently, more research to do.

Help was on hand. It came from Blackwellians, past and present, with memories, oral accounts, and anecdotes they were willing to share. And the management dispensed support services: kind words, cups of tea and the printing, and reading, of drafts. Going back to the shop, where I have now spent many hours, was the starting point for writing up these tales. It was, after all, their context: the place 'from whose bourn, no traveller returns'—or not without a hole in her pocket, in my case. And just being among such a vast number of books, where I could browse at will, reminded me, as Sir Basil had stated so many times, that books were the central plinth of the Blackwell story. In any case, as he had claimed, 'books themselves are more immortal than people'. Towards the end of his life, he had been fearful that the repository of knowledge contained in books would be taken for granted, or even sidelined, in the age of the computer. Preparing a speech for the Classical Association, in 1964, he acknowledged that the computer had the potential to expand the mind, but it would not replace books. Books were not commodities, as in other retail trades, but a way of life. Long ago, they had buoyed up the 'homesick psalmist', Basil Blackwell wrote, 'who sat by the waters of Babylon' and had 'sought solace in the writing of songs of his hopes and fears'; 'good books' Basil wrote, 'provided this unity' in a disunited world.

Of books and bookmen

A moment of truth

What then, I wondered, was a good book? As always, I found my answer among Basil's notes. He had happened on Housman's explanation, that a good book contains: 'a moment of truth' that goes 'to the core of the human mind and the unalterable element in its constitution'. Such a moment of truth, in Basil's view, was captured when Mrs Bulstrode, in *Middlemarch*, on learning that 'her husband's reputation is blasted by the discovery of some villainy in his early life ... seeks him out as he sits abjectly feeling himself perishing in unpitied misery'. Putting one hand on his, which rests on the arm of a chair, and the other on his shoulder, she says, 'Look up Nicholas!' So she espouses her husband's shame and sorrow; no more is spoken, they weep together. Against this, he suggested, the twenty-two stanzas of Browning's *Any wife to any husband* appeared 'ponderous and inadequate'. For Basil Blackwell, *Middlemarch* had an immortal quality. A line from a good book, from a classic, Basil argued, stirs the mind, whether it is 'the cruellest line in English drama: Lightborn's "And get me a spit, and let it be red-hot", Chaucer's gnomic thrusts: "Allas, Allas, that ever love was synne!" or Wordsworth's: "To me the meanest flower that blows can give, Thoughts that do often lie too deep for tear". Sentimental? Absolutely not!' Basil exclaimed, but 'a challenge' certainly.

But how is the reader to find the classics in the midst of such diversity? Who establishes them? Can they be catalogued or graded? 'The answer, as I see it', Basil wrote, 'is that delight and memory are things of the spirit and will not admit of precision or mechanical ordering'. But, he cautioned, readers must be sovereign; they must exercise choice: 'classics', after all, 'are to be found in the minds of men'. Basil reflected further on the 'unconscious selection of books by the reading folk'. 'In the natural order of things many readers in the field of English literature at any time find individually, and recognize in common, excellence in many of the same books. They have long done so and will long do so. . . . In so wide a field happily there is no question of uniformity: here is nothing doctrinaire, no forced faith. We range as freely as the bees, and each of us brings back to the common store our findings'[11].

And even in the face of literature that corrupts, Basil sided with Milton, who claimed, in his formidable *Speech for the Liberty of Unlicensed Printing* (to which Basil added the aside that its 'passionate appeal is so often made by those who appear not to have read beyond the title-page'), that books 'do contain a potency of life in them to be as active as that soul was whose progeny they are; nay they do preserve as in a vial the purest efficacy and extraction of that living intellect that bred them. Many a man lives a burden to the earth; but a good book is the precious life-blood of a master-spirit embalmed, and treasured up on purpose to a life beyond life'[12].

Taking his cue from Carlyle, who described J S Mill as 'sawdustish', Basil rejected J S Mill's idea of steering the reader. Basil had no time for the tyranny of pedagogues. Leading intellectuals were merely custodians of 'the Laputan university of Lagoda labouring in co-operation to compile a dictionary of quotations, which *ought* to be familiar', and rejecting 'any deemed to be unworthy of common use'. In J S Mill's four volumes of the *Commonplace Book*, Basil lamented, 'I did not notice any mention of Shakespeare'. He would have been all the more rattled by the idea that governments would come to prescribe the reading curriculum in today's schools. Perhaps they too should heed Milton's warning that 'God uses not to captivate under perpetual childhood of prescription, but trusts him with the gift of reason to be his own chooser'. This was not to say, however, that there should not be guides to help people discover these immortal moments of truth, wrote Basil, who loved to have the last word. But, alas, not many books were immortal: 'of the many individuals of any species which are periodically born, but a small number can survive'. Books, according to Basil, were subjected, by the general reading public, to Darwin's Natural Selection: Darwin went on to say that 'man's power of selection' would more accurately resemble Herbert Spencer's 'Survival of the Fittest'. This rubric, rather than the recommendation of any expert, was the one employed by Basil to try to explain the survival of any particular book: 'there is no guardian, or general synod', he argued, merely 'the verdict of posterity'[13].

Although Basil cautioned readers to exercise caution and vigilance, as well as having sympathy for the book, it is the individual reader's personal judgement that really counts. This belief is perfect cover for the bookseller, for anyone who wants to sell books per se, but it was also the measure Basil Blackwell used when, famously, he was a witness for the prosecution in the *Last Exit* affair. Being well-read, the Blackwells always appreciated books as things in themselves; they warned against taking them for granted, and urged others to consider the efforts that went into bringing books into their hands.

'Behind every book', Basil had explained, 'are all the bookmen: the researchers, the authors, the publishers, the typographers, the printers, paper-makers, binders, booksellers and librarians'. These, I was reminded, were the real Blackwellian adventurers: some famous, many 'unknown to fame'. They each performed different, but complimentary and interdependent, roles on the Blackwell expeditions. The explorers were scholars and students, general readers and browsers, and their sherpas were publishers, printers, binders and booksellers, and all those who go to make up the world of books. 'Now which would you like to be?' Basil asked. Starting with the author, Basil provides a guide: 'he is a free man: he is self-employed. He has the great joy of creating and of speaking his mind; but he takes great risks. Unless he is invited to write a book (and a good many authors are so invited), he has to take the chance that his work may be in vain'. And it is the writers on whom we all depend; the writers drew up the maps and provided new territories to discover.

The risk-takers are the publishers: they back their fancies. They may make a lot of money, but very many more publishers fail in business than do printers, binders and booksellers. On the other hand, not a few publishers make fortunes. Both Basil Blackwell and his father thought that, in practice, they often exercised their prerogative of choice too narrowly, using overly commercial criteria; in the process they may have rejected a good book, and opted for a marketable one. Sometimes this rejection would be down to the ignorance of the publisher; Blackwell's as a publishing house had itself made this mistake, famously failing to see the merits of *Asterix* and only by a whisker rescuing the writings of Wittgenstein, and there were other examples too. The printer on the other hand, and the binder, have to employ many workmen, and have to install very costly machines; and if the machines are not kept busy, a printing or binding works will soon show a loss. The librarian's, in Basil's view, was the happiest lot, 'though some may think it lacks the excitement which risk and enterprise provide. If he is a Public Librarian he is, to a certain extent, at the mercy of the Library Committee and of the public grant of money. If he is a College or University Librarian, he is perhaps happiest of all, should the bent of his mind be studious. What then of the bookseller?' he asked.

In Benjamin Henry's time, the terms publisher and bookseller were, as often as not, indistinct. The private presses were still in their heyday, and the Blackwells, like other booksellers, acted as 'literary agents' and published many, usually small, books which would have been discarded by the established houses; their readership was very limited and esoteric. And to advertise, and sell, their wares, the traditional bookshops compiled and produced catalogues. The first B H Blackwell had prepared catalogues, for the foreign as well as the home market, referring to the best in the tradition of antiquarian booksellers; the second B H Blackwell became known for his catalogues, making their construction into both an art and a literary form. The entries were peppered with asides, and the choice of titles implied 'guidance'. For example, Benjamin Henry Blackwell's catalogue entitled 'A Roll of English Writers' was necessarily selective, and he had employed the more avowedly academic assistance of his friend from Balliol, Dean Beeching. 'Today', Basil Blackwell explained, 'in the appropriate section of a well-ordered bookshop we should meet most books in a profusion of catalogues, from those edited with scholarly care to those covering the lists of paperbacks, which are more inclusive. The catalogues of publishers and booksellers from times past are, in their own right, an invaluable source of information about books and the markets they served; they were the bibles of the early B H Blackwells'[14].

Rebecca West, at a Foyles Literary Lunch, referred to booksellers as 'the most agreeable servants of civilization'. Whereas the publisher takes a small number of big risks in producing a limited number of books, the bookseller takes a large number of small risks in buying the stock from various publishers. He is an anxious man, for he is bound to be baffled and confused by so many new books, and he cannot afford to make many bad bargains, since his profits are small and his expenses are high. But he has the great advantage of being in immediate contact with the public who buy and read books, of talking and exchanging ideas with men and women with all kinds of interests. If ever there should have been an idle hour there is, so to speak, the wisdom of the world on his shelves which he can turn to; and the truth is that not many booksellers go bankrupt, though rarely do they die very much richer for a life's work in bookselling. It must be regarded as its own reward. But, Basil Blackwell cautioned, echoing Dr Johnson, 'No man will be a bookseller who has contrivance enough to get himself into a workhouse'. The pre-requisite for a good bookseller, according to Basil Blackwell, was the love of reading books, 'and a vocation such that he will make this as much a part of his leisure as his working life'. Tasting his wares, just as it is not amiss for a grocer at times 'To crack a bottle of fish sauce, Or stand himself a cheese', would make a full man, in the sense Bacon intended, and, Basil Blackwell added, a better bookseller.

But a good bookseller needs more than just a taste for his wares, Basil advised. They need courage, faith, craftsmanship, a love of literature, idealism and shrewdness; all characteristics his father had brought to the trade. 'Courage is needed because the Book World is full of incalculable hazards, and he who plays for safety plays also for defeat. Faith, because it is the soul of all enterprise in the Book World—the faith of an author in his writing, the faith of publisher and of bookseller, each in his own judgment, the faith of the public in all three. Joy in work, for obvious reasons, and for one less obvious: to wit, hard work is pleasant to remember, and out of such pleasant reflection in time of leisure often spring the ideas which grow to great accomplishment. Craftsmanship, because it is the vehicle of our ideas, the handmaid of the creative faculty—and craftsmanship again means joy in work. Love of literature, because without that the writing and handling of books becomes at best mechanical, at worst cynical, and either quality is pregnant with the seeds of failure. And idealism is the vital element which gives us all these qualities direction and purpose. Idealism makes the Book World go round, but, like love in the World of Men, unbridled, leads often to disaster. Wherefore, finally we must have shrewdness to govern our idealism. Where there is no vision the Bookman perishes: but how often do we see folk in the Book World carried away by their ideals—swept to disaster, and yielding ultimately disservice to the cause of Books. Now you have been warned and you can make your choice'[15]. Making up this society of bookmen are, of course, the customers! An issue in November 1946 captures the spirit of dogged service in an *Ode to our only Customer*:

> Oh, whence the gay laugh that is borne on the breeze?
> Oh, what makes Tom chirp like a cricket?
> 'Tis your latest requirements, inscribed in Chinese
> On the back of an ancient bus-ticket.
> Pray do not regret that you can't call to mind
> Date, publisher, author or title.
> With a staff such as ours, such small details we find
> Very seldom (if ever) are vital.
>
> All the items that won't be in print for ten years,
> And those that are deader than mutton,
> Lest (quite rightly) you charge us with shameful arrears,
> We will send the same evening by Sutton.
> We are happy to see a large scrawl for your name,
> Though just plain initials are better.
> And if you have three, please don't stick to the same—
> Use a different one for each letter.

> If ever you happen to change your address,
> Don't imagine that makes any difference;
> It keeps our minds nimble, in trying to guess—
> And don't ever quote us a reference.
> And when in due course you receive your account,
> We rely on you to gainsay it;
> And, when you have challenged each separate amount,
> The last thing you should do is to pay it.

These then are all Basil Blackwell's bookmen. The term itself seems outmodish but it is difficult to find another. Taking the term as read, he had a profound sense of its meaning. In 1970, attempting to put his ideas on the subject together, he wrote, 'As a bookman I have been able to watch from a point of vantage the varying fortunes of books, as some, seemingly assured of permanence, have dwindled into neglect, while others have held with promise of indefinite survival. Such indeed has been the story of famous books down the centuries; some like shooting stars flash across the firmament of literature and disappear, some fade into obscurity, some remain fixed and shine with constant light'. His predecessors, Benjamin Harris and Benjamin Henry Blackwell had all sat at this 'point of vantage' but they took no licence to dictate the choices, the tastes, of others. In fact they did much to broaden the base of the stock available in their shop, including new areas of discovery and catering for children, families and for leisured reading: reading just for pleasure's sake. By making more books more generally available, by implicitly recommending books as a genre, and publishing in areas where there was a gap, the Blackwells invited the browser to 'salute the pioneers who in our lifetime have changed the face of literature, introducing new styles and setting the reader on his own adventures'. Far from selecting, or limiting, reading, they aimed to stimulate their customers to 'read athletically'. In the choice of books, Basil's only public advice was that adventurers should, at the outset, accept Milton's admonition in *Paradise Regained*:

>   who reads
> Incessantly, and to his reading brings not
> A spirit and a judgement equal or superior,
> Uncertain and unsettl'd still remains,
> Deep verst in books and shallow in himself,
> Crude or intoxicate, collecting toys,
> And trifles for choice matters, worth a sponge;
> As Children gathering pibles on the shore.

The literary man's house of call

They have come to Blackwell's for their tools

The 'Adventurers All', that the Blackwells dedicated themselves to, were these bookmen, from many disciplines, trades and walks of life. The Blackwells helped to make them, and they made Blackwell's. But these tales would be incomplete without according a central place to Blackwell's itself as an institution. To begin with, it was simply known as Mr Blackwell's shop. Quite soon, according to Bishop William Stubbs, the Regius Professor of History and a family friend who had lived next door in Kettle Hall and for a while in Marriot House, 53 Broad Street, it became the Literary Man's House of Call. During Benjamin Henry's time the shop became an institution in his own lifetime. And not just in Oxford, but from the far-flung outposts of the Empire, Blackwell's as an institution, recommended itself. The relationship between Blackwell's the institution, and the people who created it, was, and remains, symbiotic; a fusion of the lives of these people and their place. The public at large may have had relatively scant acquaintance with the founder of the Broad Street business, Benjamin Henry, but everyone, it seemed, knew Mr Blackwell's shop. If, after his death, Benjamin Henry the man was accorded only quiet praise in public, the praise for his shop was monumental. An article in the *London Daily News* recognized that both the man and the business were identical. 'Hardly anyone in Oxford', it declared, 'will have noticed the death of Mr B H Blackwell. The average undergraduate has probably never thought of wondering if there was such a person, any more than the average Londoner inquires if there is a real Mr Marshall or Mr Snelgrove. *That is what it means to be an institution.* . . . One does not go there just to buy books: one goes there as Londoners go to the Park . . . to see and be seen. One is certain to meet friends there within a few minutes, and then even the pretence of having come to buy books is given up' [16].

Jan Morris claimed that 'Blackwell's has almost certainly become the greatest bookselling complex in this, or indeed any country'. And another (anonymous) reader was heard to say that a reader can often get a book more easily at Blackwell's than at the Bodleian. Before the shop had barely attained its twenty-first year Lord Rosebery, in conversation with Basil's father, was heard to refer to Blackwell's as a remarkable shop kept by a remarkable man. Dearer to the heart of Benjamin Henry, Blackwell's became, in his own lifetime, a place for self-improvement: a place where scholars from the university, and booklovers from the town, could read under the same roof. Mr Blackwell's small shop was there for anyone interested in books, and in the extension of their own education, formal or informal. Side by side with the Colleges of Oxford, Blackwell's had become a place of learning in its own right. Twenty years before he died, a daily newspaper summed up his contribution, 'Many men will aver that the greatest educative influence of Oxford resides neither in the Bodleian, nor schools, nor tutors, nor lectures, nor college societies, but in the excellent management and most liberal facilities of one of the best bookshops in the world—Mr Blackwell's'[17]. Blackwell's had become internationally known, by booklovers, while providing a refuge, for town and gown and the exile returned to Oxford.

'Though Dons and Schools make Pundits out of fools,
They have come to Blackwell for their tools:
And seek, to turn their dunces into Sages,
The Delphic oracle of Blackwell's pages.'
Ode to Scholarship, Poona, April 1912

A writer in the *Oxford Chronicle* recalled his first impressions of this alternative seat of learning: in its 'strange capacity for making you feel as though you were at home in a vast library, of which some generous patron of letters had given you free run, it seemed like a book shop from a happy dream; and when I went out I had rather expected that, like the "magic shop" in Mr Wells' story, it would have vanished from consciousness, leaving only a blank wall to the eye. But fortunately Blackwell's is a thing of reality, to which one returns again and again, to buy if one can, but with the knowledge that if one does not buy but only browses one is equally welcome'. Indeed, the *Oxford Chronicle* cautioned, 'we have all grown up in the habit of taking Blackwell's bookshop, like other good things in life, very much as a matter of course'.

The Bookseller, in 1956, on hearing of Basil Blackwell's knighthood, proclaimed Blackwell's as 'The most illustrious and evocative name in British bookselling'. 'Blackwell's', according to Beverly Nichols, in *The Prelude*, 'was a feast of excitement, and Cecil ran completely wild among minor poets, Fragments bound in yellow and orange . . . and thousands of French writers that he had never heard of before. How wonderful it would be to spend years at Oxford within a stone's throw of this amazing treasure house!' Literature, too, recognizes Blackwell's: Mr Samgrass in *Brideshead Revisited* is caught, by the reader, standing at the table in Blackwell's, where he was perusing the latest German books on display; and many other characters play a leading part. Among these, Oxford merits a special mention. The story of the Blackwells is more than just a footnote to the history of Oxford and the University: 'it benefits from the air of permanence and intellectualism, which pervades this ancient City of learning. . . . It has an academic flavour, the town itself is a bookish one, just as the City of Munich is a beery city. The whole town seems to smell of books—of damp bindings, musty pages, smoky leather and long-dried fish-glue. Oxford has the air of being a place where studying and reading and mental activity are forever going on'[18]. And Harold Laski found Blackwell's as stimulating as any of the colleges in either of the ancient universities, Cambridge or Oxford[19]. In an address at Christ Church, in 1954, Basil linked his life to that of Oxford, and the University—it had been his playground as a child: playing shyly with Dr Theodore Chaundy, in the late years of the nineteenth century, in what is now Trinity's rose garden. He had been instructed as a child by Professor Jenkins who had the distinction of 'declaring prophesies' or what is usually called instruction in Old Testament history. Despite Basil recalling 'an Oxford which had hardly ceased from whispering from her towers the last enchantments of the Middle Age', he did not treat Oxford as the measure of all experience. This may well have been one of the secrets of Blackwell's success.

Grace before ploughing

While the heavy ploughman snores all with weary task fordone[20]

Blackwell's was, and still is, in the field of academic bookselling, a household name. If present students from the universities as well as other walks of life are asked, Belloc style, 'Do you remember an old bookshop, Blackwell's?', the answer is usually 'Yes!' What singled out these gentile and scholarly entrepreneurs was their ability to transform one small bookshop into an empire, in a trade not usually renowned for making anyone rich. There has been much conjecture as to the secret of this success. Certainly, with their collective love of books and scholarship, and reputation for taking infinite pains, they created an empathetic environment for their customers. It has also been suggested that the Blackwells just happened to be in the right place at the right time. Any bookseller worth his salt had, in the second half of the nineteenth century, the means to satisfy consumer demand. Books were the means to nourish the minds of not only scholars, and due to the expansion of university education there were more of them, but also the newly literate. A hard-working tradesman, with application, could now benefit commercially from the prodigious growth in education; whether in the schoolroom, the workplace, the Evening and Technical Institutes, the Church, through various community schemes, or simply self-education to be garnered in the now proliferating, lending libraries. And Benjamin Henry, and his father, were just such men. Right under Blackwell's' nose successive governments urged on educational reform, adding to the curriculum subjects more fitting to the industrial landscape of late Victorian England. Britain was no longer the only workshop of the world and the Government cast a nervous eye at the more advanced technical education systems in Germany and America, who were fast stealing a march on their more traditional British cousins. In Oxford the repeal of the Test Acts swelled the ranks of scholars, as the University was released from the straightjacket of the established Church; Dons could come from other denominations. Added to which they were permitted to marry and live outside the Colleges. Academia could now be a family affair.

Generations of graduates kept Blackwell's in the family, taking their memories of happy times in Broad Street, that unofficial college of the University, to their new posts. The establishment of the first Empire universities took many of these scholars, who in their student days had known Mr Blackwell's little shop, to destinations far from parochial Oxford, carrying with them the Blackwell's flag. Indeed, 'as scholars, as intellectuals, as zealous evangelists going out to convert the heathen, few generations can hold a candle to the Victorians, many of whom had deep associations with Oxford (University)'[21]. Thus, while the Blackwells themselves may not have adventured further than the find of a rare antiquarian book in some musty library, their reputation secured the backing and sanction of the Empire. Long before the age of distance purchasing, buying on the net, Blackwell's customers had no need to be physically present in Oxford, providing the interested parties had received the catalogues, since they could take advantage of the mail order service. Having made their purchases, remotely, the books were then despatched by parcel 'to post or sea and ocean without rest'. Bookshops the world over compared themselves with Blackwell's. And to have more books on a subject than Blackwell's was the ultimate accolade. Walter Goldwater, the proprietor of the University Place Bookstore on 12th Street, New York, had aspired to reach this gold standard. An old acquaintance of Blackwell's had written of Walter's ambitions, which all started on a visit to Oxford. Walter Goldwater, together with his wife, Eleanor, who owned the Corner Bookstore in the same city, had visited Blackwell's to check out the extent of their African section; his own collection of books by black writers had set his shop apart from others. Unused to the ramble of Blackwell's, he fixed on what he thought must be the African section, intending to buy such an amount of books that his stock would out-rival that of Blackwell's. When he had pulled several hundred books off the shelves, he finally caught the attention of an assistant. 'Would you', the clerk enquired, 'like to see our African section?' Walter Goldwater never forgot how many more books Blackwell's had than he had[22].

Basil Blackwell, and his sons, independently, attributed the firm's success to the habit of constantly ploughing back the profits for the next generation, fructifying meanwhile for the benefit of the staff and community. Benjamin Henry had handed on the equivalent of £300,000 (calculated in the money values of 1974) and Sir Basil handed on ten times this sum to the next generation. Each of the Blackwells passed on more than just wealth: Benjamin Harris joined bookselling to the opening up of education, and the development of the public libraries; Benjamin Henry's 'quiet genius' made him an acknowledged master of the trade, what his apprentice Fred Hanks called 'the master of a vineyard where literature was undoubtedly the most significant shoot on the vine'. Basil Blackwell had magic and inspiration, and two sons trained to follow in his footsteps. They all believed in the tradition of service; service to their staff and customers, tailored to their individual needs. In its time Blackwell's has been an innovator, at many levels, from introducing a paper recycling system, they introduced the idea of issuing shares to all staff in 1921, which came to fruition in the forties, and, much earlier, they had instituted a life pension scheme; they gave their staff a dinner hour, in 1921, at lunchtime; and another hour for a cooked tea, from 1881; they daringly replaced the quadracycle with a motor van, in 1921, and chairs were placed in the shop, for the comfort of the ladies, who were a relatively new group of customers; they managed to reconcile the production of fine books with mass demand while constantly battling with the local authorities over the expansion and modernization of the Oxford shop, and the road traffic schemes (*plus ça change!*). The dot com age would not have surprised them. Even in the Sixties the importance of computers was not missed on the Gaffer; he was always ready to combine the old and the new. Computerisation though, as with any modern device, was not, if Basil Blackwell had anything to do with it, 'to be allowed to blind his staff to the fact that good bookselling begins and ends with personal service'.

From the beginning, in 1846, this service had been opened up by Benjamin Harris to include the export of books. As America, and Germany, industrialized, so their universities were founded, and expanded. And their students came to Oxford. Going back to the new world, or to the far-flung outposts of empire, Blackwell's soon became an institution; by word of mouth, its reputation made its success. Benjamin Harris's early efforts were redoubled by his son. To begin with, especially, the public at large knew very little about Benjamin Henry, the man, but everyone, it seemed, knew Mr

Blackwell's shop. If, after his death, Benjamin Henry the man was accorded only quiet praise in public, the praise for his shop was monumental. An article in the *London Daily News* recognized that both the man and the business were identical.

For many an undergraduate Blackwell's became an integral part of the ritual of university life, 'where the only exercise is the "Blackwell Crawl" which occupies very well that awkward interval after a lunch party and before one can decently appear at tea'[23]. It was allegedly said, at the time, that no undergraduate could be said to have completed his university career unless he had been mistaken for an assistant in Blackwell's. One admirer of the Blackwell's cult anthropomorphised the figures of the Sheldonian as habitués of Blackwell's: 'The quaint old heads that front the Sheldonian Theatre, where degrees are taken and prize poems recited, look across the road to one of the pleasantest bookshops in the world. Is it not the usual and recognized haunt upon wet days—of which our dear city gives us a plentiful store?'[24]. An anonymous translation of Theogis suggested that Blackwell's was contentment itself: 'When atte my neede I sought the Black Wells's Store, Contente I knew was never mine before'. And the shop was immortalized by the Poet Laureate of the day, John Masefield:

I seek few treasures, except books, the tools
Of those celestial souls the world calls fools.
Happy the morning giving time to stop
An hour at once in Basil Blackwell's shop
There, in the Broad, within whose booky house
Half of England's scholars nibble books or browse.
Where'er they wander blessed fortune theirs,
Books to the ceiling, other books upstairs:
Books, doubtless, in the cellar, and behind
Romantic bays, where iron ladders wind.
And in odd nooks sometimes in little shelves,
Lintot's and Tonson's calf-bound dainty twelves[25].

In his turn, the young Basil Blackwell, too, acquired the 'Blackwell's habit'. And it was a habit he never tired of. Treading in his father's footsteps, Basil Blackwell never deserted either Blackwell's or Oxford. His commitment was rock solid, even though he could have had several other 'lives': joining the ranks of the major London publishers or the academic world. Quite simply, Basil's life was the life of Blackwell's; it had been thus from his birth and was to continue to the end of his life. The writer Laurence Clark Powell discovered the symbiotic relationship between the man and his firm. He had arrived late for an interview with Sir Basil to be greeted by the Gaffer himself 'in his office lined the shop's own publications'. 'You have been here a long while', Powell ventured. Sir Basil pointed to the ceiling 'I was born in the room above'[26]. By the second half of the twentieth century there were few who could recall the 'old' Mr Blackwell, and for the majority it was the figure of Basil Blackwell, who was literally born over the shop, which dominated. Jan Morris wrote that, 'no one has gone on record to cast any doubt on the verdict of history that attributes the expansion of the Blackwell's empire, bookselling and publishing, to the genius of Basil Blackwell. On Restoration Day 1889, the twelve sculptured Emperors on the palisade of the Sheldonian Theatre, in Oxford, pricked up their ears to hear the joyous sound of a baby's first cry from an upstairs window opposite. Master Basil Blackwell, son of the promising young bookseller, Benjamin Henry Blackwell, was coming into the world in a second floor bedroom above his father's modest shop: and prescient as these Romans were, for all their mouldy masonry, they interpreted the omens as propitious. And', she wrote, 'they were right'[27]. Doubtless there were other voices, which, if heard, might suggest a different verdict, but such alternatives sources have not as yet come to light.

When Basil Blackwell was knighted, in 1956, Blackwell's was claimed as 'the most illustrious and evocative name in British bookselling'[28]. It was a moot point in some quarters as to whether Sir Basil's knighthood was for the man or for his shop. Tributes came from across the world and, all in the same vein, conjoined the names of Sir Basil and Blackwell's[29]. In Sir Basil's view, this recognition was misplaced, 'it was in the glory of the books that it resided'. 'As I see it', he wrote, 'the status of bookselling in our economy remains much as I found it when I entered the trade. True bookselling—not merchandising—remains in the middle parts of fortune—an arduous business requiring qualities of intelligence, diligence and enterprise, which in many callings would win greater material rewards. For this, I think, is as it should be. For in this grasping age when the world of men appears to be divided between those who strain for more profits and others who strain for more pay, there is, as I see it, a third estate, unorganized, unvocal, unpredatory, being the commonwealth of those whose commerce is in sharing delight in the noblest products of the spirit of man, in the visual and scenic arts, in music . . . and, need I add, in books:

> "In books we have the compendium of all human experience. We may use them or neglect them as we will, but if we use them, we may share the courage and endurance of adventurers, the thoughts of

sages, the vision of poets and the rapture of lovers, and—some few of us perhaps—the ecstasies of the Saints."'

And it was, so often, to Blackwell's that people turned to satisfy their appetite for books. When Basil Blackwell was awarded an honorary doctorate, the Public Orator expressed surprise that the preferment had been so long in the coming. 'Some people unknown', he suggested, 'have wondered why Sir Basil has not already been honoured?' 'Well', might have come the reply, 'he hasn't written a book yet, has he?' The Orator had replied that 'so far as I know he (Basil Blackwell) has not committed such an act of indiscretion, although he has ensured that a great many books of the highest quality have got published. But you must be aware, members of Congregation, that if it were not for the existence of this, his magnificent shop, where learned books are sold to every part of the world, you would be scribbling your lubrications in vain.'

Another aspect of the shop's success was its tradition, its timelessness. The external look of the shop is still instantly recognisable from Victorian drawings and photographs. But inside it is a different story; Blackwell's had moved with the times. Adam Fox, an old and honoured friend of the Gaffer's, briefly Professor of Poetry at Oxford, had written a poem about the biggest extension of all, the 'new room underground': The Norrington Room. He had sent his poem to a close friend, Lou Levitas, with a picture of the Norrington room turned upside down. Lou Levitas, with Adam Fox's permission, sent it to Sir Basil. Sir Basil, chacteristically, 'was amused', although Fox had feared that he would not be. Basil thanked his old friend and speculated 'Why didn't we think of turning this Room upside down before? It looks so much more splendid. Here, you see, is the Professor of Poetry's eye "in a fine frenzy, glancing down from heaven to earth and earth to heaven" and showing us a thing of beauty—"such tricks hath strong imagination"'[30].

> Oh dear, oh dear! I was a clown,
> I had the picture upside-down,
> And to myself I said dismayed,
> So many books, so well displayed,
> And yet, although it's all so grand,
> It's puzzling. I don't understand
> A gallery above the floor
> At height, I guess, of three-foot-four.
>
> Much higher up six shelves of books
> Impress me greatly, but it looks

3 An upside down view of the Norrington Room.

> As if, when they were being made,
> Someone forgot the balustrade,
> And, if I get to them at all,
> (I can't tell how) a nasty fall,
> As far as I can see, may be
> The fate of careless, browsing me.
>
> When vertical I turn my eyes
> I have another great surprise
> Books horizontal there are spread,
> Which should, but won't, fall on my head.
> And that big oblong with no end
> (No doubt an architecture trend)
> Stays there suspended in the air,
> But how on earth did it get there?
>
> Well, I'm no engineer, I own;
> I'll have to leave the thing alone.
> So down I turn my eyes once more
> And view the man-holes in the floor
> As wishingly numerous they,
> But what's their purpose I can't say;

And just beyond a colonnade
Gives shelter from perpetual shade.

And all this in the open air,
Although the weakest not set fair,
And I forecast, to judge by looks,
A wet night fated to the books.
Comes this from Blackwell's, famed for sure,
This nightmare built at such expense?
You ass, of course not. Turn it round,
And there's the new room underground [31].

Basil Blackwell, in his heart was more than a little afraid of the huge increase in the size of the firm. But he knew that the foundations were strong; it was financially very secure and it continued in the hands of those who were capable of ploughing a straight furrow. The family name, B H Blackwell's, first appeared in 1846 above a small shop on the outskirts of the city of Oxford. Sadly this founder, Benjamin Harris Blackwell, died young, and it was left to his son, Benjamin Henry, to re-establish the business. Overcoming family hardships, with the backing of an indomitable mother, Benjamin Henry re-opened 'Blackwell's' in Broad Street. When Benjamin Henry Blackwell opened his door on New Year's Day, 1879, in a space twelve-foot square, he was told by Frederick Macmillan that it would surely fail 'as it was situated on the wrong side of the street'. Ten years from its foundation, the shop had passed its struggling stage. By the end of the nineteenth century Mr Blackwell's little shop had become a legend in his own lifetime. Benjamin Henry Blackwell died in 1924, and his son, Basil, continued to build the reputation of Blackwell's, both as a publisher and a bookseller. Sir Basil Blackwell was the man who, more than any other, witnessed and controlled the expansion of the business in the twentieth century. In turn Sir Basil Blackwell's sons, Richard and Julian, and their sons, played their part. With the retirement of Julian Blackwell as Chairman, in February 2000, the family firm is now in the hands of the fifth generation: Philip Blackwell, as Chief Executive on the retail side, and Nigel Blackwell, Chairman of Blackwell Publishing. Frederick Macmillan's prophecy of doom had been gloriously disproved! Some things, like good books, are eternal:

'The same old work was being done
With pleasure, comradeship and fun;
And at the days-work-end for these
Even in war-time, there was ease,
And strength remaining for delight'[32].

Beset by contradictions

Do good men do nothing, when doing nothing is all that is needed for evil to triumph?

Yet for all Blackwell's success, the lives of the Blackwells were, from the beginning, beset by contradictions. The first B H Blackwell became a bookseller, his father was a tailor; where had he got the knowledge and the wherewithal? He was given to new adventures, starting out for a new place and a new occupation, but he was dedicated to keeping others on the straight and narrow. The first B H Blackwell was no Don Quixote; he didn't tilt at the City's windmills, but set out to woo them, giving the University's grandees what they wanted: good books and an outlet for publishing their work. (The University certainly didn't want any of the 'dirty trades' and the place was already awash with tailors). To begin with, he was a rank outsider; he wasn't even 'Town'; his shop was outside the City's limits, in St Clements. He became, nonetheless, Oxford City's first Librarian, and within thirty years of his death, his son, Benjamin Henry Blackwell, had opened a shop which became an unofficial college of the University. The second B H Blackwell, unlike his father, was a native of Oxford, and he loved the City and the surrounding countryside. So enamoured was he, that, even when successful, he eschewed the richer picking of the London book scene. The Blackwells went all over the place, in the mind, yet loved best to walk through Oxford's meadows setting Mathew Arnold to music in their heads.

Reading their tales, and hearing of their songs, helped me to get inside the heads of a group of Victorians who believed in redemption and the importance of the spiritual life, in heroes of the imagination as well as deed, taught themselves classics yet worked long hours leaving little time for leisure. They became part of the establishment, yet challenged the status quo; they were indeed people who made their own judgements. They lived with poverty and bequeathed modest riches; their lives were intermingled with poetry and literature and sometimes, rather mischievously, they confused fact and fiction. In their lifetime, the barriers between art, science and technology came down, a divide they hastened to remove, just as they despised social division; yet they wanted to preserve the old order of traditional craftsmanship. Their stories on these and many other subjects belong to another age, but they have resonance for today. Overhanging their youth was the threat of war: its insecurity and inhumanity, and the threat of poverty was buried deep in their psyche. If they had been here now, would they have been accused of political cross-dressing? They were 'independent-thinking';

they were Utopian Socialist, Liberal and small c, conservative, all at the same time. Like Heraclitus, they were beset by contradictions and paradoxes. They grappled with things that torment us, especially our politicians: 'Whither representative democracy?' Basil asked, 'for democracy to-day, in great matters as in small, is the precious but imperilled legacy of the nobler past—precious because it allows that every man is master of his soul and that his soul by itself has worth; imperilled because we have forgotten that the best gifts of life need ever watch and ward'[33].

Basil Blackwell, particularly, brings us uncannily back to the present. Thirty years ago he demanded to know: what was the point of holding a referendum on Europe? He was irate: 'We keep upwards of five hundred dogs in Parliament at a comfortable salary, and now are we expected to bark ourselves? Can more than one in ten people in the street, give an intelligent and valid answer to the question—in or out?' European integration was for him imperative: 'How else can we prevent, what Toynbee called, "the new wine of nationality" from making sour ferment in the bottles of tribalism? Why,' he asked, 'do good men do nothing, when doing nothing is all that is needed for evil to triumph?' Basil Blackwell's writings are full of questions: How can we redistribute resources so that poverty is banished and work is rewarding? How can we re-discover the spiritual in the midst of the material? How shall we preserve our crafts? How can we live the good life in the world, outside the monastery, with all its temptations? How can we simultaneously care for victim and miscreant? How can education be free for all, and its provision, and its teachers' pay not be watered down? How can we teach our children that education is a privilege, as well as a right? How can the tax system be made fairer to all, helping the needy while not encouraging the entrepreneur to cut and run? These and many more questions he addressed, but he never did settle the problem of pain, and suffering.

As a bookman, and a bookseller, Basil Blackwell had other, more immediate concerns too. How, for example, could academic bookselling continue to provide a living, to those in the trade, with current marketing and pricing practices? How, indeed, could we encourage people to read and write for pleasure, to become intellectual mountaineers, rather than using books simply as a means to an end? Basil Blackwell was also a counter revolutionary. Taking his cue from William Morris, whose essential argument was to show by word and deed the difference between crass commercialism and the ideals and satisfaction of the handcrafts, he helped to prolong the art of fine printing. For Morris, as it was for Ruskin, and also for Edward Ashbee and Walter Crane who were his contemporaries, this meant not only a beautiful product, but the chance to take pleasure and pride in its production. In the field of book production the hand-brake of the Private Press Movement halted for a time the headlong flight of mass production for its own sake. All these perennial worries he left with us. But he also left us with an idea of freedom; the idea that we are our own jury. We, he reminded us, have 'Liberty to know, to utter, to argue freely', and to judge the new literature for ourselves.

Although it is Basil Blackwell who is the most well-known, and who played such a key role in the development of Blackwell's, his speeches and writing give his father 'a goodly share of the limelight': 'I have less scruple in praising the father that begat me because no one knows better than I, or is happier in knowing, that ability visits alternate generations. I have full confidence in the future; but in one respect I deem that I am in no way inferior to my father. I say this because I believe it is true, and not to please you—I believe that I am as fortunate as he was in the staff that work with me, and I think that is because of the principles which guided him in business—the transcendent capacity of taking trouble, and the achievement of a day's work in the day, have formed a tradition which comes through from one to another. And so, it seems to me, we have grown into a kind of society—not a learned society, but a society meet for the people with knowledge of learning. And every one of us who is faithful to those principles—be it in the scrupulous packing of a book, or the placing of the right book on the right shelf by the youngest apprentice, or by the accurate transcription of an address or a record—each of us, whether we plan to publish, to sell, to catalogue, books, or to answer those strange queries which inevitably come to us, contributes to the cause of learning'. Those who dealt with these 'strange queries', are the real heroes of these tales; the self-made, hard working booksellers; the scholars manqués: Benjamin Henry and his erstwhile apprentices. It is interesting that the female Blackwells played no direct, and formal, role in the workplace: they earned their laurels elsewhere. Basil's daughter Penelope (Dame Penelope Jessell) showed the old family traits and earned a reputation in her own right in the Liberal Party; she was a liberal in every sense, and she too had brought up her children alone after the death of her journalist husband. The Blackwell women came from a line of strong women—Nancy, Lilla, Christine—but they played a supporting, rather than a central, role in the family firm. The Blackwells were dedicated to the education of women, yet they were too Victorian to want to see them on an equal footing in the workplace. Basil, as Gaffer, lived to see all this change; he had the vision to accept change despite his Victorian instincts.

A venial fault

A paste-pot, a pair of scissors and a little horse-sense

I have not, wittingly, tried to impose my own version of these tales; I have not 'modernised' accounts used in the text, even though some of the vocabulary, speech, expressions and ideas may, now, appear unmodish, anachronistic, even, in a few cases, politically incorrect. Basil Blackwell had very firm ideas on language, ideas he incorporated into many of his writings. He pleaded for 'a Society for the Preservation of Ancient Words and Phrases', and decried the shoddy language of the talking pictures. 'Variety, in the subtlety of the meaning of words', Basil feared was on the wane. He delighted in language and from infancy had sat at the table and learned a richness of expression from his well-read father. 'Take, for example,' he wrote, 'the verb "to carve". That word today does service for the dissection and distribution of meat or fish or fowl indifferently. Now turn to Wynkyn de Worde's book of carving and see what we have lost:

> "Thus while you break a deer, you must lesche brawn, rear a goose, lift a swan, sauce a capon, but frusshe a chicken and spoil a hen, a mallard must be unbraced, a heron dismembered, a crane displayed, a peacock disfigured; you must join a bittern, untach a curlew, allay a pheasant, wing a partridge and a quail, mince a plover, thigh a pigeon and a woodcock. . . . A pasty must be bordered and an egg tyered. Fish carving has its niceties also. You chine a salmon, string a lamprey, splatt a pike, sauce a trench, splay a bream, side a haddock, tush a barbell, culpon a trout, fynne a chevon, traunsene an eel, traunche a sturgeon, undertraunche a porpoise, tame a crab, and barb a lobster" '[34].

Was there room, I wondered, for such gourmets to discriminate the pudding? Discrimination itself attracted lively debate, and for Basil Blackwell, so many words were increasingly denied, or neutralized, in the interests of 'political correctness'. The Blackwells feared to tread where: 'they had foul ado and much struggling for that they could not tread on slippery ice.' But, if they thought it necessary, they ventured; they did not care for political correctness in any case[35]. But they did like correctness; Benjamin Henry, in particular, was a stickler, in this department; 'he fall to't yarely'. I have tried to be brisk and nimble in the use of their language. But if I have made mistakes, misrepresented Blackwellians, or anyone else, and if I have not always, for lack of knowledge, or space, included every reference, and primary source, then I would like to claim the same immunity as Benjamin Henry

Blackwell. He was always nervous that his lack of learning would cause him to make mistakes, and invoke the ire of his more select readers, and I, as a rank amateur in almost every field, share this anxiety. Sir Arthur Norrington noted this tendency to anticipate criticism, as evidenced by an entry at the head of a catalogue (12 May 1884). Benjamin Henry took recourse to the line of argument employed by the great London bookseller, James Lackington, in his *Memoirs*. Lackington's shop in Finsbury Park, 'that Temple of the Muses', had been one of the sights of London a century earlier. Lackington absolved himself from any blame in compiling catalogues, by writing of his limited role: 'I contented myself', wrote Lackington, 'with reading the translations of the classics, and inserted the originals in my catalogues as well as I could; and when sometimes I happened to put the genitive or dative case instead of the nominative or accusative, my customers kindly considered this as a venial fault, and bought the books notwithstanding.'

In his 1888 catalogue, Benjamin Henry proffered his own let-out clause: 'His (the cataloguer's) work has been so faithfully performed for him, a generation or two ago, by Brunet, Stevens, Lowdes, Dibdin, Allibone, Willis, Quaritch, and the rest of the old bibliographical guild, that all he has to do is to follow in their tracks and plagiarise at every footstep.... To compile a book catalogue in these days one only needs a paste-pot, a pair of scissors and a little horse-sense. That is the whole of the necessary equipment.'[36] And the extent of any claims Benjamin Henry would make for himself. At the end of the first catalogue, he included some lines from Pynson's *Ship of Fools*:

'Styll am I busy bokes assemblynge, ...
But what they mean do I nat understonde'[37].

I have tried to understand, and in having the presumption to take you on my journey, I hope I have not bored you. Basil Blackwell in apologizing for his own 'dog's ramblings' was very forthright: 'If in my ignorance I should follow stale scents, you in your kindness forgive me, but should I prove tedious, I shall not forgive myself.' I hope you will forgive this amateur anyway. In order to write up these tales, I have tried to be scholarly; I spent many hours in the Broad Street shops and I, too, learnt at the university of Blackwell's. The library facilities offered were just what I needed, and the service from its staff, in many departments, was peerless. Just as I finished replicating these tales, a true Blackwellian, Jo Shelton, died in harness. In his seventies, he was first in the shop, to open up, and the last time I talked to him he was boasting of his early morning cheap deal: buying strawberries for a staff breakfast. Blackwell's is still, it seems to me, a family concern: a community. And I hope that more people will come to study here. Its history, in so many ways, reminded me of one of Anne Stevenson's Oxford poems:

> 'When I am rich . . .
> I'm going to endow a college in Oxford
> Called Lost Souls College . . .
> . . . for dirty old men whose bunks
> are streets, whose chairs are drafty hedges
> there'll be beds, baths, heating, glasses
> and maybe even built-in shelves . . .
> But the highest and grandest chair (don't you agree)
> Should be the Regius Professor of Simple and
> Compound Factions . . .
> The architecture . . .
> a sculpture made of lost bikes, failed theses, fag-ends
> red tape and refused applications for grants . . .
> But when, with its petty pace, the Worm of Time creeps
> in
> (with all the blether about tomorrow, tomorrow,
> and tomorrow)
> we'll remember the Lost Souls chaplain and invite him in'[38].

For all their success, the Blackwells were often chaplains to lost souls. And their stories had resonance for me as I crossed Broad Street, and bought another copy of Big Issue. The early Blackwells had made their own adventures, and yet they had stayed, more-or-less, in one place. They were good people, with good ideas, compassion and entrepreneurial, rather than materialistic, spirit. They were Victorians, in the best sense of the word. And their lives and work are so like that of other family businesses at the time. The conclusions Margaret Forster came to, in her biography of the Carr family, would equally apply to the Blackwells. From one room in a provincial town, sprung a successful worldwide business. They had their battles, their campaigns, their victories, just as soldiers and politicians of their day did. Being religious, very devout, they had moral dilemmas too. 'When the entrepreneurial spirit clashed with religious conviction, something very interesting happened, with repercussions right down to our own time'[39]. Basil Blackwell had offered up his own thoughts on his family firm: 'some fruits gathered from the experience of a lifetime spent, in work and in leisure, among books'. 'Perhaps', he worried, 'those fruits may prove to be no more than Dead Sea apples?' In his Presidential address to the English Association he claimed no authority. 'I stand before you', he explained, 'no more confidently than the soul of Tomlinson, in Kipling's Ballad, at "the gate within the Wall, where Peter holds the keys" as he sought to answer the challenge of the stern custodian: "Ye have read, ye have heard, ye have thought," he said "and the tale is still to run; but the worth of the body that once ye had, give answer—what ha' ye done?" Tomlinson, you may remember, failed to satisfy the examiner, "And Peter twirled the jangling keys in weariness and wrath" and bade him—euphemistically speaking—seek alternative accommodation. I cry you mercy then if today I should prompt you to a like behest'.

Chapter 2
Partners in Trade

*We are bold to demand a standing among the
most important societies for the improvement of man, physically,
socially, morally and intellectually*[40]

The 'First' Blackwells:
Benjamin Harris and Nancy Blackwell

Although Blackwell's was founded by Benjamin Henry Blackwell on the present Broad Street site in 1879, it was his father, Benjamin Harris Blackwell (1813–1855), who first put the family name above the door of a bookshop. Benjamin Harris and his wife-to-be, Anne Nancy Stirling Lambert, had their own, separate, trades, and had emigrated to Oxford from London in the eighteen-thirties. Benjamin Harris became a librarian-bookseller, but he died young, having 'worked himself literally to death'. It was left to his wife to ensure that the name, B H Blackwell's, was restored[41].

Beginning in bookselling[42]

A standing for the improvement of man

Having adventures was not something the Blackwells had planned on; tradesmen at the time the first B H Blackwell was born had their work cut out to provide for themselves and their families. Benjamin Harris Blackwell was born in London in 1813, the son of Joshua Blackwell, before Wellington beat down Napoleon and the new bourgeoisie won the vote. His father was a tailor in East London, and had been married at St Andrew's in Holborn in 1808. How his sons Benjamin Harris, and Isaac, ended up in Oxford is not clear. Maybe they were looking for adventure? Maybe they were escaping the squalor of East London? The City of London had been expanding for over a century, and the success of its financiers and industrialists was having a considerable flow-on effect; but not enough of one to transform the quality of life for most of its inhabitants. At the beginning of the nineteenth century, those who lived in the East End, even if they were reputable and skilled, as Joshua Blackwell must have been, given his interest in education and the temperance movement, still experienced the same fetid alleyways, 'foul congestion of all the traffic servicing the trades and businesses; the herds of abattoir-bound beasts leaving their filth behind them, and all the other dirt

37

and pollution in this overcrowded quarter'[43]. They could not help but be numbed by the sight of paupers, literally starving in the streets, and in the doorways of the gin palaces the demon drink left its own dead, daily, in its wake. They pitied, rather than feared, 'the less than desirable elements of society, who could disappear in the myriad lanes and turnings', but 'were still prepared to fight one another for the opportunity of even half a day's casual labour'. Joshua's temperance work would have reclaimed a few souls, but 'philosophy alone can bake no bread'. His son, Benjamin Harris, sensitive, bookish and devout, was only too aware that all around him was a life where:

'Hobbes clearly proves that ev'ry creature
Lives in a state of War by Nature'.

Swift's satire, *Rhapsody*, from an earlier century, still fitted; the mean streets of London had not changed for the better, but for the sensitive they were no matter for mockery.

The Blackwells, perhaps, had read *Gulliver's Travels*, and they certainly had an ironic view of politicians. But they were more optimistic than Hobbes. Life need not be just 'poor, mean, nasty, brutal' and, above all, 'short'; it could be enlightened by education, and the human spirit. Joshua Blackwell was an independent-minded man, and he must have been keen that his sons, as rational beings, should better themselves. This meant abandoning the East End. He likely guessed that the days of the labour-intensive trades, such as tailoring, especially in England's capital city, were numbered; 'they were unable to compete with the more cost-effective—in financial terms, at least—machine production, and larger workshops were being moved out to the provinces, where there were cheaper rents, space for expansion and lower fuel costs'[44]. So had Benjamin Harris simply intended to pursue his father's trade, in more propitious quarters? Or perhaps he was attracted to Oxford because of its ancient connections with the rag trade? Benjamin Harris's wife-to-be, who came to Oxford at the same time, having also emigrated from London, was trained as an embroidress and a dressmaker. Despite his family links with the rag trade, there is nothing to suggest that Benjamin Harris ever contemplated following his father's line. And if he had looked at the street directories of the time, he would have seen for himself, that there was a preponderance of tailors.

Judged by the evidence of his subsequent activities, Benjamin Harris must have had a predisposition for a trade connected with books; and to the bookish, Oxford would have been a big draw. Three hundred years earlier, the famous printer/binder, Plantin of Antwerp, who similarly had no private means, had set up in a city where there were the facilities for practising his trade. He had written of his reasons, long afterwards, to Pope Gregory XIII: 'Access to the city is good—the many different nations to be seen in the market square.... And in Antwerp all the materials so necessary... and manpower enough to train', all flourishing by the 'University of Louvain, outstanding for the learning of its professors in all subjects and whose learning I reckoned to turn to profit for the general well-being of the public in manuals, textbooks and critical works'[45]. This was to be the story of the Blackwells, but Benjamin Harris was never to know this. Plantin had had to make his own way, beginning in trade as a leather-worker and binder. It is not known how Benjamin Harris earned his credentials, or just how he had acquired the necessary further education to be so knowledgeable about rare and second hand books; this remains a mystery, and there are no clues as to where his family found the money to possess books, in an age when they were only to be found in the homes of the wealthy. Somehow his parents had given him enough education that he developed a passion for books, and a fervent desire to help other working people to enjoy them, in the days when even basic elementary education was not statutory. He could not have been unaware of the politics of the time; these were days of agitation, before and after the 1832 Reform Bill, and his father, a man with maverick and independent traits, nurtured in him a healthy and critical cynicism of the government. Joshua was himself, doubtless, tied to his business in the capital, but he must have understood the lure of the provinces, especially for the young.

This was the new age of independence, and there was much to stir the imagination of the adventurous. Given that we know Benjamin Harris was a book-lover, and had, at least, a good basic education, which must have extended to a knowledge of classics, then it is not so surprising that he chose Oxford as his destination. And he must have been aware that Oxford had other attributes too. For all its provincialness, it provided a fertile environment, and one at the forefront of social change. As university education expanded, and other cities gained university charters, a wider breed of students came into the mêlée; and Oxford became an increasingly cosmopolitan centre, with connections in the industrial North. Although the Church still held sway in the University, its dog days were numbered. Rival religions were in the ascendancy: the industrial revolution spawned its own creed. While Darwin was already juggling with natural selection in the animal world, the railway engineer, Herbert Spencer, observed the process in the business world, and saw not redemption but the survival of the fittest. Within twenty years their work was linked with that of the impassioned Tom Huxley: now the fat was in the fire and the established Church in the dock[46]. All this was manna to the Blackwells: as it was to many of their trading contemporaries; the power of the old order was under attack. In Oxford, the young Blackwells were surrounded by those who had cut their reforming teeth in the University. They espoused the universal rights of man: to political participation, to education, to the equality of the sexes, and to the liberation of the oppressed: both the slaves of the Empire and the factories of 'Darkest England'[47]. This ferment of ideas found a ready audience, and willing participant, among the newly franchised. Some supported the rallying call of the Chartists, and others the Anti-Corn-Law Lobby, which aimed to feed the poor with cheaper bread. Oxford, at the time, had its fair share of needy: the rich bowled alongside the beggars, and the long vacation was a 'great trial to the poor or the improvident'[48].

But the great and good were not the only ones to stir things up. The London Blackwell family had demonstrated some of its own 'political' form. Disliking the politics of his day, Benjamin Harris's father, Joshua Blackwell, had turned teetotal solely to spite the Government, and rob it of excise duty! Now it was his son's turn to cock a snook at the establishment. Benjamin Harris was determined, at least, to become his own master, and to defy Oxford City's antiquated trading restrictions, by opening a small business, even if it was only a small shop on a peripheral High Street. More private motives would also have been at work. Benjamin Harris wanted to marry. Tales are told of his passionate letters to the younger Nancy. And to an enterprising couple with thoughts of marriage and children, Oxford would have seemed a more ideal spot. Compared to London, it provided a 'clean town' in which to settle down. Disraeli's dream of *'sanitas sanitatum omnia sanitas'* came early to municipal Oxford, and if there was still poverty and squalor, the meaner streets could be easily left behind; the open countryside was just a short walk away. Cows were still driven to grazing across Magdalen Bridge, and 'the hills around Oxford were studded with plumy forest and the valleys were prolific in every class and genus of herbage. Views of the Colleges and Churches of the City offered everything London may have had, and their spires were reflected in the mirror-like surface of the rivers, Cherwell and Isis, as they glided by'[49]. The young Blackwells could not fail to be susceptible to such a scene.

But was Oxford the place to set up in business? The University remained dominant, and 'Members of the University', starting with 'the Chancellor and the Duke of Wellington', topped the hierarchy amongst Oxford's inhabitants[50]. At first sight, this order of things may have acted as a damper on

4 Magdalen Bridge in 1814.

young adventurers eager to set up in business. The University itself provided only limited potential for the expansion of the retail market, and there was already a preponderance of traders. But Benjamin Harris must have looked further than the end of his nose. He saw new trends, which portended well for business. A municipal inquiry, conducted in 1832, concluded that 'the city has lately much increased in size and population, and may be said on the whole to be prosperous'. At the time, there was much talk of the relaxation of the University's ancient residential and religious laws, which would enlarge the population, and improved transport brought students from new universities in Britain, as well as from Europe and America, at least during term-time. A more all-year-round demand for Oxford's services came from local townspeople, as well as those from wider Oxfordshire. The latter came not only to buy and sell in the markets, but also to avail themselves of the wider choice of wares provided by Oxford's traders. Among the most lucrative visitors to the town were wealthy gentlemen farmers, enriched by their success in transporting high-priced corn and other agricultural products down the conveniently proximate canal network, and successful entrepreneurial types seeking the accoutrements of gentrification. They wanted nothing better than to ape the gentry of the shires, and tendered for the building of fine houses and gardens, to be furnished with all the accompanying trappings, including their own private libraries. They aspired to send their children to the public schools and the universities, both already growing in number, and thence to the professions, the Civil Service, law or politics.

For an enterprising trader, these economic and social developments, in the Town and the University, were an enticement, even though Oxford had no industrial base, and only benefited indirectly from the wealth generated by the industrial revolution. But the University, for all that it bred many a 'political free thinker', was a hot bed of reaction when it came to supporting economic development. It had been ferocious in resisting the extension of any gas works in Oxford, and had run rough shod over both the Corporation and its citizens when they had suggested that a railway carriage works, for the Great Western Railway, could be opened in Oxford. Trade was all very well, and gentlemen needed the services of booksellers, good tailors, and the purveyors of fine victuals, but an influx of manual workers was quite another thing. The University's officials were appalled by the very idea that Oxford's hallowed streets would be flooded with 'mere mechanics'. Letters poured into *The Times*, and *Punch* produced two famous cartoons. These august arbiters of public taste supported the University, and local citizens parading with placards 'urging the great benefits that would follow from the works', were lost to sight[51]. As so often in the past, Gown prevailed over Town and the idea was quashed. The University's laggardly bigwigs did, however, finally allow one concession to modernity. After much dissembling, they agreed to the extension of the GWR's branch line near Oxford, although they couldn't resist pointing out that 'a railway would be a distraction to junior members of the University'[52]. Travel up and down the line now brought business and tourists into Oxford, and the local economy benefited from faster connections to and from other great cities; and there were many more lines on offer. Coach services to London were already in operation, and 'horse-drawn omnibuses, run by private enterprise, had made their appearance in the street shortly before the railway was opened'. The local hotels were quick off the mark, and advertised 'Omnibuses to and from the Railway Stations for every train'[53].

All those engaged in the retail and wholesale trades, especially those whose goods could feed the new 'consumerism', seized the opportunities afforded by this increase in traffic. Oxford also capitalized on its expertise. It had, in the past, boasted one of the earliest of the Weaver's Gilds, and by Benjamin and Nancy Blackwell's time this had left its mark with a large

Partners in Trade 43

number of tailors and dressmakers. To cater for visitors' more immediate needs, the city centre offered an unusually wide choice of fine wines and victuals. But the trades that stood out, in this ancient University city, were those associated with bookmaking. A wide variety of skilled craftsmen were employed in this category, and as time went by: 'the medieval illuminators and scriveners' gave way to printers, bookbinders and paper makers[54]. Their numbers, however, had been limited by the 'relatively small size of their ready market'. This ready market was restricted to the University, its libraries, and local gentlemen booksellers, such as the Parkers. With a greater demand for books, coming from the educated middle classes, there was some room for expansion, and some call for more quality bookselling outlets. It was on the latter that Benjamin Harris now pinned his hopes. At the age of thirty-three, in 1846, he was to be found renting a small ground floor property, for £18 per year at 46 High Street, St Clements, where he put the name of B H Blackwell above the door. An old faded photograph shows the parade of shops at St Clements, fronted by its own open market, which was a further magnet to attract the public across Magdalen Bridge. Crossing Magdalen Bridge in 1846, the name of B H Blackwell's could be glimpsed, sandwiched between those of the trading establishments of William Loder, Pork Butcher, and Samuel Prince, Baker, and next door but one to J B Cardi, Professor of French[55]. 'That the shop was situated outside the city limits was significant, for unless he were a freeman of the City, or the son or apprentice of a freeman, no one might set up a new business in Oxford without the payment of a fine'.

The city fathers of Oxford had always taken great pride in stamping out enterprise, and protected by Oxford's lack of the raw materials required for an industrial settlement, they had maintained the psychology of a 'walled town'. Reflecting on his grandfather's life, Basil Blackwell took pride from the stand Benjamin Harris had made as 'one of a number of young adventurers in trade who refused on principle to submit to this tyranny, and opened shops just beyond the City's eastern boundary across Magdalen Bridge'. Only one of these independent-minded small businesses survived on the outskirts of Oxford's City centre: the family firm of one Henry Eagleston, ironmonger and straw-hat-maker, which kept its doors open until 1947[56]. So, in this spirited, colourful and hardworking company, began the business and literary adventures of B H Blackwell's. Although the small shop was a step away from the heart of the University, it was on a site 'not unpropitious for those times, when undergraduates' leisure was not absorbed by organized athletics, and the haunts of the Scholar Gypsy were not mere names in a fading poem but were frequented in the course of long afternoon walks'. Not by chance, it would seem, the road to Headington, Gypsy Lane, Elsfield and Shotover led past the door of B H Blackwell's shop[57]. But B H Blackwell the first, then in his thirty-second year, was not himself disposed to leisure. Competition made the going hard, with the dominant bookshops of Parker in the Broad, Thornton in the High, and nineteen other booksellers within the City's bounds[58]. Nonetheless, 'whither he went'.

Mr Greatheart

Whither! Nay, none but God knows whither

As if work in the bookshop and 'teaching', and saving souls, at night, in the Temperance Rooms, was not enough, Benjamin Harris applied for the post as Oxford's first City Librarian. The Library opened in 1854. Here was another landmark in the story of worker's education. Through poesy and literature, they could make their way through the slough of despond to the Celestial City, and the room where they could adventure was warm and free. Bunyan was a favourite, a text book for the English working class movement. Very little of Benjamin Harris's short term as the City's first Librarian is known, and the record in the City Library archives is slight. But a letter from the House of Commons, dated 14 June 1854, from William Ewart, who was the prime sponsor of the Public Libraries Act, was a portend of the future success of B H Blackwell's. Ewart had written that 'he did not doubt that the venture's progress was a good augur', and he added that: 'The City's first Librarian bore a name which Oxford will always connect with books'[59]. In earlier days, all that Sir Thomas Bodley had required for the good librarian was 'leisure, learning, friends and means', but the task of the City's first Librarian was, however, no sinecure[60]. 'One wonders', mused a contemporary, 'how Mr Blackwell and his assistant contemplated the future, in which it was their duty to be in constant attendance on weekdays, from 9.00am until 11.00pm (10.00pm in the winter months) and, after church, from 6.00–10.00pm on Sundays'[61]. But contemplate it he did.

The Public library was not, primarily, a facility for the leisured classes. It had higher purposes: ones to which Oxford's new Librarian was wholly committed, as he had already demonstrated as the Librarian of the Teetotal Society. The purposes of the 1850 Library Act were, in High Victorian rhetoric, 'that knowledge should triumph over ignorance' to become 'the means of enlightenment against utter destitution by self-improvement'[62]. Literature, art and science were now, with the establishment of public libraries, to 'belong to all classes'; especially as anyone could come to the Library after they had finished work. During the Library's first year, over 13,000 books were issued for reference, and the wide selection of newspapers—metropolitan and weekly—were widely read. Judging by the daily attendance of over 400, the Library's 'handsome room', on the ground floor of the Town Hall, St Aldate's Street, must have provided a welcome respite from the workplace, or an over-crowded family kitchen. In its interior, there was 'a neat little drinking fountain, affording copious libations of *aqua pura*' [63]. Benjamin Harris would have been more than gratified if his Library's attractions were to keep people out of the public houses. But protecting his patrons from the demon of drink was only an inadvertent duty, and benefit. His duty was also to guard the doors of the new Library 'lest any work of an immoral or infidel tendency should be admitted'[64]. More practical considerations also prevailed on Benjamin Harris, when accepting the position of City Librarian. With a wife and three children to support, he understandably wanted to bolster the very modest income he derived from his nine-year-old bookselling venture. Relying on the services of his young library assistant, Harry Collins, employed full time with wages of seven pence a week, he calculated that, since duties at that time in the Library were largely custodial, the Library being only open for reference, he could sustain both positions. But this calculus was to be to his cost. Refusing to heed the symptoms of overwork, and spurred on by the suffering of others less fortunate around him, not least by his deep concern for those affected by the atrocities in the Crimea, he looked to extend the scope of his bookselling activities, as well as tending to his library duties.

The papers were full of international news, and the tales of butchery and heroism in the Crimea sold them. Benjamin Harris was appalled by the appetite his readers had for this daily diet of horror, but the papers in the Reading Room also told more peaceful tales; tales of adventures in the expanding world of international trade. Ahead of his time, and despite international uncertainty, this young librarian-bookseller considered the prospects for overseas openings in the book trade; Britain, after all, was not the only 'workshop of the world'. In fact, 'newly emerging' industrialists in America and Germany were fast challenging Britain's pre-eminence. Commensurate with their development was a growing demand for education, particularly technical and scientific learning, which had a far stronger base in the less academically conservative institutions of America and Germany. These newly industrialized countries would stop at nothing to gain a competitive edge. The Americans aspired to overtake Britain in all fields, and Germany was fast gaining the ascendancy in the chemical engineering industries. Benjamin Harris was, rightly, convinced that their demand for educational material must, at least, equal that in the British market. Other barriers to international trade were coming down too: with the invention of steamboats, parcels of books could be carried across the Atlantic in two weeks. Since opening his shop, Benjamin Harris had traded almost exclusively in second-hand books, not available outside Britain. Now he would advertise them overseas. He set to work to prepare catalogues to inform potential overseas customers about his stock. A bill survives, dated 11 January 1853, for the production by the *Oxford Chronicle* of 250 catalogues numbering twelve pages. Somehow these catalogues found their way to other centres of learning, across the world: an invoice dated 30 May 1853 for books to the value of £4 14s, was sent to a Mr John Gooch of Pennsylvania.

All too few other stories of Benjamin Harris's life, as bookman and bookseller in Oxford, have survived. Basil Blackwell alluded to having read his grandfather's diaries, but sadly the originals have not come to light. At the time of his death there were no public obituaries, save one line in Jackson's *Oxford Journal* and a few lines in local newspapers, now in the Oxford City Library's scrapbook. We do know that his young business had been viable, but only just: he had so little fat that, when he died, his creditors, publishers, had to 'exercise generosity'. 'That they did so is, nonetheless, one sign of the esteem in which he was held, albeit that his life's work was left incomplete'. Something of the variety of his work in the book trade is captured in a story salvaged by his grandson, Basil Blackwell. Probably taken from his now missing diaries, the story provides a wistful glimpse into the daily life of a second-hand bookseller[65]. B H Blackwell, bookseller, may have succeeded in becoming master in his own house, but, when he set out to buy books in other people's houses he was at their beck and call, and he was never quite sure how he would be received. On one occasion, Basil recorded, 'my grandfather had been invited to visit the house of a local devout Quaker, to value some books offered for purchase; he was courteously received by the grave Quaker, who showed him to the room where the books were and said: "Wilt thou take tea?"' Acutely aware of not wanting to trouble his host, Benjamin Henry politely, obsequiously, declined the invitation. But, as so often must have happened, the valuation took rather longer than was expected and 'presently the door opened and the Quaker's wife came in, bearing a tray with teapot and pleasant nourishment and put it down on the table'. Basil, picturing his grandfather's relief at the sight of the sustenance, describes how he thanked her graciously. 'But almost before she had left the room, the door immediately flew open; the Quaker entered, seized the tray and carried it off, saying "Thee hasn't to tell a lie in my house".'

For someone as sober, upright and self-denying as Benjamin Harris this upbraiding must have been mortifying, especially coming from one whose philosophy of life so nearly matched his own. He was both a devout Christian and teetotal, a stance that was heart-felt and not motivated, as in his father's case, by any desire to rob the government. 'Even as a young man in his twenties, he was concerned for the moral welfare of those who were not similarly blessed with a distaste for alcohol'. Seeking to save them, he had founded the Oxford Teetotal Society, together with his brother, Isaac. His work was not confined to the Society; his conviction had made him too zealous and expostulatory to be so limited. In 1839 he wrote an article on the importance of temperance, lamenting that his efforts in Oxford were largely unsupported 'by those who should know better'. 'We have not one minister of the gospel to assist us', he wrote, 'nor one medical practitioner to attempt to dispel the delusions which are generally indulged concerning the qualities of intoxicating liquors'. 'Yet', he continued, 'we are bold to demand a standing among the most important societies for the improvement of man, physically, socially, morally and intellectually'. And this, according to the book of Benjamin Harris, librarian and bookseller, meant freedom from the demon of drink and freedom to be educated; finger-wagging and fine words would do little, compared with a process of education. His principles were put into practice, and he organised for the Society to rent 'temperance rooms'. They provided a refuge for people after work and, more importantly, a more healthy, and cheaper, alternative to the public houses. Appropriate refreshments were provided while visitors availed themselves of the facilities of the Society's fast-growing library of books. Here, as in the newly developing 'working men's clubs', they could continue, or start, their education; books could be borrowed too, and there were lectures on how to lead a healthier life, physically, morally and spiritually, without the anaesthesia of drink.

Fitting in his official, paid, duties at Oxford City Library, with the demands of his own business, and his community and church ventures, was more exacting than Benjamin Harris bargained for. In an attempt to make life easier, and to be nearer the Library, he moved his family to 3 Turl Street, which was later to be called the Turl Cash Bookshop. But if he, privately, accepted that he had pushed himself too hard, he tried fiercely to keep any fears about his health to himself. Looking back on their early life, his children had stored up memories of how he had bravely conspired to escape detection: 'When a sudden sharp pain caused him to cry out, he would try to cover-up by pretending to sing scales; he was after all an avid chorister'. His family, however, were not deceived. At the age of forty-one, before he could enjoy the increased comforts of his new abode in Turl Street, he died; the victim of angina pectoris, exacerbated by diphtheria. His granddaughter, Dorothy, recorded the bleak and shocking tales of her grandfather's death, which she must have heard from her father, or from her Aunt Matilda or Uncle Fred. One Sunday after lunch, she wrote, 'B H Blackwell the first died suddenly in his chair'. But he had left behind 'a little, rather grave, boy of seven', who was 'to grow up in a home struggling with poverty and a life in which there was no time, or room, for fun'[66]. This 'little boy' was her father. And he was destined to succeed his father, becoming the second B H Blackwell, and, in turn, his son Basil became the third in line in the family business.

Basil Blackwell later wrote to one of his grandfather's successors, as City Librarian, that his 'grandfather had in fact worked himself to death'[67]. 'He had 'pluralised as first City librarian and emergent bookseller, with any spare minutes devoted to the cause of total abstinence'. When in a lighter, more ironic mood, Basil Blackwell used to moot that his grandfather had perhaps died of 'teetotalism'. But this, Basil hastened to add, was 'a tradition which fell by the wayside'[68]. These memories of his grandfather, who had died over thirty years before he was born, became the stuff of legend for Basil Blackwell. The first B H Blackwell, the original founder of Blackwell's, a frugal, God-fearing and uncomplaining man, had died before his time, and the first bookshop died with him. His wife, Anne 'Nancy' Stirling Blackwell, was 'left with a business in its growing pains', and when the publishers' accounts had been settled and the stock had been sold 'at valuation', the young widow had little left. Benjamin Harris's executor was one Charles Richards, a bookseller, of 104 High Street, to whom his son, Benjamin Henry, was later apprenticed. Charles Richards had been a close friend, and had also worked as a librarian for the Oxford Teetotal Society. As a 'licensed appraiser', he valued, 'for probate, the stock of printed books on 15 May 1856'. The value being what it was, he tried to do his best for the family. He wrote to the publishers, Routledge and Co, explaining the circumstances of Benjamin Harris Blackwell's early death, hoping to persuade them to relinquish their claims for unpaid bills. A generous reply came back to Charles Richards by return, from George Routledge, of 2 Farrington Street, London, on June 20 1851: 'After your letter of this day we will most willingly give up our proportion of the dividend for Mrs Blackwell's use. I only regret that she should have been so badly provided for'. The letter was kept by the Routledge family, and over a century later a duplicate was sent to Basil Blackwell: 'I am sending you a

5 Benjamin Harris's gravestone in Holywell cemetery.

copy of a letter which bears the signature of your honoured firm and does honour to it, as I do now. *Floreatis semper!*'[69]

Benjamin Harris, 'tired and overworked, was laid to rest' in the public graveyard, beside the Church of St Cross, Holywell, and the first B H Blackwell's went with him. It had, of necessity, been sold to supplement the income of his wife and children. Yet he had made a name for himself, and his work as the pioneer of the Oxford City Library: 'this quaint honour', did not 'turn to dust'[70]. His grave is still 'a fine and private place', standing clear of the hawthorn and in the shade of the yew, and it is heightened in summer with purple-flowering Honesty, speckled all around. The site of the cemetery is ancient; in mediaeval times it was part of a small village of fullers and weavers, with a manor house, a green, a church and the 'holy wells', which gave the site its name. It teems with meadow life, just as it was described in the *Doomsday Book*, although its peace was temporarily disturbed during the Civil War, and again in the eighteenth century, when it was used as a cockpit and a bowling green. Merton College acquired the land, and made it available as a burial ground. Benjamin Harris's grave lies NW of the church, and a notice, by the wooden bench, points it out. At the sound of a Stanley Spenceresque trumpet, he could arise to a roll-call of many notable book people: the writer Kenneth Grahame, poets, like Maurice Bowra, brushing up on his Pindar, and Charlie Williams, Basil Blackwell's old OUP friend, and the drama critic, Kenneth Tynan. There are others too, who served the causes of the University, and far beyond: Radcliffe-Maude, for example, who founded UNESCO. Benjamin Harris's glee can only be imagined when he discovers himself in the company of the great Victorian church composer, John Stainer, hymning himself through eternity. The more modest Benjamin Harris is not forgotten; his beginnings in bookselling were the inspiration for the future Blackwell's 'empire'. Basil Blackwell reflected on the subsequent success of B H Blackwell's where: 'The first B H Blackwell, unfortunate in himself, was fortunate in his son. The second Blackwell (B H Blackwell of Broad Street), re-founder of the firm, was fortunate in his staff'. And, he declared, 'the third Blackwell (himself) was most fortunate in his staff and his colleagues'[71]. But it is doubtful if Benjamin Harris's son and grandson would have ever re-established the family name, and built on his foundation, if it had not been for the determination of his wife, Nancy.

Anne Nancy Stirling Blackwell 1823–1887

Her mission in life would be to see the name of B H Blackwell revived in her elder son, Benjamin Henry Blackwell[72]

Ann Nancy (Stirling) Blackwell had been born in 1823 in London, and must have come to Oxford with her prospective husband, nearly ten years her senior. They were married in Oxford in 1845, the year before the newly-weds started their Blackwellian adventures in St Clements. Little record of Nancy exists, save that of her marriage and various brief entries in Oxford Directories. The two chief family chroniclers, Basil and Dorothy, were not born until after her death. Nonetheless, for the Blackwell family, and for their close associates, she became a legendary figure. It was to his grandmother, Nancy, that Sir Basil properly attributed the founding of the present B H Blackwell's. 'That the Founder's wife was a woman of strong personality: of remarkable character and industry, is not in doubt'[73]. Left to fend for her family at the age of 32, 'Nancy resolved that the dreams of her dead husband would not go unrealised'[74]. Her husband, according to Basil Blackwell, had courted her with a great ardour, and she now directed her reciprocal passion to rescue his business[75]. Her sole mission in life was to see the name of B H Blackwell revived in her elder son, Benjamin Henry Blackwell. In the meanwhile, if her ambition was to be realised, there was a livelihood to be found. Casting sentimentality aside, Nancy left Turl Street, and moved her family to cheaper rented quarters, at 1 Jews Mount, subsequently called Bulwarks Lane, looking down on the terminus of the Oxford and Birmingham Canal, now the site of Nuffield College[76]. This was the age when only 'self-help' could save the unfortunate, however worthy, from the workhouse. Widowed, with three small children to support, she fell back on her old, pre-married, trade. Henceforth, until well after her son had made his way, she made a living plying her dressmaking skills and teaching embroidery[77]. Her good craftwork brought her to the attention of the Conventual Sisters of St Thomas, whose habits she helped to make. And her fine needlework embellished many a ceremonial ecclesiastical vestment[78].

Whereas Basil Blackwell claimed that the Oxford Movement gave an impetus to Nancy's 'art', her skills also caught the attention of a secular, and more lucrative, market, where she captured a corner with her elaborately sprigged waistcoats. Sporting such finery was, then, the vogue among Victorian undergraduates: 'such as might have been seen on the young Pendennis, who, during his time at the University, was rather a dressy man and loved to array himself in splendour. He and his polite friends would dress themselves out with as much care in order to go and dine at each other's rooms, as other folks would who were going to enslave a mistress ... but what follies will not youth perpetrate with its own admirable gravity and simplicity?' And the Blackwells were to profit from their 'folly'. It was due to these 'blessed waistcoats', asserted Basil Blackwell, that Nancy's children received their rudimentary education and training. And, perhaps more importantly, her efforts 'served to impress upon them the lesson of self-help, which was an article of faith to a generation who looked to Samuel Smiles rather than to Whitehall for direction and support in their lives'. Alongside her children's upbringing and education, Nancy took on the business of training others, and it was not long before the amount of work put into her hands enabled her to employ apprentice pupils. Some elderly Oxford citizens still remembered his grandmother, as Sir Basil recalled in 1954: 'I was talking on Christmas Eve to a little old lady of 99 who remembered that her sister came as a pupil to my grandmother's little school of embroidery'[79]. As the family fortunes picked up, Nancy was able to move the family, together with a boarder-apprentice and a servant, to larger, more spacious quarters at 46 Holywell Street, in 1874; a house large enough to let lodgings in term time[80].

Nancy's business success, although modest, given a household to maintain and boarders to be attended to in addition to earning a living, had enabled her 'to place the eldest and the youngest, girl and boy, satisfactorily in the world'[81]. Little is known of her daughter's adult progress, save that she was as devout as her father and brother and went off, in 1874, to teach at Bloemfontein, in the Orange Free State. Basil Blackwell remembered his grandmother's eldest son, Fred. Uncle Fred, he wrote, 'reminded him a little bit of the patriarch in Little Dorrit'. Until he retired, he had worked as a water rate collector, at a salary of £160 a year, conveniently supplemented by comfortable dowries from his two marriages. Like his younger brother, Fred 'had a fine singing voice and sang in the choir of St John's Church (part of Merton chapel while it was still a Parish)'. Basil recalled his uncle's ability to write 'a beautiful hand' and, perhaps because of this, 'he worked for Blackwell's for some years after his retirement from water'. Basil attributed the start of the Blackwell's Catalogue of Customers to his uncle, and it was this catalogue, Basil thought, 'that became the basis of our Computer Customer List of some 70,000 today' (1979)[82]. Although Fred ended up at Blackwell's, it was his younger brother, Benjamin Henry (Harry) Blackwell that 'was to restore to the list of Oxford booksellers the name of B H Blackwell. For seven years his mother maintained him during an apprenticeship, which began with the remuneration of a shilling a week; and for nine more years she helped him while he assembled the knowledge and modest resources which enabled him to open that little ground floor front shop at 50 Broad Street.'[83]

As soon as Benjamin Henry finished his apprenticeship, he was sent to manage a branch of Richard's shop at 38 High Street, from where he rose in the ranks by getting himself appointed as an assistant at the more flourishing firm of Slatter and Rose. Harry was by now earning good money, his wages rising to 40 shillings a week in 1878. Harry Blackwell, however, was intent on his own new project, and saving hard to put it into practice. On New Year's Day 1879, Nancy's wish was fulfilled; her son opened the door to a small one-roomed shop, above which the name 'B H Blackwell' was revived, and at a central site in Broad Street. 'The mother had had little doubt that the son would thrive'. Ever mindful of his mother's example and expectations, and fortified by his own abilities, training and application, he was successful from the first. Nancy, installed with her son above the shop, was able to witness at first hand the efforts of her son: 'a young man', according to his son, Basil, 'who guided his life by the discipline of the fifteenth psalm'. (And Basil recalled his father giving him sixpence for repeating it as soon as he could understand such things.) Nancy lived to see her son conduct his business 'by his belief in that aspect of genius which Carlyle describes as 'transcendent capacity of taking trouble', and by the rule 'that a day's work be done in a day'[84]. This maxim would just as well have applied to Nancy herself. Anne Stirling Blackwell, Sir Basil wrote, had been 'in the right tradition of great Victorian women, who thought more of their duty than of their rights'. With these qualities she endowed her son, and seeing him established was reward enough.

Nancy seems to have kept up her own trade, even after her son re-established the family business. The *Oxford Directory* of 1880 described the residents of 50 Broad Street as: B H Blackwell, bookseller, and Ann Blackwell, dressmaker. Her own pride, independence and pleasure in her 'art' probably precluded any letting-go. Like her son, 'she was determined that their earlier poverty would not be visited on the next generation'. He did not marry until 1886, the year before Nancy's death, by which time he was reasonably assured that he could not only provide for his mother but also for a wife and for his staff, at Blackwell's. Benjamin Henry's first responsibility had been to see his mother comfortably established, and an entry in his diary, dated 22 March 1880, announced: 'Mum and I are going to live at Broad Street'. Nancy lived with her son until she died, on the 4 June 1887 at the age of 64. Her mission in life abundantly accomplished, Anne Nancy Stirling was buried among her kinswomen, the weavers and fullers of the old mediaeval village of the Holy Wells, as was her elder brother John Thomas Stirling Lambert, 1807–1868. Beside the church of St Cross, she joined her husband:
'Some natural tears they'd drop't, but wiped them soon;
The world was all before them, where to choose
Their place of rest, and providence their guide:
They hand in hand with wandring steps and slow,
Through Eden took their solitarie way'[85].
But their way had not been so solitary, and they were not forgotten. Although her grandson, Basil, was born two years after her death, he was always acutely aware of her importance. Assembling accounts, and stories, of the lives of his family, he attempted to sum up her contribution. 'Unlike medieval historians', he explained, 'who used to speculate as to how many angels could stand on the point of a needle', it could be argued that 'Black-wellians, although not angels, did indeed stand on the point of a needle'. It

was indeed his 'grandmother's skill in embroidery which made what she did possible'[86]. Ann Nancy Stirling Blackwell had, by her own efforts, set her youngest son on the road to Broad Street, and in her own lifetime, she had indeed seen her husband's name 'revived in her elder son, Benjamin Henry Blackwell'.

Chapter 3
Merchant Scholar[87]

'This above all—to thine own self be true,
And it must follow, as the night the day,
Thou canst not then be false to any man'[88]

Benjamin Henry: the second B H Blackwell 1849–1924

Growing pains

Voyaging through strange seas of thought, alone[89]

Benjamin Henry, 'Harry' Blackwell, like his own children, Basil and Dorothy, in their turn, was born over a bookshop. After his father's death, when Harry was merely six, his mother, Nancy, had been forced to move to rented rooms, in a cheaper and less salubrious part of town, down by the canal. Here she resumed her former trades, embroidery and dressmaking, 'in order that she might prepare her young son for the task of restoring the family name'. Harry Blackwell always bore the imprint of these hard days, as his daughter, Dorothy (Blackwell) Austin, later recorded. She wrote poignantly of her father's early life: 'It must have been a struggle for his mother to maintain two boys at school', and the strains and disciplines which formed Harry's character during his early life 'must have conditioned his adult character'[90]. In both his personal and business life, he remained quiet, devout, dutiful, gentle and very 'Victorian', exercising 'a forbearance that was in no small measure the result of a strong, and rather simple, faith'[91]. There were times, however, when Harry's unshakeable faith was put to the test, and his prayers, even for others, were not always answered. This 'problem' of pain was one of the imponderables that he tussled with incessantly, as did his own children. Basil Blackwell remembered a story, from his own childhood, which illuminates the 'simple faith' with which his father endowed him. 'I was bidden with my sister to go and play in the small garden behind the shop, where there was a Ribston Pippin apple-tree, having been strictly enjoined not to nibble the windfalls. This was certainly no garden of Eden, and I do not know if my sister was the one to tempt me, but we did eat the windfalls, were caught, and put across my mother's knee, my sister first as she was the elder. I do not know whether she was spanked the harder, but she was in great distress, and I conceived the idea of asking God that some of her pain should pass to me. I thereupon prayed, and then asked her whether the pain had diminished, but she still howled loudly, and said very firmly, "No!" It was a great shock to me that such a self-sacrificing prayer was not answered.' Benjamin Henry would almost certainly have advised his son that he was 'wrong' to have asked for such a 'favour'.

Young Harry was not a child who expected favours: he was self-contained, and made his own entertainment. Cats were his one childhood passion, and, like other lonely children, he made up his own language to 'talk' to his beloved cats. Books, too, provided him with solace, and a means of escape. His appetite for books was voracious, and his avid consumption gave him the basis of an education, which he later relied on for progress in his trade. Showing a natural aptitude for books, in and out of the schoolroom, his fate was sealed; Nancy Blackwell renewed her efforts to steer him in his late father's footsteps. But given the family's financial circumstances, there were no short cuts to be had. If Benjamin Henry was to establish himself in his father's trade, he must work his passage, and acquire 'qualifications' through the apprenticeship system. Thus, in 1862, when only thirteen, Harry left Price's School. Basil Blackwell, writing of his father, imagined the pangs he must have felt 'when he was pushed out so early into the world'. To recompense himself, Harry combined the 'learning of his job' with a programme of self-education in literature, classics and music. His early familiarity with Latin came from sacred music, and he learnt, or more probably taught himself, the piano and the art of sight-singing. While still at school, and being musical, he had been accepted for Queen's College Choir and Choir School, where he had hoped to continue, even after his apprenticeship. He had also counted on his chorister's pay to help sustain him during the forthcoming difficult and long years of apprenticeship. Again he was disappointed. To his dismay his voice broke early, and his mother was 'sorely put' to keep him on his 'pay' of one shilling a week[92].

His daughter, Dorothy, in her account of her father's childhood, had been struck by the pathos of his situation. But if he was inwardly disappointed and lonely, and felt the lack of a more indulged childhood, his diaries told a different story. True, his mother was preoccupied with earning a living, but Harry amused himself with countless hobbies. In this way he established a pattern that carried him through his childhood years, and a habit that he maintained throughout his life. The range of his hobbies was extraordinary, given his lack of leisure time; there was very little evening left at the end of a long working day in the shop and Sundays were given over to the church choir. Nonetheless, he frequently escaped the city to walk in the surrounding meadows, and he learnt to row, enrolling himself in a local club at not inconsiderable expense. For social life he relied on the contacts he made through his church. The Church year had its high and low points, and there was a time and a place for the reflective, as well as the celebratory. There was always music to be rehearsed, and the annual harvest supper, the summer outing, and the festivities of Easter and Christmas to look forward to. He also found good company, and intellectual stimulation, at the Churchman's Union. Such holidays as he took, he spent cycling on a 'penny farthing' around Oxfordshire and Berkshire; riding on horseback remained the preserve of the wealthier. Before setting off on these tours, Harry would make exquisite little maps of the routes and byways. Fascinated with detail, and kept indoors by the Oxfordshire rain, he would occupy himself with illuminated missal work 'of the utmost refinement—tiny specks of gold and silver paint put on with a magnifying glass'[93]. But none of these hobbies 'surpassed the pleasure he received from reading, and acquiring knowledge'.

An apprenticeship as lengthy as Jacob's was to Laban[94]

Snatches of reading (said he) will not make a Bentley or a Clarke. They are, however, in a certain degree advantageous[95]

Basil Blackwell reflected that his father 'had only just begun to revel in acquiring knowledge and pursuing scholarship' and to feel his mind 'reaching out', when he was forced out to work. Master Benjamin Henry's childhood had been as short as his apprenticeship was to be long. At the tender age of thirteen, he was bound apprentice at one shilling a week, with annual increments of one shilling, to a bookseller, Charles Richards, at 104 High Street[96]. He was a dutiful son, and as far as the world could judge, he settled down with a good will. Although he had the compensation of being among books, it was not at all clear, in his early working years, that he 'shared his mother's single-minded desire to see his own name over a bookshop door'[97]. 'Mr Richard's shop was a queer one, one side being a bookshop and the other a wine merchant's'[98]. When trade was slack, especially, Basil Blackwell wrote, 'in the long vacations when the weeds grew in the Oxford streets and the booksellers took down their shutters and sorted and dusted their stock,' he studied the catalogues, learning the entries by heart. When seeking for further adventure, he would pause from Quaritch's catalogues, and turn to Caesar. Guided by Smith's *Principia Latina*, he adventured vicariously, accompanying Caesar to the Gallic Wars. Pausing to reflect on the state of Europe, he could not help being fired up by its injustices. He would seek his own physical relief, by taking strenuous exercise on the river or running round the meadows before breakfast. Here he was reprieved from Caesar's 'dreary themes of war', to find the rural idyll of the singing farmer of Virgil's *Georgics*.

Studious and enterprising as Benjamin Henry was, his lack of formal education led to setbacks. While at Richard's shop he had applied for, and failed to get, the post of Librarian of the City of Cardiff [99]. Nonetheless, patience was one of his virtues, and 'seventeen years went by, during which he completed his apprenticeship'. He had bided his time, but he was now more than ready for further responsibility. An opening for a manager came up at the flourishing firm of Slatter and Rose, at 2–3 High Street, and Benjamin Henry made his first move. New responsibilities did little to disrupt the former pattern of his life; he continued to combine a day's work with a programme of 'continuing education'. A page of his diary, with entries from 1879 to 1882, provides an insight into what this involved. The range of his reading is in itself worthy of note. To his earlier study of the classics, and his habitual reading of Tennyson, he added *Don Quixote*, and was moved to spend several days on Pope's *Dunciad*, a satire of Aaron Hill, which he 'started on 6 June at 6.50am'. At the same time he studied the qualities and temperaments of creative writers, using Isaac (the father of Benjamin) Disraeli's *Curiosities of Literature*, and *The Literary Character*. One 'literary character' caught his special attention: Thomas Babington Macaulay, as captured in a new study by George Trevelyan. Macaulay had first made a literary name for himself with an essay on Milton, and on early morning runs, before breakfast, Benjamin Henry would recite Milton. Milton's elegiac *Lycidas* suited his pastoral mood, as he crossed Iffley Meadow in the mists of 6.45am; two years later he had learnt this poem off by heart. Perhaps he shared the anxieties Milton expressed in the poem: the uncertainties of life, ambition and unfulfilled promise? Not for him, on his daily jaunts, the 'unreproved pleasures free', the 'nods and becks and wreathed smiles' at the hand of the 'mountain nymph Sweet Liberty', of Milton's *L'Allegro*. His preference was for the Milton of *Il Penseroso*: 'sober, steadfast and demure'. This ode conveys something of Benjamin Henry's character, with its sentiments of piety, asceticism and a puritanical obsession with hard work. Like Milton, Benjamin Henry had a passionate faith in God and free will, and the attainment of 'paradise within'. He was moved by the dilemma of *Paradise Lost*, responding to 'Milton's compassionate myth of the precarious human situation, a myth which in one way or another comprehends all that mankind has felt and thought and done'[100].

For all that 'the world was all before him', he was a young healthy man, and his sap was rising; the same page of his diary refers, in passing, to a dance and a concert, with a note, added later in 1882, that he had 'started to learn bicycling'. Harry Blackwell's youthful diaries also convey his sense of pleasure as a member, and treasurer, of the Falcon Boat Club, 'which cost me 24 shillings per annum'. In the height of midsummer, June 1877, when the light was at its longest, he went 'Down river in evening, picked up crews for sports. In Quelch's four—Annis's said to be the best and Woodward's next (three fours in all). Off to Sports, first heat, 7 o'clock, beat Annis's easily, very pleased, got plated cup. . . . To Iffley to supper (3 shillings) songs and toasts till 11; home by boat 12—a jolly day altogether. . . . I am talked of for the Regatta'. Music, too, featured in these watery pleasures: 'There was music on the river' and, on the 30 July, an Orpheus Water party: '1.15 off from the shop—started at Nuneham and then to Sandford for tea, singing all the way'. Harry Blackwell's physical stamina must have been immense; packing in this vigorous programme of activities on top of a job where he worked over ten hours a day, six days a week. On the seventh day, there was much music making too. Benjamin Henry was by now a chorister at the Church of SS Philip and James, the new parish church in North Oxford designed by George Edmund Stroud, famous not only for his churches, but also the Law Courts in the Strand. According to his diary, Benjamin Henry had been singing with the choir for 'nearly fifteen years'—almost from the time of its consecration. On Sunday evenings, more sacred and secular music was enjoyed at home with his mother, and their friends.

From now on, however, life at home with his mother would be quieter: his brother Fred, he noted in his diary, 1878, was to be married. Whatever Benjamin Henry may have privately thought of his own prospects, nothing was to distract him; his future had to be secured, and his mother's dreams fulfilled. When the librarianship door had not opened for him, made harder by the fact that his father had been Oxford City's first librarian, he pinned his hopes elsewhere. An entry in Benjamin Henry's diary for 1877 recorded the germ of his ambition: 'I have now been with Mr Rose six years and seem likely to stay for a year or two, at the end of which I hope to be able with a little assistance to open in London or elsewhere a business on my own account'[101]. A year later his intention became clearer. There was no more talk of 'London or elsewhere', and his muses, and his boating enthusiasms, were strictly extra-mural. According to his diary, his mind was now fully made up: 'I will begin business in Oxford and probably in October 79'. Hearing of vacant premises at 50 Broad Street, progress had been faster than he had anticipated. He formally agreed to take the shop on 17 October 1878, and a few days later, 25 October, he noted his previous master's approbation: 'Mr Rose thought I should do'. There, at the heart of the University and in front of the great Bodleian Library, he had at his disposal 'a shop and back room with use of cellar at a rent of £2 a month'. His commitment to Oxford was complete; sealed not only by his religious and family ties, and his firmly entrenched social pattern, but also by the re-establishment of B H Blackwell's.

During his years at Slatter and Rose, he had made many friends and contacts: the beginnings of a business network; and after seventeen years in the trade he had a wealth of experience and knowledge to draw on. More importantly, his wages at Slatter and Rose had enabled him, given his customary self-restraint, to save for his big day. Steadily buying suitable books, he had accumulated, by the autumn of 1878, a nice little nest egg, with over 700 works in his personal stockpile. The list, as featured in his diary scribblings, was an eclectic mixture, featuring Greek and Latin classics amongst 'modern' poetry and biography. Diodati, Diodorus Siculus, Diogenes Laertius and Dionysis the Areopagite, held court, in strict alphabetical order, for the *Amores* of Ovid, while Carey's Dante, 1868, vied with Drayton's eclogues in Spencerian mode. Palgrave's *Golden Treasury*, an 1875 edition, was exposed to works of English criticism by the contemporaneous Stofford Brooks—*On English Literature* 1876. A life of Chatterton, an 1837 edition, was, perhaps, a reminder of the ignominy of poverty, and a life of Bacon, an 1853 edition, an invitation to 'experience' life rather than always to explain. Benjamin Henry's collection sported the work of fellow publisher and bookseller, Henry Bohn, and, splendidly, twenty-two volumes of the 1810 fourth edition of the *Encyclopaedia Britannica* in company with three volumes of Froissart's series of *Chronicles*, 1871 edition. Henry Hallam could be found juxtaposing *A View of the State of Europe during the Middle Ages*, three volumes, 1834, with a *Constitutional History of Britain*, spiced-up by Roscoe's *Memoirs of Benvenuto Celini*, an 1822 edition. Not to be left in the shade were the Puritans of the Midlands. Their struggles were personified in *Memoirs of the Life of Colonel Hutchinson*, written by Lucy Hutchinson, his wife, in 1806. They would doubtless have looked askance at Keble's *Christian Year*, an 1874 edition bound in calf, which Benjamin Henry had acquired in exchange for a pack of cards and four pence! Conservatively valuing his 'stock' at £126 (diary entry

24 December 1878), with a nominal sale price of £190, he used the security of this 'working capital' to take the final plunge.

The name over the door

A remarkable shop, kept by a very remarkable man[102]

When Mr Blackwell's shop opened on New Year's Day 1879, it consisted of one tiny room, only twelve-feet square, with room for only one chair and one customer. From this modest beginning, with a working capital of £100, a loan of £150 at three percent, £20 worth of fixtures and fittings, a further outlay of £70 on books and £60 put aside, Benjamin Henry set out to become solvent and to provide for his future. This new merchant-trader was in good company. The little shop was established on a site that had been dedicated to trade for many generations. When, for example, his father had opened in St Clements, being prohibited from the 'inner-city', the small shops in Broad Street, numbered 48–50, contained no less than seven practitioners of diverse trades: S Seeker, in 'china', J Daly, a stationer, W H Bliss, painter and

6 The exterior of the Broad Street shop in the early 1900s.

7 An internal view of the shop in the early 1900s.

plumber, Matthew Charles, engraver, J Bradfield, plumber and Henry Lockwood, tailor. Thirty years later, Benjamin Henry joined the throng of Broad Street tradespeople, his mother, too, being listed as 'dressmaker'. Impervious to the temptations offered at No 52, the White Horse Public House, Benjamin Henry must have been uplifted by the adjacent buildings of the University, where the faces of the emperors outside the Sheldonian, and the facades of the Colleges of Trinity and Balliol, outshone the run-of-the-mill jumble of old buildings that made up Benjamin Henry's immediate surroundings. To the back were stables and haylofts ('undergraduates were still prone to equestrian exercise') and, more to Benjamin Henry's taste, the headquarters of the Churchman's Union, deriving from the Oxford Movement. Intermittently, at the back of the shop, would come 'rapid footfalls and alarming spuds' where students could, safely, put the gloves on[103].

Perhaps because of these many 'presences', and despite the existence of other competitors further down, on the other side of the same street,

8 The exterior of the shop in 2000.

'Mr Blackwell's bookshop had, from the outset, a special air about it. Those who came in from the noisy, cobbled street', chronicled a later edition of the *Oxford Magazine*, 'found quiet and an invitation, not so much spoken as conveyed by the friendly spirit of the bookseller, to scrutinise and handle the books on the shelves without obligation to buy'[104]. A full account of the shop's customers is preserved in the immaculately kept accounts of Benjamin Henry. The first entries, in 1879, list names such as: Beeching, Jowett, Macmillan, Ward and Lock, Parker, Thornton, Morrell, Trott, Goddard, Raven, Routledge, Longmans, Sladen of Oriel, Eastwood, Tillard, Clode, Hutton, Gibbs, Griffin, Hodgson, Morris, Higham, Gilbert, Norton, Drayton, Gladstone, Chatto, Sage, Brough, Hopkins, Roper Brooks, Cunliffe, Bright, Herbert, Ward, Swadling, Cassell, Darwall, Cobb, F Blackwell, Goodford, and so on. As the lists progress, the names become more familiar, and more famous, and the celebrated libraries make their appearance. The attraction for such a diversity of customers, and the pull for new undergraduates like Beeching and his Balliol contemporaries, must have been the ambiance and then the stock. The stock, mostly second-hand, was drawn from Ancient and Modern Literature. It had been chosen with good judgement and with a bias towards Greek and Latin, reflecting Benjamin Henry's love of the classics. Using the skills he had learnt as an apprentice, he compiled a catalogue to advertise his wares, and to titillate the interest of potential 'paying' customers. As luck would have it, Benjamin Henry's taste in books found a ready market. Such was the excitement generated by entries in his first catalogue, that he enticed even those not known to take exercise to attend in person at his little shop. One such customer was the formidable scholar, Ingram Bywater. Legend has it that he once said to a pupil: 'You go for walk! I have not wantonly taken a walk for twenty years'. But on receiving a copy of Mr Blackwell's first catalogue, he left his breakfast and *ran* to 50 Broad Street to secure a copy of the rare edition of Pacius' *Organon*![105] But there was more to Benjamin Henry's new life, at Broad Street, than satisfying those with a rarefied taste for the Greats.

In a commemorative address to fellow Blackwellians, Sir Basil tried to conjure up what it must have been like for his father, when he sat down alone on his first day in Broad Street. 'As I look at this assembly I am bound to reflect that if my father, in the first week of January 1879, had thought to commemorate the founding of his firm by sitting at lunch with his staff, he would have sat down alone. He would have had one guest of honour, and that would have been his mother, Ann Stirling Blackwell; and it would have been for her perhaps the happiest day in her life. Her thoughts must have gone back to Benjamin Harris Blackwell, her husband, who started as a bookseller.' Dorothy Austin takes up the account of the founding of the firm. 'Then came the time when an old lady, (a family friend, Mrs Teressa Messer of Thame) thinking him of a good type, lent him (Benjamin Henry) £300, and he opened his own shop—a counter and nothing else'. His mother's judgement was sound and Benjamin Henry's apprenticeship, self-education and application had already equipped him with 'the knowledge and industry necessary'. The tiny venture 'prospered most steadily', and brought out Benjamin Henry's natural skills—what his son termed: 'his quiet business genius.' His lifestyle was modest and 'returns from the business were ploughed back enabling it to continually expand'. Early, almost instant, success meant that Benjamin Henry did not labour alone for long. Benjamin Henry would have been the first to own that those who subsequently joined him in Broad Street were as much responsible for the success of the family business as he personally had ever been.

During his second year of trading, in 1880, Benjamin Henry took on his first apprentice. Master F W Chaundy came straight from school, untried and untested. However, being indentured gave an undertaking which was only very rarely reneged on. Solemnly, Fred Chaundy promised: 'to serve faithfully for five years, not to waste the Goods of his said Master ... not contract Matrimony within the said term nor play Cards or Dice Tables ... haunt Taverns or Playhouses'. For all this he was to receive 3s 6d a week, rising to 10s in his fifth year. Given the existence of this small remuneration, the English apprenticeship system was open to all, and gave an 'education' to those whose circumstances would have otherwise denied it to them. It was the system that had enabled Benjamin Henry, with no means, to put his own name over the door. The European system, in contrast, such as that operating in the craft *bottege* of Italy, required the apprentice to pay the master. Italian master tradesmen would only share their 'art' with those able to pay. Nonetheless the wages in England were barely more than subsistence. Returns in kind were the real benefit; Mr Blackwell's young apprentice learnt his art from one who was not only master, but who had himself started with nothing, had trodden the same path and knew intimately all its trials and pitfalls as well as its opportunities. Fred, and his brother Harry Chaundy in turn, became masters of their own shop. Master and boy worked long hours, and takings from the shop enabled Benjamin Henry to pay back his debt to Mrs Messer. Contemplating the length of his days, 'working 10.00 to 10.30 at night', according to his diary of 22 November 1881, he thought of engaging another pair of hands. Benjamin Henry's next apprentice was not only to learn the art of bookselling and the antiquarian trade, but something of scholarship too. In 1883, diary entry for 4 June, Master Fredk. Hanks came on board with Mr Blackwell and Fred Chaundy.

A month later, at his 'binding', Fred's mother made the understandable request that 'he should be a good boy'. Basil Blackwell often reflected on the similarities between the early lives and circumstances of the boy, Fred Hanks and his mother, and that of his own father and his mother[106]. Mrs Hanks, like Nancy Blackwell, was left with no choice other than to become the breadwinner when her husband died, and Fred was only six. Mrs Hanks, like Nancy Blackwell, had aspirations for her son, despite their situation, and encouraged him to 'better himself' with a little book learning. Fred Hanks presented his own account of his education at a speech he made at a *fête de champêtre* held in Appleton, where the Blackwells lived, to celebrate his Jubilee in 1933 and the conferment on him of an Honorary Degree of MA by Oxford University. On this public occasion he rehearsed a tale that so nearly matched Benjamin Henry's own: 'The only education my mother could afford to give me was that provided by the elementary schools at 2d a week. It must have been when I was about eight years old that my mother, anxious to do all she could to supplement my elementary education, thought it would be good for me to learn a little French. I remember accompanying her to a bookseller's shop, where she purchased for me with her hard-earned pennies a French grammar. This was, as far as I can remember, the first book I ever possessed.' (And it was perhaps this genesis of Fred Hank's interest which saw Blackwell's subsequently develop a Foreign Language department.) At the age of ten, Fred attended the church school of SS Philip and James. Here he added the rudiments of Latin to his beginnings in French. Reaching the age of thirteen, Fred Hanks, like his new mentor, had to combine self-education with a day's work. He also absorbed his master's love of 'hobbies'. Fred Hanks recalled that, in his spare time, he assisted 'Mr Blackwell' in taking his model steam engines to bits, cleaning them and putting them together and eventually sharing with his employer the pleasure of seeing them working[107].

Benjamin Henry's fatherly undertakings did not end with Fred Hanks. Thirty years later, Father Hanks assisted 'Mr Blackwell' in the 'up-bringing' of another apprentice who, like them, saw apprenticeship as a means to escape, initially, from poverty. Geoffrey Barfoot, recruited in 1913, later to join the ranks of the apprentice-directors, described himself as coming from peasant stock. His father had died when he was four, and Geoffrey vividly remembered his pauper's funeral. All the family resources, he recounted, had been used up in burying his grandmother. When his father died only two weeks later, there was scarce enough left for a coffin. The body of his father was conveyed on an open handcart in one of the last 'walking' funerals to be recorded in Oxford City. Shortly after Geoffrey Barfoot, Mr Blackwell happened on another likely recruit for the business, Will (Rex) King. Basil Blackwell takes up the story of Rex's fortuitous introduction, as told by Benjamin Henry. Basil's father had sat on the Oxford Library Committee, the Library Benjamin Henry's own father had helped to inaugurate, and, as part of their deliberations, they considered offers of new additions. 'At one of the meetings there was read a letter written with sly humour offering for the acceptance of the library a considerable collection of standard works in the field of English Literature "in case frequenters of the Library should still have an itch to read something after the popular papers on which the Library grant is mainly expended"'. The signature was 'W. King'. 'My father', Basil recounted, 'scrutinized the books and found them to be a poor man's library judiciously chosen, well used, and well kept—the result of many sixpences hardly come by. He sought the donar and found him to be a baker's son who had fallen out of employment by the GPO through long illness, and was recovering from a period of almost desperate poverty. In conversation he revealed a mind so stored with reading, so acute in literary judgement, altogether so manifestly the mind of a born bookman, that my father invited him to come and work in the Second-hand and Antiquarian department'[108].

In Rex King, Benjamin Henry had found a kindred spirit. The scope of Rex's knowledge, and his personality, made him a perfect Blackwellian. Benjamin Henry delighted in a mind which when touched at any point would respond with 'literary allusion, shrewd criticism, apt folk-sayings, or original aphorisms vividly phrased and presented with the somewhat wry humour of his native Gloucester'[109]. Two other men joined Mr Blackwell's staff towards the end of his life: Ewart (Edgar) Hine and Fred Stevens. Both Ewart Hine and Fred Stevens became members of the Board of Blackwell's under the Chairmanship of Benjamin Henry's son, in 1952. Fred Stevens recounted that the promotion from office boy to director had been beyond his wildest dreams. Sadly Rex King had died young in 1950. Together with the earlier apprentices, these three wise men passed on the collective wisdom of half a century of bookselling and a great deal more knowledge on the history of books. If they were unable to answer a customer's enquiry, the most junior would be sent over to the Bodleian and expected to return with an answer. How the academics of Oxford must have delighted in the offices of these 'unpaid' research assistants! Blackwellians had their own compensations. Bound as they were by similar backgrounds, the apprentices egged each other on, and not all the time in the long working days was devoted to serious endeavour. The Blackwellian apprentices, choral singers like the master, would sing lustily while they let off steam. When they weren't devising some test for the unsuspecting, even scaring the customers by hanging from the spiral staircase, they busied themselves among the shelves, the younger being 'trained', and kept down to size, by the elder.

In the early days of Blackwell's, when stocks of books sold inconveniently fast, Fred Chaundy, the first apprentice, had the artifice to arrange books sideways-on, thus attempting to disguise the gaps. Along with artifice, Fred Chaundy also acquired the art of disguising his reactions, especially in the company of customers. It was part of an apprentice's job to deliver books to customers and to collect them. This was done by hand, or using the Blackwell's bicycle contraption. Being sent out to deliver books to customers provided variety, but it also afforded opportunities to see more than a young apprentice bargained for. One such encounter provided a well-loved story for Blackwell's annals. Fred Chaundy had been sent to collect some books from the rooms of Charles Dodgson, in Christ Church. Calling early, Fred found the author still in his bedroom. Hearing the door, Dodgson emerged clad only in his shirt. Turning his back, he stooped down to recover a pile of books from the floor. But his shirt was only a 'cutty-sark'—it had no tail. This provided a sight for sore eyes no doubt, and a tale to enliven the long days in the shop, even though, in accordance with the Victorian philosophy of a young person's proper place, staff were expected to be seen and not heard. At Blackwell's both Master and Boy were the soul of discretion, and kept a discrete distance from customers. But they were ever on the front foot should customers require assistance. Customers were sovereign. They were to be made to feel at home, but left 'unmolested to browse round the shelves'[110]. Whatever impression this practice may have conveyed to the customer, the reality, viewed from behind the counter, was very different. Nothing was casual. Books were not sold as a result of chance encounters among dusty bookshelves. Booksellers, worth their salt, had to 'know' the stock, committing all the titles to memory (a task now performed in seconds by the computers that adorn modern booksellers' counters) so as all the better to advise, when called upon. Benjamin Henry was a taskmaster in this respect; he had learnt by heart the great catalogues of Bernard Quaritch, and his apprentices were obliged to do the same.

Quaritch's legendary catalogues inspired Benjamin Henry to devise his own extensive, and painstakingly precise, catalogues. In this way, customers could be enticed into the shop, and those from further afield could be kept informed, on their own doorsteps, by post. 'Catalogue No 1' has been preserved, and was reprinted in 1973 to coincide with the issue of No 1000. Reading through the original catalogue, it is easy to see where Benjamin Henry's preferences lay. Given his veneration for the classics, it was no surprise to see them leading the field. The catalogue included a number of nineteenth century texts, grammars and dictionaries that were the stock of university students. Among these day-to-day tomes were a few very fine earlier editions, including two Aldines (5s and 5s 6d.) and a Baskerville (5s). Over two-thirds of the items in the catalogue were less than 5s; only forty-five cost over a £1 and these were often in two volumes. The author's love of Oxford also shaped the choice of books on offer. A large selection of books included Loggan's *Oxonia Illustrata* (1675), which at £5 was the most expensive single volume in the whole catalogue. Even better investments were Piranesi's *Le antichita romane* (1756) in four volumes at £5.10s and the first edition of Hobbes' *Leviathan* (1651) at 18s: the retail price of these items would now be several hundred times higher. Perusing the catalogue, the eye of Sir Arthur Norrington, the author of the centennial history of Blackwell's,

No. I.   JAN., 1879.

CATALOGUE
OF
SECOND-HAND BOOKS
IN
Ancient and Modern Literature;

Comprising many that are Curious and Scarce, and a number of valuable and interesting Books relating to Oxford, including the works of Loggan, Williams, Skelton, Ingram, and others; being a portion of the Stock of

B. H. BLACKWELL,

On Sale at exceptionally Low Prices for Cash, at

50, BROAD STREET, OXFORD,
(Opposite the Sheldonian Theatre).

2d. in the 1/. DISCOUNT FOR CASH off New Books published at 2/6 and upwards.

Libraries and Small Collections of Books Bought for Cash.

Second-hand and Scarce Books, not in Stock, sought and advertised for free of charge.
ORDERS BY POST PROMPTLY ATTENDED TO.

9 The cover of catalogue No 1.

happened on what could have been an early day parenting manual, item 230, published in 1654 and marked 'very rare'. Used to the student community of the 1960s and 70s, Norrington must have enjoyed the irony of the entry: Thomas Hall's '*The Loathesomeness of Long Haire*, or, *Treatise wherein you have the question stated, etc., with the concurrent judgement of Divines, both old and new against it; with an appendix against Painting, Spots, Naked Backs, etc.*, 8s 6d'![111]

Blackwell's catalogue of 1886 displayed a more expensive selection of scientific and general volumes. Dr Radcliffe's Physic Library had been re-housed in the newly built University museum in Parks Road, Oxford, and Blackwell's was the recipient of some 800 volumes of overflow, some containing the bookplate of James Gibb, architect of the Radcliffe Camera. By the mid-eighties, new books began to feature alongside their second-hand rivals, and soon tipped the balance of sales. Catering for the Christmas trade in 1894, Benjamin Henry produced a general catalogue, with something enticing for the 'whole family', 'for all tastes and all ages': poetry, drama, religion, history, biography, reference books (the *Encyclopaedia Britannica* in twenty-four volumes), almanacs and annuals, including one for football! Adult titles, 1,500 in number, included the major Victorian novelists, with the notable exception of Trollope whose reputation had sadly collapsed at the time of his death in 1883. Added to the hall of fame were those of the younger generation of writers: Hardy, Kipling, Meredith, Lytton, Lever, Harrison Ainsworth, F Marion Crawford, Marie Corelli, Hall Caine and many who are long since forgotten. 'Who', asked Arthur Norrington, reviewing the lists for the 'Blackwell's History', 'can remember Amelia E Barr's *Feet of Clay* or *Love for an Hour is Love for Ever?* Among the extensive list of children's books was the 'gift pack' entitled *Our Little Ones' Library*, done up in a case with silk ribbon, at 1s 6d. No less than forty-seven of G A Henty's historical tales were there, accompanied by such names as R M Ballantyne, G Manville Fenn, W H G Kingston, Jules Verne and *Alice in Wonderland*. Included in the list, a sign of the times, was L T Meade's *A Sweet Girl Graduate*[112].

Foreign texts were now to be found on Mr Blackwell's shelves, and the catalogue of 1895 included Spanish, French, German and Italian texts. Benjamin Henry had been appointed by the Oxford Union Society to provide foreign books for their library, and a note informed customers that 'B H Blackwell having agents in the leading Continental Cities is enabled to obtain Foreign Works, not in stock, with the utmost promptitude and at the lowest rates'. Just as Benjamin Henry relished the inclusion of texts in other languages, so he delighted in providing a selection from the fine and applied arts, a special interest of his own. The catalogue of 1912 advertised the reproductions of the great masters in the recently revived 'Arundel and Medici Prints'. Judged by an entry drawing attention to a *Madonna and Child* of Filippo Lippi's, the description of the artist's feelings of 'romantic passion' may have reflected those, deeply hidden, of Harry Blackwell. By the turn of the century, the sales of new books exceeded the second-hand. Taking their place beside the antiquarian specialities were new tomes of science, medicine, economics and technology, the Loeb parallel translations from Latin and Greek (1906) and two famous series: World Classics (1901) and Everyman's Library (1906). For light relaxation the reader delighted in: *Nostromo, Mr Polly, Zulieka Dobson, The Scarlet Pimpernel* and *The Four Just Men*. Their children were treated to *Peter Rabbit* and *Wind in the Willows*[113].

Judging by this eclectic selection, old and new, Benjamin Henry's 'bookish place' could not fail to have broad appeal. And at the turn of a new century, Benjamin Henry's ardour, to educate and attract readers from far and wide, was undampened. And there was also plenty to attract those who were not able to present themselves in person, in Oxford. By 1913, overseas trade accounted for 12 percent of sales, and it continued to grow in importance. Moreover, Benjamin Henry's skill in 'knowing his market', so successful at home in Oxford, was now applied to the selection of works that might appeal to his overseas customers. American libraries took notice of a selection in leaflets he prepared in between 1902–3. Among the offerings were 542 mid-seventeenth century tracts, quarto leather-bound, detailing the Civil War and the Commonwealth, priced at $350. But America was not, as yet, Benjamin Henry's biggest overseas customer. He had taken a special interest in the educational fortunes of a new group of undergraduates, training for the Indian Civil Service, the Indian Institute having opened at the end of Broad Street in 1884. Such was the bond that developed that Blackwell's outdistanced all its competitors in the supply of books to India. Every Monday morning, the Indian mail would arrive by P & O, and Benjamin Henry would join the mêlée in the stockroom. Under his supervision, books not in stock were ordered that day, to be despatched no later than the following Thursday. Other forthcoming 'Commonwealth' customers also featured high on Benjamin Henry's list of priorities.

Rhodes Scholars, starting to arrive in Oxford from 1903, could find refuge and familiarity amongst Mr Blackwell's shelves, precious commodities for any stranger off the streets of Oxford, cold and wet as they often were. This hospitality did not go unrewarded. When Rhodes University in Grahamstown was founded in 1904, the librarian, who had known Blackwell's as an undergraduate, looked no further than Benjamin Henry. He wrote back in response to the librarian's request, and the spine of each of the books consequently despatched was blocked with the inscription 'Rhodes University'. Soon, similar relationships were built up in other African universities, as well as in New Zealand, Canada and America. These new friends may, at first, have been more of a burden than a benefit. Clifford Collins of the University of Canterbury, New Zealand, wrote of his embarrassment at the 'meagre purchases', which 'for decades could hardly have covered the printing and postage costs' incurred in servicing the library[114]. But, as was his way, Benjamin Henry did not see things solely in a commercial light. If he had any motive, other than the spread of knowledge, it was to shore up the future by putting his family business on a broader footing. And his policy, towards these new customers, turned out to yield a very lucrative long-term return.

But Benjamin Henry's interest in pastures new was never at the expense of his commitment to Oxford. It was, after all, from this solid home base that his success abroad stemmed. Oxford habitués were just as keen as ever to ruminate in the Elysium fields of Mr Blackwell's little shop. In this respect, despite the vastly different stock, nothing had upset the status quo or diminished Benjamin Henry's reputation one jot. Albeit tucked away in a provincial city, among the old cobbled streets of the University, Blackwell's attracted favourable comparisons with the 'more established' shops in the capital. 'Elsewhere', it was suggested: 'a bookshop is no longer a literary centre, it has become a pleasant, flowery pasture. If it has lost power, it has gained in beauty. How gay it is within! Every colour of the rainbow, every kind of shape and size greet the eye and whet the palate of the literary ruminant. Yes, these would be the golden days of browsing, only—well, the bookseller seems to mistrust the browser. "Are you being attended to, sir? Seen the latest novel, very strong, sir? Puff's essay just out".' 'So', the account went on, 'the rascally attendant, a plague on his importunity, confronted the customer: Why must we who have an air about us of good feeling, a certain distinction of garment, a shiny hat, perchance gloves, be less at our ease than the merest stall hunter? Shall Martin B—, the friend of Elia, read two whole volumes of *Classisa Harlowe* unmolested, and we be eyed askance if we read a title? But I know a shop or two where I can escape this insult to my honesty. There is an old-fashioned window down in Piccadilly behind which there is great wealth not dragon-guarded . . . But higher still do I laud the Sosius of

Oxford, where I may stand from morn to night unchallenged, finding the newest books from all the world before me, and I should ask for one not there, be it in the language of the hairy Ainu, some all-knowing one can tell me its price and the publisher'[115].

Despite changes made by Benjamin Henry to accommodate the ever-increasing range of titles and customers, his business, in the pre-First World War era continued to resemble the original, in spirit and atmosphere. But it was, nonetheless, much increased in size. There was nothing new in this trend. Given the almost instantaneous commercial success of the business, Benjamin Henry had been under pressure to expand from the first year of trading. Within a year of its founding, hardly any of the books included in the first catalogue could be found on the shelves. Business was already on a sound financial footing, with a turnover of £1,267. 2s.11d in 1879, rising to £1,841. 9s. 3d. in the second year of trading. Such was Benjamin Henry's success, that the two rooms which made up the shop were already brimming over, and, as Basil Blackwell recorded: 'the shop was too small for the customers. It was literally a standing order that when more than three were present the apprentice (Mr F W Chaundy who had joined his father in 1880), had to go outside'. A visit to Mr Blackwell's, 'the literary man's house of call', was now an established custom. It is on record that Oliver Wendell Homes, emerging from the Bodleian, clutching an honorary degree, made straight for Mr Blackwell's. 'Finding a copy of his *Poet at the Breakfast Table* (2 volumes), autographed it and presented it to the proprietor'. He also asked for a copy of his *The Autocrat*, 'but alas! It was out of stock'[116]. The turnover was fast, and the shop was as popular among students as the 'learned'. In the sales ledgers are the names of many whose 'early purchases shadow forth the careers of those who made them'. Here against H C Beeching are set Hazlitt's *Fairy Mythology*, *The Dream of Gerontius*, and Rosetti's *Ballads and Poems*; against A C Bradley *Sir John Browne's Works*, folio, and Shakespeare's Jahrbuch 12 volumes; against W H Hutton *Massinger's Works*, Clarendon's *Rebellion* and *Imitatio Christi*; against J St Loe Strachey *Letters of Junius*, Morley's *Burke*, Bagehot's *English Constitution* and Boswell's *Johnson*[117]. The rising tide of books overflowed to the point where Benjamin Henry determined to expand his premises. Next door, at 51 Broad Street, was a tailor's shop, and, wrote Sir Basil, 'before long it was a case of *cedant libris togae*'. By 1883 sales were running at £3,000 a year, and they were to rise to £15,000, including a stock of over 10,000 volumes, before the end of the century[118].

Benjamin Henry now felt confident enough to purchase the freehold of No 50, also acquiring the lease of Lockwood, the tailor's, at the rent of £40 a year.

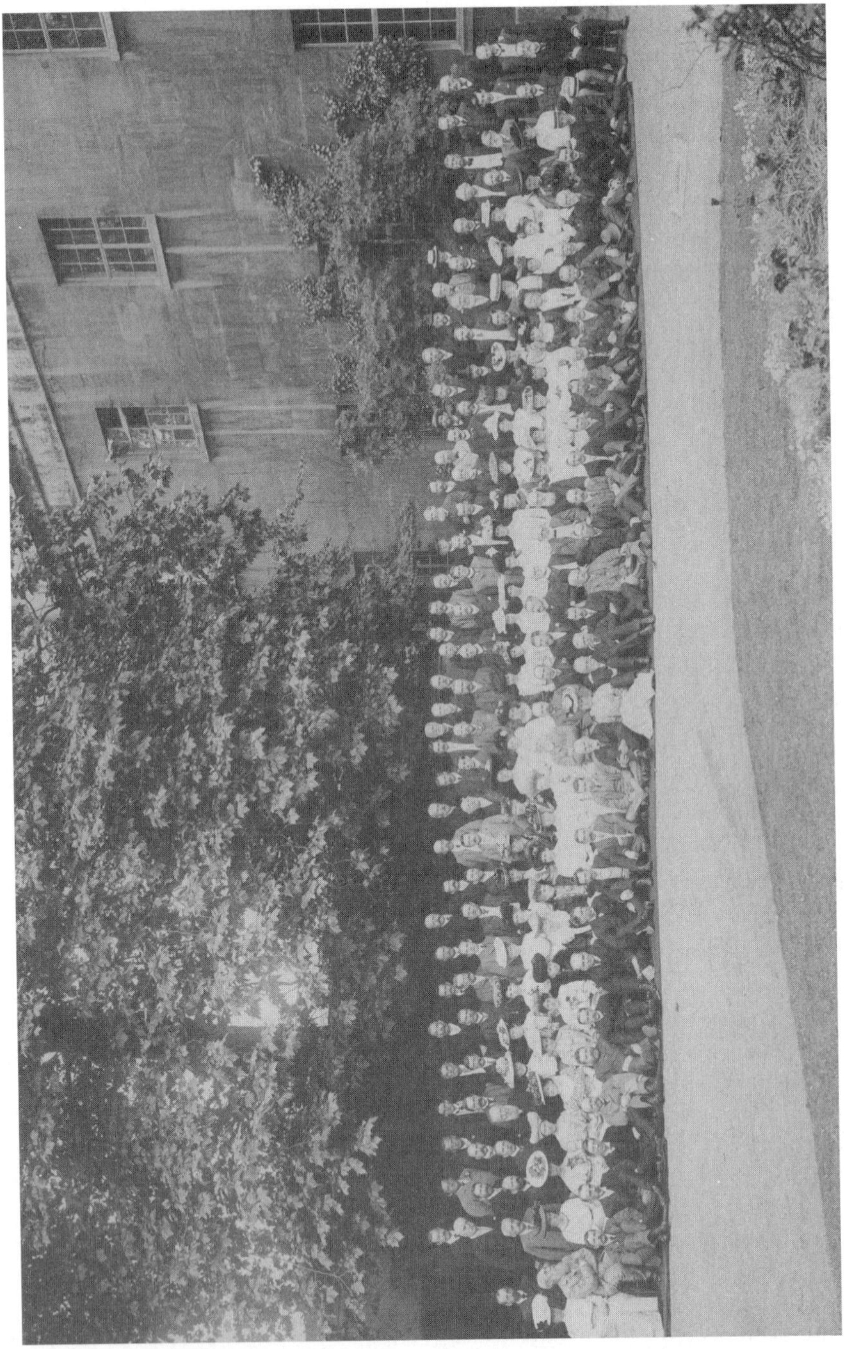

Merchant Scholar 75

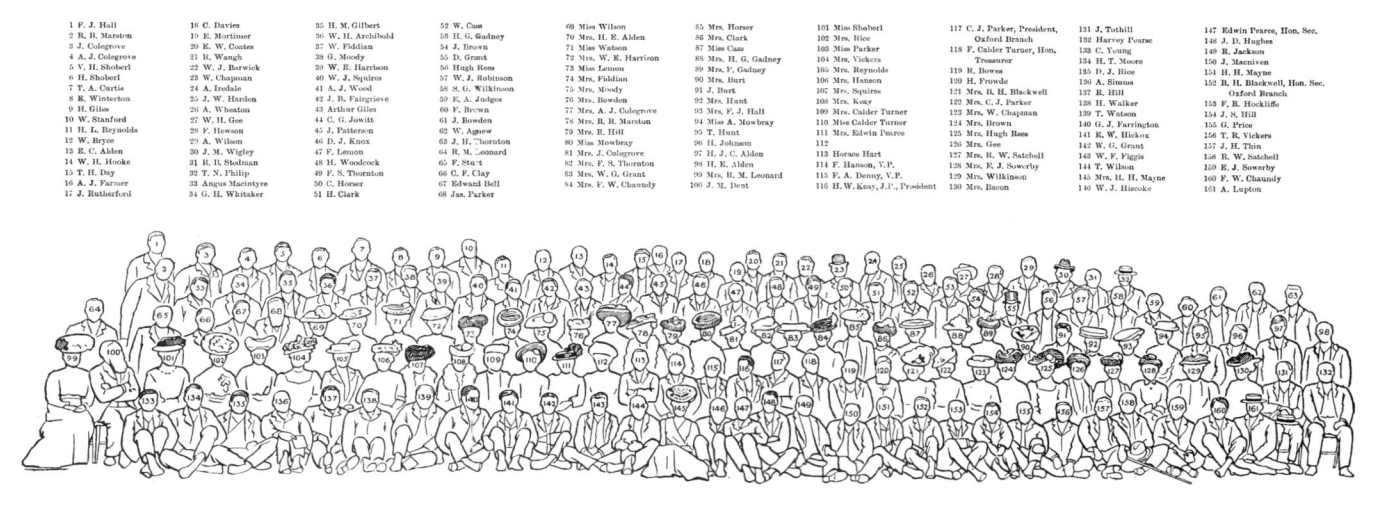

10 The participants in the Ripon Hall Conference in 1906.

1 P. J. Hall
2 R. R. Marston
3 J. Colegrove
4 A. J. Colegrove
5 V. H. Shobert
6 H. Shobert
7 T. A. Curtis
8 E. Winterton
9 H. Gilso
10 W. Stanford
11 H. L. Reynolds
12 W. Bryce
13 E. C. Alden
14 W. H. Hooke
15 T. H. Day
16 A. J. Parmer
17 J. Rutherford

18 C. Davies
19 E. Mortimer
20 E. W. Coates
21 H. Waugh
22 W. J. Barwick
23 W. Chapman
24 A. Iredale
25 J. W. Harlon
26 A. Winston
27 W. H. Gee
28 F. Hewson
29 A. Wilson
30 J. M. Wigley
31 R. H. Shadrum
32 T. N. Philip
33 Angus Macintyre
34 G. H. Whittaker

35 H. M. Gilbert
36 W. H. Archibald
37 W. Fiddian
38 G. Moody
39 W. E. Harrison
40 W. J. Squires
41 A. J. Wood
42 E. R. Fairgrieve
43 Arthur Giles
44 C. L. Jowitt
45 J. Patterson
46 D. C. Knox
47 F. Lemon
48 H. Woodcock
49 F. S. Thornton
50 G. Bower
51 H. Clark

52 W. Coe
53 H. G. Godfrey
54 J. Brown
55 D. Grant
56 Hugh Ross
57 W. J. Robinson
58 S. G. Wilkinson
59 E. A. Judges
60 F. Brown
61 J. Rawdon
62 W. Agnew
63 J. H. Thornton
64 R. M. Leonard
65 F. Slater
66 F. P. Clay
67 Edward Bell
68 Jas. Parker

69 Miss Wilson
70 Mrs. H. E. Alden
71 Mass Watson
72 Mrs. W. E. Harrison
73 Miss Lemon
74 Mrs. Fiddian
75 Mrs. Moody
76 Mrs. Bowden
77 Mrs. A. J. Colegrove
78 Mrs. R. R. Marston
79 Mrs. B. Hill
80 Miss Mowbray
81 Mrs. J. Colegrove
82 Mrs. F. S. Thornton
83 Mrs. W. G. Grant
84 Mrs. F. W. Chancely

85 Mrs. Bower
86 Mrs. Clark
87 Miss Case
88 Mrs. H. G. Gadsby
89 Mrs. F. Gadsby
90 Mrs. Hart
91 J. Burt
92 Mrs. Hunt
93 Mrs. F. J. Hall
94 Miss A. Mowbray
95 T. Hurst
96 H. Johnson
97 H. J. C. Alden
98 H. R. Alden
99 Mrs. R. M. Leonard
100 J. M. Burt

101 Miss Shobert
102 Mrs. Rice
103 Miss Parker
104 Mrs. Vickers
105 Mrs. Reynolds
106 Mrs. Hensen
107 Mrs. Squires
108 Mrs. Kent
109 Mrs. Caulder Turner
110 Miss Caulder Turner
111 Mrs. Edwin Pearee
112
113 Horace Hart
114 F. Hanson, V.P.
115 F. A. Doxey, V.P.
116 H. W. Kney, J.P., President

117 C. J. Parker, President,
   Oxford Branch
118 F. Calder Turner, Hon.
   Treasurer
119 R. Bowes
120 H. Froude
121 Mrs. H. H. Blackwell
122 Mrs. C. J. Parker
123 Mrs. W. Chapman
124 Mrs. Brown
125 Mrs. Hugh Ross
126 Mrs. Gee
127 Mrs. R. W. Satchel
128 Mrs. R. J. Sowerby
129 Mrs. Wilkinson
130 Mrs. Bacon

131 J. Tuthill
132 Harvey Fouse
133 C. Young
134 H. J. Moore
135 D. J. Rice
136 A. Simms
137 E. Hill
138 H. Walker
139 T. Watson
140 G. J. Farrington
141 R. W. Fiddian
142 W. G. Grant
143 W. F. Figgis
144 T. Wilson
145 Mrs. H. H. Mayne
146 W. J. Hancke

147 Edwin Pearee, Hon. Sec.
148 J. D. Hughes
149 R. Jackson
150 H. J. Macintyre
151 H. H. Mayne
152 B. H. Blackwell, Hon. Sec.
   Oxford Branch
153 F. R. Hinchliffe
154 J. S. Hill
155 G. Price
156 R. Vickers
157 J. H. Thin
158 R. W. Satchel
159 E. J. Sowerby
160 F. W. Chancely
161 A. Lupton

These enlargements were carried out partly with the help of his original benefactor, Mrs Messer, who now lent him £1,150 on a mortgage at four percent. This lucky stroke was enhanced by 'the kindness of Mr Parsons, of the Old Bank, who, while advancing him the money, shook his head gravely and bemoaned that: "he was not in banking to lend money on old houses"'[119]. This agreement to a loan may have been an act of faith on the part of the bank's manager, but it was an exercise of judgement that did not fail. Benjamin Henry seems to have been confident that the business would expand, even though there were rivals. When asked by the then Chairman of Barclay's Bank, Mr John Thompson: 'Well, Mr Blackwell, and are you capturing enough of your rivals' trade?' Benjamin's replied charitably: 'I believe there is enough for all' [120]. Almost before he could turn around, the problem of space again became pressing. The new acquisition had given only a brief respite, and the packing and storage of books spread into the patchwork of old houses of Bliss Court, sandwiched behind Blackwell's and the gardens of Trinity College. Basil remembered the labyrinth of old cottages as anything but 'blissful'[121]. There, he observed, only ferns would grow in the fetid atmosphere fanned by the breezes from the three communal 'offices' and a standpipe. Notwithstanding the environment, the elderly residents seemed to thrive, and could only be removed when nature took its course. Benjamin Henry bore their unexplainable longevity with his usual kindly patience. His diary notes the gifts of money he regularly made to them at Christmas, and fruit for the few children living in the buildings.

As each house was left empty, so it was colonized by Blackwell's. Added to these were other adjacent premises, formerly occupied by not only the Churchman's Union, but also by 'Dolly', a boxing coach. Basil Blackwell recalled the visit of the poet Verlaine to these quarters. Before he could meet his audience, Verlaine had had to snake his way through *'un dedale de chambers regorgeant de livres'*. Benjamin Henry, like his modern equivalents, knew the importance of providing a forum for men of letters, at the same time as providing an inducement to 'buy books' for his customers. Blackwell's young apprentices, too, were avid for the sight, and preferably the sound, of those who brought the old books on the shelves to life. Fred Hanks, Blackwell's second apprentice, remembered peeking though a crack in the wall as the poet addressed his audience by candlelight[122]. But bookselling and entertaining in the *'dedales'* could not continue. Eventually Benjamin Henry was able to buy 51 Broad Street, and the two houses, 50 and 51, were merged. But it was not only the bookshop and Blackwell's customers that benefited from these improvements. They enabled Benjamin Henry to remove himself, and his mother, from Holywell, and set up house in their own premises, 'over the shop'. Respectability and independence were now fully restored. His mother was provided for into old age, and, at the back of his mind, Harry Blackwell was able to make other plans of a more personal nature. Changes were afoot in the Blackwell ménage. But abroad, not all the changes were greeted with unanimous acclaim.

There were fears that the alterations to Blackwell's would change both the character and the nature of this 'literary man's public house-of-call'[123]. Public opinion, however, soon moved in favour of Benjamin Henry's decision. The new alterations were hailed in the press: 'B H Blackwell's takes the opportunity of calling attention to alterations at 50 and 51 Broad Street'[124]. Now the reader had yet more 'liberal access' to 'that favourite lounge of the lettered, Mr Blackwell's well-known and hospitable taberna'[125]. The verdict was unanimous: Blackwell's remained 'the very bookiest of book-shops, lined with shelves full of books, full of tables covered in books. . . . The very floor was heaped up with books. We browsed at leisure. No one came to disturb us or to ask us to buy'[126]. Perhaps these new alterations pre-empted those at the start of the twenty-first century, when the present shop incorporated a coffee bar and a not inconsiderable number of chairs for 'readers'. Despite the glossy covers of the mostly new books, today's Blackwell's continues to have the ambiance of a reference library: the sort of library to be found in old institutions. But like these august relatives, it is much modernized and designed to attract all comers, not just specialists. The diversity of Blackwell's customers, heads in books, sprawling on the leather sofas outside Benjamin Henry's old office, would not have surprised him. He had set the precedent. Enclosed with copies of a 1907 catalogue was a leaflet, written by Benjamin Henry, announcing: 'a room has been opened upstairs, which may be found convenient by visitors wishing to examine books, write a note, or look through the literary papers; and may in some degree supply that lack of seating accommodation which, it is feared, ladies have sometimes found noticeable'[127].

Yet for all his business acumen, Benjamin Henry was also unworldly. The hours he spent preparing and editing his catalogues must alone elevate his work beyond that necessary for commercial success. As an old man, he liked nothing better than to hide himself away, making and annotating his latest selection. Of course, this effort did not go unrewarded; it brought in the customers. Thus at Blackwell's, they had the kind of reference facility that graced the learned libraries. Indeed Mr Blackwell's shop had more the air of a free library, than that of a retail outlet. An article in the *Manchester Guardian* pointed to this tendency: 'Perceiving that they liked to be left alone, Mr Blackwell allows his customers to treat his shop as a free library. If a visitor wishes to buy a book he must say so, for he is never spoken to unless he speaks first. A courteous and expert attendant is at his disposal the moment he wants him; but if he does not want him he is left in peace, and may remain as long as he likes, and depart without buying anything. Perhaps the attraction of libraries over bookshops is that of "a goodly volume lying before you, ... that you may open it if you please, and need not open ... unless you please[128]". Mr Blackwell seems to have a natural insight into the mentality of book-lovers, who are also book-buyers'. Moreover, the overflowing shop also provided a resource, as well as an outlet, for the trade's 'producers'—the would-be writers. Many such admitted to preferring an environment where they felt less pressure, especially when the muse was being elusive.

For Benjamin Henry, considerations of cost seem to have been subordinate to his overriding passion for promoting the education of his readers and authors. Consequently, he turned a blind eye to all sorts of practices. Credit was very long in those days, and many who could well afford to pay took their time to settle up. The ledgers reveal, for example, how Dr Jowett, the Master of Balliol, bought a copy of the folio of *Diodorus Siculus* for seven shillings and sixpence in 1879 and no payment was made until March 1881. Benjamin Henry never lost faith in those who owed him money, even when they could easily afford to settle the amount. He took comfort from the words of his cashier, Charles Field, who advised: 'Oh, he'll come up'. One such was the Lord Chancellor of the University, and subsequent High Steward, whose three-figure account had not been settled since his student days. According to Basil Blackwell, Frederick Edwin Smith, the Earl of Birkenhead, had bought books 'by the yard' and had them sumptuously rebound, a practice that must have depressed rather than enhanced the value of many first editions. But such ideals did not pay the bills, or provide the means to replenish the stock. Despite Benjamin Henry's almost obsequious regard for his academic customers, his support for, and tolerance of, the reading public was just as unequivocal. From the beginning Blackwell's was known as a place where the general public could read alongside the academics and students. Putting aside the problem of those who 'forgot' to settle their accounts, surprisingly few abused the liberty afforded by this rambling shop. Perhaps this respect reflected Benjamin Henry's ability to put his love of books above mere profit. On one much published occasion 'one unlucky wight once tore an uncut page and fled dismayed'. The next day the book was displayed for all to view, 'but Sosius did but desire that next time he should use a paper-knife'[129].

This quietly understated way of making a point was typical of Benjamin Henry. He was always nervous that his lack of learning would cause him to make mistakes, and invoke the ire of his more select readers. Sir Arthur Norrington noted this tendency to 'anticipate' criticism, as evidenced by an entry at the head of catalogue 12 (May 1884). Benjamin Henry took recourse to the line of argument employed by the great London bookseller, James Lackington, in his *Memoirs*. Lackington's shop in Finsbury Park, the Temple of the Muses, had been one of the sights of London a century earlier. Lackington admonished himself from any blame in compiling catalogues, by writing of his limited role: 'I contented myself', wrote Lackington, 'with reading the translations of the classics, and inserted the originals in my catalogues as well as I could; and when sometimes I happened to put the genitive or dative case instead of the nominative or accusative, my customers kindly considered this as a venial fault, and bought the books notwithstanding.' In his 1888 catalogue, Benjamin Henry proffered his let-out clause: 'His (the cataloguer's) work has been so faithfully performed for him, a generation or two ago, by Brunet, Stevens, Lowdes, Dibdin, Allibone, Willis, Quaritch, and the rest of the old bibliographical guild, that all he has to do is to follow in their tracks and plagiarise at every footstep. . . . To compile a book catalogue in these days one only needs a paste-pot, a pair of scissors and a little horse-sense. That is the whole of the necessary equipment'[130]. And the extent of any claims Benjamin Henry would make for himself. For his part, Benjamin Henry would take little credit. At the end of the first catalogue, he included some lines from Pynson's *Ship of Fools*:

'Styll am I busy bokes assemblynge, ...
But what they mean do I nat understonde'[131].

Food for the soul

The soul of the whole past time lies in books[132]

Benjamin Henry's disclaimer 'I nat understonde' is a testament to his respect and love of books for their own sake. And since he viewed them as an unending source of knowledge, this most modest of men would never have claimed otherwise. But he was sometimes tempted to display his more than a mere mechanical interest in and knowledge of his books. He readily quoted from Johnson, Hazlitt, Macauley, Horace Walpole, Anthony Wood (*Oxoniensia*) Isaac D'Israeli, to name just a few. Occasionally he would indulge himself by including a personal comment in his catalogues: 'Suckling was among the purest, if not the very purest, writers of his day that has gained any celebrity.'

He wrote that 'J H Burton's *The Book Hunter* is a delightful book'. His indignation showed itself in the first edition of the twenty-four books of Chapman's *Homer*, when he declared 'some Ishmaelite has cut out the engraved title with scissors!'[133] Demonstrably Benjamin Henry had enough private confidence to proffer such offerings, and those who worked for 'Mr Blackwell' had no doubt of his abilities. One of his apprentices, Fred Hanks, described Mr Blackwell as the master of a vineyard where literature was 'undoubtedly the most significant shoot on the vine'[134]. Benjamin did himself attempt writing, not least his regular diary writing, but he had a business to run. His main creative outlet was therefore confined to the catalogues he wrote, seventy-two of them between the years 1879 and 1900. In his seventies one of 'Mr Blackwell's greatest pleasures' was to 'escape' to 'his little shanty', a haven where he spent many happy hours in pricing and cataloguing books and libraries[135].

Concentrating on producing these 'scholarly' catalogues, drawing on years of hard work and 'self-education', gave Harry Blackwell the chance to pass on 'the soul of the past'. It also gave him a distinction, which more than made up for his lack of formal, academic, qualifications. He was, as his son Basil suggested, a scholar manqué; reading as much as he could and delighting in the society of the learned. Always a little insecure in their company, he ensured that his own son had the benefit of a 'varsity' education. But in his own world, in the Broad Street shop, he was in good company, sharing his disadvantage with his apprentices. Like them, he never missed an opportunity for 'intellectual betterment'. Even on Sundays he disciplined himself to follow the Sunday church lessons in his own *Biblia Sacra*, which he kept in his pew. 'By this means he improved his knowledge of Latin—a language which he always regarded as being essential in as cosmopolitan a business as his was'. One of his apprentices, Fred Hanks, took his cue from his employer, and kept both French and German Bibles in his pew[136]. The early life of Fred Hanks, his second apprentice, bore a remarkable similarity to Harry Blackwell's own. Fred Hanks spoke of his formative experiences in 1933: 'My father died when I was five years old, and my mother, who was left penniless, literally became the breadwinner. The only education she could afford to give me was that provided by the elementary schools at 2d a week. It must have been when I was about eight years old that my mother, anxious to do all she could to supplement my elementary school education, thought it would be good for me to learn a little French. I remember accompanying her to a bookseller's shop, where she purchased for me with her hard-earned pennies a French grammar. This was, so far as I can remember, the first book I ever possessed'[137].

'In trade', in Benjamin Henry's time, the lack of formal education was no bar to future success. And in the case of Mr Blackwell's apprentices, there was an inbuilt opportunity to improve their education. Not only did they handle books all day, but also they had the example of a master who venerated books and learning. Blackwell's too benefited from the services of those who wanted to 'get on' in life. This was the age of the self-made, and during Benjamin Henry's time, his apprentices, more often than not, ended by joining their master as 'colleagues' round the manager's table, or, once they had served their time, setting up in their own businesses. It was also a time when mutual self-help prevailed. Fred Hanks, in turn, passed on the skills he had learnt from his master, to the next apprentice in line, Will Hunt. After a day's work, he helped teach him the rudiments of Latin and French. Under Hanks' tutelage, Will Hunt readily took on his Master's mantle, and served the cause of learning throughout his life. Although he developed Blackwell's expertise in new books, becoming a renowned specialist, he was something approximating to a latter-day research assistant. Basil Blackwell recorded that Hunt would never give up on a request for a book, and he would instruct his fellow assistants accordingly: 'If the customer knows the book, so must we, Find it!' Finding the book often involved a trip to the Bodleian Library, where Blackwell's staff were equipped with readers' tickets[138]. Hanks and Hunt were both to join their mentor as fellow directors of the firm in 1920, as did Charles Field who started off as a clerk in Blackwell's Counting House. For many years Field was Blackwell's cashier, taking over from the original, Lambert, described by Basil Blackwell as 'of sterling character', who may have been related to Benjamin Henry's mother, Nancy Blackwell, neé Lambert.

Although Benjamin Henry was fortunate in his choice of staff, he inspired their devotion and love of books and scholarship. Fred Hanks' reward, for his lifetime of dedication to books, exceeded that of his Master's. Ten years after the death of his benefactor, he was awarded an Honorary MA by the University. Benjamin Henry was never to be so recognized, but it must have been to his great joy that his son, Basil, studied Classics at university, although, unlike his father, he preferred Greek to Latin, 'finding Greek the more expansive literary vehicle'. Further afield, Benjamin Henry lent his support to the public provision of continuing education, enabling the less fortunate to have access beyond the 'normal' leaving age of 13. He became an official of the University Extension Movement and the Oxford Branch of the English Association. At home, his family had no escape from their books. Just as Nancy Blackwell had encouraged the young Harry to read, so he set an example to his own children. His daughter wrote that 'if he was not working, which he did until the small hours, then he would be found reading. . . . He was indeed a reader of all that should be read . . . and as a father, too, he was determined that his children should read'. He urged his own children to 'take advantage of their childhood leisure and read while they could'. Indeed, remembering his own childhood, Benjamin Henry had no understanding of how else children might spend their leisure times; reading for him was axiomatic. Nonetheless, as his daughter Dorothy recalled, 'we were given rewards for a good read'. He may even have regretted the princely sum of half-a-crown he awarded for the 'consumption' of Spenser's *Faerie Queene* when, as Dorothy recounts, 'my brother recited at every meal the loathsome description of the dragon's indigestion'[139].

Although his mother's ambition started Harry Blackwell on the road to becoming a bookseller so that he should re-kindle the family name, it was his own love of books that had launched his adventures in 'book land'. What was food for thought became manna for a successful business: its spiritual capital. Dorothy wrote that 'only some years ago Sir Fisher Unwin said to me that no one had [Harry's] knowledge of books.' Somehow he had the genius to translate this esoteric interest into a commercial success, although he would never have seen it in that way. For Harry Blackwell, books were objects of value in their own right, irrespective of any other advantage they may bestow or any price they may fetch. Even though he daily presided over a successful, and growing, enterprise, his love of books came first. And his knowledge of them gave Benjamin Henry the sort of inner ripeness which cannot be measured simply by the accolades of a formal education. But even Harry Blackwell had his limits. His bookishness did not extend to that most popular of Victorian preoccupations, the novel. He made no secret of his dislike for Dickens. Whether he actually read him is a matter of supposition since, reportedly, he was never 'seen' to be reading any novel, preferring essayists and poets such as Charles Lamb, Herrick and Wordsworth and all those quiet gentle writers. Benjamin Henry Blackwell's love of books is enshrined in Blackwell's, as an institution, which continues as a tribute to his memory. But his role as a publisher and his extensive help for poets, particularly 'in providing encouragement and a chance of publicity to . . . young writers' is perhaps less well known[140].

Adventurers All

Young poets, unknown to fame[141]

In retrospect it seems rather apt that Benjamin Henry attended the boys elementary school in Clarendon Street that later became the site of the Oxford University Press warehouse, since publishing, too, became his passion. If it is the name of Basil Blackwell that is most usually associated with Blackwell's' publishing ventures, then the pioneering work undertaken by his father deserves special mention. Sir Basil Blackwell, writing in 1979, stressed his father's dedication to the gentle art of bookselling but, from the very first, set out to combine it with publishing[142]. It was Benjamin Henry's assistance in bringing forth the offspring of poets 'unknown to fame' which led to the formation of Blackwell's' publishing ring. Although his role was generously acknowledged, particularly, noted Basil Blackwell, by Sir Compton Mackenzie, little is generally known of his work in this field[143]. Benjamin Henry's first adventures in publishing took more the form of disguised 'bursaries' for would-be poets. He thought nothing of working into the early hours of the next day to correct their proofs, in his own time and at no cost to them, as his diary notes, written on a page torn from an old minute book on 12 June 1882. Only too mindful of the pecuniary barriers facing those who yearned for literary recognition, Benjamin Henry determined 'to remove from the work of young poets the reproach of insolvency'. What he chose to publish was to be 'confined to such work as would seem to deserve publicity. It is hoped that these adventurers may justly claim the attention of those intellects which, in resisting the enervating influence of the novel, look for something more permanent in the arduous pursuit of poetry'[144].

'My father', Sir Basil Blackwell wrote, 'who had a deep reverence for scholarship and literature, which he had not been able to pursue as a youth, having had to start his apprenticeship at the age of 13, had a natural affinity with scholars and men of letters'[145]. Even in his very first year of business, in 1879, this desire to be associated with scholarship led Benjamin Henry to risk a publishing adventure of his own. 'My father', Basil wrote, 'soon divined that there were some brilliant young men at Balliol'. This 'divining' resulted in the appearance of the first B H Blackwell imprint. It took the form of a brochure, entitled *Mensae Secundae*, which collected together some of the verses of students at Balliol. All the way through the early accounts books there is evidence of the cost of its production: £2.8s.10d, in January 1880. H C Beeching, described as the 'wisest and wittiest of contemporaries', was the moving spirit in this new publishing enterprise, with Bowyer Nichols as accessory. Beeching, later Dean of Norwich and editor of the collected works of Benjamin Henry's great poetic hero, John Milton, became a great collector of Blackwell's second-hand books, and not surprisingly a family favourite. Shortly after his first effort came *Primavera*, another slim anthology of poems, with A E Housman, of St John's, to be found among the contributors[146]. At the same time, in 1880, Benjamin Henry rescued the Oxford poetry magazine, *Waifs and Strays*. Here the names of James

Rennell Rodd, J St Loe Strachey, J W Mackail and A E Housman were added to that of Beeching. Seventh in the publication file was *Thermopylae*, the Newdigate Prize Poem of 1881 by J W Mackail, and the Lothian Prize Essay for 1884, *The Art of War in the Middle Ages*, by C W C Oman, 134 pages, 3s 6d net.

Following the early success of his 'little poetry series', Benjamin Henry brought out separately the works of some of these Oxford poets. They were little books 'in hand printed style, by the Vincent Press, bound in brown paper or stiff cards, or with wallpaper covers'. Appropriately, the series was called *Adventurers All*. The *Daily News* reviewed the worth of the series and the adventurers of the mind who authored them, retrospectively in 1924, at the time of Benjamin Henry's death: 'Most of them have not taken the world by storm, but that is nothing'. These publications were nonetheless the vehicle by which greater 'Adventurers', such as Aldous Huxley, Meyerstein, Dorothy L Sayers, Edith, Osbert and Sacheverell Sitwell and Powys Mathers were carried onto the literary scene. Dorothy L Sayers was published in Volume 1 of *Adventurers All*, and Volume 7, *The Burning Wheel* [147], first brought Aldous Huxley to the public's attention. A first volume in a later series in the same vein, called *Initiatives*, was by Geoffrey Faber[148]. Others in the series included the ilk of Philip Guedalla, Robert Nichols, Ronald Knox and Roy Campbell with his famous poem *The Flying Terrapin*. Basil Blackwell recorded how his father continued to help his poets even during the war years, bringing out further slim volumes, quite a few of which were authored, or edited, by women. Edith Sitwell found her voice in this way; Basil Blackwell published an early volume of poems called *Clown's Houses*, in June 1918, in a paper cover, price 6d. She edited the first volume of B H Blackwell's *Wheels*: an annual poetry anthology, which came out four times between 1916 and 1919. The idea almost certainly came from Nancy Cunard, who wrote the poem *Wheels*, which was to give the series its title. But it was Edith who took the idea up, 'as something of a counterblast to Edward Marsh's *Georgian Poetry*'. *Wheels*, like many other poetry collections brought out under his imprint, was paid for by the firm[149]. 'Of the first volume, 500 were printed and 500 reprinted; of the second, 750 were printed; of the third and fourth, 1,000.' It is now a sought-after collector's series and, ironically, its volumes fetch not inconsiderable prices, as indeed do other early books issued under the B H Blackwell imprint. Blackwell's was also Sacheverell Sitwell's first publisher; he made his debut in a volume entitled *The People's Palace*, 1918. Osbert Sitwell, too, suffered a similar fate in Blackwell's' hands.

Spurred on by his son's enthusiasm, and turning a blind eye to small financial losses, especially in the promotion of unknown poets, Benjamin Henry used his earlier experience of publishing poetry to launch *Oxford Poetry*[150]. He was dogged in the defence of new writing, ignoring fashion and the critics. 'When he first published the yearly anthology, *Oxford Poetry*', wrote Basil Blackwell, 'people laughed, no doubt. That was before the war, and it is still going strong'. The *Oxford Poetry* series, particularly, has stood the test of time; it is still a well known and much collected series. *Oxford Poetry* continued after Benjamin Henry's death, and Stephen Spender made a splash with a series of poems published in the 1928–1930 editions. During Benjamin Henry's time, a contribution had come his way from one of the most famous of B H Blackwell's alumni: Ronald Tolkien. Years later, writing from his study in Merton, momentarily relinquishing his lands of myths and hobbits, Tolkien reminded Basil Blackwell of this fact. His first published poem *Goblin Feet* had seen the light of day in a 1915 issue of *Oxford Poetry*: 'So you (Blackwell's) were my first publisher', he wrote, 'as I remember with gratitude'[151]. Just as well then that Benjamin Henry did not desert his muses during the Great War. And his muses certainly did not desert him. They continued to fill the 'black wells of *Oxford Poetry*, sending things from France or the East, while Blackwell's kept up the necessary organization for bringing them out'. '*Cambridge Poetry*', Basil Blackwell recalled, 'also came out once or twice, but it died after a very few flickers; for Cambridge has no B H Blackwell'[152].

With the support of Benjamin Henry, many of his authors graduated into the lists of London publishers. Benjamin Henry would do nothing to try to keep them in Oxford. He had plenty to keep him busy, and plenty more to do on the publishing scene, especially after his son joined him. In this way, claimed Sir Basil, 'the House of Blackwell acted as a literary accoucheur to many a young genius'. Other names such as J W Mackail, Gilbert Murray, Hilaire Belloc, John Buchan, Maurice Baring, Laurence Binyon and Robert Bridges 'adorned publications of the earlier years'. They paved the way for Basil's own publishing adventures, when Compton Mackenzie, Julian and Aldous Huxley and Christopher Morley stood in the Blackwell's publishing file of the 1940s, 'linking that earlier period with the younger writers of today and tomorrow'[153]. It was via poetry that Benjamin Henry made his debut in the publishing world, but his imprint was not limited to poetry alone. His first author, Beeching, edited an elegant reprint of George Herbert's *The Country Parson* for Benjamin Henry in 1898. When, in 1885, he became rector of Yattendon, Beeching collaborated with Robert Bridges and H E

Wooldridge, to produce the famous *Yattendon Hymnal* (words and music). Arguably, this was the most notable work to bear the Blackwell's imprint. In its field, it had an influence way beyond the rural parish for which it had been prepared. And Vaughan Williams' *English Hymnal* owed much to it. Basil's youthful memory of Beeching, who died in 1919, was of 'Beeching telling us en famille that his first infant utterance was "beastly bath".' Beeching's famous contemporaries also featured in these experiments in publishing. Other more weighty tomes followed. A very distinguished book, Dudley Medley's *English Constitutional History*, came out of this same era, becoming a standard text that was affectionately known as 'Deadly Muddly'[154]. Following his spell at Oxford University Press, at Amen Corner in London, Basil needed no encouragement to continue his father's publishing work.

As the years have elapsed, Benjamin Henry's role in encouraging writers, and most of what is known of his early role in Blackwell's Publishing has been rather lost with the death of those who knew him. It was typical of this modest man, that he staked no claims for himself. At the time of his death, however, he belatedly received some public approbation. The *Daily Mail* had pronounced that: 'Blackwell did a very great service to Oxford in providing encouragement and a chance of publicity to young writers'. He would have been more than satisfied with the tribute paid to him by one of his grateful poets, who described him as 'a gentle man,' with a gentle art—'a habit of publishing'[155]. The poet Christopher Morley provided a reminder of Benjamin Henry's contribution to late nineteenth and early twentieth century poetry. Writing of his association with 'the Mr Blackwell, of B H Blackwell's', he recalled the man 'who made a habit of occasionally publishing collections of undergraduate verse'. His 'little booklets', wrote Christopher Morley, 'were bound in paper and sold (if at all) for a shilling each'. Morley remembered such volumes as *Ignes Fatui* and *Metri Gratia* by Philip Guedalla of Balliol and *Play Hours with Pegasus* by A P Herbert of New College. Herbert went on to campaign for the rights of authors, when, later, he was MP for Oxford, 1939–50. Taking his cue from this more august company, Morley took the plunge, and risked sending a little sheaf of his own rhymes to Mr Blackwell. This, he remembered was in October 1921, when Benjamin Henry was near the end of his days. But Morley was not disappointed. The elderly Benjamin Henry was as assiduous as ever, and he invited him into the office in Broad Street 'to discuss his work'. 'What I remember best of my bashful interview with Mr Blackwell senior', Morley wrote, 'besides his pink face and white hair and extreme politeness, was his asking me to put in some more commas.' He told Morley that he liked his poems but 'there don't seem to be any commas in them. Perhaps you don't use commas much in America?'[156]. Mr Blackwell's bark was worse than his bite, and duly Morley's poems came out, with or without 'proper' punctuation, under the B H Blackwell imprint.

By the twenties, Basil was itching to expand this publishing side: to improve its quality and to try and make it pay. The most profit of the worldly variety Benjamin Henry ever received from his publishing adventures was, at best, an average of less than £200 per year. It was a start, nonetheless, and the value of the goodwill he generated was incalculable. Harry Blackwell had not thought himself sufficiently qualified to go all out on the publishing side, and he was too preoccupied with the firm as a whole, but he had made sure that his son was. When Basil returned from London, and after the upheavals of the 1914–18 War, the imprint began to appear on more ambitious works, endorsed, during the last few years of Benjamin Henry's life, by the acquisition of the Shakespeare Head Press. The Shakespeare Head Press had been founded in 1906 by A H Bullen, a London publisher 'who had a dream'. According to a Mr Kendrick who was the head 'comp' at the Shakespeare Head Press, first under Bullen, and later under Bernard Newdigate, Bullen did actually say that he had had a dream regarding the press; a dream which had impressed him very strongly. In this dream he had been visiting Shakespeare's birthplace and someone had said to him 'You're not going away without seeing the book?' 'What book?' he asked. 'Why, haven't you heard of the noble edition of Shakespeare that is being printed here—the first complete edition ever printed and published in Shakespeare's own town?' this dream cried out to Bullen, 'and he was determined to set up a press of Stratford men'. And Bullen's partner, Frank Sidgwick, recorded in his diary that the dream came true[157]. A complete Shakespeare was produced between 1904–7, and Bullen published many other works of the Elizabethans, and reached out to the 'modern' canon, to include the works of W B Yeats.

Despite the quality of his work, Bullen had no head for commerce, and sadly at his death, in 1919, at the age of 63, the Press was left derelict. Bullen deserved better than this. Both Benjamin Henry and his son admired his fine printing, and his publication of *Elizabethan Lyrics and Love Songs*, which had brought them back from oblivion.... But 'Weep you no more, sad fountains': the Blackwells came to the rescue, ignoring a gloomy economic forecast and the high level of unemployment in Britain. The Shakespeare Head Press was incorporated in February 1921, and at the second directors' meeting, held in June, there was only £20 in the kitty. Happily, Basil Blackwell wrote, it was becoming good business, not simply idealism, to be generous of time and skills in the production of books.

The Press prospered for over twenty years, ensuring the production of a series of scholarly reprints of English classical authors, which 'all elegant and some magnificent, designed by the master typographer, Bernard Newdigate, delighted at once the eyes and minds of their readers'[158]. It was Basil who had put Blackwell's publishing on the map. But it was because of Benjamin Henry Blackwell's pioneering work, that the muses of the next generation, the young adventurers, looked to 'draw their draughts' from 'Black Wells'[159].

Toiling in the vineyard

A self-made man relieves his creator of a great responsibility[160]

It was not only muses who drew strength and inspiration from Benjamin Henry Blackwell, as one of his oldest friends, Michael Sadler, reminded Basil, in 1938: 'Your father's untiring, friendly and graceful kindness to young undergraduates is vivid in the memory of one of them [himself] and I see him still as clearly as I see this sheet of paper, in his surplice warbling at St Phillip and St James'; and the same sentiments were echoed by Maurice Bowra[161]. In his time, B H Blackwell became known as a man who would encourage and help anyone in the mastery of their trade; whether poets, academics, apprentices, or working people coming in to the shop at the end of a hard day. He had toiled in the vineyard until he became a master, and his example was an inspiration to others. Yet despite the esteem in which he was held, and the enormous success of his 'little shop', Benjamin Henry lived a little unrewarded, and died relatively unsung. Teetotal and modest, he ran his daily life by the conventions of the time: 'he believed in and practised discipline—cold bath in the morning and church on a Sunday. As a churchman 'he was either singing in the choir or acting as churchwarden all his life; but if challenged as to his beliefs, I think he would have admitted with a smile that he thought as the Bishop of Woolwich all his life'[162]. Indeed the pressure of work, and the need to become established in business, had seemingly left Benjamin Henry little time for personal pursuits. Fortunately the depth and extent of this quiet man's life, seen from the inside, was captured and stored in the writings and oral accounts of both his colleagues and his children, Dorothy and Basil. A closer look at the life of Benjamin Henry reveals him as a man with eclectic interests and hobbies.

Going through his father's papers, after his father's death, Basil discovered more and more about his father's 'private sidelines'. Although he kept them to himself, wrote Basil, 'my father was constantly involved in acts of charity, which established a tradition of petition that I inherited'. In one way or another, most of his 'interests' were directed towards the end of 'self-reform' and 'betterment' for the individual. This emphasis derived from Benjamin Henry's religious beliefs, as well as his own struggles as a self-made man. Deprived of a formal education himself, he willingly lent his support to the Further Education and University Extension Movements. He abominated wasted talent, and wanted to see help available for the less able, as well as the able-bodied. Drawing inspiration from the words of one of his favourite mentors, John Milton, who became blind, he developed a special relationship with the Oxford Society for the Blind. Non-confrontational as he was, he would brook no opposition from those whose vested interests frustrated his efforts to 'improve the standing of others'. His ideas were typical of the kind of reforming liberal who moved with the changing times of the late nineteenth century. It is perhaps surprising to find such a retiring man active in so many areas of public life. His acute sense of public duty nonetheless drew him out. In the very public domain of local politics, his approach was entirely consistent with the social and moral philosophy he applied to the conduct of his daily life and his business. Not all of his contemporaries, however, appreciated the merit of his ways. When applied to the conservative and hidebound conduct of local government, his policies, according to Mr Case, a don at Corpus Christi, made him 'a dreadful radical.' He stood as a Liberal for the City Council, and he was the first Liberal ever to be successfully elected to a North Oxford constituency.

In these different guises Benjamin Henry's life epitomized the balance of late Victorian life. His interest in social reform was coupled with a concern for the town and the country around Oxfordshire. In his time 'the city was still never so far from the country', and Benjamin Henry's range of 'little hobbies' reflected the rural influence that persisted in mid to late Victorian England, especially in the county towns. One of the ways in which Benjamin Henry played out his rural interests, even in the relatively built-up new suburb of Summertown, was to go to the allotments. He administered the North Oxford branch of the Allotment Society, supporting the wider aims of the Allotment Movement and keeping a keen eye on the husbandry of the locals. His interest in the up-keep of the allotments was another manifestation of his credo of self-help. As a young man and would-be scholar, Benjamin Henry had communed with nature during his early morning runs. These were solitary periods when he would daydream of scholarship and writing. He did take up the pen himself on some occasions, not least in the keeping of detailed diaries and translations of classical authors. But his favourite hobby was to associate with writers, especially 'struggling' poets. For some years he found succour as the keeper of the records of the Horace Society. Founded in 1898, 'this was a literary club with a difference. The members met, not to discuss others' works, but to rehearse their own'[163]. And who better to sit in attendance than that great listener to poets: Harry Blackwell.

Basil Blackwell recorded his father's experiences at the hands of the Horace poets: 'Each (poet) was bound to produce and read to his fellows a poem written for the occasion "in a well-known language", and not exceeding in length, nor falling below in brevity, any poem of Horace (excluding the *De Arte Poetica*)'. The list of members included such well-known names as Asquith, Belloc and John Buchan, A D Godley, St John Lucas, Arnold Ward (the Club's founder and great nephew of Matthew Arnold), H C Beeching, Laurence Binyon, A E Zimmern, Meade Falkner and W R Hardy (who invariably produced a poem in Greek). Unusually, two Cambridge men, Maurice Baring and Owen Seaman, were also admitted. The President was T H Warren and the Keeper of Records, Benjamin Henry Blackwell. After a short, but sparkling, life of three years, the Horace Club was disbanded. But it was not forgotten. Benjamin Henry, in his meticulous way, had kept an autographed copy of each of the poems, pasting them into an album at the end of each meeting. Sir Arthur Norrington wrote that these records 'served as a moving monument to Victorian wit and scholarship'. But it was also a tribute to Benjamin Henry, who was welcomed and esteemed as one of their number. He subsequently published a collection of the poems, featuring Hilaire Belloc's 'rebus' design and the motto *Sumite castalios nigris de fontibus haustus*[164]. True to form, he forbore to mention that he was the Black Well source from which his poets drew their draughts.

In his remaining free time, Benjamin Henry somehow managed to fit in writing editorials for tour guides of Oxford, rowing and singing 'glees'; Blackwell's boasted its own very successful choral society performing regularly from an ambitious repertoire. This diversity of occupations was not, however, untypical among Victorian tradesmen. But for Benjamin Henry, the practice of his trade had to come first. Like many of his fellows, his commitment to his business was based on rigid discipline and religious principle. He valued and practised self-denial, and ever mindful of the privations of his youth, his first priority was to get his infant business on a sound financial footing. Only when he had secured his future and he was satisfied that his business was securely established, the Broad Street shop having had its doors open for three years, did he turn his thoughts to private happiness. In 1883 he had met Lydia (Lilla) Taylor, whose sister, Charlotte, was the wife of

11 Lilla Blackwell in 1906.

an Oxford friend. They soon came to an understanding. Lilla too had been placed in circumstances that forced her to put duty first; they had to bide their time. Three years later, Benjamin Henry felt justified in embarking 'discreetly, advisedly and soberly' on matrimony, and Lilla, freed by then from her caring and pecuniary responsibilities by her mother's death, was able to accept. So it was that on the 26 August 1886 Benjamin Henry Blackwell, son of a bookseller, married Lydia Taylor, daughter of a Norfolk farmer, at the Parish Church of SS Philip and James. The newly-weds were by then both in their late thirties and had only the most modest of expectations. 'I have no ambition', Benjamin Henry had written to Lilla during their engagement, 'even if I had the chance to make a fortune'. He was content enough with the prospect of the help he would get from his partner to enable him to 'live comfortably and quietly, paying my way'.

Within a year of their marriage, a first child, Dorothy, was born and Basil followed two years later. Basil was always proud to have been born 'over the shop', and its cramped back alleyways stood in lieu of a nursery. But not for long. The success of B H Blackwell's allowed Benjamin Henry to contemplate the purchase of a house with seven bedrooms, not considered immodest in those times given the 'necessity' of resident domestic help. In 1896, when the children were nine and seven, Benjamin Henry was able to remove his family from their crowded quarters at No 51 Broad Street. They soon forgot the delights of the old shop as they settled into their own house at No 1 Linton Road; the house remained Benjamin Henry and Lilla's home until they died in the 1920s. In the new North Oxford suburb of Summertown the Blackwells found themselves in the company of families of academics and book people. In this new home the Blackwells raised their children and entertained modestly. Following his father and grandfather, Benjamin Henry was a strict teetotaller, although, his son Basil insisted, he did out of politeness offer 'pretty bad' wine and spirits to his guests[165]. But if the wine was of poor quality, the conversation was more reliable. His wife, Lilla, loved company, and their two children, who 'might babble and romp as they willed', more than made up for any reticence on Benjamin Henry's part. While she engaged visitors and family on every subject, including politics, even though such discussion was frowned on, Benjamin Henry's contribution would be temperate and to the point. Sparing those his contributions were, he was never dour. His silences were contemplative, rather than oppressive or foreboding, and the company, who could have been forgiven for thinking his thoughts elsewhere, would be surprised by his spicy interjections. Basil loved his father's penchant for allusion and whimsy, and recorded one of his own favourites: ' "Three times I have asked you to pass the salt", cried my sister sharply at dinner. "And thrice the brindled cat hath mewed" was the instant rejoinder.'

As a father, Benjamin Henry's most formidable form of rebuke, Basil wrote, was to flutter his napkin and say 'Bah!' 'The effect', Basil conceded, 'was crushing'. His ire was reserved for petty bureaucracy. A nagging for the non-renewal of a dog licence met with the response: 'Vide Richard III, Act V, Sc. 5, L.2.' ('The bloody dog is dead'!). A gentler form of irony was reserved for his customers. Finding the first volume of a set of Swinburne's poems missing, Benjamin Henry placed an advertisement in the *Oxford Magazine*. He invited the customer who had 'borrowed' the volume to supply his address so that the remaining volumes could be sent to join it, these volumes not being sold as separate items. Duly the missing volume reappeared. On another occasion, Benjamin Henry's advice was openly sought by an OUP representative: 'As you know so much about Ovid', the man asked shyly, 'could you tell me about Ibid?' 'My father', said the Gaffer, giving exactly the right weight to his adjective, 'was able to tell him much about the work of that *voluminous* author!'[166] While quiet wit was his hallmark, Benjamin Henry was never heard to utter any language more excessive than 'Dash it', but he patiently tolerated passion in others; the verbal political assaults of his mercurial farming-stock wife, Lilla, for example[167].

12 No 1 Linton Road from the garden.

Lilla and Benjamin Henry, although very different personalities, were devoted parents who took a very direct interest in their children's welfare and education. They were always available for their children, as they were for Blackwell's staff and the circle of friends associated with the business, the church, or those involved in one or other of their community activities. But, when not required to directly participate, Benjamin Henry would remain silent and abstracted, always immersed in some aspect of his work. Sir Basil recalled his early childhood perceptions of his father: 'as a man of middle height, slim, well proportioned and nimble at need, with hair that was sable-silvered from a prematurely early age and keen dark eyes'. 'My father', he reminisced, 'was a kindly but reticent being, whose thoughts were elsewhere and who worked long hours. He appeared briefly in the middle of the day for lunch; the next time we saw him was about seven o'clock when he nourished himself on sardines and cocoa. Then he disappeared again—until what time I can hardly imagine'[168]. This became even more the pattern when the family moved away from the shop, and Benjamin Henry was physically absent for the best part of six full days. On Sundays things were different. But they were hardly the proverbial days of rest. The Blackwell family were up and out in their Sunday best. Each Sunday Benjamin Henry escorted his family to church, where he would be found officiating, but now more usually at the new local church of St Andrew's, the ties with SS Philip and James being less after the family move to Summertown. Basil Blackwell clearly remembered the weekly routine of these Victorian Sundays, especially exacting when his father served for a term as the Vicar's Warden at the University Church of St Mary Magdalen. All was formality, and Basil 'had to don his Eton suit, stiff collar and dicky, with a brief "bumfreezer" jacket'. Regardless of the weather, the family had to walk the long mile from Linton Road to the City Centre. Bicycling on a Sunday, in those days, would have occasioned more than a raised eyebrow.

As he walked Benjamin Henry may have had his mind on higher things, but his family were more intent on the social pantomime of this ritual. The first scene was to be viewed on the approach to nearby Bardwell Road. 'As we neared', recalled Basil, 'it was customary to see the family of "Dictionary Murray" pour out of the house at the corner marshalled by Sir James in full plumage of his honorary doctorate and sons and daughters with Anglo-Saxon nomenclature, Rosfrith being one'. Arriving in good time the family were left to make their own dreams, while Benjamin Henry undertook the preparations for Matins, and afterwards counted the offertory and discussed church matters with the incumbent. The children's dreams had to be good ones since, as Basil recalled, the services were very long, intoned by a very nasal curate, and the sermons interminable. Their only saving grace, for the young and fidgety Basil, was the aura of expectation created by the Vicar's habit of publicly remonstrating with any member of the congregation 'caught napping' or simply being inattentive. This was a two-edged sword, and Basil was kept on his toes, terrified lest he be singled out. The Blackwells, Basil recalled, were however unlikely to have stood out. Albeit rather visible, ensconced as they were in the Vicar's pew, they were eclipsed by the splendour of Mr Vincent, the People's Warden. The words of the Sermon were lost on Basil as he examined the finery of Mr Vincent's silk hat and frock coat. But, as Basil's father must have pointed out, appearances weren't everything, even in those days, and more usually Mr Vincent could be found in a journeyman's apron and old cloth cap in charge of the compositors in the family's printing firm[169]. The staple clientele of the Church of England were not, it would seem, simply 'the middle classes at prayer'.

More numerous were the respectable tradespeople, and their apprentices and families, intent on educational and social betterment[170]. And the Church, too, had much to be grateful for. Occasionally, with a deprecating glance at his achievements Benjamin Henry would remind his family 'that a self-made man relieves his creator of a great responsibility'[171]. At his own mother's instigation, a very young Benjamin Henry had had a very large dose of church, and church education. It became another of his solaces, especially the chance to sing in the church choir. Music training and the art of sight-singing were skills the Victorians valued, and school inspectors gave financial rewards to schools whose pupils were well versed in the rudiments of music. Alongside his musical education, Benjamin Henry had used his time in church to teach himself Latin; and the prose of the liturgy, the bible readings and hymns introduced him to literature and poetry. Understandably he wanted his own children to benefit from the type of education that had been his own mainstay. His wife, too, had benefited from similar influences. In addition to teaching, she had played the harmonium in her Norfolk village church. As parents, both Blackwells determined that their children should observe the ethics and practices of Christianity. Throughout his boyhood Basil was greeted each morning by song; 'it was a signal that my father had emerged from his bath and was rubbing down; the song continued while he dressed, then there was silence; he was kneeling in prayer in his dressing room'. This, recounts Basil, 'was his private discipline and before his marriage, in accordance with Psalm 55, at noon-day would he pray and that instantly'. Yet he obtruded his religion on no-one and rarely spoke of it, but 'to one in daily contact with him it was evident that his rule of life was to do justly, to love mercy, and to walk humbly with his God'.

Benjamin Henry never let his devotional habits lapse. They formed an integral part of his daily life, just as reading and study did. On top of this, he had never been so busy at the shop, or in the community. His teenage children set out on their own adventures: Dorothy to follow a nursing career and Basil to university, and his wife had her own local interests. One of Lilla's great, and many, strengths was the way she let her hard-working husband have his head; she never stood in his way. She must have relished her daughter's tales of nursing life in London, and after Basil's marriage, she looked forward to grandchildren. Now in his seventies, Benjamin Henry appeared more and more remote. His grandchildren had only very hazy memories. His very young grandson, Richard Blackwell, remembered getting into trouble with his serious grandfather on at least two occasions; stamping his letter numbering machine on the red baize table-cloth in the dining room and mishandling parts of his precious model steam engines. What may have seemed like gruffness to a very young child was just Harry Blackwell's natural reticence. Especially as an older man, he was loath to say more than was needed, and as his daughter Dorothy wrote: 'What he thought he largely kept to himself'. Dorothy saw him as a 'shy and cruelly sensitive man'. That 'things and people hurt him too much' she accepts as 'a natural consequence of his inward life'. 'In short', she writes, 'he was the exact opposite of a club man, and was quiet and withdrawn in company.' His simple honesty and integrity did not go unnoticed. But it was not always received in the intended spirit. Sometimes it rebounded on him altogether. His daughter recalled that 'although as a businessman he was known for his high principles and conduct beyond reproach', he faced challenges to all that he stood for. Serving on the Oxford Town Council, as a Liberal, a stance that was regarded as suspicious enough in itself, his integrity was often regarded as a tiresome and irksome virtue. He was finally frozen out, and rather hurt, 'when they passed him over for chairman of the Library Committee for someone ignorant of books'.

Even in the conduct of his business, his integrity could be misconstrued. On one occasion, Mr Blackwell found that a rare first edition had been overlooked in the purchase of a library. He immediately wrote to the widow, who had sold the library, and sent a cheque. If he had been a different personality he could have capitalized on this lucky 'find' or proclaimed his virtue to the world. In the event, the widow grew suspicious and demanded another valuation! Benjamin Henry had no taste for argument, preferring to follow Thucydides tenet: 'that restraint impresses men most'. His manner may have given the (mistaken) impression that he expected it in others. But his wife had plenty of spirit, which he delighted in, and his colleagues too had their fair share of confidence. Despite his considerable success, Benjamin Henry was not a confident man. His early childhood experiences had emphasized the serious elements of personality, at the expense of fun. Reared according to the credo of expectation, rather than praise, it was hard for him to openly praise others, and he was never self-congratulatory[172]. But amongst his own work colleagues, this reserved and bookish man always inspired respect, affection and devotion. His daughter wrote that his staff were not fooled by his manner. They were 'always aware of his approval, and very deep affection, and no man had better service.' Members of his staff handed down their own accounts of Mr Blackwell's abiding, and sometimes salutary, influence over the family firm. The tone of these recollections is always proper: 'Mr' Blackwell was respected for his 'fine sense of values, his moral integrity and rectitude of spirit', but his staff were not so daunted that they could not refer to him with endearments such as 'our dear Founder'. Indeed the accounts which remain aimed to 'pay homage . . . to the integrity and uprightness of one of nature's gentlemen'[173].

Fred Hanks, an apprentice at Blackwell's who became a fellow director with Basil Blackwell, recalled his first encounters with Mr (Benjamin Henry) Blackwell. At the time Hanks was a nine-year-old member of the choir of St Philip and St James's, where Benjamin Henry Blackwell was a senior chorister. 'I sat in the front bench immediately in front of him. I suppose that like most boys I tried to make the most of my appearance by using some sort of hair lotion. . . . Anyhow, one Sunday morning after the service Mr Blackwell spoke to me for the first time and asked me nicely and kindly if I would mind not using this particular hair lotion. The next Sunday I obediently turned up in my usual place with my hair in its natural and inoffensive state, and you can imagine my surprise when after the service Mr Blackwell spoke to me for the second time, thanking me nicely, and at the same time placing a shilling in my hand. . . . In the course of time, hearing that Mr Blackwell required an apprentice I boldly applied, and whether the hair-oil did the trick or not I don't know, but at any rate in July 1883 my indentures were signed. . . . I hardly knew what it was to have a father, and I like to feel that by the kindly interest he took in me Mr Blackwell tried to some extent to fill that gap'[174]. Subsequent Blackwellian apprentices and Juniors also looked on Mr Blackwell as a father figure, but one cast in the strict Victorian mode where duty always took precedence over pleasure, and a job was not done unless it were well done.

However gently understated his style, manner and utterances may have been, his apprentices knew that Mr Blackwell was a stickler for scrupulous exactitude in the everyday performance of even the simplest rote task. And his high principles were applied irrespective of the position of the recipient. They were deployed without discrimination and applied equally beyond the doorstep of Broad Street. But his son Basil remarked on his father's reticence in recalling such incidents. Basil had heard tell of a run-in with *The Times* Book Club in the early 1890s, but it hadn't prevented Benjamin Henry from being regarded as one of its most influential members. Better known was his little misunderstanding with Hilaire Belloc. The situation arose when Belloc offered a collection of his essays to Mr Blackwell. Basil describes how his father then undertook to publish them. Shortly afterwards, however, Benjamin Henry noticed the self-same essays appearing in some other literary paper, and he told Belloc that he was disturbed by this! Answering this concern, Belloc replied, 'Oh, that is common form these days!' 'My father's reaction,' Basil continued, 'was typical'. Explaining that 'perhaps I am a little old-fashioned', he returned the manuscript to the miscreant. Belloc knew he was beaten and produced his *amende honorable* in recompense. Designing a rebus around his friend's name, he added a caption in the form of Latin hexameter: *Sumite castalios nigris de fontibus haustus* (From the Black Wells draw ye the Muses draughts). All was well. As a token of reciprocity, Blackwell's used Belloc's offering to adorn the covers of its catalogues[175].

Others lived to thank Benjamin Henry for his interventions. One of his later apprentices, Rex King, who became a distinguished antiquarian, recorded how Mr Blackwell would brook no short cuts, even in copying out the title of a book, with all its defects and blemishes. 'When I came to Blackwell's as a greenhorn in 1916', he recalled, 'I had the exceeding good fortune to be initiated into the art of cataloguing by Mr Blackwell himself, and I well remember that under no circumstances would he countenance the omission of the articles "a" or "the" from the title of a book: *The Poetical Works of Robert Browning* must appear as "Browning (Robert) The Poetical Works of", and never as "Browning (Robert) Poetical Works". He would quietly but very firmly maintain that "Poetical Works" might apply to all poetical works, or only a selection; whereas if the definite article was affixed "The poetical Works of...", then the complete poetical works (up to the date of publication) was indicated'[176]. If, on face value, he seemed bluff and pernickety, that was never his intention. Rather, he sought to educate his staff that they could better share in the success of the enterprise. But woe betide any employee who slipped off to the White Horse for sustenance, so

13 Basil Henry Blackwell.

temptingly placed as the public house was between the two halves of the Blackwell's shop. Although his apprentices owned to have a wholehearted respect for their disciplined and strict master, they were not so afraid as to refuse to keep 'pike' (lookout) for old John the packer 'who liked a pint'.

Shouldering responsibility for his staff's welfare—moral as well as physical—Benjamin Henry was never slow to administer a clear reprimand, if he felt it was called for. That he had no use for fools and knaves, who were not prepared to work, was clearly understood. The kind of help and guidance Mr Blackwell offered was often, at first, perceived as an unwelcome restraint, to put it in their own mild words, by many a young entrant. One of Blackwell's' band of apprentice-directors, Geoffrey Barfoot, engaged in 1912, recalled Mr Blackwell's admonition 'not to waste time and paper' when caught happily embellishing the postal ledger[177]. Benjamin Henry's attention to small things must have frustrated those who tried to take short cuts, especially impatient youth. Geoffrey Barfoot remembered Mr Blackwell tirelessly instructing him in 'the ways of string'. This was an art form taught and supervised by the Master. Past masters of the art never cut string. And Benjamin Henry never did. Basil Blackwell recalled his father sitting late at the desk in Broad Street, while his mother sat quietly untying knots in the string that had come in on parcels from outside. The apprentices were all taught how to pack parcels of books for storage in such a way that while they were protected from the dust of the stockroom, a replacement copy for the bookshop's shelves could be speedily retrieved and the parcel retied without cutting the string. Benjamin Henry never gave up on his attention to detail. A few months before his death, in 1924, he startled a young apprentice in the process of 'squaring-up' the books on the shelves. In the manner of youth, he had devised a short cut by running the palms of his hands along the wooden edges. This would not do at all. Being warned of the risk of splinters, the old man showed him the proper way to do the job[178].

Although at seventy Benjamin Henry was still a presence in the shop, and continued to cut a dash on his bike as he rode around Oxford, he was aware of a change. Whether or not this was a premonition, he shored up the future by incorporating the firm, with his old colleagues and his son among his fellow directors. He was to be chairman for less than five years. In March 1922, Basil Blackwell recalled, 'my father had the misfortune of a fall from his bike in collision with a taxicab, causing a concussion which would have been more severe but for the strong brim of his bowler hat. I watched with dismay the decline of his vigour, his withdrawal from public life. He retired from the City Council and felt bound to decline the Presidency of the Booksellers' Association, of which he had been a founding member. His mind showed signs of fatigue and an uncustomary reluctance to entertain new projects'[179]. Basil increasingly took over some of the tasks his father had performed so punctiliously throughout his Broad Street days. Although he presided as Chairman until his death, Benjamin Henry's immaculate copper plate hand was replaced by his son's, in the writing up of the Company's minutes. Not long after one of the regular directors' meetings, where no one's disquiet could be detected in the work-a-day account of the proceedings as written by Basil, he became too weak to come into the office. And so it was that the 'name over the door' passed to the next generation. On the 26 October 1924 B H Blackwell the second, at the age of 75, died peacefully at his home in Linton Road, North Oxford. How was it that this good, reserved and modest man turned a room twelve-feet square into an institution? Basil Blackwell thought of Wordsworth's words:

'That best portion of a good man's life
The little nameless unremembered acts
Of kindness and love'.

A great and lone achievement

A good man who did good things

Benjamin Henry was renowned for always doing a proper job, and he never ceased his vigilance. He neither retired from nor lost interest in his, now family, business. And he did not surrender one jot of his responsibility, presiding as chairman at the last meeting of the board of directors, which had been held only five weeks before his death. Perhaps the last word on Benjamin Henry Blackwell comes best from his son, Basil, who took over the chairmanship of Blackwell's from the time of his father's death. His father's death was recorded in the company minute book; when the next meeting of the Board took place a week later, clearly it was business as usual. Sir Basil wrote of his father: 'I used to watch my father as he sat in his chair reading in the evening, and ask myself: how is it that this man, so quiet, so apparently reclus-ive, is so highly esteemed by his friends and fellow citizens? Has he really something of greatness?' Great, in Benjamin Henry's book, would have meant the writers of the classics and *The Bible*. But his son recalled a text from Thucydides, which summed up his father's 'greatness': 'Of all the manifestations of power, restraint impresses men most'. Basil remembered the more public words that an unknown supporter had used to describe his father when he was a Liberal on Oxford's City Council: 'There is one who could stand on Carfax, and not a man in Oxford could throw a stone at him. He was, I judge, a good man and did good things'[180].

His success was due to the interplay of a number of variables; a matrix made up of personal qualities correlated with propitious timing. Unlike his own poor father, Harry Blackwell was endowed with prodigious physical good health; a blessing he passed on to his son. But there was much of his hard-working and devout father in the young Harry, and he had watched his own mother practice thrift, economy and deferred gratification. Wrenched from school and sent to work at the age of 13, a normal enough situation, he determined to better himself, engaging on a strenuous programme of self education. This application to the task in hand, while satisfying his own desire for more education, helped him during the early days of his apprenticeship. When business was rather slack he had busied himself in the long afternoons, in the absence of any customers, memorizing Quaritch's catalogue[181]. 'By this means he obtained a wide knowledge of the title and character of books he had never seen, and forty years later would come into his hands which he would remember having first learnt about in Quaritch's catalogue'[182]. When he became the owner of a shop in his own right, Harry Blackwell's personal qualities were woven into the daily practices of his business.

The discipline he had exercised in learning his trade, his natural probity, his sound judgement and application, and an extensive knowledge of his stock and his customers' needs, set the tone of his business from the start, and sealed Blackwell's' success in a trade where there were, at the time, several rivals. But Benjamin Henry's 'edge' in the trade was never at others' expense, rather it was an advantage gained by natural authority and the policies of keeping an open door to scholars, students and readers and forever taking infinite pains[183]. Harry Blackwell was endowed with all the qualities that made up the stereotypical highly successful businessman in Victorian England. Sir Arthur Norrington aptly summed up these characteristics in his history of Blackwell's. 'The English', he wrote, 'believed in the virtues of self-control, self-improvement, and self-denial, virtues mockingly admired in Clough's *Dipsychus*:

> Staid Englishmen, who toil and slave
> From your first breeching to the grave,
> And seldom spend and always save,
> And do your duty all your life
> By your young family and wife'[184].

Other personal qualities, less recognized as hallmarks of business success, suited Benjamin Henry to his chosen trade. He had written to his prospective wife that the riches of a well-stored mind ranked far above the advantages of mere wealth and mere birth.

But this love of learning, and his own life-long pursuit of knowledge, embracing both old and the new disciplines, was exactly what endeared him to his customers. He felt at home with scholars, and they warmed to him. The term 'scholars' was never narrowly construed by Benjamin Henry; he had a natural affinity with anyone who wanted to advance their education and book learning. His shop was never an elitist haven; it was open to all: Town or Gown. Like his father, starting off the Oxford Public Library, he wanted Blackwell's to welcome the newest scholars: those who could only begin their studies at the end of a day's work. While Benjamin Henry balanced the roles of supervisor and manager with those of literary host, research and information assistant, and offered school-teacherly guidance, his customers found a safe haven. 'Every book-lover', declared a leading weekly, 'knows of shops where he can browse at will . . . and one of the earliest literary hosts of this accommodating style was Mr B H Blackwell of Oxford'[185]. The *Evening Standard* of the time described the antics of those who took advantage of Mr Blackwell's hospitality: 'Undergraduates at Oxford were accustomed to spend their afternoons in three ways: either they indulged in some kind of athletics, or else they took a walk, or else they went to Mr Blackwell's shop in the Broad. When they went there they read any book that occurred to them. All the shelves were open. . . . Generations of undergraduates have done their reading there without cost'[186].

However laudable, Harry Blackwell's personal qualities would not alone have assured his success. There were, as his bank manager had pointed out, plenty of others in the same trade, even on the same street. Benjamin Henry had lost no time in reassuring his protagonist that there was room for all, but he had had his own doubts in the past. At the time of his marriage in 1886, he had written to his wife that he knew she would support him in the rainy days that must come. There was some room for his pessimism; the book trade was in the doldrums in the 1870s. In 1868, according to Basil Blackwell, the co-founder of Macmillan's, Alexander Macmillan, complained to Gladstone that 'books were nothing but appendages to toyshops and Berlin-wool warehouses'. And until the Net Book Agreement of 1900, it was only books that found their way onto the second-hand shelves that provided booksellers with a living. But as fortune had it, the anticipated rainy days did not materialize. Benjamin Henry had made his reputation in second-hand books and earned the eternal thanks of many a customer[187]. And this was especially true of those with writing aspirations. In Benjamin Henry's day, there was no clear dividing line between publishing and bookselling, and his early decision to break into publishing was a natural progression. Perhaps he instinctively understood the importance of diversification, of spreading the load. Although at the time this was no hardheaded commercial decision, motivated as it was by his irrascible independence of spirit that hated to see talent unrecognized, it became a side of the business that was to thrive when Basil Blackwell joined his father in 1913.

The small businessman had to be jack of all in his trade, and Benjamin Henry's own mastery was a source of inspiration and respect for his apprentices. A sound training, with good prospects, was a much sought-after prize by those who were forced to enter the world after only an elementary education, and this had indeed been Harry Blackwell's own plight. In this golden age of the small family-owned business, labour in the towns was plentiful, wages were low, food and housing were cheap and income tax was 5d in the pound. Added to which, Benjamin Henry's modest ambition to open up in trade on his own account had taken place against the wider backdrop of Victorian Britain at the height of its imperial glory. Having experienced the pain of industrial development, Britain was beginning to demand some of the good things of life. The wealth generated by the industrial revolution, backed up by social, political and economic agitation and reform, was beginning to manifest itself in the provision of public goods: transport, education, improving conditions in the workplace and paving the way for the development of leisure facilities and the popularising of knowledge. Chief among this interplay of factors, which turned around the fortunes of the British book trade and cleared the way for Benjamin Henry's success, was the expansion of education, at all levels of society. With this new age of enlightenment, came an unprecedented increase in the demand for books: fiction, non-fiction and those covering the new technical curriculum subjects such as economics and science.

To meet the needs of household reading, called 'the general reader' for the first time in 1862 according to the *Oxford English Dictionary*, there was an explosion of demand for translations of the classics, such as Homer and Plato, for reference books, dictionaries, histories and favourites, such as Burton's *Arabian Nights*. If this fare was too esoteric, then arrayed before the reader were the works of the great Victorian novelists, Thackeray and Dickens, with newer entrants, Trollope, George Eliot, Hardy, James and Kipling, hard on their heels. Books, of all descriptions, became part of domestic architecture in even modest homes. Increasingly skilled workers were becoming literate, and 'book-learning' became popular as never before. Books were being made available in a selection of lending libraries, as well as trade societies, local clubs and churches, and, at the turn of the century, through the Workers Education Association. Matching these developments in adult education was the establishment of another new, younger, readership, benefiting from the introduction of compulsory elementary education; the realization of an ideal for Benjamin Henry Blackwell.

These young readers now provided a whole new market for children's literature and school texts, and a further opportunity for the expansion of the tandem trades of publishing and bookselling. The new middle classes voraciously used their leisure time to better themselves, building up their libraries. Especially convenient for Blackwell's were the married academics who, settling in North Oxford, provided a ready market for the full range of books available in the shop, which now included a children's department. Families with new wealth were determined to educate their children as 'gentlemen' at the public schools. More than a dozen new public schools had been opened in the mid-nineteenth century, and there were scholarships and lower fees available at the grammar schools. Children of the middle classes also broke through into the older, traditional establishments which, straying far from their ancient foundations as places for poor scholars, had for too long been the sole preserve of wealthy aristocrats and the landed gentry. This latest breed of students were more aware of economic reality than the laid-back 'bucks' of the previous century, and the aristocracy all but gave way to this meritocracy who were prepared to work their passage. Benjamin Henry and his son Basil were of their number, as were many of their customers. The Blackwells, father and son, understood the necessity to support the new learning, and the corresponding need for well-produced, but cheaper, books.

Not to be outdone by their brothers, girls, too, began to demand to be formally educated outside the home. Brooking no opposition, even when they were branded 'un-natural', Miss Buss and Miss Beale pioneered Grammar Schools for Girls in London, catering for those of modest means typically from families with a small business or whose fathers had joined the growing ranks of the clerical classes. Their example served as a model for the Girls Public Day School Trust, who established Girls' schools in many parts of the country, also offering a large number of scholarships, Oxford High School for Girls being one such institution. The year Harry Blackwell opened his door in Broad Street, 1879, coincided with the opening of two women's colleges in Oxford: Lady Margaret Hall and Somerville. At the same time, 'poor' children, boys and girls, could now win scholarships from the local elementary schools. These developments came too late for Harry Blackwell, but they greatly benefited his children and grandchildren's generations. Much later his son, Basil Blackwell, attacked the credo of the 1970s, which tried to end the grammar school system. But in his time, the flurry of academic activity in the elementary and secondary schools served his trade well. It also broke the monopoly of Oxbridge. As more candidates sought places in higher education, a succession of new universities were founded, and the granting of degrees was no longer restricted to the ancient universities. Durham and London had been founded in the 1830s, Manchester arrived on the scene in 1880 followed, at the opening of the twentieth century, by five others: Birmingham, Liverpool, Leeds, Sheffield and Bristol.

As a generation of new graduates: teachers, academics and civil (Colonial) servants, left Oxford, they set out to serve 'Victoria's People' in the far corners of an expanding Empire or in the independent New World. And Mr Blackwell's fame went with them. The *Oxford Chronicle* demanded: 'Is there any bookshop where so much trouble is taken to get you the book you want, though it may cost only a shilling or two? Blackwell's has customers in every corner of the globe, most of them, no doubt, men and women who first knew this home of the book-lover in their undergraduate days.' This small local Oxford trader found himself at the start of a burgeoning export-import business, facilitated by land and sea transport that made possible the transmission of parcels to new centres of learning, across the Atlantic and to the 'last, loneliest, loveliest' regions of the Pacific[188]. Closer to home, he saw the importance of linking scholarship, through the distribution of books, in Europe. Sending books would hardly bring in Dante's *Paradise*, but turning their leaves could make a positive, and peaceful, contribution to healing the rifts of war: '*In quella parte surge ad aprire Zefiro dolce le nouvelle fonde di che se vede Europa rivestire*'[189]. At the first meetings of the directors of Blackwell's as a newly incorporated company, the prospect of selling more foreign books in England was a recurring theme, as recorded in the minutes. While international scholars and librarians came to regard Blackwell's as their own, Benjamin Henry stayed fiercely loyal to his alma mater. He had laid strong foundations in Oxford and he kept them in good repair, and not just in the University.

For all his support for Oxford's 'institutions', Benjamin Henry remained independent and single-minded. He was not one of those who thought that the University always had to come first, especially when it used its might to upset the efforts of local tradesmen, who were providing much needed employment. Blackwell's, of course, was exempted from this 'aesthetic cleansing'. Not so Mr W R Morris, who opened his first workshop in Longwall to howls of disapproval. Morris swallowed his pride and became a major benefactor of the University. Town was prepared to meet Gown, but Gown would not relinquish its hold over the Town without a struggle.

14 Basil Henry Blackwell and C Parker.

Benjamin Henry was often an intermediary between the two. It is interesting to speculate on whether his independent stance cost him a much-coveted honorary degree. He may not have been willing to be bought off, but he was as loyal to the University as he was to the City. The world outside Oxford held little allure for him, but he was always on hand to receive visitors, especially those from his own trade. He hosted bookselling events in Oxford, and organized charabanc excursions, through the Antiquarian Booksellers Association, to look at their establishments. For the most part, he stayed on site in Oxford. As a major worldwide second-hand market, it provided rich pickings for second-hand booksellers, especially as libraries were dispersed and modernized: and some notable scholars repaid Mr Blackwell's many kindnesses with bequests. In this way Blackwell's was able to devote an entire issue of its Catalogue (1888), entitled *Ex Oriente Lux*, to a collection donated by the late Laudian professor of Arabic, Robert Gandell. Blackwell's was, unofficially, a part of the University, and those associated with the University looked out for their own.

But Harry Blackwell also knew how to look after his own. And he always worried lest his success should steal the thunder of his fellow tradesmen. When, in 1888, he was asked to supply foreign books to the Oxford Union, he was anxious to reassure Parker, his rival on Broad Street and one who was still mightiest in the City, that this was not his doing. Benjamin Henry wrote to the librarian: 'I should like to ask, as a favour, that, if it be possible, Messrs Parker's may understand the change has not been the result of any application on my part, so that there may be no room for ill-feeling towards me'. Such was Benjamin Henry's personality. Parker's no doubt had to accept that Mr Blackwell was his own best salesman, and there were no known recriminations. In his lifetime he was hailed as one of the most knowledgeable booksellers of his day, and he turned the respect he had earned to good account. He served a term as president of the International Association of Antiquarian Booksellers, founded in 1906, with a membership of fifty in Great Britain and twelve overseas, five of them in America. He was also a founding member, in 1899, of the Oxford and District branch of the Associated Booksellers of Great Britain and Northern Ireland, serving in turn as secretary and chairman, before being elected to the National Council.

Despite his own successes, he was acutely aware of the struggles of others in the book trade. He worked tirelessly for a net book agreement, trying, as others had done in the past, to end the devil of underselling. Earlier attempts had been to no avail, not helped by an unsympathetic press. *The Times* had attacked the idea of retail price maintenance as 'this anomalous interference with the free course of competition and the natural operations of trade'. Thirty years later Benjamin Henry joined the fray, and he gently but unremittingly kept up the pressure. At the end of the century, he gained the support of authors, such as Lewis Carroll, who insisted that his publishers, Macmillan's, should not supply his books at a discount of more than 2d in the shilling, so as to leave no room for underselling. Frederick Macmillan, second generation like Harry Blackwell, lent his elbow and orchestrated a well-publicised public campaign in defence of those who tried to earn a living selling new books. He tried to alter the old allegiances of the conservative press, writing to *The Times* of the disastrous effects of retail price wars[190]. Thus Benjamin Henry found himself in good company, and this time his efforts, and those of the book trade he served, were rewarded. The Net Book Agreement was signed in 1901. At a meeting of the Association in Oxford in 1906, organized by the 'indefatigable Hon. Secretary', Benjamin Henry made a triumphant after dinner speech, and several of the most prestigious publishers feted him; among them were J M Dent, Gerald Duckworth, the great Henry Frowde of OUP and William Heinemann[191].

But Harry Blackwell, never at ease being covered in glory, was happiest working alongside his own bookmen: his staff. He also introduced measures that would provide more personal security for them. In other trades, the protection of employees was underwritten by provident societies. And Benjamin Henry set out to establish just such a safety net, not only in the wider book trade, but also under his own roof. Under his management, the lot of Blackwellians was eased in a number of ways; intrinsic benefits being as important as the actual level of wages. The introduction of holidays with pay were an innovation for those times, but there were other perks too: bonuses, a pension and a staff profit sharing scheme. These improvements for the condition of man were accompanied by Harry Blackwell's fight for a shorter working week with a half day on Thursdays, which put Blackwell's in the vanguard of those employers who strove to improve conditions in the workplace, even before statutory regulation[192]. Staff were rewarded for their hard work with promotion from within their ranks. And some apprentices rose up through the ranks, joining their master as directors of the Company when the firm was incorporated as a private limited company in 1920. When Benjamin Henry took the Chair, with his son at his side, at the first meeting of the Company, held at 41–42 Cornmarket on 22 March 1920 at 3.00pm, he was in the good company of his loyal stewards, and former apprentices: Fred Hanks, William Hunt, Charles Field, and Harry Critchley. Family firms had been converted into joint stock companies since 1856, when this type of organization received the sanction of law. For many family firms, however, this change in their status was the beginning of the end, or at least of their independence[193]. But not so at Blackwell's.

Unlike other family firms, established in the Victorian era and anxious to take advantage of the fund-raising and loss-limiting possibilities afforded by incorporation, at 'Mr Blackwell's' there remained no real working distinction between the owner and the management. For Benjamin Henry, to own, or possess, was to manage; he took complete responsibility. And the interests of shareholders, themselves Blackwellians, being either family or staff, were identical. While Benjamin Henry held 7,000 Preference Shares and 55 Ordinary Shares, and Basil Blackwell had 3,500 Ordinary Shares, the remaining Ordinary Shares were distributed to his seniors: Hanks and Hunt had 800 each, Field had 400, Critchley had 200 and Steele, Bates, Rowles, Cook, Presley and Bishop had 100 apiece At the time of incorporation, profits were running at the rate of £7,000 a year, this sum being double that of the pre-war period, and rising to £8,000 by 1922. Benjamin Henry Blackwell was the first to acknowledge his good luck, attributing his firm's success to Oxford not being a manufacturing town and therefore not so prone to depression[194]. This was not explanation enough, since the

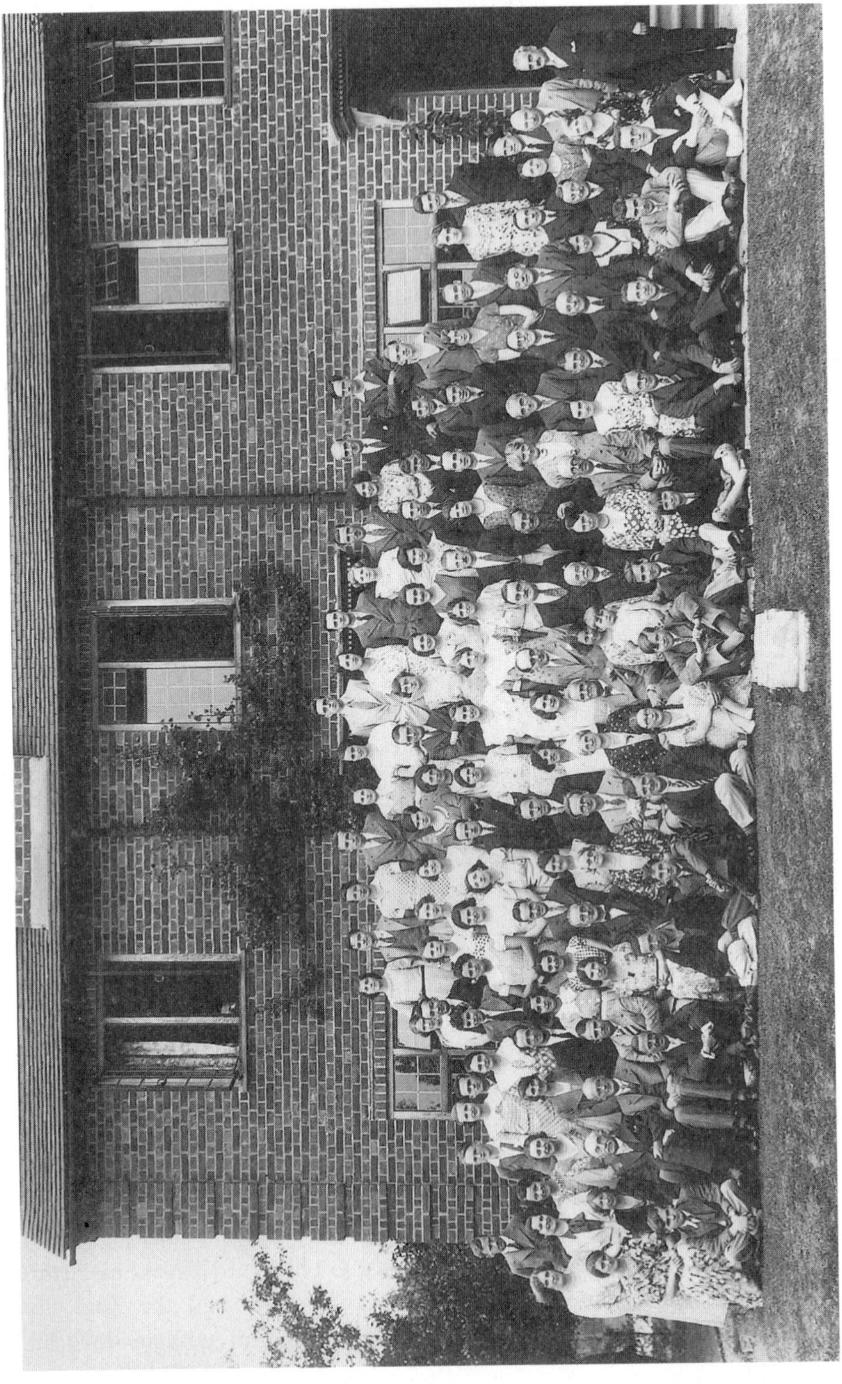

15 The Blackwell family and staff at Osse Field for Fred Hanks' jubilee celebrations, 29 June 1933.

Left to right, Top Row
Phyllis Stone, Tom Templeton, Eleanor Halliday, Frank Timbs, Marjorie Parker, Hilda Phelps, Rupert Boasten, Marjorie Soden, George Adams, Patricia Taylor, Percy Coates, Doris Ward, C W Field, Ken Clarke

2nd row down
Molly Hawtin, Willie Herman, Gladys Garrett, Kath Garrett, Irish Clifford, Honor Tracey, Mr & Mrs Piper, Miss Wern, Florrie Phelps, Marian Hemphreys, Joyce North, Art Alder, Mr Boyd, Curly Kent, Sam Knights

3rd row down
Sir Adrain Mott, Harry Knights, Ida Soden, George Bunting, Bessie Kirk, Dudley Buttrum, Freda Strange, Joan Tyrrell, Betty Vernon, George Crutch and wife, Sybil Barnes, Audrey Walker, Mr & Mrs Olliffe, Mr & Mrs Hine, Charlie Smith, Mr & Mrs Fenemore, Ruth Tucker, Peter Gray

4th row down
Irene Quartermain, Doris Hounslow, Mrs Higley, Miss Lovelace, Mr & Mrs Brimfield, Gladys Downham, Irene (Minne) Blagrove, Mr & Mrs Fred Stevens, Mr & Mrs Stan Loughborough, Mr & Mrs C W Cutler, Sam Weller, Bill Smith, Mr & Mrs King, Rignell & Kettle, Mr & Mrs Rowies, James Sherbourn, Mr Steele, (Binder) Levitt

5th row down
Kathleen, Mary Mott, Jack Thornton Snr, Reginald Hanks, Lillian Hanks, Mr & Mrs Hunt, Gaffer, Mr & Mrs Hanks, Lady Blackwell, & Julian, Uncle Fred Blackwell, Mr & Mrs Critchley, Tommy Doe, Ivy Radell, Pluck Fowles and wife

Bottom Row
Mark Innes, Stanley Dorrill, Reggie Nash, Jackie Bateson, Henry Schollick, Helen Blackwell, Richard Blackwell, Wiggins, Corinna Blackwell, Pigott Snr, Mr Barfoot, Jim King, John Alden

industrialisation of Oxford had already begun. In 1919 William Morris of Cowley had just put up his first modest factory building, where 350 cars were produced a month. The continuing success of Blackwell's was, in greater measure, due to Mr Blackwell's effective management of people, and the owner's abiding enthusiasm for new projects. Along with new projects went an equal appreciation of new technology. However much Benjamin Henry revered craftsmanship, he was no Luddite: his staff were to be trained in the joys of modern technology, and the firm would avail itself of labour saving devices. One such device, newly purchased and installed by Benjamin Henry at the beginning of the century, was a revolutionary device in the form of a Hammond typewriter. And a new age man, one Bert Steele, who eventually became a director, was re-trained and promoted to become the firm's first stenographer. And the delight of the apprentices can easily be guessed at when a spanking new Chevrolet van was purchased in 1921, for £281, making deliveries a whole new ball game.

In return for his varying good offices towards his staff, 'Mr Blackwell' had their fierce, and in most cases life-long, loyalty. Blackwell's was not just a place of work; it was a society or social community, and a source and means of betterment, where its members, having successfully completed an apprenticeship, could expect security of tenure and find convivial company on their doorstep[195]. The Blackwell's system, which could be seen as paternalistic by a casual observer, provided a society—a community—where colleagues and friends enjoyed leisure activities together, playing sport or singing with the shop's choir. They were a part of the extended Blackwell family, and, when needed, became surrogates overseeing the youthful exuberances of Benjamin Henry's children, Dorothy and Basil. When Benjamin Henry died, he remembered his extended family in his will. Each of his employees, of three or more years standing, was to receive one month's pay as a farewell gift. Throughout his life, Blackwellians, family and colleagues alike, were his paramount and overriding concern. He had what his son called 'a touch of genius', which enabled him to walk the tightrope between all the competing, and often conflicting, demands on his time and energy, and not waver or fall off.

'In his own quiet way', as his daughter recorded, 'he had time for all'. If Blackwellians loved him for his gentle concern, so also did his customers. Taking pains to help any customer was his hallmark. The shop now attracted a very eclectic bunch, and the new parcel post of 1883 saw Blackwell's books despatched to new customers, far from Oxford. Customers now ranged from working people anxious for new novels, translations and works of non-

16 Illustrations used for stationery and publicity between 1900 and 1950.

fiction; their children; the families of all of those associated one way or another with the University, as well as the traditional 'academic' customers (students, scholars and librarians); to those, across the world, who may never have visited Oxford. But despite the increasing acclaim for this little shop and Mr Blackwell's unquestionable personal achievements—a consummate knowledge of books and literature; the respect of scholars and the general public alike; and his generosity and dedication to his staff and customers—no public or academic honours came Benjamin Henry's way. His most coveted prize, 'and one for which he would have given all the rubies in the world: an honorary degree—fell to his senior assistant after he was dead'. At the time of his death, the *Oxford Chronicle*'s entry was understated: 'Mr Blackwell lived a quiet life . . . he had no clubs and no cronies. His whole life and interest were in his business.' He was the epitome of a good public servant, valued for his efficiency and less well known as a personality[196]. Certainly Benjamin Henry was a solitary man who would never have asked for any recognition, save the success of his firm. And until now no 'little memoir' has ever focused 'on his great and lone achievement on £300'[197]. He would have been thankful to remain a part of Oxford:

'Pale pink convolvulus in tendrils creep;
And air-swept lindens yield
Their scent, and rustle down their perfumed showeres
Of bloom on the bent grass where I am laid,
And bower me from the August sun with shade;
And the eye travels down to Oxford's towers'[198].

And he would also have been thankful that he had been at one with his fellows, had provided for his Blackwellian family, left a healthy business for his son and had, above all, given good measure. Looking back on the death of his father, Basil concluded:

'Now he his worldly task has done, home has gone and ta'en his wages'[199].

Yet, more accurately, the owner of Blackwell's had not 'ta'en his wages'; he had put everything into his shop and left it to the care of his son and his trusted colleagues. Thus even if the successful way Benjamin Henry fulfilled his worldly task in all its aspects has been often overlooked, the pay-off from the shop is not forgotten. It remains as his true and long-lasting memorial. And it had already become an institution in his own lifetime[200]. Mr Blackwell's shop, the institution, and Harry Blackwell, the man, seeming in the public mind to be one and the same thing, were in life inseparable. His life, and that of his family, whether blood or co-opted Blackwellians, were entwined with the shop that took his name. He had lived over the shop, his children had been born there and he had spent the better part of every working day, six days a week, in Broad Street, even after the family removed to Summertown. And after his death, when son Basil was ensconced in his father's old workroom cum office/study, Benjamin Henry's guidance continued to issue from an old photograph on the wall. For over half a century, while Basil oversaw an expanding business, the face of a more youthful man than Basil had remembered stared down from the wall of what had quickly become the new 'Gaffer's Room'. Basil could not waver or slacken off under the cool, shrewd, dark eyes of his father's gaze, and an expression that embodied pride and expectation. His expectations and faith in his son were rewarded although just what he would have made of the present multi-million pound empire can only be guessed at. When he opened his own small shop in 1879, in a space twelve-feet square, he was told by Frederick Macmillan that it would surely fail as it was situated on the wrong side of the street. Well over a century and a quarter later B H Blackwell's is still disproving this prophecy of doom[201]. The Emperors of the Sheldonian still keep their unflinching watch over Mr Blackwell's shop front, a landmark that has, even now, changed only superficially.

When Basil Blackwell joined his father in Broad Street in 1913, he found the family firm in fine fettle. Overcoming a blip at the beginning of the century, the value of sales were, by then, up to £27,000, as compared with £15,000 in 1901. Blackwell's' net profits were averaging eleven percent of sales, and the balance sheet showed positive assets of £20,000. At his father's death in 1924, and not before, Basil Blackwell took over the chairmanship of the firm, a position he held for exactly the same number of years, forty-five, as his father. Thus installed, he continued and expanded his father's interests in publishing, while broadening both the size and scope of the bookselling side and the physical buildings. In many ways he was quite unlike his father. He was more daring, more impulsive, more sociable and perhaps more of a risk taker. It was of course Basil Blackwell who was the best known of the Blackwells, and his work was recognized by his inclusion in the Honours List of 1956. His knighthood was a first for any bookseller, and set a trend for honours going to trade. During his long reign of over sixty years at Broad Street (he did not retire even in 1969 when he handed the Chair to his son, Richard), Basil kept in trust his father's endowment. The business gained in size and influence and remains, to this day, in the family.

Benjamin Henry lived through the educational revolution of Victorian and Edwardian England, and his present descendents have faced another, less easily reconcilable, revolution: the electronic information one! Yet his 'literary public house' continues to whet the appetite of book lovers, vying successfully with the many substitutes. Blackwell's has now been passed from Benjamin Henry's direct control for over three quarters of a century. His grandson is now life President of the still family-owned firm, and his great grandson, Philip Blackwell, is the Chief Executive. He would have applauded their efforts to keep the name above the door: to 'match their noble ancestors in prowesse of their owne, and by their fruits commend the stocke whence they themselves are grown'[202]. If the latest Blackwellians are less well known to the public, the same is not true for Blackwell's the shop. Like the house of Pindarus, the house of Blackwell's has been preserved. Even the present shop front would be instantly recognizable to Benjamin Henry Blackwell. And the interior, for all the changes and enlargements, exudes an atmosphere that has been undisturbed by the passage of time; as customers and browsers continue to explore his (expanded) empire. So that, even if his personal reputation has been a little superseded by that of his son, and his image shrouded in the mists of time, the main creative purpose of his life, the bookshop, remains as a living tribute. This was the sort of success Benjamin Henry Blackwell would have most wanted: not for himself, but for his family of Blackwellians and the shop full of books. All other pursuits and accolades were secondary to him. Now, as then, 'on every hand, on every shelf, the eye encounters books which in Milton's words:

> 'do preserve as in a vial the purest efficacy and extraction of that living intellect that bred them'[203].

Lydia (Lilla) Taylor Blackwell 1850–1927

Something of the country air about her[204]

Undoubtedly, Benjamin Henry was the living intellect which made the firm of Blackwell's. But for all his fine qualities, it was not just down to Benjamin Henry alone. Two women, his mother and his wife, from among the main dramatis personae, played vital roles on Benjamin Henry's stage. Notwithstanding, they were less written about, although at the time, according to his daughter Dorothy, they were often talked of. Benjamin Henry was, for all his virtues, a man of the times; he was a typical Victorian and he would not have wanted his wife, or his mother, in the front line of business. Both Nancy Blackwell and her daughter-in-law, Lilla, had in common the experience of having to hold the fort, occasioned by the untimely death of the family breadwinner. Harry Blackwell's own deprived childhood, and his memories of his own mother having to maintain a family single-handedly while earning a living, made him determined to provide for his own. But it was, arguably, his mother's ambition which set him on the road to bookselling. Benjamin Henry had had an indomitable mother, and he went on to marry an equally determined and independent-minded woman. At the time when his shop was getting into its stride, it was inevitably the influence of the younger of the two, Lydia (Lilla) Taylor Blackwell, which was the more immediate. Adversity had not sullied Lilla, and her natural exuberance and zest for life had provided a foil for her more sober husband, whilst they shared in the experiences of having to work hard and pay their own way. Nonetheless, Lilla was a free spirit, he recorded, who found it difficult to adjust herself to the stratified society of Victorian Oxford. Yet, as Benjamin Henry had written to Lilla before their marriage, he knew he could count on her for help and support. To fulfil his part of the bargain, he soon learnt to tolerate and accommodate his high-spirited wife, 'with something of the country air about her'[205].

Lilla was indeed a 'country girl', by birth, breeding and inclination. For all her husband's good offices, she remained somewhat impervious to the repressive regimes of the city. One of her many 'causes' was to inveigh against the gulf that existed between the Townsfolk and Gownsfolk of Oxford. This 'political stand' appalled and dismayed her husband, who had grown up to regard the divide as untraversible and fixed[206]. After her marriage to Harry Blackwell, and to occupy their two small children in the confined space above the shop, she would tell stories of country larks on the Norfolk farm, where she grew up. Lilla's daughter, Dorothy, fondly described her mother as a woman who was much loved, full of fun and bubbling with gaiety. 'As a child, I loved her stories about life on the farm', wrote Dorothy, 'and they were so vivid they always remained with me'. Thanks to Dorothy, we have a vivid set of vignettes of her mother. Among these was the indelible image of Lilla as a small village girl, always showing off in front of her peers. On one notable occasion, Lilla dressed up as the 'village zany'. Taking no pains to conceal her jest, she was discovered and, to her surprise and dismay, the real 'village zany' gave chase: a chase Lilla never forgot. Another of Dorothy's favourites records her mother's description of harvest-time parties held at a neighbouring farm: 'the hay cart was brought round filled with clean straw, and the little sisters laid in and covered with a tarpaulin'. These mid nineteenth century tales rekindle sights and smells now much less familiar; the horses black with sweat in the stable, the small kegs of brandy, the fun of the harvest supper when the hard work was done, and the townie cousins, visiting the country from London, to be 'initiated'!

> All sang, (and after sixty years
> The singing lingers in my ears)
> From wagon-tops, while bearing back
> The end of harvest to the stack[207].

Lilla, together with her four sisters and one brother, Jack, enjoyed a carefree and happy early childhood. They lived in a roomy and pleasant farmhouse, with French windows opening onto the lawn, and hanging creepers[208]. Lilla loved to recall the one outstanding, and rather dramatic, feature of the Taylor children's childhood home: 'the huge crater before the front door where a thunderbolt had once struck'. Typically it was this image that had stuck in the mind of the imaginative Lilla. But her image of her father was equally clear. John Taylor, as she had told her children, was a strong, thickset man 'with a golden spade-beard and kind blue eyes'. Her father, owning and farming his own land in the Norfolk village of Blo' Norton, was much respected as an honest and upright man. Guided by his granddaughter's written record, it is not difficult to 'see' John Taylor with his square bowler hat spanking through the lanes on the way to market at Diss. On rare, but memorable, occasions Lilla was allowed to accompany her father to market. Here she would wander off from the din of stock auctions, and the farmers haggling over prices, to be tantalised by the colourful displays of wares on the general stalls. Lilla's memories of these halcyon days were, alas, soon to be overlaid by those of tragedy.

Despite their cheerful demeanours, all was not well for the Taylor family. The livelihood of rural England, and small farmers in particular, was being threatened by a new government policy: the reform of the Corn Laws. It was a reform that changed the face of rural England forever; in its wake came the destruction of many small farms. Unable to contend with the influx of cheap corn from Canada, they went out of business. Sadly, John Taylor, along with hundreds of others, suffered this fate. Dorothy Blackwell recorded her mother's poignant account of the day their farm went under the hammer. Lilla had watched her father as he sat by the open bedroom window. Down below, in the farm courtyard, in front of his eyes, John Taylor could see the whole disastrous spectacle where his horses and possessions were all being sold. As so often happened when a livelihood was removed, Jack was broken-hearted and never really recovered. His death was untimely, and his good strong life largely unrewarded[209]. Lilla, on the other hand, like the husband she was to meet, was determined to find a means to overcome the family's tragedy. Typical of many dutiful daughters, and sons, of the time, Lilla put aside any thoughts of marriage and stayed on at the farm to care for her mother. By becoming the village schoolmistress and playing the harmonium in church, Dorothy wrote, Lilla was able to maintain her mother in the old farm until she too was laid to rest next to her husband in the village graveyard, in the company of other faithful old servants who had succumbed to cancer, the scourge of that part of Norfolk.

After the death of both her parents, when everything was settled, Lilla came to Oxford and was introduced to Benjamin Henry Blackwell, by her married sister Charlotte. It is interesting that of John Taylor's five daughters, it was Lilla who had chosen to provide the caring and bread-winning role. The Blackwell men, it seems, had a penchant for choosing women who could weather adversity. Benjamin Henry's own mother had maintained her children after the death of his father, Benjamin Harris Blackwell. Dorothy Blackwell wrote that she thought of her mother, Lilla, as a latter day Boadicea because she was a fearless fighter against injustice. The term would be as well applied to describe Anne Stirling Blackwell, her husband's mother. Dorothy captured other sides of her mother. Her love of fun was matched by her sensitivity and telepathic leanings. 'My mother always had a vivid dream of being in a horse fair when someone near was going to die', Dorothy wrote. Her mother described the tossing manes and red nostrils that were the portents of disaster. 'At some much later date when she, Lilla, was married and living in Oxford, she woke my father up at 2 am to say "I have been in the horse fair and Jack (her brother) is dead". And truly news came that Jack had died at that time, tragically, from an overdose of laudanum.' Dorothy remarked that her telepathy may indeed have survived her mother. In 1928, as Lilla lay dying, Basil Blackwell was telephoned from Blo' Norton by a woman he did not know, an old pupil of his mother's, to ask if all was well with Mrs Blackwell as she had been compellingly aware of her all day.

Stories of Lilla's brother Jack were the stuff of myths for her two young children, as they sat at the tea-table, above the quiet shop, where their father worked so late. They were transported by her descriptions of Jack riding high on his horse across the windswept fields of Norfolk. Dorothy wrote down these stories of 'Uncle Jack', which enable us to catch a glimpse of her mother's time, while perhaps suggesting other strains in Blackwellian blood. Subsequent Blackwells grew up in the country, and not all their adventures were in the mind. Jack was not, however, content with the cramped life of rural Blo' Norton, and he set off to seek his fortune in Canada. Strong, and used to the outdoors life, Jack looked to the wilds and 'went trapping'. He was, according to his sister's stories, in his element; 'he was a wild one'. Yet, he was still spoken well of, in his native village, many years after his death.

His fine horsemanship was legendary, as was his reputation as an amateur vet and one who would put on the gloves and take anyone on. Quick to rise to the bait, he was also admired for his compassion and fearlessness. The fields, at that time, had dykes rather than ditches, with straight walls, and if a heavy carthorse slipped in, he was boxed and helpless. Then the cry went up 'Fetch Jack Taylor'. Putting a halter round the animal's neck, and with complete control of a very steady horse, he would drag the animal inch by inch out of the dyke. One jerk would have been fatal! Lilla's stories must have encouraged her childrens' imaginings to run riot, and, in this, Basil certainly needed no encouragement. Dorothy was, at times during the London Blitz, as fearless as her forbears; she, too, was cast in the mould of the stalwart Blackwell woman, her mother and her paternal grandmother.

Dorothy, hardly known as compared with her brother, had many talents. Her aptitude for music came from both parents. She studied the piano under Dr Ernest Walker, the musical genius of Balliol, and later played first fiddle in Dr Allen's orchestra. Dorothy shared her parent's hatred of cant, and had no time for Victorian fading flowers, if such a species ever existed. Small, but strong and athletic, Dorothy competed with her brother at tennis and swimming; she was also a good horsewoman and rejoiced in long walks through the Oxfordshire countryside, as her father had done. Benjamin and Lilla Blackwell were determined that their daughter should be as well educated as their son. Dorothy was sent to Oxford High School, where she did not disappoint them. According to her brother, Basil, Dorothy 'responded to the mark-grubbing discipline of those days by a weekly score of "Red As"'. Like her mother and grandmother, Dorothy was 'a carer'. She was a formidably competent nurse, working in France during the First World War, and as a Matron in the Second. Family folk-law has it that during the endless nights of the Second World War, Dorothy acquired the habit of 'kipping anywhere'. On one occasion, as she slept on a laundry basket, she was sent flying down the corridor during a bombing raid. On her return from France, Dorothy fell for one of her brother's friends, Sumner Austin, whose ambition to be an opera singer had been thwarted by the intervention of the War. He had been training in Germany when war broke out and the prospect of a pianist wife, helped him to contemplate a return to his chosen career. Their marriage lasted for fifty-eight years, although once again war cut across their lives.

In wartime, Dorothy returned to the wards, and her husband, who was also a linguist and a specialist in German, acted as an interpreter in

Army Intelligence. After the war, they settled in the Kensington area of London[210]. Dorothy's nephew, Julian Blackwell, remembered his aunt as an intelligent and very kindly old battleaxe. Remaining childless herself, Aunt Dorothy would invite her brother's family to rare treats in London where 'we would be taken to the theatre and treated to chicken and chips afterwards'. Her husband, an intellectual and much to the Blackwell family's taste, became the family 'Father Christmas' during the festive season[211]. After her father's death, Dorothy was well provided for, but the family business passed to her brother and her mother stayed with her son in Oxford. She watched her brother continue with her father's good work, but many years later, at Basil's Encaenia, she still regretted that her father had not received a degree. Dorothy continued to live in London, and did not return to live in Oxford until the very end of her life. She had shared a happy childhood with her brother, and she had chronicled her mother's adventures to pass onto the next generation. Neither Basil, nor his sister Dorothy, ever forgot their mother's adventures. They were committed to memory, to be recorded and placed alongside those of their more sober and reticent father.

Lilla Blackwell lived with her son, and his family, for the four remaining years of her life, after the death of her husband. In her last few years, she still had the spirit, and the time, to regale her stories to her son's wife and children, the stories that had so often captivated her own son and daughter in their infancy. Basil, living under the same roof as his mother, continued to be infected by his mother's zest, verve and liveliness. As head of the family firm, Basil having assumed the Chairmanship at his father's death in 1924, his style displayed as many of her characteristics as those of his father. As an independent and original thinker with guts and confidence, and an unending fund of ideas and enthusiasms, he inspired others, as his high-spirited mother had inspired him[212]. At Lilla's death, the Second Blackwells, Benjamin Henry and Lilla Blackwell, took their place with the First, Benjamin Harris and Anne Nancy Stirling Blackwell. Taken all together, their several qualities endowed Basil, the Third B H Blackwell, with the genetic brew that gave him that touch of genius referred to by Jan Morris. While Basil and his family were to reap the rewards of the dedication and hard work of previous Blackwells, he was to inspire and oversee the growth of an empire on a scale that would have been inconceivable in his parents' and grandparents' days. Yet, like them, Basil remained a local: he was an Oxford boy born and bred. Basil became better known than his father, who had nonetheless been a leading figure in the City, and when he moved his wife and five children to the village of Appleton, he showed himself to be his mother's son. He was accepted as one who was natural to country life. Lilla's 'country-air' continues in the family house, gardens and woodlands of Osse Field, where her grandson, Julian, lives. Symbolically Osse, the name of the local stream, also means good luck. And Lilla had brought her son plenty of that.

Chapter 4
Play Days with Pegasus: Father and Son
*Tired the sun with talking
and sent him down the sky*

Seven years of holiday!

I grudge not an hour of the grammar-grind which opened for me the unforgettable pages of Thucydides and Herodotus

A former apprentice who subsequently became a director of Blackwell's, 'Father' Fred Hanks, recalled the birth of Basil Blackwell. 'There have been many memorable and momentous days in the history of Blackwell's, but I say without the least fear of contradiction that of them all 29 May 1889 was the most memorable and momentous. This day . . . stands out clearly in my memory as if it were yesterday. It was a beautiful day in the summer term, and I well remember the many frequent and anxious visits which Mr Blackwell (Benjamin Henry) made to the second floor, and his final reappearance with the announcement that he had a son. . . . I take advantage of this opportunity to express . . . our deepest sense of appreciation and gratitude for the continuance and extension of those sound traits of character and business integrity which he (the son: Basil) has inherited from his father'[213]. And Fred Hanks was as good a judge as any since it was he, not the pre-occupied father, who kept a constant vigil over the young Basil. Benjamin Henry, an old Blackwellian remarked, 'must have delighted in a son born like Minerva in full panoply'[214]. His panoply was the green cotton sunshade of an infant's pram, in which Basil was parked in the small garden at the back of No 51. And it fell to Fred Hanks's happy lot to report any urgent noises from that quarter. Later, he was detailed to employ diversionary tactics, lest the two small Blackwell children should stray into the shop on working days. But the shop was their home, in those early days, and it had its mysteries and its refuges.

Above 'History' on the first floor front of the shop was his mother's drawing room. This was a cosy book-lined room, as one would expect the home of a scholar to be, and the books, including his father's first imprints, almost hid the original William Morris wallpaper. Looking out of the windows of this pleasant comfortable room was a harmless, but exciting, diversion for Dorothy and Basil. At the sound of music in the Broad, Basil's sister, three years his elder, would yank him up bodily so that he, too, could see the sights.

He always remembered his sense of wonder at the spectacle of the circus come to town: 'there they all were, people in Moorish costume, Britannia in her chariot followed by those representing people from all parts of the British Empire . . . going in procession down the street'. For much of the time the street was quiet in those days of the early nineties, especially in the University vacations. But at the start of a new term 'all was set at six and seven'. The racket outside caused the children's adrenalin to rise, just as it portended the start of a busy time in the shop below. The din outside the Blackwell's windows was the result of horses' shoes and the iron-shod wheels of carts, coaches and growlers grinding over the cobbles with which the street was paved. In the cabs undergraduates, lounging back with all their impedimenta a-top, were being delivered to colleges and lodging houses. Basil remembered that running behind each vehicle was a young hopeful who followed the equipage to its destination, with the prospect of earning a few coppers by carrying the toff's luggage to his rooms[215]. This room, so full of happy childhood adventures, became his own office, one he occupied for over sixty years as Blackwell's Gaffer.

Unlike his father, forced to leave school and seek an apprenticeship, Basil was free to enjoy childhood and, later, secondary and higher education. On holidays, very local affairs, Fred Hanks would take Basil and his sister, Dorothy, in a basket-chair mounted on the front of the firm's quadracycle, thus initiating them to the joys of speed on the road. At home, in Broad Street, the shop below delighted the two small children. They never thought of it as a future burden. Rather, it beckoned them to play. During the working week it was off limits, but on Sundays it became a great place for hide-and-seek[216]. This childhood haunt was nonetheless to dominate Basil's adult working life. As with so many sons of a family business, it was simply assumed that Basil would eventually join his father. He had his father's love of books, and was always curled up in dim corners with a book propped up on his knee, even though his eyesight was poor, having caught measles at the age of twelve, which later debarred him from the trenches but not the book trade. Preparation for his future could not start early enough in the Blackwell household; his father, if not his mother, determined that his childhood was not to be all play. When at the age of seven Basil was sent to school, his hard-working father observed 'he has already had seven years of holiday.' Basil's education began at a small local dame school kept by Misses Wilhelmina and Sarah Mardon. So unlike his own father, Basil was nonetheless free to enjoy the privilege of formal education, beyond the age of twelve. Thus he progressed, in the company of many fellow Mardonians, to Magdalen College

Play Days with Pegasus: Father and Son

School, then a small establishment of some 100 pupils, in the early years of the Mastership of C E Brownrigg. Basil always remembered Mr Brownrigg as a teacher who, together with Mr Pullen, the usher, 'did a wonderful lot for me every day of my young life'.

A glimpse of what Basil might have seen on his daily walk to school can be extracted from a contemporary account, written by William Tuckwell in 1901. Walking down The High, towards Magdalen Bridge, he would have passed, on his right, the Old Bank. This would have served as a solid reminder of his father's present good luck, and he was not unaware of the ragged bare-footed children, surreptitiously begging in the street, who would have provided a salutary reminder of what could have been his lot. Any anxiety he may have felt coming on would have been quickly dispelled by the commotion at the nearby, fashionable Angel Hotel. Here, on any one day, 'the carriages and four of the neighbouring magnates, the Dukes of Marlborough and Buckingham, and the Lords Macclesfield, Abingdon, Camoys, dashed up to it; there stopped all day post-chaises, travelling chariots, equipages of bridal couples . . . and coaches from the eastern road. Passing the Physic Garden . . .' and the gate of Magdalen, which Tuckwell judged of debased Jacobean style, adjoined by 'a remnant of the old Magdalen hall, used as a choristers' school', he may have gone straight on past the old stables where his Magdalen schoolroom stood, to hang about 'a vast inn': the Greyhound. The inn would undoubtedly have been out of bounds, but Basil's boyish appetite may have been satisfied by the possibility of a snack. Under the nearby trees, 'then in the perfection of their stature, sate always an aged woman, Mother Jeffs, selling tarts and fruits'[217]. But lively and imaginative as he was, his attention to his schoolbooks was not lacking. Much to his father's quiet delight, and perhaps relief, Basil showed that his mind, too, was receptive to academic study. At the end of his Magdalen days, he won the Classics prize, and his first published poem, a sonnet, in traditional form, appeared in the school magazine.

ON A DEAD CAT

Come, oh my muse; and with majestic broom
Sweep thou the chords of my responding lyre,
And tell me why, without a blazing pyre
And eke unhallowed by a hollow tomb
There lies this object by the lily's bloom
Half in the water, half upon the mire,

> That skirts the stagnant stream. Say who its sire?
> And why it lies neglected? Direful doom!
> Oh! cat, for thou wert as once of yore,
> And singing this I scarce suppress a tear,
> In Memphis' fane was reverenced with awe
> Yet of thy power rests there somewhat here,
> (Wrapt in thy sack-cloth shroud), not in thy claw,
> Though lost in sight, to smell alas; too dear.[218]

Better still, he displayed a keen interest in the classics, so beloved of his father. Looking back on his life, Basil recalled that it was at Magdalen that he developed his own lifelong love of the classics, vowing that 'he did not resent the hours of traditional instruction in Latin and Greek'. He insisted: 'I grudge not an hour of the grammar-grind which opened for me the unforgettable pages of Thucydides and Herodotus'. In this sense, at least, Basil was his father's son. And this love of the classics was not just a classroom occupation. It was a resource he always drew on; not only for allusion, which he loved, but also for companionship. In later years, on holiday with his old friend Henry Schollick, Basil always took a Loeb edition of his favourite school book. Sometimes a passage in the day's news would stir a recollection of Thucydides, as on the departure of the Fleet from Portsmouth to the Falklands. On this occasion, Henry Schollick recalled, he put down his newspaper and asked, 'Do you remember the sailing of the Sicilian expedition?'[219] This love of the classics had other advantages too. It helped to secure Basil a scholarship (postmastership) in Greats, at Merton College, Oxford. And in 1907 he progressed to the University to study, or so he claimed, 'the grand, old, fortifying, curriculum of rowing and playing rugger'. Basil put his skill at the oar to good use, and during the 1920s Basil returned to Magdalen as rowing coach, passing on the expertise he had learnt as a member of the College Eight at Merton. He had won a trial cap while a student at Oxford University, but rowing wasn't everything[220]. There was much more to Basil Blackwell than rowing.

When Basil had gone up to Merton, he had been left in no doubt of the privilege of his situation. Lest he should forget it, his father's quiet, hard-working presence was ever there to remind him of the responsibilities that went with educational advantage, an advantage his father had not been able to enjoy. The massive expansion of educational opportunity had been closed to Benjamin Henry, just as it was to his lieutenants at Blackwell's. But although Benjamin Henry was not himself a 'varsity man, he had done the

Play Days with Pegasus: Father and Son 127

17 Basil Blackwell's room at Merton College.

next best thing: his work as a bookseller and publisher was dedicated to supporting increased educational opportunity for others. Education was as important to him as his religion, and his children had been willing recipients of both. No record exists of what Benjamin Henry Blackwell thought as he ushered his son over the threshold of the University. Basil was the first in the family to go to university; his father's cup was full. That education was also good for trade would not have been uppermost in Benjamin Henry's mind. The happy coincidence did, however, enable him to balance idealism and commercial endeavour; a torch Basil was groomed to carry. Meanwhile, for four relatively carefree years, Basil was unencumbered. Despite his serious father, and the weight of responsibility he felt, he was also a young blade who liked to cut a dash about town. Julian Blackwell described his father as 'a tallish, very slight, good looker with endless charm who engendered a sense of mischievousness'[221]. If Basil had gone up to university a generation before, he would undoubtedly, like the young Pendennis, have sported one of his late grandmother's embroidered waistcoats.

Salad days

The tendency in both politics and industry is to submerge the individual. Capitalism and Socialism, in theory, may be as different as heads from tails: in effect the individual finds them as near as two faces of a coin

As a youth Basil could not quite resist a little flamboyance in dress and style. Perhaps he needed to find a harmless way to break from the confines of his father's sobriety? His legacy was a complicated weave of the different strands of his parents' lives. These influences both restrained and liberated Basil, all at the same time. First, and foremost, his parents were staunch individualists. Politically Liberal, and socially liberal, they despised those who used advantage to upstage others. They had both known hardship; they had earned their livelihoods, one way or another, in 'education' and looked to the company of their fellow tradesmen as much as they ever did to the higher echelons. Lilla Blackwell, especially, had no truck with the traditional divide between Town and Gown. This atmosphere in the Blackwell household, and the tales of his parents' experiences, gave Basil an edge; they heightened his awareness of those who did not have his privilege and predisposed him to be open-minded. His father was determined that his son should go to the University, but not as a 'Toff'. Basil was one of the breed of new public school, or grammar school, students who, rather than assuming a divine right of attendance at the University, saw it as an immense privilege. Basil always reminded his own children of this privilege. His son, Julian, argued that 'going to Merton was the making of his father'. In fact it gave Basil, and his family, a new burst of confidence. Now they were truly both Town and Gown! Basil had been formed as much by the one as by the other, and arriving at Merton he maintained the family tradition of taking an independent stance. He preferred, and sought, the company of those who, like him, had been brought up with an unswerving respect for individuals, irrespective of their stations. This 'lack of side', for which his mother was renowned, stayed with him as he moved from school to university, into the publishing world and thence back through the portals of the family firm in Broad Street.

Basil's first acquaintance with Merton made him acutely aware of the divide between the privileged academics and those who served them. Revisiting his old rooms at Merton College, which he had vacated in 1910, more than sixty years previously, Basil recalled an Oxford which had hardly ceased from 'whispering from her towers the last enchantments of the Middle Age'. Casting his eye around the much-modernised Merton of the 1970s, Basil had no regrets for the 'old days' save for the discontinuance of

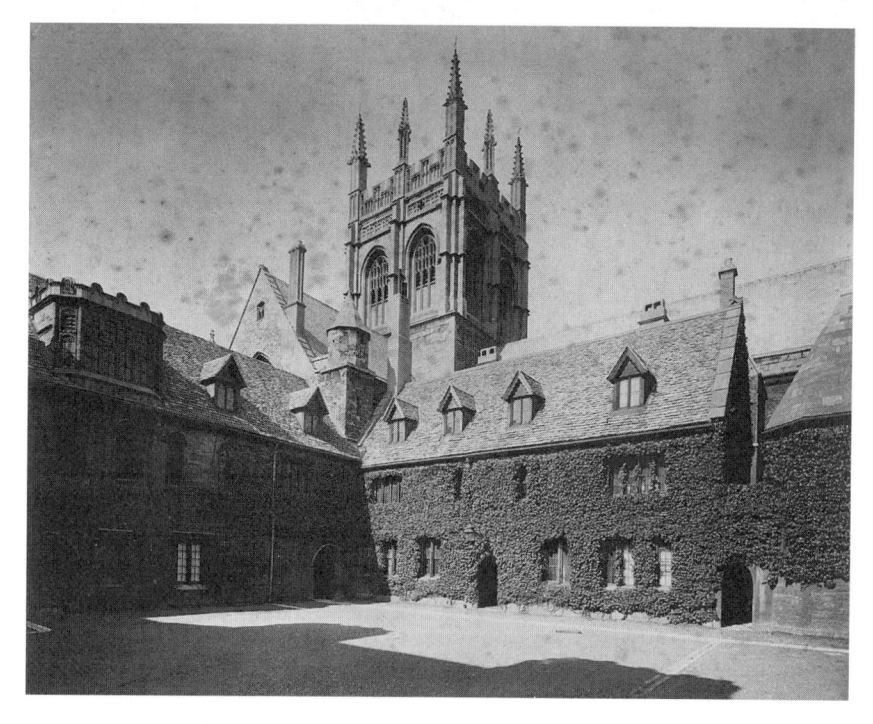

18 Old Merton buildings: 'An Oxford which had hardly ceased from whispering from her towers the last enchantments of the Middle Age'.

the tolling of the Founder's Bell, which had 'disturbed the repose of our great philosopher recluse Bradley'. But by the start of the second decade of the twentieth century, the repose of more than just Bradley was about to be shattered. Underlying what should have been a carefree student life, safe within the walls of Merton, was the disquiet Basil felt, even in 1908, about the agitations in Central Europe. Turning over the pages of the photograph album of his Merton days, he relived the feelings of insecurity and impending tragedy of this pre-First World War period. Basil reflected on the days: 'which were the golden sunset of our civilisation as Europe was poised to lead humanity into the new era of scientific savagery'. Armaments were mounting and Germany was preparing her envious challenge to British sea power. Basil was always acutely sensitive to man's inhumanity to man and he could not put the gathering storm in Europe out of his mind. No comfort was to be derived from his study of the classics, even from his favourite, Thucydides, who had tried to provide a rational basis for war. And his contemporaries gave an

19 Basil Blackwell and fellow students at the OUOTC Signal Section camp on Salisbury Plain in 1908: 'We felt that there was something extraordinary though indefinable in this quiet, shy little man, later known to history as Lawrence of Arabia'—he is seated, cross-legged, second from the right in front of Basil.

impression of indifference. As he remembered it: 'most of my contemporaries did not give any serious attention to the Kaiser's posturings'. Basil was not able to share their acquiescence. He wanted to take some action. Looking around he noticed that the Officers Training Corps was being organized in Oxford; 'I joined it', he declared, 'but cannot remember that any in the circle of my freshmen friends did so'. One of Basil's photographs, of the OUOTC Signal Section camp on Salisbury Plain in 1908, depicted him with a small crossed-legged figure sitting at his feet. But even then, recalled Basil, 'we felt that there was something extraordinary though indefinable in this quiet, shy little man, later known to history as Lawrence of Arabia!'[222]

Life at Merton, in the early twentieth century, even compared with Basil's introductory insight into the life of a trainee soldier, was not for the hedonistic. It was a rigorous daily diet of Chapel before breakfast, a light lunch (Commons) after physical exercise on the river, or on the field

20 A parade at the OUOTC camp on Salisbury Plain in 1908.

(Rugger), and Evensong at 10pm every day. Basil was awoken at seven each morning, to the music of his 'scout' clearing out the fire grate, where 'by some sleight of hand, he kept (a fire) burning all day long'. 'That fireplace was my alarum', Basil recalled. From the warmth of his bed, Basil would watch, rather guiltily, as the 'nimble and cheerful Charlie Scarrott' would rake out the cinders and enquire of the recumbent Basil 'if he were expecting guests to breakfast'? It was part of Basil's character to reflect on the life of a man: 'peace be on the good man, who combined in some measure the functions of valet, butler and chamber-maid, and worked seven days a week without the benefit of a summer holiday'. Basil recalled his further unease at the sight of his scout cycling home with 'a bag on the carrier of his bicycle in which, like his fellows, he carried home to his family the broken meats from the staircase'. When he made a tour of inspection in his eighties 'the hallmarks of the old servant/scout days were gone: the table was not aptly placed for social meals, and the fireplace was no longer in use'. These were features of Merton life whose loss Basil did not regret. Taking their place were new, more enticing traditions: the appearance of women students, for example.

Social life for undergraduates, resident in College, was an almost exclusively all-male affair. Apart from his sister, two years his senior, and her friends, and the socially acceptable acquaintances made through the local church, girls played very little part in Basil's outer life as an adolescent. In Basil Blackwell's student days almost everything had to be left to the imagination: 'to the inner fantasy life'. Little further opportunity was afforded to him as a student at Merton. 'Female undergraduates', he recalled, 'were remote mysterious creatures and chaperones were *de rigueur*'. One of his friends, on the same staircase, confessed to never having spoken to a girl during his time at Merton. But if his accounts are anything to judge by, he never missed a chance to catch even the remotest feminine stir. Basil remembered that 'a few girls, not accorded matriculation at the time, came to lectures in pairs and, in one case I recall, chaperoned by a nun. Only one of them in the Greats School took any care of her appearance; we rejoiced in her elegance and grace and discovered her name from a scrutiny of her bicycle. Verily Phoebe W. had her reward; she married her history tutor'[223]. For Basil, this was 'a proper ending for a clever girl'. Although his social judgement could be called into question, his appreciative sense was clearly not lacking. And his appetite for female Greats scholars must have been whetted, since his future wife was herself a classicist. But during his Merton days, Basil, like most students of his era, had to fall back on the companionship of other male undergraduates.

On first acquaintance, Basil found his fellow students rather disconcerting. But the fault, if there were one, was all his, he owned. He did not land on the doorstep of Merton brimming with confidence; he was unsure of his intellectual and social capabilities. He wrote of this disadvantage: 'I was some twelve months younger than most of my year; a handicap I found difficult to surmount mentally and physically'. But Basil was not easily beaten. As his first term progressed, strong and close friendships began to develop, which increased his self-confidence; perhaps too much? By his final year he reported a distinct improvement brought about by his 'mind and body beginning to set'. He ventured that such was his mental improvement, that another year may have enabled him to grapple with the philosophical side of Greats, though he modestly conceded that this would probably not have elevated his Second. In the event, Basil admitted to 'a Third in Mods (*valde deflendum*) and a Second in Greats (fair enough)'[224]. Basil nonetheless labelled his final performance as 'creditable'. Yet Basil was reputed to have an original mind, and his tutors had expected something more than just a creditable performance. If Basil's academic progress was modest, his physical prowess was not, despite his slender frame. Although he was a back-row boy in the University's Drama Society (OUDS), he could never sing, he did not have a musical ear and he did not have 'the eyes which are so essential to enjoy natural history rambles', as his father had done. So playing to his strengths, he attempted to make a name for himself in the College Eight. Basil had limbered up as a schoolboy oarsman, and he had been spurred on by the example of his father, not himself an inconsiderable practitioner at the local Oxford City Club. It was not all plain sailing, and he remembered being bumped by those who later found fame in many other walks of life, Sir Adrian Boult in the Christ Church crew, for example. To his lasting joy, Basil was lauded as the 'engine of the boat' at Merton.

Play Days with Pegasus: Father and Son

21 A day on the river.

Basil may not have done himself full justice in the Examination Halls, but his performance as a student oarsman was something to write home about: 'My strength had come fully to me when I rowed for the Eight at Six after nine days training with a delightful, rolling, splashing crew of freshmen. My sixth and last year was crowned with a bump supper'. *Nunc, nunc, insurgite remis* he had liberally interpreted as his rallying call: 'get more life off your stretchers'. And off his stretcher meant rowing. Both his sons grew to be good oarsmen, and his son Richard had asked that something of his father's passion for the sport be written up[225]. Basil had written that 'a brilliant reporter could convey the sense of excitement in watching a race, but I doubt if he could reveal the passions and prayers of the contestants unless he were writing from actual experience, and could say "Ah! The needle!"' Four lines of Virgil's *Georgics* summed up his feelings of this 'austere sport':

'*Considunt transtris, intentaque bracchia remis;*
Intenti exspectant signum, exsultantiaque haurit
Corda pavor pulsans laudumque arrecta cupido.'

22 Basil (on the right) as an undergraduate, on the Merton barge.

In this passage you can 'recognize that draining nervous condition, at once fearful and combative, which assails even the most experienced oarsman before a race'. And the next line marked the spot: '*Hos successus alit; possunt, quia posse videntur*', 'when unity of action engenders a unity of spirit which lifts a crew out of its class'[226].

Not surprising, given this passion, that Basil's studies often took second place to rowing. Basil, however, could even justify this diversion, as it linked him to the great masters, such as Virgil. As Virgil had escorted Dante away from Hell, so he would guide Basil back to his books. 'Far and away the most interesting boat race on record', he wrote, 'is that reported in Book v of the Aeneid'. Rowing, for him, 'brought you back to where you started', having achieved a goal and circumnavigated the rocks below the water line. And rowing was something that had helped him to overcome problems, as it had helped his father.

Play Days with Pegasus: Father and Son

Going up to University a year early may, initially, have put Basil at a disadvantage, but if he had waited another year he may not have met Austin Longland. Basil numbered Austin among his closest friends; a friendship that endured through their lives. Austin Longland, the son and grandson of country parsons, had, like Basil, been brought up with a degree of austerity and the clear undertaking that his first duty was to God and to his neighbour. This belief had become the mainspring of his thought and conduct, and Basil found comfort in the company of one who, like him, had had an upbringing 'early imbued with the untroubled faith and the moral discipline which was in the best tradition of devout Victorian churchmanship'. Feeling dwarfed and out of place in his freshman days at Merton, Basil had found a soul mate: 'we studied together; we rowed in the eights together; together we walked the Downs and afloat explored the upper reaches of the Thames, opening our minds to each other without reserve'. Behind his genial bearing, Austin had a spirit that Basil found at once gentle as well as firm; the latter quality being called upon on occasions when Basil's more free spirit needed to be subdued. Basil recalls that for Austin 'duty was not to be questioned, but to be done'.

23 The Merton eight with Austin Longland at the rear.

Yet, for all his high-minded idealism, Austin was as reluctant as Basil to finally put away childish things. And who better to be on the receiving end of their high spirits than their patient, if idiosyncratic tutors?

One such tutor, Basil recalled, was Walter 'Billy' Howe, who taught ancient history. As he taught, Billy Howe would allow his right arm to rise and fall to the rhythm of his words. As if this were not enough of a bate to his student audience, he emphasized his addiction by the use of alliteration: 'Thus Pericles found it impossible to pursue a policy of peaceful penetration' for 'The day for which he had been sharpening his sword found him dallying with it in his sheath'. Fascinated by their tutor's performance, Basil and Austin devised an appropriate response. They mischievously conspired to prepare their next weekly essays, for reading to him, 'in a rivalry of studious magniloquence'. Come the tutorial, Basil, first into the fray, won the comment 'Ye-e-es! Rather a tinkling symbol'. Longland, with a glint of anticipated triumph, followed with an utterance that Basil admitted 'paled my ineffectual fire'. Basil remembered that his friend 'closed with a resounding period and modestly dropped his eyes'. Sitting down, the only response he met with was a deep sigh. After a suitable pause for thought, Billy Howe declared 'Well, that's bad!' On that occasion, Billy Howe was accompanied by a fellow tutor, the gentle philosopher H H Joachim, late Wykeham Professor of Logic. Joachim was equally loath to castigate the duo. He could only offer 'Thank you; very interesting; will you have a cigarette?'

The now much-embarrassed Basil felt moved to cover his tracks by offering up an 'original theory of knowledge' in recompense. Joachim and Billy Howe did him the courtesy of listening. Joachim then fell back in his chair exclaiming 'God bless my soul!' It was suggested to Basil by Edward Burney, wittiest of his contemporaries, 'that this was the first time he (Joachim) had acknowledged the existence of either (God or soul) and, Basil added, 'I was credited with his conversion!'[227] Whatever his tutors' views of this insouciant youth, Basil wrote that for his part: 'he had only pleasant and grateful memories of the men who taught me'. Of others who taught him, he chiefly remembered 'the kindly H W Garrod, who presently turned from classics to the field of English Literature after, as I suspect, a collision with A E Housman over the editing of Manilius, and W H Fyfe, Principal of the Postmaster. 'In those days', Basil wrote, relationships with tutors involved more than just teaching; 'talking, walking and playing' was how he described their intercourse in those 'last golden days'. Still a regular visitor to his old College in his eighties, Basil wrote: 'I seldom enter my beloved College without a pang, for the names of so many of my contemporaries are engraved on the memorial to those killed in the Great War.'

Play Days with Pegasus: Father and Son 137

24 Sir Basil with the Blackwell coat of arms in Merton.

Emerging butterfly-like from the chrysalis of his undergraduate days, Basil was seen as a young blade about town[228]. But this public persona disguised his inner, more serious, side. And if his semblance deceived the truth that he had arrived so near to manhood, in the Miltonic sense, his father was there to remind him of the virtues of inner-ripeness. Education was one of the means to achieving inner ripeness, but, Basil's father reminded him, it had to be put to good account. Basil's student days were at an end, and his working life was to begin forthwith. Destiny required him to say his 'grace before ploughing'[229], and prepare to set the tally straight. His educational advantages must now be repaid by hard work. Basil's future was mapped out: he must earn his living in the family business. In all of this Basil faced a very different set of imperatives from those of his wealthier and more aristocratic student peers. But although he may have been exposed to all the temptations of Waugh's Sebastian, his was not to be Basil's way. In this he was also his father's son. His father's success came from dedicated hard work, side by side with those who had learnt and practised their crafts and trades on the job. For all his fine education, Basil was brought up to esteem the individual craftsman who relies on the work of his hands in order to 'maintain the fabric of the world'.[230] The relationship between master and worker had fascinated Basil as he watched his own father. In his father he saw the embodiment of Aristotle's dictum that a virtuous man must first have a virtuous teacher to show him the way.

One such virtuous teacher, and mentor, was Basil's father's apprentice, 'Father' Fred Hanks. Over the years 'Father' Hanks rose through the ranks, from an indentured apprentice to become a director of Blackwell's. When Basil took the helm at Blackwell's, after his father's death, Fred Hanks was his guardian, even more so than when he had watched over the infant Basil parked in his pram at the back of the shop. Basil's admiration for Hanks owed much to the philosophy of William Morris, who had had an almost reverential attitude towards the craftsman. Later, when Basil took over his father's publishing interests, his admiration for Morris reinforced his determination to produce fine books. Basil remained acutely aware of the debt he owed to those craftsmen, whose capacity for taking trouble had made the family firm's reputation and success. They also influenced the way he subsequently developed the family firm, expanding the scope and the quality of both the publishing and bookselling side with some of the finest craftsmen, such as the distinguished printer/scholar Bernard Newdigate, and A H Bullen, of the original Shakespeare Head Press. Other craftsmen, too, attracted Basil's attention, and he was passionate in his support of his father's efforts to help struggling wordsmiths. Such seminal concerns may have weighed down the more feint-hearted. But not Basil; he had a lightness of touch. His outward life was far from all work and no play. The contacts he had made as a student opened new doors, ones far from the orthodoxy of life in his parents' house. As a young working man, he cultivated an ever increasingly varied and wide circle of friends, making social, economic and political contacts from many walks of life, which lasted a lifetime. Perhaps he was one of those who early demonstrated that networking was a social form to out-rival the old school tie? Yet he remained aloof from any particular sect, upholding the habit of independence that he had inherited from his teetotal father and his lively countryish mother. This did not, however, preclude a little dalliance. Garsington, in its heyday before the First World War, provided just such an outlet.

Basil's strict upbringing did not prevent him from being attracted by the allure of the Garsington Set, but he claimed never to have succumbed. His interest in their antics, he insisted, was solely cerebral. Interviewed shortly before he died, he reminded the journalist from the book world of 'this fact'. When asked about his connections with Garsington, it is easy to imagine Sir

Play Days with Pegasus: Father and Son

25 J M Dent in 1906. The Dent Memorial Lectures were founded in his memory. Sir Basil's was the first lecture of the series.

Basil's mischievous grin as he nipped in the bud the perpetration of any myths. Yes, Basil remembered Lady Ottoline Morell's soirées, and especially Lady Ottie herself. 'A very kind soul, Lady Ottie', he recalled, 'she loved taking care of young men . . . helping them in their early years: she came to the conclusion I was a young man to be helped'. Eventually, cautioned Basil, 'I had gently to indicate to her that I was getting married and in a fairly substantial position!'[231] He would however have been the first to acknowledge the importance of mingling with the intellectuals, scholars and writers who had graced Lady Ottoline Morell's salons. The ideas of such Garsington habitués as Bertie Russell, the Huxleys, and the Keynes brothers, to name but a few, shaped the 20s and 30s. And Basil claimed that they helped to form his psyche. Their ideas stemmed from and spread through the intellectual circles of the universities, lending support to the movement for economic and social reform, which came into its own after the Second World War, and especially after the depression of the 30s. Garsington had boasted its own political hangers-on: a serious lot. Figures such as Butler and Beverage, who, like Basil, were more sober products of the elite education system, and were on hand to harness idealism.

Sieving through all these influences, Basil constructed his own brand of political ideology: capitalist and socialist all at the same time[232]. In his Dent Memorial Lecture, he tried to explain his emerging personal philosophy:

'the tendency in both politics and industry is to submerge the individual. Capitalism and Socialism, in theory, may be as different as heads from tails: in effect the individual finds them as near as two faces of a coin'[233]. Later on, as Chairman and Chief Executive of the family business, Basil 'extracted from these two systems the means to run a business where the individual benefited from both systems'. Although he had great sympathy for the Socialist Utopianism of William Morris, his own mixture of the two dominant ideologies never fitted that of any specific political party or political sect. If a tag could be attached to his beliefs, the term 'old-fashioned liberal' would have been the most apposite. His belief in this 'mixed' approach stayed with him, and, to his mind, became even more important; those who had come through the Second World War, he had written, would never accept the treatment meted out to the workers at the end of the Great War. Liberalism, as a philosophy, after the school of Hobhouse rather than Mills, as seen by Basil Blackwell, gave people choice. This principle of choice had to be upheld, especially as the Liberal Party was already coming under threat from Labour. Basil was not convinced that socialism could combine the economic imperatives of private enterprise with concern for the individual. As a student he eschewed party political activism; he never developed a taste for the political fray, and had no use for Britain's adversarial system. He preferred direct democracy: upholding the freedom to speak his mind without reserve and rancour. Democracy was never a dead letter; for Basil, it was something to be aspired to, in the workplace and in all everyday dealings. Politics was not the only area of public life he found wanting; his greater wrath was reserved for the bureaucrats. He fumed at the idea of an individual's affairs being left in the hands of undemocratic officials, for whom business perforce must be digested in advance and prepared for quick dispatch; where there was no time to spare for debate. Bureaucracy, in Basil's opinion, was only less evil than dictatorship.

    Basil started his working life as an idealist, and, later, he lamented the size of modern bureaucracy, as he did modern enterprise, and modern finance: 'whither the human scale of the craftsman, of the individual, had gone'. But at the time, the bravado of the freer, modern orthodoxy, which was infecting Edwardian England on so many fronts: the fight for greater equality, for universal suffrage, for women's social and political rights, for education, for better living and working conditions, the introduction of a redistributive taxation system and greater literary, artistic and creative freedom, were to be applauded from a safe distance. And Basil kept his head below the parapet. As soon as he had finished at Merton, he was dispatched to learn the publishing trade at the London office of Oxford University Press, at Amen House. Of all his early manhood experiences, the time Basil spent there, as a trainee publisher, was perhaps the most formative. He may have lacked the leisure time to be drawn into the political and social issues of the day, but he dug into a rich seam that provided the resources from which he drew ideas for his subsequent adventures.

'An insight into publishing'

Tired the sun with talking and sent him down the sky[234]

Towards the end of Basil Blackwell's time at Oxford University, Sir Henry Frowde (an old friend of his father's) suggested that he spend at year at the Oxford University Press (OUP), in London, to gain some insight into publishing. On a September morning in 1911, Basil made his way to Amen Corner, 'there to spend one of the most delightful years of my life'. Basil relished the freedom to dawdle in the London Library and the British Museum Reading Room. Here he had 'all English literature to choose from, and drank insatiably of that pure fount so refreshing after the close and anxious studies of the Oxford School of *Literae Humaniores*'[235]. Basil Blackwell recalled his generous initiation to the Book Trade at the hands of Frowde. He was exhilarated by Frowde's invitation to complete the selection of *A Book of English Essays* for inclusion in the World's Classics, and to see it through the press. 'The task of selection had been three parts done by Stanley Makower, before his death, and mine was to complete it; and I was to share the honour of the title page'. In Sir Basil's view, The World's Classics were without doubt the 'pathfinders for the Everyman Library launched by that shrewd idealist J M Dent ... serving the same market, that great boon to poor students, the Home University Library'[236]. Grant Richards had launched The World's Classics at 1s, and one year later the series had passed to Henry Frowde, publisher to Oxford University Press, and unequalled seller of Bibles.

'Basil's chair', at a high desk in a small narrow office, had recently been occupied by E V Rieu, departed to India to explore the prospects of a publishing outlet, and its next two occupants were Geoffrey Faber and 'Gerry' Hopkins in succession. Adjoining Basil's narrow office was Veve Collins, nicknamed 'Vera Historic', who he assisted in choosing samples to peddle around schools and universities. Collins edited texts to cater for these important markets, and was particularly interested in providing books for sixth formers and undergraduates—a growing market that he understood ahead of his time. Basil described him as 'dedicated, kindly, humourless and pedantic. . . . Rigorously punctual, Collins would return from lunch, cherishing against six o'clock the unburnt half of a cigarette'. If he were lucky, and he had to be very lucky, he would not be noticed by the resident of the inner sanctum, the legendary Henry Frowde himself. Frowde was a numinous figure with a spade beard, always dressed in a grey frock coat, except on occasions when a blue serge suit appeared, signalling a luncheon appointment. On such momentous occasions, the cloakroom was out of bounds for a good two and a half hours. Basil remembers Frowde being guarded by a church-warden-like secretary, one Curtis, who was responsible for the bible side of OUP, who should always be approached, rather than Henry Frowde, in matters pecuniary. The subject of wages, always a delicate one, could be broached if Curtis was appealed to in the right way. Curtis, allegedly, interceded by communicating that you were plagued with religious doubts and needed the aid of the great man inside. That good man, Basil was advised, would then be at pains to set you right, in return for which the supplicant had to make his thanks for the intervention with the assurance that all difficulties had been removed. The removal of these 'little difficulties' was said to be worth 5 shillings a week![237] When occasionally Frowde crossed the threshold of his office, he passed 'silently to and fro the office recognizing nobody; but when my father came to visit him I was invited to join in the conversation, and on these occasions he would ask my opinion of Humphrey Milford—did I not think that he was a man of singular ability? I always agreed!'[238]

Amen Corner had also afforded Basil with the chance to appreciate something of the typographer's art. On the floor above Henry Frowde's office sat the kindly Frederick Hall, trained as a printer and later to succeed Horace Hart as Printer to Oxford University. Sir Basil claimed to have been taught the rudiments of the trade from this Master. He remembered his introduction to the mysteries of book production, such as casting-off. No matter what the department, Basil's lasting impression of Amen Corner was one of reverence for scholarship and enthusiasm for any books which might advance its cause. During this time he had little contact with the Oxford base of OUP, knowing the great 'Chapman' as only 'R W C' who occasionally employed a green pencil in sign of disapproval: 'then we believed and trembled'. Over the years Basil earnt Chapman's esteem, but he modestly wrote 'I have always thought that both he and Milford esteemed my ability beyond my deserts'[239]. To his eternal delight, Basil was invited to stay on a few further months 'to instruct a young Oxford graduate: that was Geoffrey Faber', he recalled with a chuckle[240].

In the Second World War, when OUP moved to Oxford, Basil recaptured the ethos of his old London days in occasional meetings with his former colleagues, the poets Gerry Hopkins and Charlie Williams. When re-united, wrote Sir Basil, and had conditions allowed, they would have 'tired the sun with talking and sent him down the sky'. Benjamin Henry, however, was not a man to relish his son at leisure. He wanted Basil to come into the family firm, and help to continue and expand his own publishing efforts. After his spell at Amen Corner, Basil needed no enticement to take on a role on the publishing side. Finally on New Year's Day 1913, following his spell of sixteen months at Oxford University Press, Basil Blackwell joined his father in Broad Street. From this time, until the Thursday before his death in April 1984, Basil's feet hardly touched the ground. But Basil Blackwell never cut the ties with his alma mater and on his eightieth birthday, The Gaffer—as he had become known—was given Henry Frowde's coffee pot and an OUP tie. When he had left Amen House, the publishing world was as important to Basil as the bookselling world would become. Even when he took over as Blackwell's gaffer, at his father's death in 1924, he was still deeply involved with publishing, and, in just over ten years, he had finished a stint as the President of its Association.

Handing over the Presidency, in 1936, he reflected on the twin trades of publishing and bookselling. 'If I were bidden to sum up human life in a phrase', he explained, 'I should say that life is experience understood too late; and now that the tale of my days as your President is told, I feel come upon me somewhat of that belated wisdom which is the tantalising heritage of man'. Looking back on publishing as the established, and successful, bookseller he had become, he admitted 'I find that the publishers have shown a truer understanding of our (booksellers) difficulties than we have had of theirs; I find that misunderstandings for which there was no need, have from time to time hindered the work which publishers and bookseller together have undertaken. He suggested, predictably, that the 'one thing at least we might do to mend matters' would be to increase the participation of the individual. Rejecting the idea of an *advocatus diaboli*, he argued for grass roots democracy: 'we must offer to pay for the fare to London of one member of each branch of the Booksellers' Association, should he need it. By the same token, let us insist that one member from each branch shall in fact attend each meeting of the Council. For democracy today, in great matters as in small, is the precious but imperilled legacy of the nobler past—precious because it allows that every man is master of his soul and that his soul by itself has worth; imperilled because we have forgotten that the best gifts in life need ever watching'.

Basil started his 'publishing watching' as a small boy, when he would see his father's 'authors' creep, or sometimes, sweep, up the stairs. He became a watcher-in-earnest at OUP, and a custodian when he, later, became the President of the Publishers' Association. From this 'helm', he found it harder to steer a straight course.

> 'For a ship's captain whose time was spent in watching and stopping leaks,' he explained, 'might well come to think that his vessel was unseaworthy and in present danger of sinking. But now that my voyage is over, and my harbour is in sight, I find, almost with wonder, that the ship still treads the waves. I mind me that in the course of my Presidency more publishers than booksellers have foundered, and that for all the worries and struggles which have beset booksellers in these hungry years, our fellowship has not dwindled but grown. We stand a small and slighted unit in a world distraught by folly and false gods—a world in deadly danger of overwhelming ills. Nevertheless, we stand as ministers of Literature, that slow invaluable cause where truth is enshrined in beauty and for ever by the miracle of written speech. So by the waters of Babylon some homesick Jew, brooding on the fate of his little nation, now ground between the huge millstones of Assyria and Egypt, now swept entire into exile as the whim of the great conqueror, set pen to parchment to leave for us a song of everlasting beauty, which stirs our hearts to-day, when the might of Egypt is remembered in its tombs, and Babylon lies in a mystery beneath the desert dust'[241].

Dusty the old rooms at Amen House may have been, but they had revealed the mysteries of publishing.

Joining his father in Broad Street in 1913, Basil ran the publishing side as a separate branch of the parent company. Within seven years of joining his father, he was stretching his wings, and the imprint on the books became 'Basil Blackwell', rather than 'Blackwell'. Seeking for further adventure he joined forces with his old Merton College friend, Adrian Mott. Adrian Mott had replaced Dorothy L Sayers as editorial assistant, 'who had been more memorable for her literary fame, than her editorial gifts'. Basil had employed Dorothy Sayers, in 1916, when he met with a 'tall, very slim young woman, dressed in a formal blue serge costume with informal yellow stockings'. Basil Blackwell dispensed with her editorial talents some three years later, with a mixture of relief and reluctance and described her employment as 'like harnessing a race-horse to a plough'[242]. Adrian Mott was another kettle of fish, he was steadfast; the brother Basil had never had, and always wanted, and 'the keeper of his business and aesthetic conscience'. Adrian Mott, for his part, claimed that he never understood business, especially the 'mysteries of finance'. 'My role', he wrote, 'in the day-to-day running of the firm was a minor one: my work has been almost entirely editorial, or sub-editorial'. Their first mission, in partnership, was to rescue the Shakespeare Head Press, formed as an offshoot Blackwell company in 1921. But this was no commercial undertaking. A year later the two friends entered into formal partnership as Basil Blackwell and Mott Ltd, incorporated on 13 March 1922.

Under the B & M imprint, Basil added scope and depth to his father's range, and profit into the kitty. To works of poetry, and a smattering of successful new classics, he had added such treasures as *Joy Street*, a series of children's annuals, which ran for 13 years and introduced contributors such as Belloc, Chesterton, de la Mare, Farjeon, Mackenzie and A A Milne[243]. It was at Blackwell's that Enid Blyton was first published, but there were disappointments too. Blackwell's only received the crumbs from Blyton's table when she hit the big time, and Richard Blackwell was later to turn down *Asterix*! Yet some of Basil's proudest achievements were to be found among children's educational books, of which Marten and Carter's *Histories* were perhaps the most famous. At first, Adrian Mott recalled, 'B H Blackwell Ltd, retail, still in Benjamin Henry's time was a little inclined to look on the publishing side as a naughty baby brother and an infernal nuisance about the house—but that time soon passed'. Basil attributed B & M's coming of age, and its passing into the serious ranks of publishing, to its staff. At the beginning, in 1922, the staff in addition to himself and Adrian Mott, consisted of S T Fenemore, three girls, and an odd-job boy. The 'girls' were the famous Gladys Lovelace, the 'Auntie Glad whose comfortable presence smoothed away many difficulties', Mabs, who everyone had 'a soft spot for', and Vera Higley. 'Poor Vera Higley', Adrian Mott reminisced, kept up a hopeless struggle to reconcile the opposing interests and bitter theological differences between 'The Modern Churchman' and 'Blackfriars'. But she was the firm's 'unofficial and unpaid welfare officer; disentangling love lives and doctoring collywobbles'[244].

The lynch-pin of any organization, at the time, was the odd-job boy; he had to do anything and everything, and uncomplainingly, and moving from pillar to post, willingly, he became the eyes and ears of the place. The first 'odd-job boy', Frank Fogden, was not one such; he was never to be found when he was wanted, but preferred to find a hidey-hole where he could play his ukulele. Frank was soon released from his other duties. He was replaced by 'James', as Basil called him, and from 'odd-job boy' he rose to become a Director, and Secretary to the Company. James Sherbourn, from nearby Witney, was a classic Blackwellian: he was self-educated and a self-starter.

26 The cover of *Joy Street*.

Born into a family of nine children, he watched his father struggle to keep them all on his railwayman's wages. But James was very keen on books, and libraries, and 'he had extraordinarily neat handwriting'; 'this came in very useful, later on, when he annotated, and drew maps, diagrams and marginal drawings' for Carter and Bretnall's (B & M's Geography series). *Man the World Over*. His first job was to fetch Chelsea buns from Week's shop, in the Cornmarket, for the Directors' tea, and they 'noticed' him. Meanwhile, down in the stock room, he prided himself on his physical fitness: 'Six foot of whipcord and spring steel'! He was the world's optimist and only once was he known to be depressed: 'for a week he went about with tears in his eyes when a football team he supported lost a cup match in an early round[245].

Licking the assembled company into shape was S T Fenemore, or 'Fen' as he was known. He organized everyone, including the directors, and kept the warehouse like a new pin. Adrian Mott, writing in 1954, recalled him instantly: 'he was brisk and dapper, with a precise turn of mind and a short turn of phrase: "Keep moving, don't let yet braces dangle", he would command'[246]. Fen was a workaholic and set the old bindery on its feet, but at heart he was a poet, and followed the fortunes of others; when Edith Sitwell's *The Mother* was selling so slowly it might have had to be pulped, he bought six copies, giving them as presents to his family and colleagues[247]. There were other characters associated with B & M, who loomed large in the collective memory, such as Bertie Ashcroft, the printer. Adrian Mott recalled him clearly: 'Besides being one of the finest printers in Oxford, he was a bit of a villain. Personally I like villains—I should have very few friends in this City if I did not. If ever the black market returns, Bertie would be the man to know. I believe there is still a bit of a racket in nylons (this was still the time of rationing) and not wishing to risk an action for slander, I can only say that I have no proof he had anything to do with it'[248]. In the company of these rich characters, whose stories he loved, Basil attempted to pass on some of the insights into publishing he had gained at Amen Corner.

Prompted to adventure

The constant discovery of the unknown, the encouragement of talent, or even the finding of genius; the excitement of the calculated risk and the vindication of judgement[249]

Basil's exit from full-time publishing in London had done nothing to diminish his ardour, and he too took up with his father's poets; he was now to play Pegasus, in Oxford, as his father had done. At the end of his life, Sir Basil

Blackwell always acknowledged that 'my aspiration to establish an independent publishing business sprang from my admiration of my father's achievements'. 'It was', he asserted, 'his example which prompted me to adventure'[250]. Benjamin Henry had sailed against the wind in giving his support to work that would not otherwise have been published. Although the Poet Laureate, Robert Bridges, had impressed on the young Basil the importance of his father's contribution, he cautioned Basil against departing from the quiet paths of bookselling for the more perilous seas of publishing. Basil Blackwell was in awe of Bridges. 'One had to walk delicately with him', Basil recorded, especially after he had visited him in his garden at Boars Hill to be greeted with the nipping end of a pair of secateurs, rather than an outstretched hand. On another occasion, Basil found himself embarrassed: 'My undertaking on the part of an unknown author to invite the Laureate to accept a copy of his book left me with difficult letters to write'. Bridges would have none of it. But neither Harry nor Basil Blackwell were to be intimidated by either the likes of Bridges or the might of the, more conservative, grand publishing houses. In any case, neither Bridges, nor the grandees of publishing, would have given a second glance at the amateurish manuscripts Basil and his father garnered. In this case, as he so often did, Basil left financial considerations at his door, and Bridges' warnings unheeded. And his independence of mind and enthusiasm served to overcome the rigidities of the publishing scene. Like his father, he was responsible for sending on their way famous names in scholarship and literature. To his father's lists he added the names of authors ranging from J R R Tolkien, Graham Greene, Wilfred Owen, Harold Acton, and Gilbert Murray, to Laurence Binyon and John Buchan; and this is the short version of the list.

As soon as he joined the firm in 1913, Basil oversaw, for his father, the publication of the first volume of *Oxford Poetry*, edited by the great Fabian economist, G D H Cole, whose ideas on guild socialism, and his 1913 major work, *The World of Labour*, were as attractive to Basil Blackwell as those of William Morris. Sherard Vines was also an editor, and the series contained early work by Philip Guedalla, Ronald Knox, Michael Sadleir and A P Herbert. Such was its reputation that, later on, it survived even the privations of the Second World War. Cultivated by his father, Basil had been planning such a venture from the end of his student days, in 1910. And, in the letter and the spirit of his father, there was much more to his efforts than just a new adventure in publishing. His support for poetry was symbolic. He wanted the voices of pre-war Europe to be given full vent, 'before our civilization was convulsed by World War and the era of new barbarism began'. He judged his first volume to contain poetry which was 'formally correct, graceful, melodious, with occasional examples of brilliant parody and occasional lapses into sentimentality'. It marked, for Basil, regrettably, 'the end of an era in poetry'. Thereafter, 'Poets were quick to see that the old order was giving place to the new, and that rhymeless utterance, in broken rhythm, sound best to express the shaken spirit of the age'. 'So began', Basil wrote, 'the new poetic cult to which we are heirs today; austerity and pregnant phrasing reign; content prevails over form, melody is banished'. Looking back, over nearly six decades, he asked 'How many poets now submit themselves to the disciplines of the sonnet?' But he was ever contrite and conciliatory: even if modern poetry did not satisfy Shelley's prescription, he was loath to condemn the entire genre[251]. He masked his dislike of the modern genre behind a cloak of ignorance; 'I am ashamed to have dropped out of the current of modern poetry', he later wrote, but 'The fault, dear William, is not in your verse, but in myself that I can't understand. . . . I am suckled in a poetic creed outworn, and cannot catch up now'[252].

As poetry went through its sea change, Basil's sense of disconnection, and his incomprehension, intensified. If he had been of a different disposition, he 'would have used Housman's razor', he had written to an old friend by way of an apology at declining an invitation to write a foreword for a new poetry volume. 'Fortunately, I use an electric razor', he added, 'otherwise, I should, in the act of (such) shaving, end up like the old man in *The Pardoner's Tale*:

> 'And on the ground, which is my moodres gate
> I knokke with my staf, bothe early and late,
> And seys "Leeve mooder, leet me in!"'

His friend, L F Herbert, had already written to admonish him: 'It is his belief', he replied, 'that most of the new book of poems was "deeper and its parameters more complex". . . . Herein it is my belief—expressed with all due humility—that you may have fallen into error, . . . a simple experience is susceptible of simple transmission, but a compound one calls for intellectual process to sort out and convey its component and transferable parts'. He took Basil to task over his condemnation of clever poems: ones where the form has sired the idea. By implication, those of Pound and Eliot must have come into Basil's mind, since Herbert's rebuttal mentions them by name, and, he adds, 'I do not think that any of these poems have been so conceived'[253]. He told Basil that he had not 'previously heard about Housman's razor, but if he meant slashing to attain perfection, he is merely repeating Horace's reference to the use of the file. I do assure you that I have used that instrument to the best of my ability, but I don't pretend to the goldsmith's perfection of a Horace or Housman. Also I have the uneasy feeling about both that, in the sense . . . they might well fall into your category of . . . Heresy!'

But all this lay in the future. Back in 1913, Basil's first volume of poems, under his father's imprint, met with success, and, much to his surprise, it was reprinted. Indulging a passion for poetry and encouraging literary experimentation, was a tendency that had made his father quietly famous, especially his support for those on the starting blocks[254]. Dictating some memories of his early days in publishing, Sir Basil reflected on the inheritance bestowed on him by his father, which empowered him to act 'as midwife for the literary efforts of Oxford undergraduates'[255]. Basil continued to 'notice' their achievements and readily included women writers in his ranks. A St Hugh's graduate, Phyllis Hartnoll, who worked for Blackwell's before she went to OUP, was ever grateful to Basil Blackwell for the recognition she received with her Newdigate poem of 1929[256]. Later he included women authors in equal measure with men. When attempting to launch the publishing house, Basil Blackwell and Mott, into the popular market, he introduced Blackwell's 3/6 novels. Here women excelled. The novels were of a very different genre that met with more varied success; their authors, too, were much less predictable in their ways as well as their writing. One of their number, a female author, a Miss M (Margiad) Evans, surprised the relatively youthful Basil when, greeting him with apologies for being late, she attributed this to a visit to Elliston's to buy underwear, and she informed him that it had been charged to his account[257]! Charging to his account was indeed a feature of Basil Blackwell's publishing; his father too had paid up front for many a poet. Yet, his publishing adventures went from strength to strength. With his father still at the helm, Basil added other series, and other famous names; ones reminiscent of the Great War, that had been debarred from publication, saw the light of day. Wilfred Owen's poems were first published in *Wheels* (1919), only five others having reached publication before his death: a childhood competition winner in an evangelical magazine, *Song of Songs*; in *The Hydra*: *Miners*, *Futility*; and *Hospital Barge at Cerisy* in *The Nation*[258]. Basil discovered and published other writers' first works, in both *Wheels* and in *Oxford Outlook*, both anthologies having been launched between 1916 and 1919. The series were, usually, edited by a team, although not always with team spirit.

Among his teams of moving spirits were such, subsequent, notables as Graham Greene, Cecil Day Lewis, John Sparrow, John Betjeman, Harold Acton, Gilbert Highet, L P Hartley, Beverley Nichols, the Huxley brothers, Roy Harrod, and the redoubtable Richard Crossman. They included the

Play Days with Pegasus: Father and Son

earliest published work of Stephen Spender, Dorothy L Sayers, Louis Golding, Edmund Blunden, A L Rowse, Guedalla, James Laver and L A G Strong[259]. They found themselves in the good company of poets such as Sassoon, Meyerstein, Powys Mathers, the Sitwells, and Christopher Morley, with his *Eighth Sin*. Harold Acton was greatly to the fore as a poet, in those days, 'he was an exotic bird of plumage' and the envy of undergraduates when they looked in at Mr Blackwell's shop-window to see the multi-coloured binding of his first book of poems, *Aquarium*[260]. Acton edited for *Oxford Poetry*, and *Oxford Outlet*, or *The New Oxford*. One of his contemporaries, Peter Quennell, another Blackwellian editor, and a would-be poet, reflected that Acton brought a cosmopolitan flavour to the proceedings: 'An English household and the English educational system still limited our view of life . . . when the Oxford term ended, we went back to our prosaic English homes. Harold returned to La Pietra, with its cypress avenues, romantic garden statues, and his collection of original Benvenuto Cellini coins, designed for a "fastidious pope" who was probably as adept as Acton in knowing "just how far to go too far"'. With valiant intrepidity, Acton, and Quennell cast their net wide: 'our contributors included poets we had read and admired, and some we did not know at all, and of whom we never heard again. Our collection, whatever its merits may have been, was decidedly unorthodox, as the book critic of *The Cherwell* pointed out: "The editors of this year's *Oxford Poetry* . . . have fulfilled their difficult task with a somewhat surprising result; they have not taken the icing off the cake; they have given us a cross section of it. . . . Their selection has been admirably catholic"'. On its pages were the very funny and vulgar poems of the flamboyant Brian Howard, Acton's rival aesthete and friend-enemy. John Betjeman remembered one of his offerings, 'with an enjoyably absurd line', in which he compared a piece of furtive music to the sound of biscuits being rubbed together[261]. From tea table allusion, these young, post-war poets travelled to more powerful prosody. Acton ventured far:

> 'When frigates from long voyages
> Drift into harbour, then I see
> Whirled momentary mirages
> Of inspissated greenery—
> Mazed mangroves casting their aerial roots,
> And diamond water-shoots
> Embroidering the air.
> And in the drowsy hanging-gardens there
> Roam slowly-swaying elephants'[262].

While Huxley looked closer to home:
> 'But I look out of the window and find
> Much to satisfy the mind.
> Mark how the furrows, formed and wheeled
> In a motion orderly and staid . . .
>
> . . .
>
> And here's a market-garden, barred
> With stripe on stripe of varied greens . . .
> Bright gardens, flower starred,
> And the opacous colour of beans.
> Each line deliberately swings
> Towards me, until I see a straight
> Green avenue to the heart of things'[263].

To their, now well known, names were added newcomers such as Claud Collier Abbot and Clifford Bax, the Georgian-toned Richard Church and many more. Basil's motive, in promoting young poets unknown to fame, certainly wasn't money. Spurred on by his father, publishing these slim, and usually rather highbrow, volumes was a risk Basil Blackwell was more than prepared to take; these adventures provided food for the soul, which was just as well. All the early series are now prized collectors items, as is *Adventurers All*: 'a series of young poets unknown to fame'[264]. Many of his poets were already making a name for themselves: the first volume of a later series, *Initiates*, Basil Blackwell recalled, was devoted to Geoffrey Faber[265]. Volumes of *Oxford Outlook* attracted the editing interest of Julian Huxley (Volume VII, 1921), Harold Acton, C Day Lewis and W H Auden (Volume VIII, 1926), and Volumes X and XI included contributions from Louis MacNeice. The series ceased publication for a time, but reappeared as the *New Oxford Outlook*, 1929–1936. Its list of authors made even the London publishers envious. Basil Blackwell remembered that Stephen Spender, who had edited the 1929 volume, and whose poems also appeared in several other volumes, had from the start 'intimations of immortality'[266]. Volume VII (1921) attracted the editing interest of Julian Huxley. Volume VIII (1926) attracted offerings from the likes of W H Auden, Harold Acton and Day Lewis. The 1931 Volume was edited by Isaiah Berlin, A L Rowse, Douglas Jay and Richard Goodman, and the 1933 edition by Emlyn Williams and Patrick Monkhouse.

Despite all Basil's good intentions to give writers a chance, the passage of these volumes was not always smooth. The vicarious time traveller can only guess at the rivalry and in-fighting that must have gone on among the editors, 'as they chose whose works were to be singled out for publication, in each issue, and those whose were not!' An inkling of this wrangling can be gleaned from a letter from Stephen Spender to Basil Blackwell, where he describes some of the horse-trading. Spender speculated whether or not Wyndham Lewis would still publish his poems in his next issue of *The Enemy*: 'I daresay he won't because he may have quarrelled with me'. Or was it to be a quid pro quo for the four poems he (Lewis) had lifted from *Oxford Poetry*? Spender rhetorically muted the legality of this—did it breach copyright? Spender, writing from Germany, where he lived after going down from Oxford, and boasting of his sun tan: 'brown all over!', lamented that Louis MacNeice, who was a co-editor, had run off with the manuscript for the next issue of *Oxford Poetry*. The poems were, in any case, 'rather depressing', but he felt confident 'we can choose the only acceptable ones from a very poor selection'[267]. 'Poor' maybe viewed from Spender and MacNeice's poetical heights, but Basil was not a man of so little faith. He was not part of the hierarchy that ordered the ranking of poets; as he pointed out: 'as one coterie became established, so another was on its way (out)'. He just wanted to get their selections into print; on the proviso, of course, that he judged them to be 'worth the candle'. It's a miracle that Basil did not fall out with the whole tribe of them! But 'falling-out' was not his way, if it could be avoided. In any case, his role was different; like his father, he was merely acting as an entrepôt, and did not enter the fray as a public critic.

Much more should be written of the Blackwells' early poetic endeavours, but, unfortunately, as Basil wrote to a colleague at Magdalen College, 'When the present bookshop was rebuilt in about 1937, many records and files were destroyed in error'. Among them were the records of his early adventures in poetry publishing, including *Oxford Poetry*[268]. But, he claimed, his memory had served him well; he had, after all, been Blackwell's 'exponent of originality in the poetry field', to wit, a sales representative. 'I used to go to London with two or three—not very important—books in my bag, and go round the booksellers: it was a good experience. And then I went out into the country, to the West Country, the Midlands, equally good experience'. This combination of the practical side of the business with inspirations for its development was typical of the way Basil worked. But the publishing imprint would not survive unless it could be made profitable; the old Blackwell habit of bearing the costs of publication had to go, although it never did, totally. While he was always ready to take a risk, even Basil could see that running Blackwell's publishing as a holiday home for lost, and impoverished, poets was not a long-term proposition; his 'poets unknown to fame' had, in any case, scarpered to London. Sense prevailed over flights of fancy when he saw his 'names' appearing in the lists of Macmillan, Cape, Faber, and many more: '*Sic vos non vobis mellificatis apes*', he declared—'thus not for you, ye bees, ye honey make'. But out of the frying pan into the fire.

Basil, and his partner Adrian Mott were as idealistic as each other. And before they settled down to earning a living in the commerical world of publishing, they undertook an excursion into the realms of fine publishing. 'In the false dawn of hope and idealism, which followed immediately on World War I, when men looked for a 'World safe for Democracy' and the League of Nations deemed to inaugurate a new and nobler age, 'there can have been few publishers who were not moved to encourage the generous enthusiasms of visionaries'. One such visionary was E R Appleton who approached Basil, and Adrian Mott, his editorial assistant to see if they could turn dreams, and visions, into reality. Together, they conspired in the preparation of a monthly review, 'which was to herald and interpret the new age: it was to be called *The Beacon*'[269]. Both Basil Blackwell and Adrian Mott grew up in this new age: it was a propitious time, and this timeliness, 'being in the right place at the right time', goes some way to explaining the success of Blackwell's ventures (publishing and bookselling). Before, during and after the Great War, the demand from the reading public was burgeoning; as did their quest for self-improvement. This increased the popularity of books in general, and the Classics in particular. Yet these Classics, at the other end of the book market, were usually issued as finely printed works of art; there were too few of them, and they were seldom affordable by the general public. Basil was determined to find a way 'to put these good books into their hands' while supporting the printing crafts. But all this was for the future. At the start of their odyssey, these two friends from college days, were attracted by the idea of a counter-revolution.

Supporting fine printing would put them in the vanguard; the 'handbrake' of the Private Press Movement halted for a time the headlong flight of mass production for its own sake. 'No changing of place at a hundred miles an hour, nor making of stuffs at a thousand yards a minute will make us one whit stronger, happier, wiser', Basil wrote. 'There was always more in the world than men could see, walked they ever so slow; they will not see it for going fast . . . it does a bullet no good to go fast; and a man, if he truly be a man, no harm to go slow; for his glory is not at all in going but in being. And if we modify this a little, remembering the bitter bias Ruskin felt against his own materialistic and mechanical age, and also add to 'the being' the extra Morris joy in handling and making, we being to appreciate the need for, and the ideals of, the arts and crafts movement'[270]. Basil hastened to explain these ideas: 'William Morris set the book printer a standard he could not hope to reach, and . . . widened rather than diminished the gap between the ideal book . . . and the book of every day.' But surely this was not the point; the patterns and styles set by Morris could not be maintained, indeed it was not necessary or important to maintain or even imitate them; the important thing was the statement of aims and practical solution in one man's eyes. Modifications to the doctrine by later artists and perhaps in line with modern production needs would have to be made, but the message had been seen and understood. The proof of this is to be seen surely in the non-private press books that followed in the wake of the first wave of enthusiasts. The books from the Pelican and Nonesuch Press; the books issued by Symon's own First Edition Club; the standard library editions from the Shakespeare Head Press; the books from the University presses; the various hard-backed pocket editions offered by many of the regular publishers; and finally, the advent of the ubiquitous Penguins, from Allen Lane, which commenced their incredible mushroom life only in 1935. 'For the success of these books must, in part, be due to the care and attention which is lavished on their design and production. This meticulous attention to detail stemmed from Morris and Emery Walker, was codified by Newdigate and Meynell and then brought to modern mass-production fruition by Tschichold and Schmoller'.

Basil's opportunity to join this rarefied world of fine printing came with the virtual bankruptcy of A H Bullen's Shakespeare Head Press, and an invitation to take it over. The invitation probably came from the typographer Emery Walker, whose work was already greatly admired by the youthful Basil. Basil set off, with Adrian Mott, to see the press for himself, and as a result it was purchased for £1,500, and incorporated on 21 February 1921. Passion was high as Basil Blackwell and Adrian Mott set out to 'develop the ideas which had inspired its (SHP) founder'. Basil had always admired the work of Bullen; Bullen was a scholar. From his earliest school days he had shown a keen interest in the Elizabethan scene both in song and story, and this interest developed in time into a passion which was to last him the rest of his life. He had set up as a publisher in 1889 but even before this he had been actively concerned in the publication of the works of Day, Marlowe, Middleton, Thomas Campion and many other Elizabethan and Caroline writers. In partnership, first with H W Lawrence (1891–1900) and then with F Sidgwick (1900–07), he issued a large number of books, including the poetry for the *Muses Library* series. *The Concise Cambridge History of English*

27 The clerk of Oxenford from the Prologue of the Shakespeare Head *Chaucer*.

Literature lists Bullen as being the producer of a delightful *Lyrics from the Song Books of the Elizabethan Age*, issued in 1886 and the first of a long line of similar collections. Bullen's work attracted the great typographer-to-be, Bernard Newdigate, into the fold, who was invited to join the 'Stratford men' as aesthetic and technical adviser. 'Whereas Bullen was an amateur, albeit an inspired one, Newdigate was a professional. With his arrival, the concept of the new Shakespeare Head image began to appear'. Basil equated the Shakespeare Head Press with the flowering of Newdigate's typography; from a purely aesthetic viewpoint Newdigate was the press, for its lifetime: 'Bullen may have had the dream, the scholarship and the vision; Blackwell and Mott the faith and the courage—and the money—but it was Newdigate, who organized the words, shapes and patterns that were the books, and it is because of this superb organization of the words, shapes and patterns that the Press is best remembered'.

To make money from fine printing was a Herculean task, and one never really accomplished. Basil must have known from the start that it would be a labour of love. At his first meeting with Basil Blackwell, Bernard Newdigate calmly informed him that he never made any money. Basil recorded his first impression of the man he came to admire so much: 'He called to my mind first and always a descriptive passage in Dickens. . . . As I contemplated the great brow, and the bald dome fringed with hair, the 'circular spectacles' . . . and 'the beaming eyes twinkling behind those glasses, I was perforce reminded of "the man who had traced to their source the mighty ponds of Hampstead". And indeed there was something Pickwickian in his innocence. . . . his enthusiasm for antiquity; but his was the spiritual

Play Days with Pegasus: Father and Son

dignity and remoteness of the later, post-Fleet Pickwick'. But Newdigate had a scholarly pedigree too; he was of the same kin as Sir Roger Newdigate who had founded the Oxford (Newdigate) Prize for English verse, and many of these poems had been published by Blackwell's. Bernard Newdigate, born ten years before Benjamin Henry opened Blackwell's, was another son destined to come to the rescue of his father's business. Newdigate's father, the son of the third Earl of Dartmouth, who had trained and worked as an Anglican priest, was converted to Catholicism, and to the enthusiasms of a Benedictine monk, Fr Strutter. This modest monk, who had founded St Gregory's Press of Stratford-on-Avon, where he ran 'a halting enterprise printing devotional books', was more renowned for his faith than his business acumen, and Bernard Newdigate's father sank his capital into the venture. But the move did not gladden the heart of his mother. His mother, the daughter of Sir Henry Boynton, Ninth Baronet, looked askance at the family's finances, and feared for her ten children's futures.

Bernard's education had its similarities with Joyce's Young Man, in *Portrait of the Artist as a Young Man*. In 1878, he had been sent to the northern Jesuit public school of Stonyhurst, in order to start his spiritual as well as his secular education. This establishment laid its emphasis on the classic Catholic Jesuit teaching system focusing on 'the Elements, Figures, Rudiments, Grammar, Syntax, Poetry and Rhetoric', and the Jesuits moulded his character. He continued to study philosophy; he read seriously 'and this self-inflicted diet of scholarly reading was one of his most remarkable features'. For all that he was scholarly, the ancient universities were closed to him; at this time it was still impossible for a Catholic to obtain a normal university eduction, although Newdigate did take the external London BA degree at a later date. Sensitive to the family's financial difficulties, Bernard set about preparing himself for the Civil Service examinations. But Newdigate was not destined to be a Trollope-like clerk. His father, meanwhile, had gone ahead, in 1888, and purchased the Press, moving it to Leamington, 'under the style of the Art and Book Company'. Here the publishing side was developed, wrote Basil Blackwell, 'but by 1890 it was showing symptoms of collapse and Bernard decided to come to the rescue'[271]. Training himself on the job, with the help of artists and printers, he was introduced to Emery Walker 'that good genius of printing for more than forty years'. Newdigate often admitted to Basil that 'he learnt more about the conditions of fine printing from Emery Walker than from any other source'. He learnt that red ink alone did not make for an impressive title page, that the unit of a book is not one page, but a pair of pages, and that it was preferable to use 'bigger type

The Tales of Canterbury
The Prologue

Here bygynneth the Book of the tales of Caunterbury

WHAN THAT APRILLE WITH
HIS SHOURES SOOTE
THE DROGHTE OF MARCH
HATH PERCED TO THE ROOTE,
And bathed every veyne in swich licour
Of which vertu engendred is the flour;
Whan Zephirus eek with his swete breeth
Inspired hath in every holt and heeth
The tendre croppes, and the yonge sonne
Hath in the Ram his halfe cours y-ronne,
And smale foweles maken melodye,
That slepen al the night with open eye,—
So priketh hem Nature in hir corages,—
Thanne longen folk to goon on pilgrimages,
And palmeres for to seken straunge strondes,
To ferne halwes, kowthe in sondry londes;
And specially, from every shires ende
Of Engelond, to Caunturbury they wende,
The hooly blisful martir for to seke,
That hem hath holpen whan that they were seeke.

b   1

28   The opening page of the Prologue from the Shakespeare Head *Chaucer*.

solid than smaller type leaded'. Newdigate had very high standards in printing and in the quality of paper he used, lamenting the mean grey paper used in the Government's printing establishments. The mandarins cannot have taken his criticisms too much to heart, since Newdigate was appointed to the Board of Education to assist in the inspection of printing classes. Having learnt his craft at his father's small press, out of which the Arden Press grew, taken over by W H Smith in 1905, Bernard came to the assistance of Bullen.

When Basil took over the SHP he 'inherited Newdigate', and he began his own apprenticeship in the art of fine printing. But he had also had to submit to the idiosyncrasies of the Master, letting him have his head, even when it made no commercial sense. Yet the books designed by Newdigate 'remain as a monument to his ability as a designer showing a recognizable technique using very simple means', Basil wrote. But what was the Newdigate technique? 'A steady eye for the minutest detail, a disciplined use of a good and fitting typeface, and a complete understanding of the unity in the book page(s). Added to this he always had a feeling for a period and flavour and married typeface, illustrations and page format to fit the spirit of the job in hand. In the beginning he favoured the Caslon type and was, in all probability, its greatest exponent but he took other typefaces, particularly the new Monotype revivals, in his stride'. The secret of the Shakespeare Head books, Basil surmised, 'is probably just this: quite impeccable tailoring of the subject to be printed. Colin Franklin says that Newdigate, like Morris and Cobden Sanderson before him, imposed his will on the book and perhaps this is so. But there is, I think, a more subtle distinction than this. The Doves Press manner is coldly formal: shaping with the chisel; Morris is more human but still carves at it; Newdigate is the subtler, a more delicate clothing for the words'. One of the earliest books produced under the new Blackwell/Newdigate partnership was the *Loves of Clitophon and Leucippe*, published in 1923 and printed on Kelmscott paper, with a few special vellum copies. 'This was a fine beginning to the new order', Basil observed, 'and the style of Newdigate is already apparent: close word spacing, judicious leading, strong title page opening, crisp letterpress on fine white paper'.

Although not so learned a man, perhaps, as Bullen, Newdigate matched him in familiarity with Elizabethan literature and even surpassed him with his knowledge of the families and characters of that era. 'Among all the good things he produced for the Shakespeare Head Press, perhaps the most characteristic are the sturdy, unpretentious editions of Defoe, Richardson and Fielding. . . . Out of all his work there shines an almost child-like integrity', Basil wrote. Stanley Morison, in a notice of his death, praised 'his high appreciation of the work of others, which led him to seize the opportunity of commending in print the merits of other people's typography, raised the reputation of others at the expense of his own. He was himself quite indifferent to praise, and discouraged attempts of other writers to give publicity to his own work... Hence, after a lifetime of effort to inspire trade printing and publishing with the ideals of the Arts and Craft movement, Newdigate remains the most under-rated of typographers'. His *Book Production Notes* remain; they appeared in the *London Mercury* from 1920 to 1937 'and formed one of the most valuable critical analyses of printing and book production during this time. Obviously many of the comments and criticisms appearing in the texts would have interest for only a typographer and printing enthusiast today[272]. Writing ten years after his death, Adrian Mott wrote that 'of all the men I have ever met I think perhaps he (Bernard Newdigate) was the one I most admired. The quite exceptional uprightness of his character, his charm and his genius were unique'[273]. When Newdigate died, the Shakespeare Head Press, for all practical purposes, died with him; the War Office had commandeered the Oxford building in 1942. Basil Blackwell deeply mourned its passing, but Henry Schollick, his fellow director since 1931, didn't want to look back: 'The time, the place and the man are gone'. 'Perhaps this is how it should be... and yet... who knows'.

For Basil Blackwell, what became the Newdigate tradition stemmed from its associations with Morris, and Kelmscott. The Shakespeare Head *Froissart*, for example, produced in the year 1927–8, was connected with Morris; a Kelmscott edition had been planned, but had never progressed beyond a trial double page spread and a few other scraps. Basil wrote that 'in this book the gentle hand of Emery Walker can be felt pushing Newdigate, and the pages, into their 'right and proper shapes'. The text moves from page to page at a steady pace and the shoulder notes and decorative shields fit neatly into the tale. 'These brightly coloured shields do not dominate the pages; they are adornment only and, as on the uniformly different title pages, one gets the feeling of restrained order. Though it is possible to be slightly mean and criticise the letter-spacing of the larger capitals, set in the Fred Griggs Campden types, on some of the title pages'. The Newdigate *Chaucer*, published between 1928–9, was a more flamboyant exercise, livelier and with more calligraphic flourishes between the stories. The Lynton Lamb illustrations redrawn from very early editions and some French sources, add a touch of lightness and gaiety to the pages. For some of these illustrations, and so continuing the Bullen hopes and traditions of using 'Stratford men', the local art school provided students who could colour and 'also lay gold with very fine results, and some pages have a sort of mediaeval golden magic feel'. In his book on the private presses, Colin Franklin compares the Shakespeare Head *Chaucer* with two other editions from the *real* private presses, viz, the Kelmscott and the Golden Cockerel. In his final analysis he comes down in favour of the Stratford version on the basis of its simplicity and careful planning. That is a difficult decision to make, but I think he has a point even though comparisons are very difficult. Basil attempted some comparison by looking at all three printings where they dealt with the same point in the story—the *Prologue* with Chaucer's description of the Monk and the Friar. 'For my own taste, the Newdigate version is to be preferred although it does smack of the children's book and the fairy tale just a little. The Cockerel is perhaps nearer to the Chaucer words, illustration-wise, except that the hearty earthy, sexual Chaucer overtones are muted, I think, by the coldness of the Gill illustrations, complete as they are in their human and branchlike intertwining. The Morris page is not easy to compare due to the lack of an appropriate illustration, but in some of the other illustrations appearing in the Kelmscott, the Chaucer feel is missing'[274].

Turning from Canterbury, Bunyan's *Pilgrim's Progress* was put out by Cresset Press in 1928. Designed by Newdigate and printed at the Shakespeare Head, it is a large 35 × 25 cm edition in two volumes. 'It has', wrote Basil, 'a strong black feel throughout and is complete with ten full page illustrations by Blair Hughes-Stanton. The illustrations are good, and give it a fitting liturgical feel. Apart from it being 'primarily a type book', it was according to Basil, a typographer's tour de force. Two volumes of the Venerable Bede's *History of the Church of England*, produced about this time (1929), show the same developing style and are akin to the work Newdigate was producing for Cresset Press. Chapman's *Homer* was produced between the years of 1930–31 with over fifty wood engravings by John Farleigh, 'and this', Basil claimed, 'demonstrated that the Caslon was not always inevitable or necessary for a superb design. In these books Newdigate used the newly-available 16-pt Centaur to excellent effect. I think we have tended to underrate Newdigate and his typographic achievements, and this under-rating is not only of our time. Bruce Rogers himself felt this and wrote in tribute of Newdigate'. Malory's *Le Morte D'Arthur* followed, in 1933, 'perhaps a little less fine, but knowing the subtle interpretations of Newdigate for tenor and time, it is probably deliberately coarser and a more rugged feel prevails. The woodcuts reproduced from the Wynkyn de Worde folio of 1498 match the text well, and the whole book has an emerging strength showing through. 'I started to read the proofs of Malory, with an old prejudice against the double column, but presently began to find that Newdigate's wizardry had made the page easy—pleasant—charming to read.'

The Shakespeare Head *Decameron* has over a hundred illustrations produced in facsimile by R J Beedham and Miss E Joyce Francis. The illustrations derive from those used in the edition printed in Venice in 1492, by the brothers Gregorii and are the work of that great school of Venetian book illustration which flourished between 1490 and 1499 (the date of the Aldus *Poliphilus*). The Books indeed have a distinct Venetian flavour 'with their apt use of long lines of Monotype Poliphilus capitals, printed in blue and closely word-spaced, starting each chapter. In this instance the use and positioning of this type was the happy choice of Henry Schollick. The Ben Johnson *Poems* (1936) were edited by Newdigate, an indication of his scholarly ability. 'Set in 12-pt Caslon, with running heads in Italic caps, including swash letters, this book again shows the care he lavished on poems, for each poem is beautifully positioned and each pair of pages perfectly balanced'. Many compositors have a rule of thumb that poetry should be set to the measure of the longest line, but that necessarily drives the poem too much to the left, and gives the page a lopsided look. To judge of the middle I find it convenient in practice to hold a short length of brass rule, or some other convenient straight edge, vertically from the top of the type script of the poem to be set to the bottom and to move it right or left until it divides the poem approximately into two equal parts, the meridian at which the straight edge rests will then determine the middle of the measure to which the verses are to be set.... The make-up of poetry, also, requires the exercise of care and a certain nicety of judgement to make sure the facing pages balance one another'[275].

The completed works of Drayton, one of the unfinished ambitions of Bullen, were finally produced when the book *Michael Drayton and his Circle*, written by Newdigate himself, appeared in 1941. He had previously designed and printed the first four volumes of the *Complete Works of Drayton*, and upon the death of the American editor of this edition, John William Hebel of Cornell University, he had, in co-operation with an English scholar, Kathleen Tillotson, completed the fifth volume. His own sixth volume was in the grand scholarly tradition of a long line of scholar-printers Aldus, Caxton, Plantin, and will surely have granted him a place in the printer's Valhalla. 'So for twenty years', Basil wrote, 'until the outbreak of the Second World War, the Shakespeare Head Press was engaged in a series of books, some glorious, all dignified, which included the work of authors ranging from the Venerable Bede and Chaucer to the Brontes and Anthony Trollope.

Basil Blackwell did not lay claim to the achievements of the Press. The Press had inherited the 'incalculable benefit of the typographical genius of Bernard Newdigate'[276]. Newdigate's reputation was well known within the literary trades; John Betjeman, for example, had written to Basil that he wished that his letter-writing could be 'as spacious and gracious as the typography of Newdigate'.

Yet, never very far at the back of Basil's mind, and especially H S Critchley's, was the need to solve the business equation. Basil was fully aware that it was almost impossible in practice for the Press to make a profit. Bernard was what Basil described as 'a fidget printer' who was 'capable of altering the imposition of a whole book after it had gone to machine'. Mr Kendrick (the composing room foreman) famously described Newdigate as 'fidget printer; fit to break your heart . . .', and Emery Walker (who was himself not easily satisfied) told Thorpe that Newdigate had 'once over-run (adjusted throughout) a page six times before he was satisfied'. Try as he might Basil could not restrain his friend's perfection. 'So', Basil recorded, 'we had to ask for an estimate, formally accept it, and leave Newdigate to dedicate the profit to getting it right!'. 'Fortunately, the books that the Press printed were profitable and Basil 'devoted some of the profits to sustaining the Press, or at least to saving it from making a loss. Trying to foil what Basil described as 'Newdy's constant improvement touches' led to the decision to publish a uniform series of Eighteenth Century novelists: Sterne, Fielding, Richardson, Defoe, and later the Barchester Novels and the 'Definitive Bronte'. While they did succeed in limiting the illustrious printer's 'corrections', they were still subject to what Basil called 'Bernard's costly minute touches'. Somehow Basil had to find a way to use his publishing house to produce affordable Classics, rather than just works of art for the 'luxury' end of the market. Basil had sought the advice and help of established writers, such as T S Eliot. In a letter to Basil, Eliot praised his efforts and promised to do what he could to attract the attention of the public: 'in the papers to which I have entrance'. He took 'the liberty' of suggesting 'texts which are not of great length and which are practically unobtainable': Marlowe's and Golding's translations of Ovid, Philemon Holland's selections from Livy, Suetonius or Pliny, selections from Donne, The Martin Marprelate Tracts, Campion's and Daniel's *Treatises on Versification*, Gawain Douglas's Virgil, Underdowne's *Heliodorus* and Nashe's *Terrors of the Night* and *The Unfortunate Traveller*[277].

Finding the means to produce such a collection may well have given Basil night terrors, but a chance to 're-issue the unobtainable', was a bait he could

29 The Gaffer in his Broad Street office, *c.* 1935.

not resist. But how could he reconcile higher moral purpose, and craftsmanship, with mass production? But Basil dreamed his dreams: 'For someone so interested in literature', Basil wrote, 'it was a natural step to graduate from authors who had just started their careers, to authors who had finished theirs'. He was convinced that he could combine the traditional craftsmanship of fine printing, and produce Classics at a high standard, but in larger quantities, and, consequently, at a lower price. He found a model in the recent commercial success of cheap sets of books being made available, in the thirties, to the new reading public: they were putting out sets of the Classics,

Play Days with Pegasus: Father and Son 165

Dickens and Shaw 'at bargain prices'. With this much homework under his belt, Basil, the risk taker, plunged in; not in a modest way with a short book or two, as Eliot had suggested, but with his Shakespeare! It was the Press's, one volume, *Complete Works of Shakespeare*, which Basil treasured above all others. This represented a marriage, and an early experiment, in combining fine printing and mass production. There was another advantage too, it may be just the way to tame Newdigate's 'wizardry'. If Newdigate makes works of antiquity 'easy-pleasant-charming to read' could his skills not also be used in the production of texts already in great demand by the general public? Basil's mind was hard at work. He began to ask himself if Newdigate could endow a one-volume Shakespeare with merit?

Newdigate seized on the suggestion. The one-volume *Shakespeare* was commissioned in 1934 and was produced as a complete edition of 1260 pages, in a production run of 50,000 copies, to be sold as 6s. each. This was no limited edition and was printed by Billings of Guildford, and the speed of production did not allow any Newdigate 'fidgeting'; its success ensured a reprint, two years later. The 9-pt Plantin of this setting, with its neatly-letter spaced small capitals, for all its smallness of size and cropped ascenders and descenders reads more easily than the larger Caslon setting of the Bullen Shakespeare. After weeks of trial, Newdigate came up with a typographical solution for combining the whole corpus of Shakespeare into 1260 pages, each page having two columns. In the event, the Bard's plays were condensed into 1,170 pages. The next problems: how many to print and what price to charge, were quickly dispensed with: Basil boldly rang up the printers and asked how many they would have to print to sell at six shillings a book. Undaunted by the answer, 50,000, Basil placed his order. The venture proved to be a great success, staggeringly, since it coincided with terrible economic depression of the thirties, the book went to a reprint, in 1937. 'In 1940', Basil recalled, 'our dear enemy destroyed the moulds, and the book was re-set leisurely'. Newdigate, now an invalid 'kept at home', read the proofs 'improved the setting, and wrote a short life of Shakespeare to introduce the plays. 'He lived to see the new edition, and saw that it was good'[278]. Basil deeply regretted that the edition, eventually, went out of favour. He wrote of its history to an old friend: 'I published the one-volume Shakespeare in 1934 at the price of 6s, in an edition of 50,000 copies, and I insisted upon the chronological order of the plays which, as you justly observe, enables one to follow the development of the poet's mind and style. I am at present in the last Act of *Romeo and Juliet*—an immense leap forward from *Love's Labours Lost*, and establishing the master. Most editors and publishers of one-volume Shakespeares have followed sheepishly the order in the first folio: Comedies, Histories, Tragedies, and I revolted from that in going for a chronological order. I have never been thanked for it until I got your letter to-day—at least, so far as I can remember. I would be very happy to see this edition returned to print, but since the last War there have been two editions of Shakespeare, and the Shakespeare Head text is no longer to be deemed canonical, though good enough for intelligent amateurs'[279].

Parting with anything to do with the Shakespeare Head was very painful: it had prompted many new adventures in publishing and its 'beautifully produced books' had whetted the public's appetite for 'finer fare'. For ten years following the Depression, imported to Britain from America, the machines at Shakespeare Head lay idle; there was little call for fine printing. The success of Blackwell's educational publications, especially the Marten and Carter Histories, provided cover for the ailing press. It limped along, producing limited editions, but to no avail. In 1938, as recorded in the firm's Minute Book, the Directors decided that 'the market for fine books of a literary character had practically ceased to exist'. Basil always regretted the short, albeit glorious, life of the Shakespeare Head Press. The name of the Shakespeare Press was preserved, and used for putting out children's books; a successful venture which included works by Enid Blyton. But the world of Bullen, and Newdigate, was no more. Writing about Bernard Newdigate, after his death, Basil had nothing but praise for Newdigate, both as a man and a colleague. Writing Newdigate's obituary for *The Times*, June 1944, he marked the passing of a man who resembled his own father: modest, virtuous, a man with no extravagance in him whose speech was short, simple and pointed, and someone who would have 'gone to the stake for his religious faith'. No one who knew him, Basil wrote, 'would hesitate to say "Here was a gentleman". Those worthy to judge in these high matters might use a greater title'[280]. More saint than sinner, he had given Basil 'twenty-four years of fellowship' as a scholar-printer in line with Caxton, Aldus and Plantin. Basil also looked to Newdigate as an antiquary, and 'no mean expert on the literature of the Elizabethan Age'[281]. Together they adventured in the printing and publishing of books, 'all elegant, some magnificent, in the right tradition of English literature, and all the spice of scholarship'[282]. Years later, when he had more time on his hands, Basil wanted to provide a more permanent memorial to the man who had inspired him, Bernard Newdigate[283]. He set about documenting his life and work, and writing a full account. At the same time he determined that Newdigate's 'collection of noble books and its commentary might be lodged permanently in some place of ready access for the instruction of 'any one who should study to achieve or to recognize excellence in printing'[284].

Some praise for Shakespeare Head, and the other Blackwell publishing ventures, must go to the publishers, as well as the various craftsmen, from writers to typographers, who made the imprint famous. Basil had attributed the survival of Shakespeare Head, 'less to our competence as publishers than to Appleton's gift of inspiring others with his ideals', to Ernest Parker for his insights 'into the bread and butter' side of the business, to Henry Schollick for his immaculate management, to Henry Critchley 'for his eagle eye that kept him to the strait and narrow path if ever he was tempted to some dubious financial expedient, such as cooking the accounts or wangling the Balance Sheet'[285], and to Adrian Mott 'true friendship, and an ear to bend in troubled times'. Nowhere, in Basil Blackwell's writings or rambling does he claim a shred of credit for himself. There is no list of 'I did this or that'; no showy c.v. Adrian Mott, however, had this to say: 'In my life I have had two outstanding pieces of luck. The first was when I married my wife. The second when, in 1920, I agreed to start a small publishing firm together with Basil, based on the prestige and connections of the great book-selling business which his father had built up. What I personally owe to our Chairman—and I think it is true of all of us—is a great deal more than I can put into words. He bore the burden and the heat of the day: his ability, initiative and hard work brought us through the difficulties of the early years, his kindness and understanding help for all those who needed it, made our firm the happy community (it is). Very seldom, have I ever seen him shaken out of that urbane dignity we know so well'[286]. But the story of the Shakespeare Head Press, wrote Basil, 'pleasant as it is, is only a minutiae in the history of British book production. The printing of books is endless (notwithstanding the advent of the computer and that monster's possible progeny,) and the printers of books many, but in this myriad company both the books produced at the Shakespeare Head and the people who caused them to be printed have made a notable contribution to the design of books and to the dissemination of the printed word. For this much we should be sincerely grateful'.

Basil's efforts in publishing, as always, were motivated by much more than profit; his ambition was 'to put more books into more hands'. Ten years after taking over the family business he set out to review the entire publishing industry in the United Kingdom. While serving a second year as the President of the Booksellers' Association, in 1934, he enlisted the help of Sir Stanley Unwin for a conference devoted to the new book market. Gaining the support of Stanley Unwin was an accolade; he was a much tougher operator than Basil, and favoured an incremental, rather than inspirational, approach. But he, too, believed passionately that the book trade should be continually improved[287]. Come the Conference, hosted by Basil, an informal weekend attended by some fifty publishers and booksellers at Ripon Hall, Oxford, 'the weather was wonderful'. And this augured well; between the social interactions of this group of friends and acquaintances, they found the time for serious talk. One of the delegates was a young man of 32, called Allen Lane. Encouraged by the deliberations of the weekend this young man resolved to make his mark in the publishing world. In conversation with Basil, sitting under an apple-tree in the Blackwell's orchard at Osse Field, Allen Lane's ambition hardened. A year later, in 1935, Allen Lane launched the imprint which was to change the face of British and international publishing—Penguin Books. These brightly coloured paperbacks, described as 'intelligent books for intelligent people', sold for less than a packet of cigarettes. Within two years the first ten titles, including Agatha Christie, Beverly Nichols, and Ernest Hemingway, were supplemented with more heady fare, six paperback Shakespeare's and the first Pelican entitled *'The Intelligent Woman's Guide to Socialism, Capitalism, Sovietism and Fascism*[288]. Basil claimed that his part in this piece was merely one of 'a dumb sort of catalyst'[289].

Basil was never 'dumb' but he was adept as a catalyst. Granted he didn't try to compete with the 'big boys' in London, but he made enviable inroads in specialist markets. For him, the publishing of schoolbooks was particularly rewarding. His father had started the Blackwell interest, spurred on by the introduction of compulsory elementary education, the Foster Act, in 1870. Like his father, Basil was convinced of the need to extend education, at all levels, and to find, and publish, books to push the process along. The Fisher Act, which added a year to the school leaving age, was about to come into force, and it called for something new in elementary school books. It was his new colleague Appleton who encouraged, and, excited, Basil's interest in publishing them. Basil decided that a little market research was called for. 'What were the current books like? I was wholly ignorant. I visited a local educational supplier and spent £1 on an armful of them for examination. It was a shocking experience'. He lamented that 'the dominant consideration was one of cheapness, and to this were sacrificed the contents physical and intellectual'. Reacting to this morass of 'hack work, shoddily produced', Basil thumped his desk and cried 'only the best is good enough for these children!'[290]. Help was at hand, 'Appleton, with whom I discussed my experience, introduced me to his friend E H Carter HMI, who encouraged us to enter the field, and undertook to advise us. In publishing the idea is of the

Play Days with Pegasus: Father and Son 169

first importance, it must be right and apt; with this in mind I discussed the project with Will Hunt, whose generous soul readily responded, and asked him who was the best man to undertake a history series. He recommended an approach to C H K Marten (a long-standing friend of Blackwell's), Lower Master of Eton, whose histories for public and grammar schools were outstandingly successful. I made the journey to Eton and opened my mind to him. He caught fire and so did the Headmaster, Cyril Alington, who gave him 'sabbatical leave' to set the work in motion. 'There were four volumes in the series and I remember that for a considerable period they were selling, each of them, at the rate of 1,000 per week. It was a good foundation on which to build an educational list'[291].

The master in the educational field was J M Dent, and Basil aspired to emulate him. And he wanted to find someone of similar calibre. It was his colleague Appleton, who first introduced him to Ernest Parker, educational manager of Collins. Rumour had it that Parker's contract there was due for renewal; he didn't renew it. 'I have no doubt', Basil wrote, 'that we should have come to grief if he had'. Ensconced at Blackwell's, he soon found his feet, and his shrewdness and expertise won over Harry Critchley, already on the Board; Critchley was an astute operator, and not easily taken in. But Basil had backed another winner, and Parker was offered a directorship of the infant firm of Basil Blackwell and Mott Ltd. 'It was one of the wisest and happiest decisions in my business life'; and recalling him, 'the word *vibrant* was the first to spring to mind. He was voluble, cheerfully aggressive, endowed with a brilliant mind and, seemingly, complete self-assurance'. Better still, he was an insider in the education world; he had been a teacher before joining Collins, and he had a teacher's nose. Above all, Basil wrote, 'his enthusiastic spirit drove him to make an immediate impact on any company he might meet; he must seek to dominate it by brilliant talk; he must always be scoring points. Often, an old teacher's trick, 'he would begin by shocking' and 'then winning those whom he encountered'. 'He was not the easiest of colleagues, and occasionally I had to say '*C'est ça*', but our debt to him was immense'. The famous children's annual *Joy Street* was his invention, and 'he guided the somewhat indeterminate policy of the Shakespeare Head Press towards the series of reprints of Eighteenth Century novelists and other profitable ventures. He combined a mind fertile in ideas with the genius of a superlatively successful salesman. After the death of his beloved wife, who kept her rare beauty well into middle age, Ernest Parker said "the word is to carry on sergeant" and so he did for a year and then collapsed. For two years we did our best to restore him, but the stern fact emerged that his "vibrancy" and urge to dominate were prompted by an extreme sense of insecurity. The force of his will had snapped and he lost even the management of such automatic actions as walking or the use of knife or fork. He began to make attempts on his life and at last succeeded'. Two stepsons appeared to be the only surviving relatives. Basil Blackwell hailed Parker 'as the driving spirit behind B & M's educational ventures'. Adrian Mott recounted that 'only once did I know him diverted from his purpose: when I found him with a young and particularly beautiful authoress, her arms around his neck, brazenly wheedling an extra ten per cent royalty out of him'.

When Ernest Parker died, in 1933, Henry Schollick, a newcomer enlisted only a year before, was appointed to replace him, as a director of B & M. 'He had taken to the trade as a natural and, whereas Parker had infused the infant business with his inspirations, Henry Schollick was more of an engineer: a builder who could develop the publishing side'. Unlike many of Basil's recruits, Henry Lightbrown Schollick was not a self-educated man. But, in common, he had made his own way; he had won a scholarship to his local grammar school and then a place to study PPE 'at the small, but beautiful, Oriel College, Oxford. How different this must have been for the young Henry, as compared with his home in Blackburn, Lancashire?' After a brief spell in the retail trade, in Glasgow, Henry Schollick moved to Collins and thence to Blackwell's. Basil counted it a lucky day when the redoubtable 'HLS', or 'Uncle Henry' as he became, started on a three-month probation. Sir Adrian Mott, too, had recorded his impressions of the inimitable Henry Schollick. 'To get Henry was an extraordinary piece of luck for the firm. His rugged exterior—slightly reminiscent of Rocky Marciano—hides a heart of gold. With his giant brain and his infinite capacity for the evasion of income tax he had done more than anyone else except the chairman for the prosperity of the firm'[292]. He caught the Blackwellian bug, and never left, except to travel the country in a vintage Austin Seven, from which he displayed Blackwell's wares, while making the firm many friends. Distinguishing himself in the book trade, he served on the Council of the Booksellers Association, from 1939, and later he became one of Blackwell's vice-presidents. His first and most important task was to re-evaluate Blackwell's as a publisher. Looking back on this time, Sir Basil, at the age of eighty, was still excited by the memory of the twenties and thirties: 'stirring times in the organization of the book trade.... and one with a foot in each camp was deemed to have something useful to contribute'. He makes no mention of Blackwell's part in the explosion of activity in the publishing world. Rather, he praised Unwin's initiatives, together with those of the society of Bookmen, Hugh Walpole's innovation, and the founding of the National Book Council, again Unwin's brainchild.

Such contacts, and organizations, provided 'days out' to London for Basil, and late nights back on what was, jokingly, called 'the fornicator's express'. These halcyon days were, temporarily, interrupted by the outbreak of the Second World War, when B & M was seventeen years old. Inevitably the War brought change, Basil wrote, 'and some things were sacrificed'. To his deep and everlasting regret, it put a stop to most of his *'belles lettres'* and fine printing. He commented ironically that 'somehow the poets who had been so vocal about the Civil War in Spain became strangely silent when the really big one started'. More worryingly, opportunities had dried up on the bread and butter front of schoolbook publishing, too. In its wisdom, the London County Council, a very important customer, stopped buying books at the outbreak of war. Their schools had all been evacuated; there was, at the outset, no compensating increase in sales elsewhere, and turnover fell by a third. Basil recalled that 'it survived . . . and fared no worse than others specialising in educational titles: badly at first, remarkably well thereafter. In September 1940, the future looked so gloomy that it did not seem a great disaster to the Directors when, on 27 September, German bombs destroyed all B & M's unbound stock of school and children's books, held by Billings, the Guildford printers. The loss was, after all, partly covered by the (compulsory) War Risks Insurance scheme, and they congratulated themselves further on being able to offset some of the rest by selling the sheets of slow-moving books, warehoused elsewhere, at 2d a pound for wrapping purposes! It seemed a sensible decision at the time, but they soon lived to regret it. And they were not the only publishers to read the omens wrong. Oxford University Press, for example, well provided as they were with slow sellers, happily pulped 'surplus' stocks of many books that would have sold fast in the future. They even proposed to reduce their enormous unbound stock of the *Oxford English Dictionary*, 'but an Air Raid Warden demonstrated that the tons of sheets, formed into a hollow square, made an exceptionally secure Wardens' Post in the Jordan Hill warehouse in North Oxford, and the *Dictionary* was reprieved'.

Despite the setbacks in the early days of the war, the trade recovered, and an upturn in sales took place very quickly. In the second year of the war Blackwell and Mott's turnover shot up by nearly £4,000 and, like other publishers, they began to ration their customers, since the shortages of paper and of labour made it impossible to keep pace with the demand. Profits soared, too, from under £500 a year before the war to nearly £9,000 by the end of it, only to be swallowed up by the Inland Revenue by way of Excess Profits Tax. And there are no prizes for guessing Basil's reaction! The vagaries of the British tax system left Basil quietly seething, 'and the young publishing company with a liquidity problem; having to pay taxes on time restricted the company's real growth, receipts from sales could not be used fast enough to replenish the shrinking reservoir of stock, and some of the unemployable cash had to be stowed away in such things as the War Loan'. For the Annual General Meeting in December 1945 the Gaffer asked Henry Schollick to produce a report on the last war year, and this report reflects very clearly the course of wartime publishing. In 1939 the company had consumed fifty-three tons of paper. In 1945 its ration was twenty-three tons, though Uncle Henry's 'careful husbandry' had added fourteen more by special licences for 'essential' books and by other subtle, but lawful, means. On this paper, fifty-one books, twenty new and thirty-one reprints, were produced in the face of great difficulties in finding printers and binders to manufacture them. Geoffrey Barfoot, and S T Fenemore, had worked like Trojans to cope with a turnover nearly twice as large as before the war, with a depleted and mostly inexperienced staff.

Through all these difficulties, and on top of all this publishing activity, there were more projects underway. After the fall of France, in 1940, it had become impossible to import French (or German) texts for school and university use, and a new series was initiated by Blackwell and Mott, with two Oxford professors as editors. It gave the firm, as Henry Schollick remarked with satisfaction, 'an entry into the select preserves of the set books formerly produced by the University Presses', and it was to go on bearing useful fruit. Thirty years on the social sciences, and humanities, became still more important to Blackwell and Mott when it acquired fifty per cent of the shareholding of the publishers Martin Robertson and Company Ltd. Ian Robertson had died tragically young; David Martin, whilst still only in his early thirties became a director of Blackwell and Mott and, on the departure of Jim Feather, managing director.

It is an irony that Basil, someone who so hated the war, and who kept a file on the horrors of the concentration camps and the conditions facing POWs among his papers, should, however contingently, profit by it. His rationale was different. Two devastating wars, coinciding with the growth of universal education, had had a civilizing effect. People were not content to be merely cannon fodder: they were more critical, better informed, and, at all levels of society, more aware of their rights, as well as their obligations. Locke had finally won the argument with Hobbes: rational man prevailed over the 'state of nature'. What the war had clearly shown was the need for more and better scientific research, in all areas from physics, to electronics and medical science. Basil Blackwell turned, with the help of Henry Schollick, to developing the 'seriously academic' side of publishing, extending the range of Blackwell's publishing to cover scientific works, leading, eventually to the establishment of Blackwell Scientific Publications in 1939. 'Here was an endeavour that may have seemed presumptuous, being undertaken as it must 'in the very shadow of the largest and most learned publishing house in the world—Oxford University Press'. 'If David were not to slay Goliath, but to live in prosperity with him, how might it be done?' Basil asked. Outside intervention came when, after the fall of France, in 1940, it became impossible for the universities to import European books and this provided 'an entry into the select preserve of the set books formerly produced by the university presses'. These enterprises succeeded by establishing a niche in a market that was otherwise dominated by the giant London publishing houses. The academic side of Blackwell's was a venture that was to go on bearing useful fruit. It included coups of the magnitude of the one pulled off by Henry Schollick, when he had the foresight to secure the world rights for the posthumous publication of the works of Ludwig Wittgenstein[293]. For Basil Blackwell this, he recalled, 'went hand in glove with our main bookshop activity in serving the needs of scholars and scholarly librarians the world over'[294].

Such a ready market of authors and students had existed from the early days at Blackwell's when former Oxford graduates went out to serve as professors, lecturers and librarians and, remembering their happy times at Blackwell's, relied on the connection to furnish their needs in books. Earlier the series of Rhodes scholars started coming to Oxford, and they too had carried back, especially to the United States, 'an affection for The Firm which expressed itself in their seeking to obtain from us their needs in books'[295]. And so began a long and happy connection between Blackwell's and the academic world in America, a link which is still as strong today.

Tied and committed as he was to Oxford, Basil Blackwell claimed that his own contribution to the publishing world was relatively modest in scope. The great names may have forsaken him, but none the less he had established his own place in the market. The area he marked out for his own may have been limited by the dictates of geography, but it neither diminished his ardour as a publisher nor his support for writers in need of a publisher. One of the most moving examples of Basil's own writing describes the visit of a poor (and in fact dying) man, who cycled over from Swindon with a manuscript of Oriental tales in translation. The story of Alfred Williams, and that of Edith Barfoot elsewhere, typifies the approach that Basil, and his father, took to 'publishing':

'Some years ago there reached me through the post a typescript on thin green paper, bearing the impress of a hard-worn typewriter. The accompanying letter stated that the work was a translation from the Sanskrit, that the Professor of Sanskrit at Oxford had written an introduction, and that if we should decide to publish the book and thought that pictures might be able to add to its attractions, a certain young artist might be able to make them for us. The letter was signed Alfred Williams. The translator's preface showed that Alfred Williams could write English. The Professor's introduction testified to his scholarship. The address typed on the letter gave the name of a village near Swindon, and the best course seemed to be to invite Alfred Williams to come over to Oxford and discuss the matter. He replied that he would be happy to come, and on the appointed day he arrived punctually, a man seemingly in his fifties and with a charming smile. As soon as he entered my room I was aware that I was in the presence of a rare spirit, but being slow, and often wrong, in my estimate of men, I could not tell what lay behind the serenity, the cheerfulness and the gentleness which both his face and his manner revealed. Our discussion raised no difficulties. He would revise his typescript according to my suggestions, and bring it to Oxford again in a week or two to meet the artist in my room, and to complete the preliminary plans for publication.

He courteously excused himself from lunching with me, for he was anxious to be getting home. When was his train? He had bicycled. I thought that a meal between two rides of twenty-seven miles could hardly be amiss, but let it go at that, and proposed a day for the next meeting. A look of pain came into his eye as he asked me, very gently, if the day after would be equally convenient, for his wife had just undergone a very serious operation of doubtful value, and the day I had offered was that on which he was to bring her home from Swindon hospital. So "the day after," and the hour of 2.30 was agreed, and Alfred Williams went his way. At noon of the day appointed came a telegram: "Alfred Williams died in his sleep yesterday." It was signed by a name unknown to me, and there was no address. Two or three days later I was asked if I would see someone who "wanted to tell me about Alfred Williams"; and there entered my room the man (as I soon learned) who had sent the telegram. He was stone-blind. He told me that he had been Alfred Williams's closest friend, and that he felt I ought to be told the whole story. He felt it was due to his friend and due to me, and as he sat before me with the strange stillness and slow speech of the blind, this honest man spoke words that made my ears tingle. "Heart failure?" I supposed. "Well, that's what the doctor said, but I'm afraid it was starvation . . . that and bicycling into Swindon every day, and then that hill up to the hospital to see his wife. You see, we found his bank book, and since Christmas he has spent only twenty-six pounds (it was then late June), and there was little left.

Even so Alfred Williams had saved a bit, for we found in a drawer a pound note pinned to a bit of paper on which he had written 'for port-wine for Mary'; and I fancy he was starving himself to give her comforts in hospital. "And she? Was her operation successful?" It was a forlorn hope. It's a cancer, you see, and she can't last long. She had been looking forward to coming home, and her husband had promised to come for her early on Friday. She was sitting at the window looking out for him when the news came to the hospital that he had been found dead in his bed. They did not know how to tell her, and she sat there waiting and waiting . . . Now she's home, and so near gone that, when I sit by her bed, sometimes I strain my ears to hear if she is still breathing, and can't hear a sound; and I'll say gently, 'Are you there, Mary?' and she'll whisper, 'Yes, Harry.' And so, bit by bit, came out the story of Alfred Williams and his wife Mary; how a country boy, like Jude the Obscure, he was set to work in the fields, but his thirst for learning drove him to the town of Swindon, where after the day's shift in the Railway Works, he taught himself Latin and Greek (and not only after the day's shift, for he used to chalk on the frame of the steam hammer which he tended the characters of the Greek alphabet, that he might learn them while he worked); how he began to write poems, which being published won him some fame as 'The Hammerman Poet'; and so, leaving his forge, he devoted himself to Literature, helped and encouraged by the village girl he married; how they set up their house literally, by taking bricks out of a lock in the derelict Berks and Wilts Canal, and using them to build with their own hands the house where they lived almost unknown to their neighbours, but sufficient unto themselves, he for Letters only, she for Letters in him'.

But the sales of poetry even before The Great War were small, and even with the help of articles and lectures, can have provided but a stepmotherly portion to this devoted couple. In 1916 Alfred Williams, being near, if not beyond, the age limit, volunteered for military service, and after a rejection on grounds of poor health, succeeded in enlisting as a gunner. He was drafted to India, where he began to explore the great literatures of the East and to teach himself Sanskrit. On his return to England he pursued his studies, and out of them had come the Translations which he had offered me. 'They thought a lot of him in London,' said the blind man, 'and only last week (the last time he was with me) he told me that the Prime Minister had written to tell him that it had been decided to grant him a Civil List Pension and sent him a cheque for £50 to carry him on for the present. But I fancy he knew what was coming for him, for he came over to me and gripped the arms of my chair so hard that I felt them tremble, and said, "Harry, it's too late."' He had learnt by then that his wife's case was hopeless. And now his wife's one care was that his Sanskrit books, the great Lexicon, Grammars, etc., should be given to the University Library. Could I help her there? I asked if it would be a comfort if I went to see her ('It would indeed'), and arranged to meet the blind man at the house in South Marston a day or two later.

I found the little house built with their own hands, and entered the sitting-room. Small, clean, furnished with the bare needs for sitting at table for food or work, austere as a cell, it contained Alfred Williams' books. They stood on a small desk by the window, eight or ten books, the nucleus of a Sanskrit scholar's working library. There were no other books to be seen; and it was manifest that to equip himself with these costly volumes he had sacrificed all his Greek and Latin and English books. I went upstairs. The bedroom was as bare as the room below. In the bed, the clothes pulled up to her chin, lay the dying woman. The ivory skin was drawn tight on her face, and her neck was wasted almost to the bone. Only her eyes moved. Beside the bed sat the blind man, and between them on the floor was a case containing all Mary Williams's earthly treasure. I was asked to open it, and there was the revised typescript which Alfred Williams had promised to bring to Oxford. There was nothing else in the case save discarded sheets of the same work. It was all of a piece with the sense of finality which possessed that house.

Mary William's first care was for the Sanskrit books, and I promised to see that they were well bestowed. We then spoke about the typescript, briefly, for it was clear that words were costly in that room, and I said I would lose no time in producing the book. We had spoken simply and with a kind of unearthly serenity about the books and the typescript, but as I took my leave I felt that I must tell Mary Williams that I should always remember gratefully my meeting with her husband, for he was one of those who left you a better man than he found you.

Like summer tempest came her tears.

'One of the best,' she whispered.

I left the house and drove home on that summer afternoon with that sense of awe which once or twice in a lifetime takes a man, when, for a moment, and without desert, he is caught up in the high triumph of one of the rare spirits of mankind'.

Basil's philosophy of publishing was inspired by idealism, but it was also tempered with business shrewdness. Although, he argued, 'the idea is of the first importance, it must be right and apt to the time'. All these elements of his philosophy underpin the richness, quality and variety of the Blackwell imprints. In his first Dent Memorial Lecture, in 1930, Basil Blackwell attempted to define the labyrinthine 'art' of publishing. 'The publisher', he outlined, 'peculiarly needs to be equipped with the qualities of idealism and shrewdness. He must recognize literary merit—more, he must discover it—he must have a flair—he must anticipate by just the right narrow margin the changing tastes and interests of the reading public (and in that sense he must have something of the journalist about him)—he must lead while seeming to follow. One lobe of his brain must be devoted to literature, scholarship and art; the other to adroit bargaining—bargaining with author or his agent, with printer, with paper-maker, with bookseller, with publicity agents, and not uncommonly, with other publishers'. He expanded his thesis: 'The publisher is open to criticism if he does not make and maintain personal contact with as many booksellers as possible; for booksellers are his points of contact with the public.... Booksellers are always ready to give advice ... and their advice is seldom wide of the mark; for they are tutored daily by the public we all seek to please'[296].

But what of the unsung of the publishing world—the authors whose manuscripts are rejected? What art form did Sir Basil advocate for dealing with this most painful of duties? As in most things, Basil Blackwell was never at a loss for words or ideas. When a refusal, not 'rejection', was called for, he had as his model the obsequious formula of a Chinese firm, as reported years ago by a Hong Kong correspondent of the *Central News*: 'We read your manuscript with boundless delight. By the sacred ashes of our ancestors, we swear that we have never dipped into a book of such overwhelming mastery. If we were to publish this book it would be impossible in the future to issue any book of a lower standard. As it is unthinkable that within the next 10,000 years we shall find its equal, we are, to our great regret, compelled to return this divine work, and beg you a thousand times to forgive our action.' No doubt in practice, Basil had his own inimitable way of letting people down lightly. For his part, Basil, too, had to adjust his sights. For just over a decade, he had indulged his love of publishing. But his publishing adventures were, to some extent, to be curtailed by the death of his father in 1924.

Chapter 5
The Gaffer
A man should serve the trade by which he lives[297]

Basil Henry: the third B H Blackwell 1889–1984

John Newsom rose to his feet and called on the assembled company to 'drink the health of the Gaffer!' Recalling the occasion in his eighties, Basil reflected on this impudence from which he had never recovered

At his father's death in 1924 Basil Blackwell inherited the family business, taking over immediately as chairman. Despite the period of mourning, it was business as usual. The Board met the very next week and appointed Basil Blackwell to the chair, not giving a thought to any other role for B H Blackwell the Third[298]. Serving his father's trade was a role for which Basil had been prepared. He had had seven years of 'apprenticeship' in the firm, and 'since the formation of Blackwell's as a Limited Company', he wrote, 'I have been seeking to prepare myself'. Yet although the wind was set fair, the transition from publishing to managing all aspects of a busy bookshop was not as easy for Basil Blackwell as it was generally supposed. Later in life Basil Blackwell reflected on his early days as chairman. 'Hitherto in my ambition for some individual achievement in the book world I had spoken, understood and thought mainly as a publisher. Now, having already established the independent firm of Basil Blackwell and Mott, with the imprint: Basil Blackwell, Oxford. . . . I had to give half my mind to bookselling affairs, in the conduct of the business and in the public affairs of the book trade fulfilling the dictum of that great and good man and mine own familiar friend, David Roy: "A man should serve the Trade by which he lives"'[299]. Whatever ambivalence Basil may have felt at 'the cardinal change in my business life' he accepted, relished even, his lot. Basil Blackwell never looked back with regret at the turn of events, which tied him irrevocably to Oxford. 'Compared with the excitements of publishing', he wrote, 'the task appeared to be simple: I was in charge of a well-trained crew'.

Basil was not alone at the top. His father's helmsmen, Basil's fellow directors, remained to guard the well-established traditions of 'Mr Blackwell's' and to keep the daily show on the road. They were well aware of Basil's ideas for innovation and change: they had peppered the deliberations of the Board, at their weekly meetings. Basil's enthusiasm had been a perfect foil for his father's caution, which had increased in his later years. His was a mind fresh from university, and the London publishing scene. While Basil proposed, and the board considered, his father had not been disposed to take any precipitate action. Although the guiding spirit of his father still prevailed, Basil was now master in his own house, and he looked ahead to further adventures. He had good grounds for optimism. The family firm, in the mid-twenties, was in fine fettle; despite the aftermath of the First World War, and the gathering gloom of depression hanging over the manufacturing sectors, Blackwell's was able to continue without facing financial hardship. Basil, taking his cue from his father, attributed Blackwell's continued success to 'Oxford not being a manufacturing town', and an oblique reference was made to the unlikelihood of any industrial action[300]. But Basil, like his father, also knew that the continued success of Blackwell's was vested in its staff. 'We must attribute the general advance of the firm', he wrote, 'to the excellence of the staff, whose members combine so happily a team spirit with pride each in his individual department'[301]. Basil's older colleagues had known him from infancy, and his early life had been centred on his father's shop. Basil felt comfortable there, and his staff felt comfortable with him. He also found common cause with them. Despite not having started from positions of privilege, but working so close to books, they exuded a scholarly air that coincided with his own. Basil knew he relied on them for the everyday management of the firm, but he also recognized the potential of others who had joined the firm more recently: 'every novice had a director's fountain pen in his pocket' he observed. These new recruits, even if 'their heads were empty at fifteen', were soon to have them filled up by those who knew their trade from the bottom up[302]. And there were to be no exceptions: learning the trade from the bottom up was a maxim to be applied to Basil's sons and grandsons, when they later joined the firm.

Trusting in the company, and good judgement, of his own highly trained craftsmen and tradesmen, it only remained for Basil 'to keep on course with a light hand on the wheel' and to 'be prepared to sail beyond the sunset'[303]. Well on course, Basil Blackwell dreamt a little and reflected on bookselling as a trade. His ideal, however, is one that is increasingly difficult to recognize today. In his day, it combined the roles of bookselling and publishing, even those of literary agent. 'A bookseller, and particularly a university bookseller', he wrote of this eclectic of occupations, 'lives with his mental vision dazzled by a dome of many-coloured glass in the illumination of a host of different disciplines. On every hand, on every shelf, his eye encounters books which in Milton's words "do preserve as in a vial the purest efficacy and extraction of that living intellect that bred them", some yet to prove their worth, others by the spontaneous acclaim of generations of readers established as classics.... He surveys at once the garnered wisdom of the centuries and the latest tidings from Pioneers, like Wordsworth's Newton, "voyaging through strange seas of thought, alone". He watches the advance of new disciplines, the persistence of the old; he harbours all, touches many, but grasps none. He is essentially *a sciolist*; but he meets and talks with learned men who are masters of their subjects'[304]. If this mindset conditioned Basil's idealized view of his trade, it did not stay his hand when it came to making changes. When the third B H Blackwell took over the helm, in the turmoil and excitement of the 20s and the 30s, he oversaw what he called 'a challenging time'.

The book and publishing trades, whether Basil liked it or not, were changing rapidly, and the social and economic problems of the period were not without their impact. Basil Blackwell recorded that 'the period was a stirring time in the re-organization of the book trade'. His world was being redefined. 'Under the impulse of Stanley Unwin ... the institution of The Society of Bookmen (Hugh Walpole's invention) and the founding of the National Book Council (Unwin the begetter)', he wrote, there began 'a new era in the relations between publishers and booksellers'. Basil's own species was not yet totally obsolete: 'one with a foot in each camp (as Basil Blackwell had had) was deemed to have something useful to contribute'[305]. And having a foot in both camps kept Basil on his mettle, was put to good account in the development of Blackwell's publishing side, and gave him a chance to catch up with his old cronies, now useful business contacts, from his own publishing days in London. In return he reaped the reward of 'many precious friendships' and received the collective 'wisdom' of the book and publishing trade. Basil had a vision, and a flexibility, which could encompass developments in both sides of the trade: publishing and bookselling. These were the talents that started to mark him out in the trade, far beyond the Broad Street shop. On home ground, he was now very much the Gaffer, and not only at home it would seem! Within six years of taking over from his father, when Basil was still in his thirties, he was becoming known affectionately as 'The Gaffer'. This was not a sobriquet usually associated with youth, and not one that had been applied to the second B H Blackwell. Basil's father was always known as 'Mr Blackwell', but not, Basil insisted 'out of dread'. The public appropriation of 'The Gaffer' came via John Newsom (the famous educationalist and author of the Newsom Report), who had been a close student friend of Basil's. Basil conceded that although the term was not unknown, its usage was restricted to a few of his staff. Then the cat was well and truly let out of the bag when Basil rashly invited John Newsom to be his guest at the Annual Bookseller's Association dinner in Newcastle, in 1935. Ignoring convention, and the fact that he had not been asked to speak; Newsom rose to his feet and called on the assembled company to 'drink the health of the Gaffer!' Recalling the occasion in his eighties, Basil reflected on this impudence from which he had never recovered[306].

Blackwell's young Gaffer was in his element, and drew great personal pleasure in being able to preside over an enterprise where he maintained close personal contact with all his staff. His was a thoroughly modern 'open-style' of management, where there was little room for hierarchy and where all apprentices 'had director's pens in their pockets'; they had every chance to end up on the Board. His father had drawn his managerial colleagues from the 'floor', and this tradition continued. In 1969, when Richard Blackwell took over as chairman, there were no less than five former apprentices serving as directors. In the thirties, managing the shop in Oxford was a less formal affair than later, when as Blackwell's grew in size, the 'Thursday director's meetings', began to be attended by what Basil described as 'a formidable body of executives'. For the first twenty or so years of 'life under the Gaffer', these weekly management meetings could not have been more different. The Gaffer was assisted in his deliberations by what he called 'the triumvirate', that is by Hanks, Hunt and Field, and from 1938 they were joined by Henry Shollick. He described these 'meetings' as 'quiet hours of fellowship, coursing the ship and charting new courses'. Basil Blackwell always feared that the business would grow too large to keep this human touch. But in his heyday, he had nothing to fear. His was a gentle and humorous style, which impressed even those observers who hailed from across the world. A Chicago journal, entitled *Drake a Day*, interviewed Basil Blackwell on a visit to Oxford in 1925. Basil, insisting on walking slowly up the stairs and taking everything in his stride, mischievously remarked that the Americans had a penchant for speed: 'to rush upstairs instanter'. 'What', he enquired, 'becomes of all the time you save?'

But for Basil, the luxuries of life at the top of his own, more gentle and comfortable, apex brought with it the responsibilities of the future. Thus after a decade of leadership, Basil presided over a re-structuring of Blackwell's. On the bookselling side Basil clearly felt that there was a need to move with the times, and that 'some modernisation of methods and some extension of the buildings' were called for. Oxford passers-by watched in consternation as the re-building programme at nos. 48–49 Broad Street, and the inclusion of the newly acquired nos. 50–51, commenced. He also had to face the reluctance of the local bank, when the then Chairman of Barclay's Bank, Mr John Thompson expressed his doubts about lending money to 'buy an old house' (50–51 Broad Street). The manager even went so far as to raise doubts about the ability of Blackwell's to survive: 'Well, Mr Blackwell', he demanded, 'and are you capturing enough of your rivals' trade?' Basil responded adamantly: 'I believe there is enough for all'[307]. But neither the book-browsing public or the conservative banker needed to have worried.

The Gaffer was resolute that the changes taking place were to be limited solely to the physical structure of Blackwell's, as he hastened to reassure his customers. 'Of late', he explained, 'we have been hard put to house a business which has been growing in volume and in scope. One after another every room had been occupied by books or the apparatus necessary for modern business, until we had reached a stage of development unknown since the earliest days of the shop; where its area was no more than the ground floor of 50 Broad Street, and if more than four customers were within, the apprentice had to stay without. . . . We feel safe in promising that the sprit of the shop will be unchanged, for that spirit is derived more from our customers than ourselves; and whether they write to us from regions near or far, or visit us for the immediate supply of their needs or to spend their time browsing undisturbed (and these last we now thank for their patience during the past difficult months, when we have had perforce to play hide-and-seek with the stock), our care will be to deserve that graceful tribute paid to us on a recent, and we hope not privileged, occasion, when a master of felicitous phrase referred to Blackwell's as "surely one of the most pleasant of the unofficial departments of the university" '[308].

In the publishing arena there were corresponding developments, with diversification into binding, in 1938. Subsequently the four small binderies, acquired by Blackwell's, were amalgamated after the Second World War into the Kemp. Later, in 1954, Basil encountered the same doubts about the future of his firm when he introduced another stage of modernisation, to be reiterated yet again when his new hidden empire, the Norrington Room—the brainchild of his son, Julian, was revealed. Whatever his private worries, Basil asserted that these developments no way compromised the atmosphere of Blackwell's—and in any case they could not, from the outside, be seen[309]. Sir Basil maintained that none of the alterations and acquisitions that he had overseen, compromised or changed 'the sound business principles upon which the firm was built'. And of these sound work principles, it was the philosophy of service that remained paramount[310]. Like his father, Basil Blackwell led from the front; he worked long hours, and his staff, never to be found in the shop later than 8.15am, would find him already at his desk. And the Gaffer's pattern persisted even as his firm continued to grow in size.

Throughout his life, and continuing when Basil took a relatively back seat on giving up the Chairmanship of Blackwell's in May 1969 at the age of eighty to become life president of Blackwell's, the ethos of personal service and 'slow time' pervaded the firm's atmosphere. And the firm's reputation of caring for its customers remained intact. From the first, Blackwell's philosophy had been one of 'benign neglect'. Now, as in the past, Blackwell's customers were left alone to meet their friends and to browse at leisure, free of any obvious enticements to make a purchase. As if by osmosis, the right book would often fall into the right hands or an old hand would find something he had never seen before[311]. When making a complaint, the customer would as often as not find wrath deflected by the personal attentions of the Gaffer himself. That is not to say that the Gaffer was ever obsequious. He did not subscribe to the view that the customer is always right, rather he emphasized their rights to impeccable service, explanation and apology. His letters of explanation or apology to customers 'were often masterpieces for he had a marvellous style, clear and concise, with a great economy of words, a genius for the *mot juste*, the appropriate reference, and always with a delightful sense of humour'[312].

Nor was his concern for people limited solely to his clients, the book buying public. Sir Basil demonstrated his deep commitment to the 'human touch', staying in direct contact with his staff. 'Blackwellians', as he called them, knew their Gaffer as a man of habit and ritual, whether on the daily round or to mark the festivals of the calendar, and this predictability was reassuring in their community. Every morning, after the post had been opened by his secretary and several helpers at 7.30am, (the shop opened at 9.00), the Gaffer would read it and then distribute the contents to the various departments 'always accompanied by one of the attractive young ladies on the staff'. 'He would bring us post-girls beautiful rosebuds that he had picked from his garden that morning and we'd pin them to our dresses'. 'Every Christmas, after our usual office party, we would all line up in the main shop to shake Sir Basil's hand after he'd thanked us for all we'd done during the past year, and he would give us a crisp new £1 note' (a little ceremony that went on throughout Sir Basil's time even though the value of the pound became symbolic rather than real)[313].

If this image of the Gaffer, metaphorically patting his workers on the head, smacked of paternalism—a dirty word in the modern commercial world—then he was unashamed. During an interview he tartly informed his audience 'I am prepared to stand on the Day of Judgement and say it (paternalism) was effective'. It depended, he explained, on 'mutual loyalty'. 'Most of our staff who built up the business had a loyalty to my father and later to me, as we had to them'[314]. In fact the Gaffer had no thoughts of his staff as menials, rather they were later day archimandrites, superintendents of their own endeavours 'a sort of society of men contributing to the cause of learning, even if they only packed books, transcribed addresses and records, or placed books on shelves'[315]. The Gaffer owned up to finding himself a little pompous at times[316]. Even if it was a brand of benign paternalism, the Gaffer's brand of the 'human touch' was legendary, as well as successful.

The late Hugh Williamson, publisher and printer, recalled that throughout the seventy years of his working life at Blackwell's, the Gaffer always had time for new friends in his workplace, be they clients, staff, potential customers or authors. Added to which, many of his former staff have recorded the warmth with which they were received when they joined the firm, in whatever capacity. Somehow he managed to convey the impression that he had time to listen, despite the obvious presence of files and typescripts that had to be attended to. Williamson describes the typical scene: 'Up would go both arms in cheerful welcome, paper work would be set aside for the moment, and there was always something more to be said, even if it would have to wait until another day'[317].

Although renowned as something of a gentle soul, Basil had his own style when it came to taking a stand. A cycle of reminders, taking over a year, was dispatched to those whose bills had not been paid. Even so, a face-to-face confession with the Gaffer, in his upstairs office, would often result in yet more time being granted. The postscript on the Gaffer's final dunning letter summed up his attitude. It took the form of an apocryphal dialogue between Socrates and a friend. 'How then Socrates', the friend would ask, 'shall we recognize the truly just and generous man?' 'It is he,' Socrates replied, 'who, being reminded of an obligation, is able gracefully to thank his creditor for prompting him to do his duty'[318]. And its authenticity was never doubted! Although gentle chiding was his more usual form, if needs be, he could be made of sterner stuff. This less well-known side of the Gaffer was occasioned by an uncharacteristically combative bout with a famous writer, who, in Basil's opinion, had perpetrated a deceit. The Gaffer's opening letter, October 23 1934, was more of an invitation than an indictment. It read, from Sir Basil's copy:

> 'Dear Mr Shaw,
>
> When Constable and Co. published *The Complete Plays of Bernard Shaw* at 12s 6d net, they assured the trade that there would be no reprint. This statement was freely used by booksellers in selling the book to their customers.
>
> The publication of *The Complete Plays*, by Odhams Press for sale solely to subscribers of the *Daily Herald* (at 3s 9d plus six tokens) has placed those booksellers in the unfortunate position of having deceived the public.
>
> It must be admitted that the new edition differs from the "Complete Edition" in containing three more plays (though this is small consolation to the original purchasers!); but apart from these extra pages and the WARNING FROM THE AUTHOR, apparently the new edition is in fact a reprint from the plates of the Constable's edition. I can hardly suppose that Constable gave the booksellers their assurance without your consent. It would help those booksellers (already sufficiently penalised) who are charged by their customers with a breach of faith, if you could arm them with a statement exonerating them from complicity.'

Bernard Shaw would have none of Basil Blackwell's polite wheedling. He responded, 25 October 1934, like a hornet:

> 'Dear Mr Blackwell,
>
> In future, when a customer asks for a book of mine, say "Thanks very much," wrap the book up nicely in paper for him (or her), take the money, give the change, say "Thanks very much" all over again, and bow the customer out.
>
> If, out of pure gratuitous incompetance, you prefer to enter into conversation and give unsolicited assurances, of an obviously idiotic character, about my business intentions, you do it at your own risk; and if it turns out subsequently that I never had any such intentions, you will have to exonerate yourself as best you can. I have given Constable a letter to the effect that they took no part in the *Daily Herald* transaction except to oppose it with all their might. I can do nothing for the booksellers but to tell them not to be childish.
>
> In America I have lately had two copies from 50,000 copies of each from Book Clubs, to be given away to their members *for nothing*, as a bonus. Of course I accepted both. I am looking forward to an order

from Woolworths for a six-penny edition. Would you, Basil, refuse any business if it came your way?

And have you no bowels of compassion for the millions of your fellow-countrymen who can no more afford a twelve and six-penny book than a trip round the world. You should see some of their letters. I am really surprised at you. When we met at Bumpus's, you seemed quite an intelligent youth.

Faithfully etc.'[319]

Basil Blackwell let the snub go. His style was ever to avoid 'cross words' if at all possible. But he had doggedness down to a fine art. In the late fifties, a little difficulty with the Post Office showed him on good form. Change in the service, provided by that bastion of the State, had threatened the collection of Saturday's parcels from Blackwell's. The Gaffer's 'packers' worked on Saturday mornings, and he was determined that the fruits of their labour should be dispatched. 'He asked the Post Office several times, nicely, to collect the parcels', remembered his son Julian. 'Meeting with continued resistance, he adopted a different strategy. The next Saturday there was an urgent call for a collection, to the Oxford main depot, from the small Post Office on Broad Street. Somehow all the post boxes, within half a mile of Broad Street, had been filled by the start of the day. No one could post any letters. Added to which, ten sacks of parcels were blocking the entrance of the little post office, and the counter hand had received a call, from Blackwell's, to say that ten more were on their way. Duly the Post Office collected the parcels, and the Gaffer was merely heard to observe: "not a cross word passed between us"'[320]. Such a style of business management may have deceived the outsider into thinking the Gaffer was a relic from a by-gone age. An article in the *New Yorker*, in 1964, described Sir Basil as a man who 'lives and behaves and even sells books as though he were under an injunction laid down by the last will and testament of the departed century'[321]. But these rather 'old-fashioned' touches, however deeply meant and felt, reveal only one side of the Gaffer of an expanding enterprise[322].

It suited Basil to be hailed as someone 'who practised and held to the good traditions of the past'. In his wily way, he knew that this image was indispensable to Blackwell's: it was good for trade. Despite his highly individualist approach, Basil was firmly rooted in the present, and in his concern for the future of his business. If running a business, in the new commercial order of the post Second World War era, meant accepting the necessity of change, then change he must. Baulking at first, the Gaffer gained confidence from the advice of Will King, who had been recruited by his father and was the epitome of everything a good bookseller should be. This 'scholar-bookseller' had written to the Gaffer in 1950 that their kind were now an anachronism 'in this giddy age'. 'It was only in Victorian days,' he wrote, 'that a bookseller like the one depicted in Beatrice Harraden's novel *Ships that Pass in the Night* could ejaculate that as long as he had a shelf full of Gibbon and a box of snuff he was content'[323]. If the Gaffer was disquieted, the public never knew. While Blackwell's 'comfortable transformation' began, the customers in the shop were left undisturbed[324]. Ensuring their content was, after all, sound commercial sense. However important the human side was to Sir Basil, and however 'right' the customer or needy the author, he never lost sight of commercial imperatives. In considering a manuscript for publication he would ask himself 'Will the world be poorer if I do not publish this?' while hastily adding 'Will I be the poorer if I do?'[325].

Fear of being poor was something deeply imprinted on Basil's subconscious. Usually he was more than ready to take a risk if it would help a writer, poet, colleague or fellow tradesman. But when it came to the high finance of the sixties, and ever more expansion of the family business, Basil showed his origins. Much to the chagrin of his son, Richard Blackwell, he reverted to the attitudes of his Victorian father, who, with his very sober and penurious Victorian up-bringing, prevailed over a system of bookkeeping that bore no relation to the modern management of capital. This side of Basil led his wife, and his son, to insist that when it came to money, 'Basil had the mentality of a village grocer'. When Richard became chairman in 1969, Sir Basil could not readily accept the modern theory that money existed on paper, and that the proceeds for expansion could be created by merely adding a few noughts. He disliked the fact that financial management was making bookselling a 'scientific business' where 'every shelf must pay for itself'. 'This', he bemoaned 'is not my world'. Basil would sooner have had on his shelves books like *The Hand of Ethelberta*, surely, 'the most obscure and unsaleable of Thomas Hardy's novels; he had, at the time, eleven copies of this 'classic' in stock'[326]. Notwithstanding his love of books in their own right, he had always been frightened about finance: he was, reputedly, never known to draw out a full year's salary. He feared that the whole firm would collapse if he did. This mentality was not born of meanness; Basil Blackwell was noted for his generosity in dealing with others. If any in his field were in trouble, he would do what he could. When a rival firm, Dulau and Co, was threatened with liquidation, Basil moved quickly into the breach: 'It has been my good fortune to be able to invite Mr F W Chaundy, Chairman of Dulau and Co Ltd, to carry on under the same roof which covered him when, as an apprentice to my father, he started his career in the book trade sixty years ago. The House of Blackwell will do its best to make sure that the customers of Dulau shall not be the losers by the disaster which has overtaken that old and honourable firm'[327].

The Gaffer's generosity to his fellow booksellers, and his loathing of unfairness, did not start with Dulau. A few years before, the Gaffer had promised to shore up his old friend Charles Parker, of 'Parker's'. When Blackwell's opened in Broad Street, Parker's was the monarch of all that it surveyed, or at least a leading light in the rarefied company of real 'gentlemen booksellers'. Charles Parker came from an old, well-connected and very scholarly stable. His ancestor, Samuel Parker, Bishop of Oxford under James the Second, had founded the business. His grandson was put on the map in 1784, when Boswell recorded his visit to the Oxford shop. Several *cousins* later, Parker's was the mouthpiece for writers of the Oxford, or Tractarian, Movement. In the literary sense, the Movement had influenced the work of Basil's hero, William Morris. This alone would have been reason enough to offer assistance. Basil willingly promised Charles Parker 'to do his best if anything should happen to him'. In 1937, seven years after his friend's death, Basil was called on to fulfill his promise: he undertook to raise half the sum required to keep Parker's afloat, but the company kept its own identity and for the time being, Parker's and Blackwell's carried on in 'amiable competition'[328]. In 1939 Basil helped his other rivals, on the other side of the street, Joseph Thornton and Son, to resist the iconoclasm of Oxford's town planners. They wanted a face-lift. Everybody else, or so it seemed, wanted to stay their hand against this 'muses bower'. Miltonic sentiments prevailed: the House of Thornton's was spared. A decade earlier Basil had expedited another rescue; this time the hero was a distressed maiden. Always susceptible to womanly charm, Basil listened sympathetically to the entreaties of a granddaughter of the well-respected firm of booksellers in Bristol, William George and Sons. Her elderly father was unable to manage the firm; she was now its mainstay, but wanted to be free to marry. Marry her clergyman she did, and the name of George's was preserved, although Blackwell's was to assume responsibility for the conduct of the business.

Acutely aware of the trials of others, and particularly the difficulties of small booksellers, Basil Blackwell counted himself fortunate in steering a prosperous business that seemed to grow almost organically. Even during the Second World War there was no let up, either on the bookselling or the publishing side. On the 15 January 1941 Barclay's Bank, the Old Bank on the High, acknowledged the receipt of a definitive copy of the Blackwell's

Mailing List, as of 1 January 1941, deposited for safekeeping because of the threat of air raids[329].

BLACKWELL'S MAILING LIST 1 JANUARY 1941

Colleges and Institutions in Oxford University	88
Libraries & Institutions in Canada & USA	751
Libraries & Institutions in British Isles	1713
Libraries & Institutions in British Empire (except Canada)	417
Libraries & Institutions in Neutral & Non-Belligerent Countries in Europe	51
Libraries & Institutions in Countries outside Europe (except British Empire & USA)	111
Individuals in Oxford & District	812
Individuals in Canada & the USA	4430
Individuals in British Isles	9040
Individuals in British Empire (except Canada)	1739
Individuals in Neutral & Non-Belligerent countries in Europe	63
Individuals in Countries outside Europe (except British Empire & the USA)	473
Newspapers & Magazines who 'review' catalogues in Literary columns, in British Empire, British Isles & the USA	48
Members of the Book Trade in the British Isles & Neutral and Non-Belligerent countries in Europe	294
Members of the Book Trade in the British Empire, the USA and other countries outside Europe	187
Addresses of Libraries & Individuals held in abeyance for various reasons, in British Empire, the USA, and other countries outside Europe	259
Addresses of Individuals in British Isles, held in obeyance for various reasons, chiefly through being on Active Service, or request for catalogues to be withheld during War for reasons of paper economy	637
Addresses of Libraries & Individuals in Italy	168
Addresses of Libraries & Individuals in Belgium	105
Addresses of Libraries & Individuals in Holland	305
Addresses of Libraries & Individuals in Denmark, Norway & the Baltic States	87
Addresses of Libraries & Individuals in France, Switzerland & Rumania	392
Addresses of Libraries & Individuals in French Colonial Empire	29
Addresses of Libraries & Individuals in Germany, Poland & Czechoslovakia	281
Total	22,480

A decade later, under the Gaffer's direction, the size and scale of Blackwell's growth was unprecedented in the bookselling business. A Mervyn Davies, a journalist from America returning to his old haunts and finding Blackwell's to be three times its former size, sought an explanation of this growth and the unprecedented increase in the sale of books. All that he could extract from the Gaffer was a modest attribution of the expansion to the war. 'People',

Basil Blackwell reasoned, 'had woken up to the fact that the war might have taken from them their own heritage'. 'As a result', he argued, 'people developed an entirely new and avid interest in reading books about art and architecture and the English countryside generally, as well as English novelists like Trollope'[330]. This romantic view of success was none the less tempered with an acute awareness of the advantages brought to the organization by the more invisible hand of sound financial management. This had been a tradition established by Benjamin Henry Blackwell, who saved up for his stock, before he opened the shop, and later shared with Harry Critchley, a founding director of B H Blackwell Ltd. John Critchley took over from his father as the firm's financial and legal advisor, assisted by the sagacious C A 'Uncle' Palmer, who Basil described as the 'conscience of the firm'. Palmer subsequently became company secretary, and George Wareham, who had come from Cambridge University Press, replaced him as chief accountant. These financial wizards brought the family business into the present, but they were Blackwellians through and through. Despite the complexities of modern business, they remained true to the firm's original ethos: retaining profits in the firm, shunning extravagance and resisting the pull of outside capital. Of their wisdom, the Gaffer was in no doubt. But without the work of the front line, the booksellers in the shop, they would have had nothing to account.

Sir Basil paid many tributes to the debt he owed: 'for the work and achievement of these good men'. Among these was his most senior 'in-house trustee': Fred Hanks, his father's second apprentice, who had started at Blackwell's in 1883. His was the hand that had literally 'rocked the cradle' of the infant Basil. Father Fred Hanks had shared an enthusiasm for the classics with Benjamin Henry, and to his delight his young charge grew to be another initiate. Under his guiding hand, Blackwell's recruits were exposed to the secrets of the Ancients; he had written his own introduction to the subject entitled: *On the Handling of Classical Books*. With the help of this 'classical catalogue', the greenest junior could be trusted to order lists of Greek and Latin classics. Teacher and scholar, he did not go unrewarded. Ten years into Sir Basil's time as Gaffer, Father Hanks was honoured by the University, with an MA, *honoris causa*, and Blackwell's with the accompanying title: 'one of the most pleasant of its (the Universities) unofficial departments[331]. As the classics were to Father Hanks, so were new books to Will Hunt. When Basil Blackwell became the Gaffer, he looked exclusively to Will Hunt, known affectionately as the 'Rhino', for advice in this field. Like Fred Hanks, he was another of Benjamin Henry's apprentice-directors, but his span was not to be as long; he died of cancer in 1938. Publisher's representatives up and down the country missed the sight of this Blackwell senior, who was always gravely attired in morning dress to receive them. Basil was devastated by the loss. He penned a tribute, published in *The Bookseller*, where he tried to spell out the debt he owed:

> 'Oh loyal heart farewell!
> How much I dare not tell
> Of me is lost with you . . .
> . . . So, for all the thanks I gave
> In life, still at your grave
> Your debtor I—
> You taught me how to die.'

These two loyal Blackwellians, Fred Hanks and Will Hunt, together with Charles Field, Benjamin Henry's second chief cashier, were the three founding directors of the newly incorporated Blackwell's, who had sat with Basil alongside his father in 1920. Other Benjamin Henry 'boys' became prominent in the organization during the Gaffer's time. Geoffrey Barfoot, appointed as an office boy in 1912, Edgar Hine, an apprentice from 1917, Fred Stevens, an ex-army boy who came to Blackwell's back room in 1920, who was instrumental in founding the firm's famous Periodicals Department, and George Bunting, who joined as the post boy in 1925, were all later to be appointed to the Gaffer's board of directors. As different as chalk and cheese, they were devoted to Blackwell's, and to keeping the young Gaffer on the right track. There must have been high jinks at the Gaffer's Thursday meeting, especially should the dreaded phrase 'modernisation' come up. The actual details of these lively councils have not come to light. They were locked up at the time and labelled 'Personal Property of Mr Basil'. But George Bunting was known for his Luddite tendencies. He regarded any labour-saving device, or labour-saving method, as indicative of a lack of moral fibre, and not very privately, the Gaffer, at least, agreed with him. A portrait of the busy life they subsequently shared together, in Broad Street, is preserved; left behind in Muirhead Bone's pastel of the shop's interior, circa 1950. There for the entire world to see, at the Royal Academy exhibition of 1950, was a day in the life of the Broad Street shop and its inmates. In the maelstrom, the Gaffer espied at least one of his stalwarts behind the Blackwell's counter: the earnest face of Edgar Hine.

Edgar Hine was singled out by the Gaffer as 'one who informed the spirit of the serving staff'[332]. He could have informed, and enthralled, us with a *Peacock Pie* of the coming and goings in Broad Street. Conspicuous, at the time, were the retired Prime Minister Asquith, the then Poet Laureate,

Robert Bridges, John Buchan and Walter de la Mare. Edmund Blunden's presence would have served to remind Hine of the luck Blackwell's had had in surviving *After the Bombing*. In his mind's eye, he could recall the Blackwell's devotees of the war years: J B Priestley and W B Yeats. Duller moments could have been relieved by fantasy, prompted by the sight of J R R Tolkien, taking a short break, in Blackwell's, from Merton and mythology. Hard on his heels came Robert Graves, brewing his own version of the Greek and Hebrew myths. Summoned back from his day dreams by Bells, Hine was to observe the unfolding of the next generation of literary giants such as the Poet Laureate of the seventies: John Betjeman. For his part, Betjeman declared that he had learnt more among the second hand shelves at Blackwell's, than at Marlborough or Magdalen[333]. Alongside were the 1948 Nobel Prize winner, T S Eliot, Stephen Spender, C Day Lewis and W H Auden, accompanied, no doubt, by the likes of Christopher Isherwood, Louis MacNeice, William Empson, George Fraser, Angus Wilson and many more, without even beginning to record the famous Oxford scholars who, like Sir Basil's old Mods tutor, Professor Garrod of Merton, took their daily exercise perusing the Blackwell's shelves.

As others joined the firm, although not necessarily by the apprentice route, they, too, became witnesses to the changing academic and literary scene. And they also became 'pillars of the Blackwell House'[334]. Not only did they do much to ensure its commercial success, they were also scholars, albeit of the college of Blackwell. Edward East, for example, had come as an apprentice in 1923, the year before the death of Benjamin Henry, taking over from Blackwell's great antiquarian bookman, Will King, who had died in 1950. That 'King' of the antiquarian trade, according to Hugh Dyson, Fellow and Tutor in English at Merton, counted himself lucky for 'finding himself in one of the better colleges—the one called Blackwell's'. Hugh Dyson wrote that for Will (Rex) King, whose famous diaries were used by Basil Blackwell to write his many notes and speeches, the whole working world was a great university. His successor, Edward East, served as a freshman and became a senior fellow of the same university. When Edward East retired in 1973, his Gaffer paid tribute to him: 'Your mastery of book-lore is acclaimed by biographers and collectors in all parts of the English speaking world, and your integrity has won the confidence of learned libraries small and great from Bodley to Folger'. In the same year, he, too, received an Oxford MA, *honoris causa*.

To those who had arrived in his father's time, the Gaffer added his own prodigies. Hearing of a Cambridge-trained man, Frederick Dymond, from

Heffer's, which is now owned by Blackwell's, the Gaffer seized the opportunity to co-opt an expert to kick the newly created music department into life. Under the direction of Frederick Dymond, the music department became the largest and busiest of its kind in the United Kingdom. Others came to Blackwell's from different callings. Christopher Francis is a notable example. He had acquired a wide knowledge of theology while studying to take orders. Failing to find a religious vocation, he brought his knowledge to Blackwell's and, in 1952, went straight to Theology. Theology had become a backwater, and Christopher Francis breathed new life into its dusty stock. He was another cast in the scholarly mode, and he devised a new classification system for his comprehensive Theology catalogue, running to well over a hundred pages. His encyclopaedic knowledge of the subject was known to, and willingly made available to, theologians all over the world. In Oxford, the theologian Henry Chadwick, revered the name of this Blackwell scholar: 'For two decades, Christopher Francis has been integral not only to one of the greatest academic bookshops, but to the serious study of religion and theology in the world'[335]. His expert advice was given as readily to visiting Prime Ministers as it was to students. David Ben Gurion, the first Prime Minister of Israel, was an admirer, and a keen Platonist, and one of his visits caught the attention of the *New Statesmen*: 'In an age of barbarism it is a pleasant thought that anyone who penetrated to the back rooms of Blackwell's last week and spied a little white-haired man on the top of a step ladder would have seen a Prime Minister indulging his favourite vice'. His fame may have spread, but Christopher Francis was a true Blackwellian; he had no ambition outside of this literary house. He was rewarded with a vice-presidency of Blackwell's in 1980, and an MA, *honoris causa*, from the University. His crowning glory was the production of his own work of scholarship: the *Catalogue of Theology and Church History*, 1978.

This tradition, of scholarship, manqué or not, continues in many of the present Blackwell's shops, in other university towns and cities. Busy behind the scenes are would-be writers biding their time, just as Dorothy L Sayers had in the Gaffer's and his father's time. Departments are still run by specialists, some of whom joined the company in Sir Basil's day. He had lamented the passing of the old system of apprenticeship, which had given way to a more haphazard method of recruitment. None the less, the pattern was not dissimilar: new entrants were often those who wanted to advance their own education, 'sometimes', Sir Basil had explained, 'not being able to afford to go to university'. Now, in the twenty-first century, Blackwell's relies on students supplementing their fees, as well as authors and adult students in part-time education. Their interest in the society of other bookmen is no less avid than in Sir Basil's day. This society of 'bookmen' increasingly includes women, making the term an anachronism but one for which there was no easy linguistic substitute. He had witnessed this social revolution, beginning in earnest during the First World War, when the men were called-up. As the twentieth century progressed, women played an increasingly important role in this hitherto world of 'bookmen'. Even in his father's day, a few women had penetrated this male world. Dorothy L Sayers had been trained as an editorial assistant, and young women poets had been as confident as their male counterparts that Blackwell's would look sympathetically on their works; several Newdigate Prizes were awarded to women, and women edited and contributed to the various Poetry Series put out under the, earlier, B H Blackwell's imprint. Women writers, outside of the workplace, were one thing, but a woman working alongside men in the shop, or its offices, was, at least in the beginning, a bit more problematic; and the situation needed some getting used to. The Gaffer, later, recalled that the first young woman to work in the office, and to undertake secretarial duties for his father, 'had proved too upsetting for the male staff', and the second 'a discreet red-haired maiden who lived in the odour of sanctity', was claimed by the holier estate of matrimony. At the third attempt, his father had struck lucky. Maggie Warner earned her full title as the Chairman's Secretary, and a place in the Gaffer's memory.

The shortage of hands during the war years led the young Basil Blackwell to advise his father to actively recruit girls, as well as boys. When the young Gaffer took over, he, and his wife, cultivated relationships with local secondary schools, and judiciously indulged in a little talent, or rather potential, spotting. Later on, many of his much admired recruits came via this route, but in 1928 the new Gaffer found himself a young candidate, who became his 'peerless secretary of nearly forty years'. Miss Eleanor Halliday came from Milham Ford School; with the strong recommendation of a headmistress much admired by the Blackwell's, one Miss McCabe. Eleanor spent her first two years in the Foreign Department, only to be whisked away for higher things. Her first task as the Gaffer's secretary was to submit to his personal instruction in shorthand and typing. She never left this post until she died, prematurely in 1968, of lung cancer. At the time of her death, a journalist from *The Bookseller* was moved to comment on how he was brought to tears by the death of a woman he had never met. The Gaffer preserved her memory in a bequest to the library of Magdalen College School. Past tributes to the men of Blackwell's were now joined by the Gaffer's heart-felt acknow-

30 The Gaffer and his secretary, Eleanor Halliday.

ledgement that in going, his right hand woman, Eleanor Halliday, had taken with her 'half his competence'[336]. She had been the perfect link between the publishing and the bookselling side of Blackwell's, 'with her encyclopaedic knowledge of the affairs of both'[337]. Basil had been supported by supremely competent women, both at home and at work, yet he professed ignorance 'as to just how they could juggle so many things' and didn't accept that they should have an equal footing in the formal management structure of the firm. His secretary had reached the top of Blackwell's administrative ladder, but during his time there was a very heavily reinforced glass ceiling on the bookselling side.

Young male staff, recruited in the same way as women, straight from school, could, if they suited and applied themselves, be speedily promoted. Phil Brown, from Bicester School with a creditable spread of CSEs, recounts how he came in at the bottom, as all beginners in bookselling at Blackwell's did, in the WB (wants books) department, only to take charge of WB, under Edward East. Here he learnt the stock, as the old apprentices had under Benjamin Henry Blackwell. Within a year he was recruited to Rare Books. Nearly ten years before, Ken New had been the first trainee bookseller to be recruited under the new 'school-leaver' system. He may not have been an apprentice of the old school, but, he recalled, 'it made no difference'; 'my initial training, and accompanying sense of commitment, was the same as if I had been indentured'. Ken had been spotted at Oxford High, he had finished his 'O Levels', and he wanted to get into the work force, rather than stay in the sixth form and go to university. He had thought of librarianship as a career, and he reckoned Blackwell's would give him a good start. Ken started at Blackwell's in 1957, and he is still there. On his first day he was sent, as the apprentices always were, to be 'trained-up': distributing books around the shop and handling 'selected mail orders'.

Within fifteen years the employment scene changed radically, and women were to be found in the management structure. And the Gaffer, as he always remained, even though his son was now chairman or the 'Governor', had began to adjust to the mood of the sixties, and early seventies. Women were not only in the running for management, but they were being recruited as mature entrants, rather than straight from school; going back to work was becoming essential. Women needed to provide for themselves, or at least to supplement the family income[338]. A stickler for the old order of the working week, the Gaffer had to adjust to patterns of work that were better suited to working mothers: part-time and flexible hours. Whatever his misgivings, he was worried about women being out of the home; his grandmother had earned the family's living, but her workshop had been at home. He accepted that change was ineluctable, and he adjusted with the times. The present manager of the Norrington Room, Ann Day, started her career at Blackwell's, as a 'mature student'. Her children were of school age, and she was less than half as mature as her eighty-year-old employer.

Despite his misgivings, and his concern for working mothers, the new system brought pleasant surprises; several of his favourite early recruits returned. These, like his Secretary, Eleanor, had, in the sixties, been recruited straight from school to work on the administrative side. One of these recruits, Angela Melvin, currently taking early retirement, just short of her sixtieth birthday, recalled 'the halcyon days working for Blackwell's under the Gaffer's regime'[339]. 'The Gaffer', Angela urged, 'was a joy to work for'. She had counted herself privileged to work with someone so full of 'quips and jollity': 'he had a quotation, a story, and a joke for every occasion. His favourite tease of any raw recruit, she recollected, was 'do you know the difference between an elephant and a letter-box?' Put on the spot, and not wanting to appear incapable of deciphering the code of what must be a seminal test of potential, the initiates invariably replied 'they didn't'. Gleefully he would inform them: 'I won't give you a letter to post then'. On rare occasions when Angela had encountered his displeasure, she knew that she only had to play a waiting game: 'his bark was always worse than his bite'; any sharp rejoinder of 'What's this all about' was soon followed by a reassuring smile and the restoration of harmony. Typically, it was the Gaffer's idea of a joke to accuse Angela of 'being idle' 'because I was the opposite, or so he said'. Angela had been recruited by the ubiquitous 'Fuzzy', from the East Oxford School, having completed her Certificate of Secondary Education, and was soon 'noticed' by the Gaffer. When his secretary Eleanor died, he turned to Angela for secretarial support, until she was posted to Blackwell's Publishing as secretary to Jim Feather, who had taken over from Henry Schollick in 1971.

After taking a break when her son was born, Angela returned to the Blackwell fold. At the Gaffer's Ninetieth birthday party, he, as the oldest Blackwellian, stood alongside Angela who was holding her infant son: the youngest addition to the Blackwell 'family'. Being a member of the Blackwell family, Angela asserted, was meant literally. And there were regular excursions to the Gaffer's home at Appleton. Like his mother, the Gaffer had no

31 Angela Melvin with her son and Sir Basil—the oldest and the youngest of Blackwellians.

side, and, when it came to his staff, no snobbery. All his employees, and their own families, were welcomed as guests: 'they had access to the swimming hole and the squash courts and the children, of all ages, were fed on Christine Blackwell's delicious home-baked cakes'. 'Lady B', Angela recalled warmly, was as enthusiastically welcoming as her husband. On one occasion, Angela had rung to ask if she could bring a man to swim in the pool. Lady B responded without reservation with a 'bring as many as you like'! The Gaffer's wife, more of a friend, was proud of her beautiful garden and liked nothing better than to share it, submitting her guests readily to her husband's 'guided tours'. At other times, as the shadows lengthened under the buddleias, and Basil left off from his incessant scything of the long grass, the chattering insect life would be drowned out by the sound of madrigals, performed by the Blackwell's singers and led by the educationalist John Cutforth.

If madrigals were a little too esoteric, then would-be musicians, with or without sight-reading skills, could try hand bell-ringing, as an alternative. This was an inclusive society, and had none of the social exclusiveness that is, perhaps unfairly, associated with other, nearby, musical venues. The Blackwell's were never patronizing: Basil Blackwell deeply resented any such idea. Traditions, such as the annual Christmas box did pass by the 1970s; the Gaffer accepted that the younger staff no longer wanted to queue up to shake hands: he was aware that it smacked a bit too much of the old benefaction system. His motive was not to hang onto the past, although he liked the old traditions, but to create an *esprit de corps*: to keep the family members together, to maintain a real family firm. If any family members were sick, and in need of convalescence, they were put up at Osse Field, and attended by the Gaffer and his wife[340]. One measure of the Gaffer's success in creating, and maintaining, an extended family, asserted Phil Brown from the present Antiquarian Department, 'is the way, nearly twenty years after the Gaffer's death, the eyes of Blackwell pensioner, Jim Broadbent, filled with tears at the memory of his days in the family firm'. Others remembered the parties, the outings, the celebrations and the annual children's Christmas parties, complete with Father Christmas bearing presents. But although Basil and Christine Blackwell were both 'nurturers', membership of the clan also carried with it reciprocal duties and responsibilities. The Gaffer's expectations, of all Blackwellians, men and women alike, were much as they were under the old order of things, irrespective of the loss of the formal bond. The old master-apprentice system may have slipped away, but his standards were as exacting as his father's. His regime would have matched that of any leader in the modern business world: a distinctive house style, rigid procedures to be complied with, long hours, strict confidentiality, and, ahead of his time: open management, bottom-up and clear lines of communication.

What was on offer, to tempt staff into Blackwell's, would match the best in modern corporate recruitment: training on the job, fees paid for further education and relevant qualifications and good promotion prospects, with international and national opportunities, as well as locally, in Oxford. There were extra travel allowances, three weeks paid holiday, bonuses, an extra week's salary for everyone at Christmas, and a pension scheme, guaranteeing half salary on retirement. To keep staff fit, there was cricket, football, hockey, table tennis, a sailing club and, for the less athletic, a philatelic club and membership of the Blackwell's Singers. All new recruits were now issued with a handbook 'Your Career at Blackwell's'. The booklet explicitly emphasized the 'career ladder': from the bottom rung, as a trainee, to a director's chair: 'The Company's aim is to promote from within. In fact, all the directors have grown up with the firm and the majority joined us straight from school.' What Basil Blackwell would have thought of the contemporary business practices, in the public and private sectors, of bringing in outsiders, new blood, can only be guessed at. It would have been at odds with his concept of keeping things in the family. Although the Blackwell's handbook stressed the family nature of Blackwell's, 'new arrivals have merely left one family to join another' and 'there are several families with two or three members on the staff and there are many cases of people marrying someone also working in the firm. Indeed there is one serving who is a product of such a union', it was a modern standardized document.

Unlike the earlier guides produced for apprentices, of which Fred Hanks guide to the classics was legendary, the more modern document projected an image of the Blackwell's brand across all its aspects. A version from the mid-sixties introduced the recruit to the bookselling trade and, bearing the Gaffer's own stamp, emphasized that the main qualification for success was finding books and book people fascinating; paper qualifications were not necessary. The Gaffer always preferred to educate his own staff, although entrants with Advanced Level GCEs did receive a higher wage. This policy preserved a link with the Blackwell's of Benjamin Henry's days: learning on the job. In this way, generations of Blackwellians were initiated into the literary life of the City and the academic life of the University: acting as sounding boards for authors, visiting academics in their rooms, taking short hand notes, delivering proofs to the printers, as well as serving the general public behind the counters[341]. Now, as in the past, new entrants were invited to 'imagine that there is excitement to be had from imparting the latest information about publications to the scientist, the philosopher or the man in the street. Whoever they are you can gain something from them and, more important, they should gain something from you'. This, latter, rider conveyed the underlying assumption of service. Service was the hallmark of Blackwell's success, and there was no dispensation: interest in books and people and hard work were axiomatic. Stress, if Basil Blackwell knew the word, was a positive challenge and anxiety a problem to be shared!

In the Blackwellian family, there was a place for everyone, provided everyone knew their place. The rewards for those who stayed the course, however, were, in the Gaffer's view, 'greater than those in the more commercial world', and more than just wages. First as students of 'Blackwell college', then booksmiths in their own right, the staff, as they became known, continued to act much as they had in Benjamin Henry's time: they were researchers to the University, and represented the repository of knowledge of the earliest to the latest books, and the sources these relied on. On a daily basis they were the Gaffer's Fellows; like his Merton College colleagues, they were his friends, confidants, advisors, co-conspirators and, in his old age they became his minders. But, recalled some of the present staff, recruited in the Gaffer's time, 'it was never all work and no play'. Filling lulls had long been a feature of life at Blackwell's, and the Gaffer's own father, for all his sobriety, had turned a blind eye. And this was a tradition that continued throughout the Gaffer's time. The Gaffer was himself complicitous; on a sunny afternoon he might urge his staff, especially his overworked personal assistants, 'to take a frisk'. Sales staff too were given ways of escape: Phil Brown remembered being sent off on the Gaffer's shopping errands, and not being asked to account for 'any delay in returning'. When the doors closed on the public on Thursday afternoons, Phil Brown and his associates played cricket on a pitch that had the benefit of a 'good run-up', positioned as it was, and very appropriately, in the English department, on the ground floor. Screwed up balls of paper sufficed for these games and similar ones of 'footy'[342]. Another favourite sport was to hang out the front windows and watch passing *hoi polloi* on their way to University ceremonies. Viewed from the upstairs windows of the shop, the Blackwellian paparazzi had a bird's eye view of processions down the Broad where they could spot royalty, politicians, poet laureates and other notables. There were the fire alarms, too, set off by the pipe-smoking Tom Templeton, in those less thought-policed days. It had been Templeton's way as a young apprentice, joining in 1926 at the start of the Gaffer's rule, to attempt to lure young ladies down to the safe where he had to deposit the company's ledgers at the close of each day.

With all their iconoclasm, the Gaffer relished, and treasured, the company of his fellow bookmen every bit as much as his father had. And the fold extended to all those associated with Blackwell's trades: authors, binders, contract printers. 'They were all such characters' and had their own signature tunes: there was, for example, 'old Broome, the printer from St Clements, with his squeaky boots'[343]. Few were barred the inner sanctum of the Gaffer's office, where he would listen to their concerns and tales; if comfort was required he would sharpen a pencil and trigger the mechanical sharpener's jingle 'A Double Diamond Works Wonders'. A former secretary remarked on his 'gift for smoothing things over', a spell he used on staff and customers alike. The Gaffer received his fair share of complaints, she remembered, but he had the knack of turning the table: 'the complainant usually ended up thanking him'. Otherwise he had a stock of limericks to lighten a tight situation, and he never, infuriatingly at times, acknowledged 'a negative situation'[344]. Part of his appeal was his positive up-beat manner, but his greatest attribute, as a gaffer, was his unstinting appreciation of those on whom he depended. He spoke publicly of the debt he owed to them: 'How grateful I am for my good fortune in spending my life among books and bookmen'. Many of those who entered through the Blackwell's route made bookselling their life-long career. Bookmen, up and down the country, especially members of the two Book Trade Associations, became Sir Basil's most precious friends. He spoke of the 'public spirit and devotion over the years that have built up our Association from little more than a guardian of the Net Book Agreement to the dignity and the influence it enjoys today'[345]. Just what qualified someone as a bookman was hard to pin down.

The business of bookselling, wrote Sir Basil, is midway between a trade and a learned profession. Whereas other retailers work by weights and measures, a bookseller is concerned with an individual book. He regretted, 'given their knowledge, years of learning and specialisms', that they were not remunerated as they would have been in other professions: 'It may be taken for granted', he argued, 'that the brains, energy and long hours required of the bookseller would yield far richer results if applied in most other forms of business'. Basil Blackwell, like his father, was a man who wore many hats: a scholar, bookseller, publisher, and servant of the wider community. How did he keep all these balls in the air? In an interview shortly before his ninetieth birthday the Gaffer described himself as an 'acrobat on top of a human pyramid... everybody is doing his best to support me, I am supporting no-one, but smiling and accepting the final applause.' He saw himself as a willing player of the game, and one who had the good fortune of 'never being found out'[346]. In this, he kidded himself. His wife had 'found him out', as had his children and his many friends, and his staff had the measure of the man: 'Well, your staff have found you out long ago Gaffer. The atmosphere of love and affection . . . will be reinforced by our desire and that of our customers and the world in general to pay homage to the . . . best Blackwellian of them all—our Gaffer'[347]. At the congregation for the conferment of his honorary doctorate, he was described as a 'Jupiter of Booksellers'.

A Jupiter of booksellers

It is not amiss . . . to crack a bottle of fish sauce, or stand himself a cheese

What made Blackwell's such a continuing success? How is it that a one-room shop branched out all over the place, and became a household name in the academic world? This was a question Basil had addressed, in reviewing his father's achievements. He came up with an answer that was a mixture of being in the right place at the right time, his father's unique personal characteristics, the dedication of Blackwellians and their love of books, and scholarship. The same could just as well be said of his custodianship: he gave Blackwell's his own magic, but he knew he had been more fortunate than his father. He had, in so many ways, lived a charmed life, and he received the public recognition that he thought should have been his father's due. On the occasion of his admission as a Doctor of Civil Law, he was proclaimed: 'a veritable Jupiter of Booksellers'. The Public Orator instructed the congregation on his achievements as a bookseller. 'I chanced to be going down the Broad, as is my custom, when suddenly I saw Jupiter emerge from the doors of that famous bookshop. Do I mean Jupiter? You think I am out of my mind? Not at all. The ancient Romans used to invoke "Jupiter the God of Hospitality" or "Jupiter who sends the rain" . . . why shouldn't we salute the "Jupiter of Booksellers today"' [348]. A librarian at the Bodleian, a student at the time, never forgot the sight of two grand old men, Sir Basil Blackwell and Sir Harold Macmillan, in conversation as they processed leisurely down the Broad. In this student's book, Sir Basil Blackwell ranked, at least, in greatness with the University's Vice Chancellor [349]. But was he a Jupiter? His assessment was very different. He knew that his, Blackwell's, success rested on the shoulders of others. As the Gaffer, and as a man, he relied on the formidable support of his wife, his right-hand man, Cuthbert White, his family, his sons and grandsons who joined the firm, and above all, those who 'served the trade by which he lived': his loyal staff. His father had bequeathed him a flourishing business, and left him in the safe hands of the apprentice-directors, who

32 The Gaffer alongside the Muirhead Bone picture of the Broad Street interior.

in turn trained the next generations of apprentices and, after 1956, school-leavers. Writing notes about his life, for his friend Thomas Norrington, Basil confessed that the burden of running the companies would have been intolerable without the help of his able and devoted colleagues.

At the centre of his world—the bookseller's world—were the books themselves: it was books that held the supreme, and commanding, position in the Blackwell's empire. It was books that made a bookshop so different from any other retail outlet. They were a very different, more durable, kind of merchandise. Their sale was a different matter too. The bookseller had to be a connoisseur, and a bit of a scholar, and if these qualities could be combined with the right stock, the right books, then he could succeed. Seizing any spare moment, to read, think and write, he reflected on the nature of bookselling. Finding any time to do other things, was itself a symbol of Blackwell's continuing success. His father could never, and would never, have strayed from the helm, and although, as the Gaffer, Basil was never far away: he was chairman of the board and frequently available on the shop floor, he did have more leisure time than his father, and much more than his grandfather. He used some of this time to reflect on the nature of bookselling in general and the success of Blackwell's, in particular. An anatomy of his father's success had suggested many, interwoven, reasons for the success of Blackwell's. But, Basil recognized, that was yesterday. None the less, many of the same factors which had helped his father still counted: the continuing growth of higher education, the ever-expanding demand from the general reader, the opportunities for growth in the export market, and the success of the publishing side to exploit specialist, niche, markets, at home and abroad. Underpinning all of these was the continued goodwill and recognition that Blackwell's enjoyed across the world.

In the academic bookselling world, Blackwell's had become a 'household' name; the success of the brand was unshakable. Yet, the Gaffer reflected, for all its success, Blackwell's was not a law unto itself: it was a member of the book and publishing trades, and there were many changes afoot there; it was subject to economic and political forces, and, above all, it had to operate in 'the market'. This concept of the market was a red rag to a bull as far as the Gaffer was concerned. It was a tyranny: it determined the profits of the book trade, a trade where profit margins were notoriously low, and the vagaries of the tax system cut them to the quick, it had put the pound under pressure, and it was devalued. It made people greedy, its invisible hand created a have and have not dichotomy, among wage earners, who had previously been united, everyone from doctors to teachers to hospital porters, posties and dustmen. It was putting the welfare state at risk. Its misdistribution, its market failure, prompted the subjection of everyone to price and incomes policies. To top it all, the free marketers called for an end to the system of retail price maintenance, the mainstay of small shop owners. There was no end to it. Acutely aware of the suffering and difficulties of others, the Gaffer, however, had to admit Blackwell's was, surprisingly to him, 'doing very nicely'. By the nineteen seventies Blackwell's had grown to become one of the greatest, and most complex, bookselling concerns in the world. To what could this continued success be attributed?

Although much of the credit for the success of Blackwell's must go to its staff, to the hard work of the new generation of Blackwell's—Sir Basil's sons and grandsons—and to the legacy left by Benjamin Henry Blackwell, it must also go to the Gaffer. He would never admit to his part in the piece, but he played a pivotal role, bringing Blackwell's from the Victorian age into the late twentieth century. When he had assumed control, in 1924, his enthusiasm, and acceptance of his role, was wholehearted. And his style of leadership suited a new, more independent age. Girded up by his team of stalwarts, his father's apprentice-directors, he was able to affect an aura of benign, but enthusiastic, neglect. He left his staff to get on with the job. But although he was not seen to be directly interventionist, he rarely missed a trick. With eyes in the back of his head, and the same eagle eye for detail that his father had had, he would pop up, as if from nowhere, with an idea, a wry suggestion and occasionally a 'Gaffer's encyclical', especially if a customer had complained. In short, he knew his staff and customers, and they knew their Gaffer; they felt valued, and 'listened to'[350]. They returned the compliment by maintaining a deep loyalty to Blackwell's. The Gaffer received letters from all over the world; from people famous and unknown, the tone of which gave the impression that the sender was an intimate friend. In old age, for example, letters would arrive asking if he was still in good health, even though the senders would often not have seen their 'friend' for forty years or more. An American, Andrew Witner, wrote in 1984 to Corinna Wiltshire (Blackwell), who by then was acting as personal assistant and secretary to her father. Finding himself immersed in pleasant memories of Blackwell's in the Forties, he began wondering how Sir Basil was. A letter from Corinna reassured him, and he wrote back: 'I can now feel that relief which Chekhov felt when he found out that reports of Tolstoy's death were false. In my case it was my imagination which had to be set at rest. . . . I am pleased to hear that your father sensibly has decided to go on till he drops'[351].

As president, rather than chairman, of Blackwell's from 1969, the Gaffer had told everyone that he was taking 'an easier ride: I came in on only four out of six mornings and delayed my arrival until 9.15. At other times, being a man of leisure', he spent this 'leisure' popping into the shop, where he would entertain the staff and old acquaintances, and make new ones. Manifestly, an encounter with Basil Blackwell, however chanced or brief, was not to be forgotten. This was his continuing part in the Blackwell magic. When he talked to someone, and nearly always when he wrote a letter, the recipient was made to feel all-important: someone whose opinion, and individuality, counted. The Gaffer's possession of such, 'management' and 'customer-relations', skills must have had an incalculably positive effect on the firm's fortunes. Commercial *savoir faire* also played a crucial role in the continued success of Blackwell's. The Gaffer had always known that Blackwell's needed to keep several balls in the air if it was to keep afloat. He was not just master of his father's old shop, but of associated shops, a thriving worldwide periodicals business, two publishing houses and a bindery. He also relied on a very buoyant mail order outlet and export trade. Blackwell's had, in a relatively small way, become a multi-national company in its own right. But through all this the Gaffer was seen close to his roots, and remained true to his convictions.

For him, it was books that mattered. They were their own best publicists, even in a time when the power of advertising seemed invincible. Books were the personification of the individual, the voice of the spirit. Basil still believed in the eternal power of the individual spirit. It is this, argued Sir Basil, which guaranteed the survival of bookshops, 'while one sees in towns up and down the country individual grocers, chemists, bootmakers... gradually being driven out, absorbed or submerged by multiple shops and trade combines, the bookseller remains, poor often maybe, but at least individual and master in his own shop[352]. This rationale, underpinning the success of bookshops like Blackwell's, did not help most other small businesses, who were pushed off the high streets by the supermarkets. Their fate was ever a salutary reminder of Keynes maxim that 'in the long run we are all dead'. He was ever watchful of those in the book trade with, what he called, 'a supermarket mentality'. For the time being, the Gaffer felt that the book trade was safe enough, not least because of the training and professionalism of its members.

This 'career structure', and safety net, did not, however, according to Basil, obtain in the publishing world. Publishing, no less a part of the Blackwells' success, had always had pride of place in the Gaffer's working life. And he was more than disconcerted by what he saw as its bastardisation. He was scathing in his criticism of new entrants to the field. 'It is', he observed, 'one of the curiosities of the British book trade that no credentials are required of those who elect to practise the hazardous business of publishing. There are no chartered or certified publishers; the name in the imprint on the title page suffices to proclaim the publisher. It is a kind of amateur status, and has been so since the term "bookseller" has been restricted to the retailer of books. The bookseller-publisher of earlier times normally had served his apprenticeship to the trade; to the publisher in his own right'[353]. Basil's father, of course, had been a self-starter with no formal training in publishing. But, Basil explained, Benjamin Henry had been inspired not by profit, but by a love of literature and a passion for helping those who may not otherwise have made it into print. He was less a publisher, more a channel of communication. And the scope of his endeavours, until his son Basil expanded the publishing side, was modest. 'In the absence of formal training', Basil asserted, 'family tradition and heredity have been the conditions most apt to success in a calling where patient merit counts for less than the spirit of adventure, and ideas count for more than elaborate instruction'. But, Basil warned, without 'vision' the publisher 'would perish'. 'Such', he cited, 'has been the exemplar of famous publishing dynasties, acknowledged to be the glory of their time'[354].

Explaining the nature of his own vision, Basil Blackwell drew more on the eternity of books, and those who handled them, than on the vagaries of publishing. He reflected that 'the status of bookselling in our economy remains much as I found it when I entered the trade. True bookselling—not "merchandising"—remains in the middle parts of fortune—an arduous business requiring qualities of intelligence, diligence and enterprise, which in many callings would win greater material rewards.' His reflections on the subject of bookselling were undertaken for pragmatic, as well as cerebral, reasons. He played a lead role in his trade, and he was often asked to write papers, and to speak on subjects connected with his trade, or his involvement with books. All this writing and speech-making meant he had to do his homework. And doing his homework, *qua* reading books, to get information, as well as for pleasure, was another source of his success. He wrote, prolifically, for example, about the special nature of bookselling[355]. Going back to basics, he asserted ' "Tis a good reader who makes a book." So, unless my memory deceives me, wrote Emerson, and with truth. No less truly, I suggest, 'tis the good bookman who makes the good bookshop. If that be so, there is good hope of better bookshops in England as the years pass, for the Englishman is changing his habits in the matter of books. It took two World Wars to make him do it (in the nineteenth century the nation might claim one of the finest literatures had also one of the smallest reading publics in Europe), but the fact is not in question that for one new book that was sold to Englishmen at home in 1938 two are sold today. In 1938 we might have said, with an echo of Dr Johnson, "No man will be a bookseller who has contrivance enough to get himself into a workhouse." Individual booksellers were trading at a loss, and proprietors of family bookshops warned their sons against following this calling, and they themselves were anxious to sell out while they still had something to sell'.

In trying to analyse the successes, and failures of the book trade, Basil was troubled by the paradox of bookselling, one that so often bedevilled his fellow booksellers—and he had experienced a similar paradox in the land of fine publishing. 'Paradoxically', he wrote, 'the better the bookseller, the less likely he was to thrive—that is if we understand by "better" the man with a wide knowledge of books, who loved them and enjoyed reading them and was ready to discuss them, and to put them in the way of the public by striving to maintain a stock representative of the best new books in a wide range of subjects. Not enough were bought before they became obsolete, and his sales were not sufficient to enable him to sustain even a modest proportion of unsaleable stock (British publishers do not supply books "on sale or return").

If then the function of a bookshop was to sell books for a profit, economic logic forced upon him the conclusion that his hope of survival lay in adopting the method of the bookstall, which is, very properly: "Here are some books; choose from them or leave them, ask no questions, but having chosen, depart and trouble me no more". So, we may say that the public got the bookshops it deserved. But today the Englishman is not ashamed of being seen in a bookshop, and a new relationship between bookseller and customer, or rather the renewal of the relationship of a more gracious age, may well come to be. Sir Thomas Bodley required for the good librarian learning, leisure, friends and means, and I suggest these qualifications are no less requisite for the bookseller, if he is to fulfil his proper function'.

Fulfilling the proper function is, however, seen differently in the computer age. Ken New, who started at Blackwell's under the Gaffer, and is now a senior bookseller in Theology, explained the current problems. 'In the age of the computer the bookseller is at a loss, unless he can find the title on the screen'. This, of course, depends on the quality of the data in the bank. Handling books, is, of course, an adjunct, 'you simply know the book because you picked it, maybe looked at it, handled it and put it on the shelf'. If you did this, you will remember. But you may not have touched the book, and even if you are responsible for ordering new books, and dealing with the publisher's reps, you still may not have seen the books. Now, increasingly, all you have to go on is a publisher's blurb'. For a good bookseller, this situation will not suffice. Traditionally, the bookseller, the species the Gaffer knew, was an expert. A look at his criteria for a good bookseller provides as good guide as any to the enduring qualities of good bookselling, as relevant now as in his day. 'Their learning, or booklore', he explained, was 'based primarily upon the knowledge of a set of four facts in respect of as many new and current books as his memory could hold. In so far as he can remember the author, the title, the publisher and the price of any new book he saves himself the time employed in consulting his books of reference. But an annual output of 10,000 in U.S.A. normally compels constant recourse to reference books; and these constitute a little library in themselves. Nevertheless he must have them, if he is to supply the information, which any one of his customers may seek, and if he is to get for his customers quickly any one of the books for which he may be asked. A bookseller cannot hope to keep in stock more than a small fraction of the total of new books current at any time, and his function is rather to provide than to have on his shelves the books for which he is asked; and the time saved by knowledge and memory is of the first value in winning for him that leisure which is so necessary, if he is fully to perform his function'.

A bookseller's work is never done. And the Gaffer, like his father, was demanding. 'If he has a sense of vocation . . . his (the bookseller's) leisure is devoted to reading: reading the books, and about the books, that he handles everyday, at work. If, additionally, he believes that he cannot buy anything "one half as precious as the goods he sells", his reading will be at once a duty as well as a profitable delight. It will make him, in Bacon's phrase, "a full man" and a better bookseller. It is not amiss for a grocer at times: "To crack a bottle of fish sauce, or stand himself a cheese". Consequently, he will be able to commend their flavour with authority to his customers. It is proper that a wine-and-spirit merchant should taste and test the precious liquids he supplies, though he is unwise if he devote his whole leisure to potation. But the more of his stock a bookseller can absorb, the better for him and for his customers. But, again, he must have leisure for discussion and trading of opinions with the good bookmen who frequent the shop. So he grows in knowledge and wisdom in his craft. Such practice naturally prompts an interest in books no longer current, and it may be claimed that no bookshop should be without a second-hand department—that intellectual lucky-dip, which is the delight of the book-collector. Here the bookseller must have the knowledge, with a difference—knowledge of author and title, of course, but also of the rarity of a book and of the interest it has maintained with readers or collectors. One might perhaps say that he must have a knowledge of the history of the book. Such knowledge guides the bookseller in buying and pricing his stock of second-hand or (as the Americans very sensibly say) used books. There is a further advantage in the handling of used books, which, if they be of sufficient rarity and interest, are graced with the epithet antiquarian, in that in this business there is some latitude in the margin of profit, and the possibility of occasional windfalls, while in the case of new books the narrow and rigid terms of supply do not follow'.

Basil Blackwell expanded on his theme: the good bookseller gains other intrinsic benefits, too, from his work. He is not only an expert and an antiquarian, 'but he also educates, and develops, himself: knowledge and reading develop personality'. But none of these qualities, Basil warned, would be of much use if the character of bookshops is lost. 'However mechanically efficient a bookshop may be . . . the essence of a good bookshop is that it should have character'. Squaring the circle, Basil suggested that the character of a bookshop is synonymous with the personality of the bookseller. Blackwell's had first found fame as 'Mr Blackwell's little shop'; its stock was well selected, it welcomed all, and it let the customer browse: this was the character of both the shop and the man. His father, and his shop, had attracted 'kindred minds, which in their turn will aid and enrich his mind; and so a bookshop may reflect in its stock and atmosphere a kind of corporate personality representing and fostering the cultural character of its locality. Such is the effect of 'friends' coupled with 'a well-ordered bookshop'. 'There is an air of good cheer as the public sample the books which they may or may not choose to buy; for though his stock is for 'consumption off the premises' a bookseller deems it right that his clients should taste, and sometimes absorb freely, before deciding what to take away. A happy murmur is heard as the customers discuss them or subjects prompted by them with friends they may meet there, or with the bookseller. Here is the freedom and good fellowship of the tavern'.

Bookshops have also been great depositories of stories, and sources of the Gaffer's. 'Sir Walter Scott, in his autobiography, tells of his search as a boy for old songs or romances on the dusty shelves of a shop in Parliament Square. It was in this bookshop of James Sibbald 'a man of rough manners but of some taste and judgment' (no bookseller need take exception to such description) that he had 'a distant view of some literary characters' and 'saw, at a distance, the boast of Scotland, Robert Burns'. There is the bookseller performing his best function—his shop is the meeting place of good bookmen, young and old. This picture of the youthful Scott brings to mind another, of a young Scotsman, James Boswell, taking tea in the parlour of the bookseller Tom Davies ('Sir, Davies has learning enough to give credit to a clergyman') when Dr Johnson, the Great Champion of literature, was seen through the glass door making 'his aweful approach'. Was any such meeting ever richer in its literary sequel? Would this introduction have been made if Davies had not earned the malicious criticism of a contemporary: 'His concern ought to be with the outside of books; but Dr Johnson, Dr Percy and some others have made such a coxcomb of him that he is now hardly enough to open volumes, turn over their leaves, and give his opinion of their contents.' This criticism could well be levelled at the modern trade of bookselling, Basil had lamented. But the problems are as much to do with means, now, as the quality, or lack of it, of the booksellers. Basil feared that: 'in an age of mass production the practice of bookselling is obsolete. A good bookseller will try to keep on his shelves one or two of the best books in most subjects—he cannot afford capital or space for more—but for the most part he will be asked for books which he has to get in specifically for his customer. Each book is an individual, and calls for individual handling; and there may be several handlings or transactions in the supply of one book. It has to be identified, ordered, handled on receipt, handled when passed to the customer, and, if the customer does not pay for it there and then, it has to be recorded in the ledger, and the account has to be sent out—perhaps on several occasions. The whole process is disproportionately costly to the contingent profit.'

How can the modern bookseller survive? Basil asked. The modern bookseller may, in compensation, look to order, and sell, books in quantities 'which involve him in no more labour than the supply of single copies; but the tendency today in Britain is for such purchases to be made with public money, and the trustees of such funds are expected to exercise a certain *force majeure* in buying under privilege, at special and unremunerative rates! They little know the cultural harm they do. The bookseller has further to contend with the paradox that the more difficult a book may be to sell, the smaller is the margin of profit allowed by the publisher's terms of supply; and, naturally enough, in most subjects the more excellent the book the less popular it is likely to be'. But even in this age of cut-pricing and fierce competition, he wrote, the bookseller still loves a good bookman. 'The best customers are those who, feeling a thirst for reading, drop into a bookshop and pick off the shelf or counter a book which takes their fancy, pay for it and carry it off under their arm. These are good bookmen, the cultural partners as it were of the bookseller, who guide him in the apt selection of books for his stock, encourage him to inform them by catalogue and prospectus of books appropriate to their interests, help to afford him the essential leisure for reading and discussion, and between them make a bookshop an intellectual exchange in a sense which no school or college, and certainly no Public Library, (where 'silence is requested') can hope to be'. Blackwell's was, however, often considered to be a 'rather agreeable library' and the Gaffer received letters addressed to 'Blackwell's Library'. Blackwell's was also many other things. The success of Blackwell's bears a remarkable resemblance to Basil Blackwell's description of good bookselling, and a good bookshop.

But Basil had written most of the foregoing accounts before Blackwell's reached its zenith, in the Sixties and Seventies. Perhaps the writing was intended as a *modus vivendi*, or, more likely, it was a reflection of the things Basil saw happening before his eyes in the shop: an account of 'the practices of good bookmen'. Staff, who still remember the Gaffer, stress his modesty, and these Blackwellians thought it typical of the man that he should question the idea of being a Jupiter of booksellers. He liked to think of himself as a Gaffer who enabled others to do things. His accounts do not take his own personality into account. Yet, his particular characteristics, his personality, must also have added to Blackwell's success. Other elements of his personal success are even more intangible. They are bound up with his reverence for books. He went on writing, and speaking, on these themes, trying to encourage his fellows and debunk the sharks. But he always wanted to elevate the mundane concerns of trade, to another level. He was a dreamer, and a parable-maker. 'For in this grasping age when the world of men appears to be divided between those who strain for more profits and others who strain for more pay, there is, as I see it, a third estate, unorganized, unvocal, unpredatory, being the commonwealth of those whose commerce is in sharing delight in the noblest products of the spirit of man, in the visual and scenic arts, in music . . . and, need I add?—in books. It is this commonwealth, which we serve, and in serving win our reward. "All the glory of the world would be buried in oblivion unless god had provided mortals with the remedy of books." So wrote good Richard de Bury in his *Philobiblon*. And how truly! For in books we have the compendium of all human experience. We use them or neglect them as we will, but if we use them we may share the courage and endurance of adventurers, the thoughts of sages, the vision of poets, the rapture of lovers, and—some few of us perhaps—the ecstasies of the Saints. . . .' He ends his explanation by quoting the *Proverbs* of Solomon: 'Happy is he who has found wisdom and the man who has found understanding: for wisdom is more profitable than silver, and the gains she brings are better than gold'[356]. But the gains of wisdom, Basil extolled, were also to be found in a source other than books.

Private pleasure
Marion Christine (Soans) Blackwell 1888–1977

Happy is he who has found wisdom and the man who has found understanding: for wisdom is more profitable than silver, and the gains she brings are better than gold

Overseeing the smooth running of the publishing and bookselling business was only one side of Basil's life, although Basil Blackwell would have owned that his chief pleasure was a love of books. Indeed in his entry for '*Who's Who*', he listed only reading under recreation, and in this bookishness Basil resembled his father. But there was nothing of Benjamin Henry's reclusiveness about him. As a personality, Basil had a great deal of his freer thinking and out-going mother about him. What he needed was a companion who could keep the balance between these two sides of his personality. And Marion Christine Soans, who Basil married in 1914, turned out to be just such a person. In her bearing Christine gave an impression of severity, she had cut her hair short at a time before it was still not quite the done thing for 'young ladies', meeting with her father's disapproval. But far from being an early 'flapper', she had more the air of the schoolmistress about her; certainly she looked very competent[357]. A successful classicist in her own right, with a first from London University, she was a woman after Basil's own heart. When they met Christine had no thoughts of matrimony. Following her own interests, she was working for the Greek scholar Gilbert Murray. He was an avid, and eloquent, champion of women's rights, and other liberal causes; like Basil, he had struggled, in vain, to save Europe from war.

The urbane, spirited, fair-haired Basil, put paid to any ideas Christine may have had on the subject of a long-term career. He was the sentimental one, and, as resolved as John Donne had been 'to live with thee and be thy love', he won her over. Accounts of their courtship vary. Lady Blackwell always insisted that it was she who had brought Basil 'to the point'. Her husband remembered 'proposing one Saturday afternoon—to an entrancing maiden with the brightest of blue eyes and a pastel rose complexion which never faded.' Being interrupted by one of the apprentices, Geoffrey Barfoot, he had to resume the dialogue, but to positive effect. After her marriage to Basil Blackwell, and with the arrival of a brood of children, she largely set aside her academic pursuits. But she never put aside her love of books, or her enthusiasm for the classics. Basil, in his Victorian way, didn't on the whole think of women as great readers, 'for women generally are not kindly disposed to books, which lie about and harbour dust, and cost money which might be better spent. A woman collector of rare books is rarissima avis'[358]. He must, of course, have been generalising, for his experience of women, and Christine in particular, was quite other. But for Christine Blackwell there was, perforce, more to life than books. Firmly rooted in her house and garden, Christine, who was generally known as 'The Mimi', became the rock anchor of the household. Here, her knowledge of Greek epic and drama again came in handy: the works of Euripides, for example, represented ordinary people, especially women, 'with impassioned sympathy'[359]. And she needed bags of this, but not so impassioned, to tame her energetic husband.

Basil was forever 'in a frenzy of ideas and activity'. Their youngest son, Julian, has a strong memory of how his mother saw her husband. She had described Basil 'as someone of irrepressible physical and mental energy', which created an aura of excitement around him. Her letters to Basil, on the rare holiday occasion when she had to go on ahead, reveal the extent of her devotion and contain teasing invitations not to forget her. For all her romantic attachment, Basil was not to be allowed to forget the exigencies of

33 Christine Blackwell—our lady of the daffodils—taking time out from taming her husband in the early 1970s.

'child-rearing'. Christine wrote from Ramsgate, pleading with him to come soon, not least to help her curb the manners of her eldest son, prone to throwing things at the dinner table, and to prevent her eldest daughter from 'being above herself'. If Christine's married life was far from rarefied, her husband, if left to his own devices could quite easily have slid off in that direction. Controlling the children probably came second to reigning-in Basil, and providing a soft-landing for his inspirations. Her husband's flights of fancy had to be contained, and moulded in such a way that the demands of work, and the needs of a large and growing family, could be properly met. And to do this she had to be bossy[360]. In adulthood, Richard Blackwell too assisted his mother in the role of 'Basil's minder'. He explained: 'My father is a rare spirit, but he needs somewhat grosser spirits to look after him and keep his feet planted on the ground'[361]. As a seven-year-old, when his parents left him behind on a business tour to the US, Richard had kept them informed of home news: an extensive account of Eights Week, and informed his father 'when I am a man and go to Merton College, I am going to row . . . when I grow up I am going to help you in your business'. In fact none of the children went to Merton: Richard went to New College, Penelope to Sommerville, and Julian to Trinity, but all of them were his 'minders', in one-way or another. But none so convincing as Christine's, whose feet were indeed firmly planted.

This aspect of her character was personified by her gardening. In the early days of their marriage, she had readily helped her in-laws in the garden of Linton Road. Now, in the old garden, which had been started from scratch by Benjamin Henry and Lilla, there is the remains of the old orchard, and the hard, early, fruit of plums can still be seen[362]. So Christine progressed from Euripides to bottling plums, and making chutney: art forms not to be so lightly dismissed! Basil, too, learned to grapple with the craft of horticulture. In his married ardour, he submitted to being told to deal with the spuds and watch the pears[363]. More often it was Christine who had to run the show. Basil, after all, had to have his head, and he had at the ready a phrase from Ecclesiasticus: 'a scholar's wisdom comes of ample leisure and if a man is to be wise he must be relieved of other tasks'. And when at home, Basil was forever occupied with his reading and his study. But for his wife Basil would make time, in the midst of his unceasingly active interest in a myriad of things, for their lively family life, which, by 1929, had grown to include five children. To contain their lively progeny, fresh air and fields were called for; they swapped North Oxford for village life in Appleton. Designed around the principles of William Morris, the house appeared modest and bare. Furnished with heavy unpolished oak tables and chairs, it had the look of a rambling cottage[364]. It must have been a haven of freedom for the young Blackwells. Basil often observed his brood of five children, romping down the street, sometimes barefoot, and characteristically referred to them as 'the Philistines'. Christine's father disapproved of the children's local accents and they were, according to her own accounts 'in need of a good deal of disciplining'[365].

But Philistines the Blackwell children were not. They inherited their parents', and grandparents', love of books, and provided a testing-ground for Basil's developing interest in children's literature. Just as his own father had urged him to read the classics, Basil wanted to make good books available to his own children, and to all children, irrespective of their financial background. Both parents set great store by an academic education, and this was as important for the three girls, as it was for the two boys. Julian Blackwell remembered a ferocious argument when his elder sister Penny (Dame Penelope Jessell) was roasted for not working as hard as she might. But a broad education was just as highly valued. While the house boasted a large, and always expanding library, which fed the children's minds, it was also a haven for their physical development. From the early days of their move to Appleton, with a houseful of schoolchildren and a toddler underfoot, Christine set out to create a house and garden that would cater for all their needs. Although the success of the family business meant that Christine had help in the house, there were no short cuts. Running a house in the thirties and forties meant mountains of hand washing, growing and preserving vegetables and fruit, chopping enough wood on a daily basis to replenish the coal fires, which fuelled the hot water system, cooking for a family when there were food shortages and somehow finding spare resources to feed and entertain an army of business acquaintances and friends.

Christine Blackwell, probably because of her logical training, gave herself wholeheartedly to the organization, and the provision of these vital back-up, home-making, services. During the Second World War, these services were extended as she found room for evacuees and their relatives. Throughout the war years, she worked tirelessly for the cause; she dispensed, and shared, anything she had: everything from constructive advice to extra rations of fresh fruit and vegetables she had grown in her garden. Her energy and strength was a mainstay of the local village community. All this invisible woman's work did not go unnoticed: it left her husband free to run a successful business and to participate in public life. Her supporting role was paid tribute to when Basil received the Freedom of the City. The Leader of the Council publicly regretted that the scroll, given to Sir Basil, did not also bear her name. But, she was reassured[366]; the City would henceforth regard her as 'an honorary, honorary citizen'. Yet, throughout all this activity, Christine always had her academic interests and training to fall back on. She was far from a drudge. Basil, something of an intellectual snob, relied on her to enliven their family holidays. With her knowledge of classical myths and stories she re-created the ancient world for her husband, and he, on these holidays, inhabited, once more, this real world, which kept him occupied while they motored around Europe.

At home, domestic calls on her time did not prevent Christine from helping her husband with work directly connected to the family business. Her contacts with local schools helped to find promising recruits for the firm. Her judgement, according to her husband, was immaculate. One or two of the girls recruited in this way, and much admired by both Christine and Basil Blackwell, still, to this day, work for Blackwell's. Invariably, these fresh schoolgirls, so carefully selected by Christine, were immediately noticed by her husband and promoted on the administrative ladder. In some cases they returned to Blackwell's, after temporarily leaving to bring up a family. These former recruits, men and women, still provide a living memory of Blackwell's as an institution, and of all those associated with its adventures. They would be invited to tea at Osse Field, with their families and friends, and Christine would keep a close eye on their progress. Christine's natural empathy helped to bring out even the shyest of visitors, and, when needed, ease any of the social difficulties of her husband's business contacts. Most memorable, Basil had written, was the way she broke the spell that bound May Morris so firmly to the past, and to the ghost of her father (William Morris): 'My wife, whom to know is to love, could coax May Morris into shy merriment and persuade her to rehearse delightfully a nocturnal argument of cats'[367]. Christine's support for her husband's work sometimes extended to more directly academic pursuits. The indexes for the two volumes of Morris's *Collected Works* were her handiwork, as was the index to Newdigate's (Blackwell's) *Froissart*. Julian Blackwell recalled another occasion, when his mother's indexing of Sir John Chandos's book *Bernard du Guesclin* provided the proceeds to buy a Canadian canoe, for her family's adventures on the local stretch of the river.

Mucking around on the river was indeed a much-loved pastime; the whole family would set off together, Christine would organize a picnic worthy of five hungry children, and Basil would scull. These expeditions were, on occasions, combined with visiting friends, particularly lonely ones like May Morris. Christine would occupy the children, while Basil rowed the family 'up the sixteen miles of lonely Thames that winds between Kelsmcott and Appleton'. Summer holidays were family affairs. At times Christine would venture ahead of her husband, if he were bound by unavoidable business commitments, and write home most days giving an account of the children's

34 Basil on holiday.

doings. From the tenor of her letters, she gave the impression that she found it hard to cope: 'oh for the male parental eye', she wished. But this was all part of her skill of dealing with Basil. He was never excluded from the family, even if he did have to work long hours. One of her letters reveals her concern for children who were not closely connected with their own parents[368]. She may have managed her brood alone, and even tolerated sharing a bed with her eldest daughter, but 'when will you ever arrive?' she wrote to Basil. For Christine, holidays proper only started when Basil was safely ensconced on the beach complete with bucket and spade. Their early family holidays were spent with Christine's parents in Ramsgate. Later, and with five children in tow, they would often rent a house in Anglesey or Cornwall, and friends would join them nearby. Swallows and Amazons style, the Blackwell gang would then declare war on these friends, a pastime which absorbed them whatever the vagaries of the English weather. On winter evenings the family had to be content with board games and books. The Christmas festivities broke the routine of school, homework and reading. Christine would organize a rigorous programme of family performances. Set in the sitting room, with the library curtains pulled across, the Blackwell Thespians would bring to life the hero king 'Croton Hoton Thologos', and there were productions of home-spun plays too[369].

Under Christine's directorship, no one, however retiring, was spared. Sir Adrian Mott and his family, regular visitors, were not excepted: 'I have had very great pleasure and suffered intense agonies, from her famous hospitality', Adrian Mott wrote. 'There have been frightful occasions, at Osse Field, when she made me dress up and try to act in plays!' Once she even went so far as to insist on my playing the flute (fortunately behind the scenes), to the alarm and despondency of all concerned.' Sir Adrian's special favourite was Basil and Christine's daughter Corinna; who radiated the Blackwell charm. Not discounting her intellectual influence, the family and the local community saw Christine as an earth mother figure. She distributed the benefits of her wisdom, and at times the cut of her tongue, together with the fruits of her horticultural labours, to everyone—she had no time for 'side'[370]. Somehow Christine juggled this mixture of working, friends, children, husband and

35 Basil with his family.

young family. She gave unstinting service to the community, and combined endless fund-raising with the making of a huge flower and vegetable garden. This was her world, a world where her children, and subsequently her grandchildren, played, and one to which her husband escaped and recovered his equilibrium. Now, over 20 years since her death, the garden at Osse Field still bears her mark, and its beauty and variety has not been subdued by the vociferous woodland and scrub from which it was claimed[371]. Christine was fortunate enough to have some assistance in taming this garden, in the person of Cuthbert White. The Whites of Appleton ruled the roost in the village and Cuthbert White was a legendary figure in the lives of all the Blackwells, and as iconoclastic as his employer and friend, Basil. Cuthbert, like the Blackwell men, delighted in circumnavigating bureaucracy, and single-handed took on Oxford's one-way traffic system (a tendency he must have passed on to his young charge Julian Blackwell who is still carrying on this family tradition). When he wasn't helping Lady Blackwell, Cuthbert used to drive Basil around. The two conspirators would take delight in always arriving at any function in good time, a feat that could, more often than not, only be accomplished by driving the wrong way up the streets. Christine Blackwell enjoyed their insouciance, and when the two friends and conspirators were not leg pulling, they shared a keen interest in bell ringing.

Just as Fred Hanks had guarded Benjamin Henry's two small children, so Cuthbert was surrogate parent to Basil and Christine's. He was of particular importance to their youngest son, Julian. Being the youngest, and like many last, later, children, Julian was at the same time benignly neglected and over-indulged by his mother. Meanwhile, his father, in the 1930s, was never busier with the family firm and had little time to oversee his youngest. At the hands of his elder and better siblings, Julian received even shorter shrift, and he was left to his own devices, rather like his paternal grandfather as a small boy. Julian would kick his heels in the garden until Cuthbert rescued him, whereafter he would put his restless energy to good account. He was trained by Cuthbert to chop the firewood, and later took on this role for his father and mother. This occupation remains his favourite. But at the time, any other activity was eclipsed when he was invited by Cuthbert 'to help him tinker with the family motor'. Should there be a problem with the motor, Cuthbert would instruct Julian to perch on the front of the bumper, facing away from any on-coming traffic and cling onto the headlights. His job was to listen for the 'wrong clinks', while Cuthbert drove the offending machine rather too fast through the surrounding country lanes. Christine was not a nervous mother, and she was too busy to notice the minutiae of her youngest offspring's adventures. For his part, Julian revelled in his relative physical freedom. Spending long afternoons on the river in his own small boat he was free to 'be a bit frightened' to avoid his censorious siblings and it was the place, above all, where he could sort out his childhood fears and dream of greater things:

'. . . But the prince,
Laomedon's great son, beholding all,
Is rocked upon the mighty sea of cares;
Hither and thither his swift mind he parts,
Speeds it all ways, and sweeps the round of thought
As when from water in a brazen vat
A flickering beam, shot by the mirrored sun
Or bright moon's image, flits from side to side
O'er all things, and at last up-mounting strikes
The fretted ceiling of the roof on high'[372].

Not every young boy (Julian had not yet been sent off to Winchester) would appreciate Virgil's mastery of simile, and Julian probably felt more like Ratty, 'Believe me, my young friend, there is nothing—absolutely nothing—half as much worth doing as simply messing about in boats'[373]. Back home, he would come home to a warm kitchen, a fresh-backed cake and his mother's affectionate, and not too demanding, or penetrating, enquiries. Christine spoiled her youngest; she was a woman who knew what was needed of her, both as a mother and a wife; she would fend off her husband, when he wanted to push her youngest into some more cerebral activity and remind him not to be too hard a task master.

Dissimilar in temperament, as his own parents had been, Basil and Christine enjoyed sixty-two happily married years. Julian Blackwell insists that his parents were never heard to quarrel, and Basil could never recall a day when they wouldn't have married each other again. 'During those years', he recorded, 'we never put out the light if there was the slightest discord between us . . . and the light was always put out'. Another thing too, Basil hastened to add, was the 'kiss at parting, kiss at meeting—however short the parting'[374]. Basil was a stickler for routine; a rigidity that could, at times, make him a hard taskmaster. But Christine had the measure of him. She ignored his early morning rituals: getting out of bed at five-thirty to swim in the Osse Dyke Brook. Basil had enlarged a tributary to form a swimming pool, where he customarily took a dip: come rain, shine, or thick ice. When the weather permitted, he would perambulate in the adjacent woods and then, when warmed-up, disport himself naked on the lawn. There he would commune with his muses and out-sing the dawn chorus. His children would hear him as he bounded back up the stairs to the rhythm of some favourite from *Hymns: Ancient and Modern*. Impervious to his eccentricities, Christine preferred to stay in bed. Basil was expected to get his own breakfast, for which Christine funded him to the tune of £1 a week. Returning home, after work, Basil would make the walls shake as he yelled, 'Home! . . . Mimi, the Gaffer is come!'. Christine's response was more circumspect. Taking her own time, she would come down the stairs to kiss Basil, and then go out to potter in the kitchen while he would go and read or take a 'soak'[375]. Much restored by this Wordsworthian period of positive solitude, he would then join his wife in her garden.

It is not difficult to imagine Basil's pleasure in the garden of his wife's making. For her 'it was roses, roses all the way'[376]. He liked nothing better than to be seen scything the long grass at the front of the house in his oldest clothes. From time to time, Christine and friends would inveigle him into a day's outing, especially if he could see the work of Morris, and those connected with the Arts and Crafts Movement. On one occasion he was diverted to the beautiful church at Kilpeck. Basil never made it inside the door; he fell into deep conversation with the sexton, who was scything the long grass. Christine had to drag him away and, ever practical, she went in search of the nearest market, for provisions. He could hardly wait to get home to sharpen his blades. This obsession with scything and chopping must have come from his mother, and his son, Julian, still lists 'chopping wood' as his favourite hobby. Christine liked to have Basil out from under her feet, especially if she was cooking for visitors: but she expected him to come into line when she was ready. Still scything in the front garden, as their guest came up the driveway, Christine would reprimand him: 'Basil, people will think you are the gardener', to which he replied, 'I am the gardener'.

None the less delighting in his days of wine and roses, he found much needed relaxation as his wife's odd job man in the garden. He may not have been a very reliable one though; he was as keen to dream and reflect. Straying away from the house, he dawdled in the adjoining meadow and woods. Here he had the jocund company of daffodils, bluebells, wood anemones, and the wild flowers of early summer, safely propagating in the long grass. There was a trout stream at the bottom of the garden, and a well-stocked kitchen garden, an orchard of some two hundred apple trees and flowerbeds brimming over with hundreds of rose bushes. Every day, in the season, Basil would arrive at his desk with a posy of his wife's roses. He countered any opposition to this practice by insisting that flowers always humanized his workroom at Broad Street. And they were also offered as gifts to his young female staff.

These frippets, as he called them, and he got away with it, were hardly that. They were the younger members of staff who showed the most promise and whose loyalty and fresh intelligence helped him to read the minds of the new generation of book buyers. Basil insisted that he was much more interested in their minds than in other of their accomplishments. Using a term like frippet, to describe women colleagues is unthinkable today, but Basil was a Victorian. He would have been bemused by our distaste; his unmodish usage, he insisted, was meant to convey a sense of distance, respect and verbal playfulness. Undoubtedly, though, he was a man who enjoyed loving friendships. And he could see nothing wrong with this. His old friend, Arthur Norrington, wrote to him: 'I do think warmth and feeling is positively good for us, and the lack of it is bad for us.'

The full flood of his warmth and affection was reserved for his wife. No one was competition for 'The Mimi'. Christine's own warmth bound the family together, blunting the edges of Basil's ego and the excesses of his imagination. Christine was always on hand to reign in her husband's imaginary flights of fancy. She simply wouldn't let him get away with too much creative embroidery of the truth. She had openly admonished Basil when he invented a story for the Shakespeare critic, Wilson Knight. The Ghost in *Hamlet*, according to the school of Basil, did not speak, but was invented on the insistence of the theatre manager to help the audience. 'And, pray, how do you know that, Basil?' Christine asked. Basil parried 'that he knew it exactly the same way the Catholics knew the Virgin went to heaven in the flesh—through the imagination'. 'And I hope you told Mr Knight', came Christine's rejoinder, 'that it was a flight of fantasy'! Some of Basil's wilder ideas and projects may well have been designed to tease Christine, and she could be relied upon to rise to the bait with her tart 'Rubbish Basil!' which, according to Henry Schollick, was not far removed from Dame Alice More's 'Tilly vally Master More'[377]. That Basil would never openly concede defeat, and never admit to being changed, vindicates Christine's supreme skill in managing him. Torn between the demands of his inner world and a fast changing outer one, she saw her primary role, according to Julian Blackwell, as that of preventing Basil from needless worry. Throughout their long life together, Christine and Basil were bound together by a fierce loyalty to one another, and a clear sense that no one should ever be let down. He always maintained that there was 'never a day when we would not have married again'. 'She, a skilled tactician, let him have his head, or let him think he had it anyway'. And so this partnership continued until they could indeed both be likened to Mathew Arnold's 'bright and aged snakes'. Christine termed this period 'injury time'. They agreed that 'be this long or short, this time was to be reckoned as a bonus'[378]. Shortly after their sixty-second wedding anniversary, Basil wrote, 'my beloved was gradually withdrawn from us as life ebbed. Her courage remained invincible. Now the tide is in full flood, bringing the numerous treasures of precious memories. *Laus Deo*'[379]. Her garden remains as a tribute:

    'While by the rosebed gay you stood, and
    Revelled in the multitude' of blooms with unfamiliar names, and tints
    And folds new-found and sweet,
    We wondered much at the rich poser which
    Breeds so many and many a flower
    Not like the myriads known before, and
    Each one lovely and complete'[380].

Public duty

That portion of a man's life
The little nameless unremembered acts
of kindness and of love[381]

Basil Blackwell's concept of public duty stemmed from his belief in a God. Duty to God, Basil wrote, was his 'anchor in the tempestuous days of wavering faith and permissive—or shall I say—licentious society; and the anchor held'. Basil wrote 'of his loyalty to those twin duties set out in the Church Catechism: My Duty towards God (surely the loveliest sentence in the language) and My Duty towards my neighbour'. Such sentiments had been at the root of his parents' faith, and its simplicity had never left him. Gaffer, generous and humorous in dealing with the shortcomings of others, was a harsh self-critic, as his father had been. Some insight into the standard he aspired to can be gained through the writings and notes he left behind. His deepest respect was reserved for those who demonstrated their duty to others: to the community and in the workplace, and who showed compassion and willingness to make sacrifices[382].

As a young student Basil had thought to play his part should there be a possibility of war breaking out. While at Merton, Basil had joined the Officers Training Corps, and shortly after he joined the OUP in London Basil was contacted by the War Office to see if he could be counted on in the event of a war. His subsequent medical explained the consternation he had felt during his student soldier days, when he had never succeeded in hitting the target during rifle practice. Basil had attributed this failure to a lack of skill, but now he learnt that it was due to his bad eyesight. At his army interview Basil stated his willingness to serve but had to own up to his disability. Poor sight was not, however, the only bar to military service. At one of his medicals he had heard the two doctors discussing other symptoms! These, Basil surmised, could be put down to the bouts of fever, which had first beset him travelling around Greece in 1909. As a result he 'was courteously rejected', but Basil, ever the optimist, was determined to overcome this set-back; kill-or-cure, he settled for a routine of rowing and swimming, and during the War he 'joined-up' as a special Constable for the City of Oxfordshire. Thwarted in his attempts to serve in the field, Basil busied himself at his trade [383].

The richness and diversity of his busy life as the Gaffer of Blackwell's, and the father of a brood of children to be settled in the family's new house at Osse Field, Appleton, did not stop Basil Blackwell from casting his net further. In public and civic life, he was every bit as dutiful as his father, but his sense of what constituted 'community' extended way beyond Oxford and its surrounding countryside. Perhaps because of this wider horizon, his attitude to private acts of charity was less indulgent. While very much his father's son, Sir Basil was of another generation and held even more strongly to the view that work and education combined, rather than various forms of hand-outs, were the realistic cures for poverty. Sir Basil was often the butt of his own stories, and his attempts to see-off the stream of supplicants who continued to present themselves after his father's death did not turn out as he had planned. 'Presently', wrote Basil, 'I gave my mind to the possibility of helping them to help themselves. I offered to equip one of them with the apparatus of a window cleaner and enlisted a number of Oxford residents who promised to engage him regularly. He thanked me profusely for my good offices, but seemed to have serious reservations: "Unfortunately, when I gets up a ladder I turns giddy". I saw the light; I made the same offer to each of the lame ducks in turn. They all turned giddy up a ladder; so I was rid of them'. If this result did not exactly accord with Basil Blackwell's sense of public good, it left him freer to concentrate on those who needed help in his trade.

The wider public good was something that had troubled Basil from his student days at Merton. He was always haunted by the memory of the two World Wars, his imagination perhaps all the more vivid, and fearful, because he had been unable to serve in the front line. After the Second World War, he was influenced by those who wanted, if possible, a more permanent settlement in Europe. In 1953 he published a short pamphlet by Lionel Curtis, of All Souls. Curtis argued the case for closer political, as well as economic, relations with Europe, but the traditionalists were trying to evade the issue. He, by contrast, wanted to ensure that it was not evaded, and he had support from the business community, as well as academics and politicians. Churchill had been dismissed from office at the close of the War, and he carried forward his campaign in favour of European unity from the Opposition Benches. In 1946, Churchill had published his latest thoughts on the subject, in a short pamphlet: *A United Europe. One Way to Stop a New War*. The chairman of Barclays Bank, at the time, warned 'that there would be no prosperity until free nations merged their national sovereignties in one international state so strong that no aggressor would dare to challenge it in war'. Basil was at one with Curtis in believing that world wars are the inevitable consequence of the fragmentation of human societies into national states. They wanted, like Churchill, for the 'prison doors to clang open' . . . and for the captives of Europe 'to walk into a joyous world'. It was only in relatively recent history that, as Toynbee had remarked, the new wine of nationality made its 'sour ferment in the bottles of tribalism'.

Taking on the politics of Europe, was not, however, a campaign Basil had time to pursue, for he agreed with Curtis that 'everyone will find the issue difficult and no one more so than the English'[384]. But the English were also, to Basil's mind, paradoxical. Although they could be so small-minded, and they resisted all the early moves towards a European Community, they were defiant in the face of injustice[385]. How was it, Basil asked, that a nation that had given itself to the fight for freedom, 'that saw the terrible truth that injustice breeds injustice in an unending and unbreakable chain', could be limited in its conception of solutions? How often in later years, he wrote, have I watched the nations of the world caught in this ineluctable coil of mischief breeding? As he watched, he reflected on his student days when he had tried to wrestle with the Greek poet, from twenty-four centuries ago, Aeschylus Agamemnon, and how he had been irritated by such pessimistic sentiments as 'The sinful deed begets more in the likeness of his own kind'. In more recent times he was reminded of this credo. And supporting the move for closer European co-operation may, he hoped, go some way to breaking this mould. With these sentiments in mind, Basil despatched a donation to support the local, Oxford, pro-European lobby, during the run-up to the Wilson referendum in 1974[386]. Support for wider economic co-operation, albeit from behind his desk, fitted with Basil Blackwell's Liberalism, and his loathing for the nationalist conflicts that had bedevilled mankind's history. On another plain, Basil hoped that 'books', from the great traditions of European Literature, a 'common heritage of learning', would 'extend their healing power'.

By the early eighties, he was prepared to participate directly in party politics, something he had been loath to do in the past. He offered to support the Liberal Party, as did his daughter Penelope, who had hoped for a Parliamentary seat. Labour was in disarray and unelectable, and Thatcher, who he blamed for re-inventing the old divide, between 'them' and 'us', seemed unchallengeable. This situation, to Basil's way of thinking, threatened the principles of participatory democracy; some other alternative had to be offered up to the electorate. His thinking at the time was summed up by a fund-raising letter he had received from Lord Lloyd of Kilgerran, (Joint Treasurer of the Liberal Party): 'The Liberal leader, David Steel, and I and our colleagues, believe that the future of our nation and our way of life, the survival of our democracy and our institutions and the prospects for our children are all under threat and the threat comes from within. More and more people are joining us in the view that the greatest threat to the things we hold dear comes from our own failures, not from the actions of others. Of course, it is a difficult and dangerous world. There is competition from German and Japanese manufactures, a scarcity of oil and other resources and a reemergence of the Cold War. But we should recognize that most of our troubles are of own creation—and that we have actually been making them worse year by year, to the joy of our enemies and the disbelief of our friends'. In particular, the letter continued, 'we have put up with a system of industrial relations which divides companies into "them" and "us". The result is low productivity, low investment, lost markets and lost jobs'. As a consequence, it expanded, 'we have perpetuated an electoral system which divides us in the same dangerous way and produces weak governments elected by a minority of the people'.

The tone of the argument sounded so familiar, and it was as infuriating for Basil Balckwell, as it would be for his successors. One of the chief worries, for a businessman, was the inability to predict government policy, an early version of no substance—all spin perhaps? Lord Kilgerran's letter summed it up: policies 'have chopped and changed ... so often that no-one feels confident to plan ahead with a strategy for the future. Instead of accepting the principle of a "mixed economy", successive partisan governments, of one "side" or the other, have failed to grapple with the (economic) problems, and "a once proud and resilient people feels increasingly demoralized and cynical", and beset by industrial decline. "Only twenty-five short years ago, Britain had a motor car industry larger than the rest of Europe put together. Now we import the majority of our cars—most of them from Europe. . . . Once we had the largest motor-cycle industry in the world; now it has almost disappeared". Time was, he pointed out, when Britain had "a share in one quarter of all the world's trade—now it is 8% and still shrinking. . . . A textile industry which led the world in product and design . . . is a mere shadow of its former self". And so the sad litany went on: In "shipbuilding, general engineering, paper, electronics, chemicals, sugar processing, steel, large companies and small" and in the wider economy the "lifeblood of this country was seeping away and being replaced by expensive transfusions of foreign imports". "And when North Sea Oil runs out, we shall not be able to pay for those". After years of political misjudgement, and missed opportunities, our time has almost run out. Our whole economic political and social system is threatened. We must do something NOW to deal with the crisis facing all of us.'

Basil felt impelled to contribute to a reconstruction, especially as his business did not seem to be unduly beset by these ills. He had no time for 'the natural party of government' who had done far too little for private industry. Agreeing with the letter, Basil, too, had a problem with the alternative: the Labour Party, at the time divided by the ideology of 'half-baked', and much misinterpreted Marxism. Basil's prescription for recovery was akin to David Steel's: 'In January David Steel outlined a Ten Point Plan for national recovery. It called for a coherent economic and industrial strategy, built on a reformed political system. The response from all sides was encouraging. The swing of the pendulum towards the extremists must be arrested. We have all been the losers from it. But now the Liberals are being joined by others who share our view. A great alliance to change British politics is in the making'. Of much greater interest to the independent Blackwells was the chance to break the stranglehold of the established parties[387]. Basil duly sent a contribution to the SDP, and the accompanying letter:

'I must thank you for your letter of 28 July, which I have read and read again with growing approval, though I am sorry that it has reached me after the eleventh hour. That is to say, I have been hoping for an utterance of this kind for a long time; but last year, giving up hope of it, I joined the SDP as a life member: life membership doesn't mean very much in my case. At the moment I can only say that I hope that the Liberal Party—or *disjecta membra* thereof—will coalesce with the SDP and set about recruiting the vast body of moderate opinion which is unable to express itself to-day. It is very difficult to get enthusiastic about moderation, but this, I think, is what we must achieve, working for the moderate majority. For the moment then, you must count on me as looking with lively sympathy from the touchline; but in my ninety-third year I don't count for much[388].

Democracy for Basil Blackwell was never a dead letter, it was something to be aspired to, in the workplace and in all everyday dealings. Handing over as President of the Publishers Association in 1936, he spoke of this ideal, in a wider sense. But he was deeply worried about a lack of democracy in his own back yard. 'If I were bidden to sum up human life in a phrase, I should say that Life is experience understood too late', he ventured, 'and now that the tale of my days as your President is told, I feel come upon me somewhat of that belated wisdom which is the tantalising heritage of man'. Having started expansively, he soon homed in, but with customary delicacy: 'Looking back, I find that the publishers have shown a truer understanding of our difficulties than we have had of theirs; I find that misunderstandings for which there was no need from time to time have hindered work which publishers and booksellers together have undertaken; and I believe we shall be wise if we take thought to set on our Council one whose duty it will be to make clear to us what the Publishers think in all matters which are of moment to both sides of the Trade. I do not suggest that we should renew the office of *advoactus diaboli*, but I see a risk that our Association may lose something of its democratic nature. The tale of attendance at our council meetings on the part of two of three branches gives me to believe that either members think that the business of the Association can be left safely in the hands of the officers, or that our council meetings do not afford scope for single members to speak their minds. If the first be true, I am sorry, for that way lies mischief. Bureaucracy is only less evil than dictatorship. If the second be true, then too am I sorry, for the blame is partly mine. I fear that the business of the Association may have grown so much that such a big body as our Council, meeting so rarely, cannot deal justly with it'.

Basil was concerned that modern life made no time for the niceties of 'democracy: for open discussion. The business perforce must be digested in advance and prepared for quick dispatch. There is little time to spare for debate'. In his own publishing assembly he wanted a participatory democracy, not an autocracy: 'let us insist that one member from each branch shall in fact attend each meeting of the Council. For democracy to-day, in great matters as in small, is the precious but imperilled legacy of the nobler past—precious because it allows that every man is master of his soul and that his soul by itself has worth; imperilled because we have forgotten that the best gifts in life need ever watch and ward. It is not easy for the President of the Association to keep unwarped his view of the bookselling trade; for safeguarding is the chief end of our body, and a ship's captain whose time was spent in watching and stopping leaks, might well come to think that his vessel was unseaworthy and in present danger of sinking. But now that my voyage is over, and my harbour is in sight, I find, almost with wonder, that the ship still treads the waves. I mind me that in the course of my presidency more publishers than booksellers have foundered, and that for all the worries and struggles which have beset booksellers in these hungry years, our fellowship has not dwindled but grown.... We stand a small and slighted unit in a world distraught by folly and false gods—a world in deadly danger of overwhelming ills'. But, Basil thought, these dangers could be overcome because in the bookselling and publishing world there was a unity: 'we stand as ministers of literature, that slow invaluable cause where is truth enshrined in beauty and for ever by the miracle of written speech'[389]. And the cause of democracy, in the book trades, had other foes needing to be vanquished.

Knight of the Ring

If they (the Ring), Basil Blackwell vowed, can run me off by setting a price, I can run them off!

Public duty, for Sir Basil, extended beyond the physical and intellectual boundaries of the Oxford scene, to the wider publishing and bookselling industry. Always an individualist, he was determined to bust any system, however well entrenched, which imposed unfair trading conditions on his fellow tradesmen. And conflict, rather than co-operation, was making the antiquarian book trade in his own back yard into a battle zone. Serving as a member, and as President, of both the Publishers and Booksellers Association and the Association of Antiquarian booksellers, Basil determined to end the stranglehold of the 'Ring'. Blackwell's, from the earliest times in Little Clarendon, had relied on the sale of second-hand books, and antiquarian books continued to hold the fascination of Basil, when he had joined his father just before the First World War. In retrospect, he explained that his partiality, like his father's, lay in the fact that antiquarian books 'perhaps even more than new books, made for a close relationship between scholars and booksellers'. Basil had urged his father to expand the antiquarian side of things, and was frustrated by his reluctance. 'Why then', Basil had asked his father, 'especially when the Blackwell's collection was doing so well, were the stocks of antiquarian stocks so depleted?' Basil ventured 'that they should replenish the stocks', only to be exasperated by the 'Ooh No! You can't do that!' issuing from his father. Basil's countering 'Why!' was silenced by his more experienced and conventional father. 'The Ring!' Benjamin Henry Blackwell cried, 'The Ring wouldn't have you!'

The Ring, in the antiquarian bookselling business was a well-established fact; it had done its worst long before Benjamin Harris started to trade in old books; the legendary Bernard Quaritch had railed against it in a confidential letter, in January 1880. But as the book trade expanded, and the status, and the opportunities to buy private libraries changed, its machinations harmed smaller dealers and infuriated those trying to earn a crust and 'live' peacefully with their fellow booksellers. Basil, full of youthful verve, was determined to get things out into the open, and to wipe the booksellers' slate clean. At the same time, of course, he wanted to restock his antiquarian department. 'In 1922 the diligence of our cataloguers and the response of our customers has impoverished the antiquarian book stock, which was normally refreshed by casual offers of private libraries or smaller lots of books for purchase'. But how to do it? He would, he assured his father, go to the book auctions and 'buy' some stock. His father, ever practical, poured cold water on his ambitions: 'Impossible', he replied, 'we should be outbid by the Ring'. He explained, Basil wrote, 'that at auction sales, especially in the provinces, an informal group of prospective buyers with common interests would agree not to bid in competition, but to leave the bidding to one of their number who, in the absence of informed competition, would make considerable saving in the total cost of his purchases. After the auction the group would meet in private, usually in a pub, and bid in competition for the lots which their representative had acquired. The gross amount bid for the books in their private auction would exceed considerably that achieved in public sale, and this surplus would be shared by the members of the group, who thus individually would be able to acquire some of the lots at approximately their true market value, together with a bonus in cash from the settlement at the end of the day. In view of this gross surplus the Ring's agent could afford to 'run off' single competitors by bidding above the market value for individual lots'.

'I soon learnt', Basil later admitted, how members of the Ring were able to replenish their stocks at my expense: 'which was all very nice for them'. But far from being quashed by his father's warning that taking on the Ring would be futile: it only served to fire up Basil's sense of injustice. Initially, Basil refrained from differing with his father, who by then was getting towards the end of his life; out of filial respect, he bided his time. Quietly he made his own assessment of the situation. His father, until very recently, had been a prominent member of the Antiquarian Booksellers Association, and had served as its President. During their deliberations, as the minutes, written in Benjamin Henry's tidy hand showed, there had been much private wailing and gnashing of teeth on the subject of the Ring. But it all smacked too much of a gentleman's agreement, for Basil not to make a fuss. Whereas the Association did not recognize the Ring, their rules did not specifically condemn it, and so, 'it was not very hard to conclude that it did not protect its members'. One of the reasons for founding the Association had been to protect its members from financial hardship, and donations were granted by the committee, but it was more of a Friendly Society for social protection, and a social club, than a pressure group daring to enter the political fray[390]. Shortly after he took over at Blackwell's, and hearing of a good library up for sale in the West Country, Basil vowed: 'if they (the Ring) can run me off by setting a price, I can run them off'. Basil, still an unknown quantity in those days, set his trap; he would infiltrate and 'break the Ring, right under the noses of the book barons'.

Basil enlisted the help of a knowledgeable assistant, asking him to mark up the catalogue, awarding a top market price to each book on the list[391]. The assistant was then dispatched to the auction with instructions to bid for each of the books at these 'high' prices. 'Bid for every item', Basil insisted, 'you'll make nothing out of it. . . . They'll start running you off . . . and you'll be content to be run off!' Basil observed of his rivals 'that if they ever tried it on me again that is what I should try on them, and they've gone to all that trouble and expense for nothing'. But all this did, in practice, was to bid up the money ceiling for each lot. There was a moral victory, perhaps, for the Ring would get no surplus, but the honest dealer seldom got his books this way. 'So an uneasy *modus vivendi* was established'. But, for Basil, there was to be no collusion with the more unscrupulous members of the book trade: 'I stuck fast to my principles; I wouldn't budge, I wouldn't go into the Ring'. Elected as President of the Antiquarian Association, in 1925, Basil saw his chance to break this collusion; he issued a circular to all booksellers asking them to declare that they would not operate in the Ring. But more was called for than 'Scout's Honour'. But this wasn't enough either: Lord Darling's Act of 1927, outlawing bidding agreements, proved to be inoperative, and attempts at remedial measures, such as Basil's 'infiltration' strategy, were left to individual dissentients.

By the mid 1950s the collusive bidding at auctions began to attract uncomfortable publicity, especially after a major trade journal went to the wall. Articles, castigating the Ring, brought the revenge of the less upright members of the trade, who refused to renew their subscriptions. A vigorous protest ensued. Basil dashed off a letter to *The Times*. He always maintained that 'it was my letter in *The Times* stating my intention to compile and publish a list of Booksellers who would state in statutory declarations that they had no part in the Ring, which moved the Association to add to their rules'. A flood of correspondence followed. Basil led from the front, and signed a legal undertaking to say that he had never, and would never, take part in any ring. But the support he hoped for, from members of the trade, was not forthcoming. By the closing date for inclusion as a signatory to the informal agreement, there were only sixty-seven signatories to the declaration, out of a total membership of some 300[392]. There was general acceptance that debunking the Ring would take more than a gentleman's agreement; strengthening the Auction and Bidding Agreements Acts would require the support of 'more than the Antiquarian Booksellers Association . . . which has long been embarrassed by a skeleton in its cupboard', and only capable of the sort of weak reaction of other establishment bodies when faced with a complaint by one of its members, such as the British Medical Association[393]. But Basil, *The Times* applauded, was no 'general practitioner'. His very vocal opposition had let the cat well and truly out of the bag. And it became more than just a one-man crusade, as *The Times* has termed it. Basil's stand was supported now in many, public quarters: it inspired a riot of articles in the national, and international press and questions in the House, surprising at a time when Suez was brewing and taking the limelight. 'One Honourable Member, catching the Speaker's eye, demanded that the Joint Under-Secretary voice his strong disapproval of these brigands and advise how good people could be protected from their maraudings'. Basil Blackwell claimed that as a result of the affair of the Ring, he was almost immortalised when he appeared in Hansard as 'the gentleman in Oxford to whom we should all be grateful' in a speech made by the then Home Secretary, Lord Lloyd George[394].

In consequence of all the unwelcome publicity, the Association decided to include in its rules a formal disapproval of the practice, and Basil did manage to persuade the publishers of the *Directory of Second-Hand and Antiquarian Booksellers*, to place an asterisk against the names of those who had signed the 'Directory of Saints'. Thirteen years later the Ring was noticeably up to its old tricks again. And there was a renewed public crusade to face-out the Ring. The 1927 legislation was, finally, fortified by the 1969 amendments. And the Ring was, finally, illegal[395]. As far as most people knew, Basil noted, the antiquarian business settled down to a cleanish future. And, he added, 'even if the malefactors escaped the law, they would have to contend with an association who would ask for the culprit's resignation[396]. Yet the gestation of legislation had taken time, and its toll, and the mere fact of it being illegal did not stop it. Everyone, Basil wryly conceded, knew of the continued existence of the Ring, just as 'Catholics know of the existence of

Hell without exactly knowing who is in it'. The Ring was, however, driven to operate more clandestinely and less effectively. 'I am told', Basil wrote, in 1969, that the Ring still operates, but cautiously. 'At any rate', he delighted, 'the harlots are off the streets'[397].

Naturaliter Oxoniensis

According to an ancient custome and laudible use of this City of Oxford used yearly at this day, ye shall give prayse to Allmightie God for certen benefactors late of this Citty departed out of this life to His mercy. And also pray unto God for the preservation of the good estate of some yet living . . . [398]

While Basil Blackwell accepted that he had to 'let young genius stretch its wings elsewhere'[399], he felt no such imperative. This did not, of course, extend to holidays, and to business in London or elsewhere. But however stimulating he found excursions beyond Oxford, he was always drawn back by the physical love he had for his native city: its rivers and rural environs. He was never parochial, just firmly rooted in the place where his family had thrived; such was the extent of their good estate that Basil Blackwell felt that he owed fealty to Oxford. The family firm was part of the Oxford landscape: both as a presence on Broad Street and in its intellectual circles. But the Blackwells were part of the City's commercial life too. And Basil never forgot this. Oxford had been his grandfather's adopted city, where the name B H Blackwell was first established and his children born, and he never hankered after the streets of East London. Like his father, Basil was born over a shop in Oxford. And here he spent his childhood and his working and public life. Basil grew up enjoying the country and the town, and from his earliest years he imbibed his father's enthusiasm for Oxford and Oxfordshire. Benjamin Henry had written of his love of Oxford and its attractions in local tourist booklets, and he had more than demonstrated his commitment, involved as he had been in such a wide variety of local causes. As a child, Basil would listen to his father hymning the great chroniclers of Oxford, most usually Matthew Arnold's words: 'Lovely all time she lies'. This was a family trait that continued. On the night of Christmas Eve 1940, on his way to take a turn at fire watching with close friend, Henry Schollick, they strayed up the pathways, as they had often done in old days. Turning into Broad Street, Basil disturbed the peaceful night with his own joyous incantation:

> 'And that sweet City with her dreaming spires,
> She needs not June for beauty's heightening,
> Lovely all times she lies, lovely tonight!'[400]

After the war, in rare periods of solitude, Basil would row up the river in his double-sculling skiff, pondering on the beauties of the countryside from the comfort of the 'Rose Revived'. Basil continued to be drawn by the local rivers and backwaters, long after they were claimed by modernity. Well into his seventies, Basil would pull strongly away from the landing stage to the hum of aeroplanes overhead, on their way to a local runway. 'The old wooden weirs and bridges' he wrote, 'were replaced by concrete, and locks had replaced rollers for the benefits of motor boats'. If 'as part of the passing of an age', Basil wrote, 'folks lounge on the decks of cabin cruisers while they speed heedlessly about the stream, soothed (I suppose) by the tawdry music which normally invades their homes', then the loss was theirs. Basil's labours were accompanied by the crescendo and diminuendo of music heard 'at water-level'. His ear was trained to pick up the sounds of swaying rushes, 'the plash of sculls patiently dipped, and the quiet mirth of the little eddies as the blades are pressed home'. His body reaped the rewards of 'stimulating fatigue of muscles rhythmically employed in the skilful economy of rewarding effort; ... the deep content in healthy weariness and the sense of achievement at the day's end. In the dark winter months, Basil was restless, like 'the heavy elms' waiting for 'the uneasy wind' to rise and the oncoming of 'the daylight new born. . . . in the midst of corn'[401]. Such joys, and compensations, had been known to Basil's father in his heyday, and continued to delight his own children, especially his sons who both became oarsmen.

But the forces of change, the urbanization of the countryside, had not made Basil weary of Oxford. Aside from rowing, his other great enthusiasm, publishing, was to be enjoyed mostly within its boundaries. At the very start of his career, when he had joined the firm in 1913, Basil's dreams of publishing had dominated his ambitions. But Basil was not to be so easily lured away. The calls of Oxford were over-riding. Resisting all overtures, and refusing to be drawn to London, except for a 'gap year' at Amen Corner, Basil wrote that 'the bookshop anchored me to Oxford'. Basil threw himself into the task of developing the local market: catering for a broad church of taste and interest and, mindful of 'newer' subjects, finding openings that the larger publishers, outside of Oxford, neglected. Although he accepted as inevitable 'that young genius would stretch its wings elsewhere' his judgement was shrewd. Oxford was to his mind a place where certain books would perhaps 'do better than in London'. At the very end of his life he told a journalist that he was never tempted away from Oxford, not even when his own poets, whom he had discovered and nurtured, forsook him for the metropolis. Asked if he regretted not having established a London imprint, his answer revealed his deep affection and ties to Oxford: 'in the end I had to say "Well I can go to London and fight it out, but I can't do that and stay in Oxford at the same time." And so I let it go'[402]. This stickability paid off for the firm, and for Basil Blackwell personally. During his lifetime, he became one of the most esteemed Oxford citizens of his generation[403].

Respect for Basil as a *naturaliter Oxoniensis* was matched by love for him as a personality: as an Oxford character. 'When not working in his shop in the Broad', wrote Jan Morris, 'he was frequently to be encountered. If not addressing literary meetings or showing eminent foreign librarians round the Oriental Department, then he would be eating and drinking'. This he did moderately, but merrily, in his favourite High Street restaurant, the local wine bar or, if it was lunchtime, at Merton. Feeling at ease with Oxford, city and county, Basil did much to straddle the divide between Town and Gown. This so-called 'gulf between' was something that had exercised his mother, who berated her husband for his deference to the University. Basil was proud of his roots as a son of 'the town'. His own career, first as a scholar and then as a tradesman, the Gaffer of Blackwell's, welded the two together. Sir Michael Sadler, his father's friend, returning to Oxford from the civic University of Leeds, and inspired by the lack of division there, enlisted Basil Blackwell's help in promoting contacts between Oxford's City and University.

Basil Blackwell left behind an account of one such, nearly disastrous, attempt to weld together Town and Gown. His help was enlisted by L R Farnell, Rector of Exeter College, Oxford, who wanted to approach the wealthy W R Morris, the car manufacturer, to provide funds for the establishment of a Chair of Spanish in the University. Farnell was not noted for his tact; in fact Sir Michael Sadler once said of him: 'If we had him as a pet hippopotamus we should be immensely proud of him but we should not welcome him into a china shop'. Dismissing Basil's advice, that Morris should be approached through a close friend, Farnell wrote a letter to Alderman Sir Hugh Hall, the Conservative agent, suggesting that since Morris had wrecked Oxford with his factory, 'the least he could do would be to make a generous contribution to the University to whom his presence had been so prejudicial'. Hall's sensitivity was equal to Farnell's: he sent a copy of the letter straight to Morris. Morris's reply, Basil Blackwell recorded, was 'a masterpiece of its kind ... which equalled in severity, and very nearly in dignity, Johnson's letter to Lord Chesterfield. It concluded: 'this is the first approach that had been made to me for support for a University undertaking. It will be the last'. But mean-spiritedness was not Morris's way. Sensing this, Basil called on the help of local tradesmen, who had more understanding of business, to keep the door open with Morris. The local diplomat, Hall the Tailor, found a way round; Morris donated £10,000 to the cause[404]. Sir Basil's friendship with this Morris, who became Lord Nuffield, inadvertently helped the establishment of Blackwell Scientific Publications; in fact it probably owed its existence to W R Morris's benefaction to the Oxford Medical School in 1936.

When it came to the tribalism of Oxford, the ancient feud between Town and Gown, Basil Blackwell practised what he preached. Later, Sir Maurice Bowra, writing of Blackwell's, marked it out as a place where Town and Gown were friendliest. Anyone who knew anything of life behind the scenes at Blackwell's, could have produced primary evidence to support Bowra's view; the staff at Blackwell's were Town, and proud of it too, but, in the main, they served the University. Their Gaffer was Town and Gown all at the same time, and he had as warm a relationship with his staff as ever he had with other Fellows. His special favourites were the porters, packers and cellar men 'the oldest inhabitants of most old English book firms'[405]. Basil loved to hear their stories, and to find out how life was treating them. At the same time, and despite the fact that academic books were the firm's business, he gave short shrift to any academic figures that tried 'to ingratiate themselves with pomposity or pretensions'. When he thought it was called for, Basil could turn his frustration on both Town and Gown, especially, prophetically, when they dragged their feet over measures to improve the local environment. He was a trustee of the Oxford Preservation Trust from its foundation, and it was one of his great disappointments that although citizens and academics alike paid lip service to the great good it achieved, relatively few gave it either practical or financial support. He saw plenty of the ins and outs of private, as well as public life, during his years as an Oxford Magistrate.

After fifteen years of service as a Justice of the Peace, Basil was appointed to the Chairmanship of the Bench. He was also Chairman of the Juvenile Court and the Discharged Prisoners Aid Society for Oxford and the adjoining counties, combining this as one of the Visiting Justices of HM Prison in Oxford. He would take his friends with him on his visits to the prison, and introduce them to his 'acquaintances'. When prisoners were nearing release, he would help them, if he could, to find work, writing them references and providing other kinds of support[406]. During his years helping offenders, or as a magistrate, he was never known to be pompous. In Court, he would stare anyone up before him straight in the eye, knowing full well that he couldn't see him or her through his reading glasses. Sir Basil insisted that he recorded all the names of those who came in front of him, especially the juveniles, and if they appeared again he would count it as a failure, on his part[407]. Invariably they came to look on him in a positive light, but not always. Adrian Mott remembered a garden party where Basil nearly came unstuck. 'At a College (Merton) garden party, he was intent on talking to a very pretty American girl when she suddenly discovered that he was the unsympathetic beak who had fined her twice for bicycling offences. Never have I seen a woman so angry: in that decorous company she told him off like a fish wife. Never have I seen the majesty of the law so flouted, or its representative so taken aback'[408]. But not all of those Basil came into contact with could defend themselves, or attack, so vociferously. Basil had a great weakness for the underdog, especially those he entertained in front of the Bench, and he dined out on their stories.

Basil could never resist an opportunity to tell stories, and the stories of those who came up before him on the bench intrigued, as well as troubled, him. For public consumption, he would 'edit' and embroider them, often turning them into cautionary tales, or 'parables'. 'Now the other day', he would begin; 'I had to deal with a boy who was in great trouble. He could not keep his hands from picking and stealing, nor his tongue from evil speaking or lying. His parents said they had done all they could to get him right and failed. His schoolmaster had done all he could and had failed, and then he had been to see a wise and clever man called a psychiatrist, who told us what was wrong with him, which, in fact, we knew; but he did not tell us how to get him right. Now all that was left was to send him to a school specifically set up to deal with boys who cannot learn to behave properly'. This depressed Basil; sending people into custody, especially the young and impressionable, usually made a bad situation worse. Certainly he had little time for retributive justice, and he made his own study, and analysis, of the social causes of crime. As usual his approach, when he wanted something done, was diplomatic: 'To my mind the British people have no more admirable characteristic than their constant care for improvement in the administration of justice and in the treatment of convicted law breakers'. And, he wrote, we had moved a long way from the days, before 1780, when the death penalty could be imposed on adults and children alike for 200 different offences. By his grandfather's time, transportation had, largely, replaced the death sentence. He cited the sentencing records of the Stafford Prison Register for 1834: Will Biglen, 14, for stealing one silk handkerchief sentenced to transportation 7 years, Matilda Seymour, 10, for stealing one shawl and one petticoat—transportation 7 years, Thomas Bell, 11, for stealing 2 silk handkerchiefs—transportation 7 years. But, Basil noted, minors were still treated as harshly as adults: Lord Norton writing to Sir William Harcourt in 1881 makes reference to a child of 7 who had been sent to prison. 'On entrance you come to the male felons' ward and yard in which are both the tried and the untried—those in chains and those without them—boys and men—persons for petty offences, and for the most atrocious felonies . . . they were employed in some kind of gaming and they said they had nothing else to do.' The Jailer told him 'that in an experience of nine years he had never known an instance of reformation; he thought the prisoners grew worse, and he was sure that if you took the first boy you met with in the streets and placed him in his prison, by the end of the month he would be as bad as the rest and up to all the roguery of London.'

In Basil's view, 'to sentence a child to such an experience was in fact to sentence him to moral death'. But no amount of factual information, either historical or current, could be as persuasive, he wrote, as the accounts to be found in literature. *The Old Curiosity Shop* provided Basil with ammunition: 'It gives a glimpse of that shockheaded, shambling, awkward lad, Kit Nubbles, accused by Mr Sampson Brass of stealing a £5 note, who, in half an hour afterwards was committed for trial and was assured by a friendly officer on his way to prison that there was no occasion to be cast down, for the sessions would soon be on, and he would, in all likelihood, get his little affair disposed of, and be comfortably transported in less than a fortnight.' And indeed the prospect of transportation might well appear comfortable to a boy whose elder brother could have been one of the five children aged between 12 and 8 years who were condemned to death at the Old Bailey in February 1814. Oliver Twist was luckier, he had a benefactor: with many interruptions, Mr Brownlow contrived to state his case, observing that, in the surprise of the moment, he had run after the boy (Oliver) because he saw him running away; and expressing his hope that, if the magistrate should believe him, although not actually the thief, he was connected with thieves, but he hoped he would deal as leniently with him as justice would allow. 'He has been hurt already,' said the old gentleman in conclusion. 'And I fear,' he added, with great energy, looking towards the bar, 'I really fear that he is ill.' 'Oh! yes, I dare say!' said Mr Fang, with a sneer. 'Come, none of your tricks here, you young vagabond; they won't do. What's your name?'. . . . 'How do you propose to deal with the case, sir?' inquired the clerk in a low voice, 'Summarily,' replied Mr Fang. 'He stands committed for three months—hard labour of course. Clear the office.'

Social reformers were beginning to urge the Home Office to segregate young and adult offenders, and to develop 'the true principles of correction, as distinguished from retribution'. The next landmark, Basil wrote, came in 1880. 'Sir William Harcourt, when Home Secretary, was appalled by the number of young folk who were sent to prisons ... He had no easy task in winning the approval of Queen Victoria, who was "disturbed by what she felt was his undue tenderness to offenders ... she would have been forewarned of these numerous remissions"'. It was a tussle between the old idea of retribution and the growing belief in reformation.... The hand of his Royal Mistress perhaps may be seen in the grant of discretion to magistrates to substitute a whipping for imprisonment in the case of indictable offences. The birch was not plucked from the magistrates' hands till 1948. The juvenile system, Basil explained: 'separate hearing of children's cases in a court having Chancery rather than criminal jurisdiction', had its origins in America in 1878, but an Act, in 1905, saw the first session of an English Juvenile Court in Birmingham; other towns followed the lead. It was a fixed obligation for magistrates in the Juvenile Court not to think first of punishment, but to think and think and think again how to bring it about that this young law breaker shall not offend again, and further shall not *wish* to offend again. The Children's Act—'we might almost call it the Children's *Magna Carta*', abolished imprisonment of boys and girls under 16, and ordered the establishment of Juvenile Courts substantially as we know them to-day'[409].

The central cause of crime, in Basil's book, was a lack of broad education, in schools, the home and the community. 'Once upon a time, long, long ago', he recounted, 'a simple race of Indians lived in a meadow at the foot of a mountain, and there they had everything they needed except water, and when they needed water they had to go up the mountain by a steep and narrow path to a spring, which was in a cavern some way up. And then one day there came among them one who appeared to be a magician. He called himself Psycho the Wizard, and he said, "You need not give yourselves the trouble of going up the mountain to fetch the water. Leave it to me: I will bring the water down into your houses. All you have to do is to turn on a tap and have all the water you want"; and he was as good as his word, and they lived very happily for a long time, until one day there came a time of great trial. A great frost came, harder and longer than anyone could remember, and when they went to turn their taps on no water came out; and they gathered together and said, "If we have no water to drink and none to cook with, or wash with, we shall surely die. What can we do?" And then one of the oldest of them said, "I remember when I was a boy we used to go up a steep and narrow path up the mountain to a spring in a cavern and fetch water for ourselves. That spring never failed." And the young ones rose up and said,

"Why were we never told of this spring?" And the old ones said, "We had clean forgotten about it." So. . . . But I feel quite sure that you are clever enough to finish the story for yourselves'.

If the 'old ones had clean forgotten about it', then the juvenile system provided a chance to remind parents of their obligations: 'The parent or guardian is required to attend at the Court with the offender. At the end of the presentation of the case, if the plea, or the Court's finding is Guilty (the words 'conviction' and 'sentence' may not be used) the police record, if any, is read, and then the Court has to take into consideration reports on the home, and conduct of the youngster, both generally and at school, and the progress of his schooling'. Basil would have liked to have introduced 'the suspended sentence', which operated in the USA, France, Italy and, I believe, most countries in West Europe'. For Basil, it was the adults who were to 'blame' if children went, seriously, beyond the law. He derived his 'evidence' from his experience in the adoption court, 'I constantly had cause to admire the providence which finds for the helpless infant the devotion of two worthy adoptive parents whose union after anxious years has proved to be barren'. 'It was very rare', he noted, 'for their prodigy to appear in the courts'. He was all in favour of 'binding the parents over . . . to give security by recognisance for the good behaviour of the offender'. He advocated 'binding them in a substantial sum; and it is important that the sum should be forfeit if there should be further misconduct'. Schools too, had a duty to ensure attendance, and he was all for 'prosccuting local authorities who failed in their duties'. The whole justice system, especially for the young in trouble, presented Basil with another of his 'individual versus collective good' conundrums. He noted:

'There are no juvenile delinquents
Here is a young creature in trouble
How manage that not only will he not offened again,
But that he won't want to offend again?
Compassions—understand why he offended.
Correct the circumstances which induced him to offend
Or help to overcome them.
Question: Which did sin, the youngster or his parents? [410]

His work as a magistrate, and the number of sessions over which he presided, grew in the sixties, when his eldest son took over the day-to-day running of the family business. In his time, this aspect of his public life became well known, and his views were sought by penal reformers, as well as national and local experts. He wrote copious notes on the issues, and, as ever, he looked to literature, and writers, for analysis and resolution. Dame Edith

Sitwell wrote to Sir Basil, in 1964, praising 'the wonderful work' he had done for Oxford's 'juvenile delinquents'[411]. His work with the young was not restricted to those in trouble. It was an exercise in systemic, or 'joined-up thinking'. 'What the young needed was a good education, and security, especially if it wasn't forthcoming, for whatever reason, from home'. He had watched the changing fashions in education with a mixture of admiration and horror: admiration for the opportunities given by the reforming post-war governments, and horror at the, later, attempts of governments to remove opportunities for poorer children. He was ever mindful of his own father's struggles, and those of so many of the Blackwellian apprentices, and he deplored the idea that the best (formal) education should be restricted to those who could afford to pay[412]. He had an eye for the local 'scholarship boys', and he, and his wife, cultivated the head teachers. He was always on the look out for 'suitable candidates' creaming-off promising youngsters, often from Oxford High School (Boys), to staff his shop; 'school leavers' had, since the mid-fifties, replaced apprentices.

In this way, such 'scholarship boys' came to work at the shop, rather than 'stay on at school and go to the university', although the universities were, in the sixties, expanding as never before. Parents conspired; this was still the age of 'get a good job with prospects'; children could live more cheaply and 'safely' at home. At the other end of the scale were the public schools where 'staying on and going to university', preferably The Universities, was the norm. Basil had remained in close touch with his old school, Magdalen College School, which subsequently benefited from his lifelong interest and commitment. As a graduate, Basil had continued to row until he had, what he described as: 'the grace to decline a seventh year. . . . whereafter I took to coaching young hopefuls from my old school'[413]. 'When the very existence of Magdalen College School was in danger, in the twenties and thirties, there was no large body of Old Boys on whom to call for support'. 'Had it not been for the help given by John Johnson, the University Printer', wrote Basil, 'the school may well have ceased to exist'. And Basil played his part. From 1944 he helped with the governing of the School, serving on the School Committee for the next twenty years. During his time as a governor he pushed the introduction of scholarships and bursaries, and after the war, as the school grew and prospered, 'it was able to provide places for boys from many different backgrounds'.

In 1966, when the new school buildings had been completed, Basil Blackwell wrote to Master: 'my aspiration of forty years has been achieved . . . it is now time to leave (he was by then seventy-seven)', or, as he put it, quoting Horace: '*Nunc arma defunctumque bello, Barbiton hic paries habebit*'. On special occasions, Basil continued to lunch at his old school until the end of his life; he was always adept at finding a good lunch. In the City of Oxford it seemed as though no door was closed to him; he was an established, if not always establishment, figure. But the welcome he found in Oxford was every bit as wholehearted outside of Oxford. On his move from North Oxford, to the rural village of Appleton, in 1929, he became a 'local' almost overnight! From the start, the family got stuck in, supporting local initiatives and the local community; Christine's work, particularly was described as 'tireless'. So much so that no one remembered that they were newcomers! Basil, in any case, always maintained that he had a natural aptitude for (John Donne's) *country pleasures*, and his children played in the lanes as country children always had. His mother had told him tales of country life, and she had introduced him to the 'lores' of the countryside and something of its larder; his own children became as adept as any child from either far-off Blo' Norton or nearby 'Lark Rise'.

It was always easy for the Blackwell children to escape their busy parents clutches, when it wasn't meal times. They had their own provisions: they picked blackberry, sloe and crab-apple, and found sorrel for a starter. They declared friendly war on other local children, and used conkers and stones embedded in snow, in season, like anyone else. During the real war Basil commanded the area Home Guard, and at other times, when and if required, he waged war on local bureaucrats: he was chairman of the parish council, churchwarden, school manager and member of the village hall committee. For fun, and to make up for his lack of musical skills, he had a go at bell-ringing at Appleton church. Every year, without fail, he could be heard chanting (he could never sing) his favourite mantra: 'There's a hole in my bucket' at the annual 4 March Bell Festival! In 1976, when the number six, 'Laurence', bell was recast, it was paid for by the Blackwell family and named 'Gaffer' as a permanent memorial to a man who was much loved[414]. The inscription on the newly cast bell read: '*Laurenti vocor, ore meo saepe ille sonabit. Mi reduci Gaffer nomen opesque dedit*', being liberally translated as: 'St Laurence bell am I, his voice and mine the same. Restored by the grace of Gaffer, I now take his name'. This local honour, given by his adopted village, was treasured by Basil.

It had been alleged, by Graham Greene's wife, that this enthusiasm for bell ringing may have immortalized him, reincarnated as Dorothy L Sayers's Lord Peter Wimsey. This is not, however, certain. But Basil Blackwell was honoured in a variety of other ways, both by the City and the University.

The Gaffer

36 The Freedom of the City.

At an informal meeting, 1 December 1968, the Council was to consider the following motion: 'That this Council in pursuance of Section 259 of the Local Government Act, 1933, hereby confers upon Sir Basil Blackwell the Honorary Freedom of the City of Oxford in recognition of his eminent services to the City over many years and as an expression of the honour and esteem in which he is held'[415]. It went through on the nod. The leader of the council described Sir Basil as 'one of our most distinguished citizens'. His work, in all its aspects drew praise: as a bookseller, publisher, magistrate, his contribution to Oxford's causes, his support for the City Library, his work for the Preservation Trust, and his wider contribution to Britain's export drive. But, above all, came praise for the man himself: 'as an enlightened employer'; 'known as a person of integrity and kindness, nationally and internationally'. He was, in the view of the Council, 'an Oxford, and an Oxfordshire, man, not merely a man of the University' and one who had become 'an institution in his own lifetime'[416]. An old friend, from Basil's father's time, now at an advanced age and living in a service flat, wrote to remind him how proud his parents would have been: 'and perhaps are'[417].

Basil himself saw it as a vindication, 'and a happy ending to a family history that began in Oxford 125 years ago'. He had often regretted that his own father and grandfather did not, under the older legislation, the City's Charter of 1197, qualify for the Freedom of the City[418]. Their temperaments were such that they would probably not have been exercised, on their own account, but they would perhaps have been more covetous, as well as proud, of the University honours that came Basil's way. In his sixties, he was awarded an Honorary Fellowship of Merton College. Horace's words: '*Hoc erat in votes. . . . nil amplius oro*', summed up Basil's feelings, but, unlike Virgil's husbandman, he did know his good fortune.

For Basil Blackwell the Merton Fellowship represented the summit of his personal achievement, 'This was my dearest wish: I ask no more'. In his view, Merton had already given him much to be thankful for: friendships from undergraduate days, a partner: Adrian Mott who the Gaffer regarded as the 'keeper of his conscience', contact with generations of Fellows, from different disciplines and age groups, and the continuous hospitality of the Common Room, where he frequently took his lunch. As a token of his love for his old College, he assembled a collection of the printed works of Aldus Manutius, the late 15th century Venetian friend of scholars, with whom Basil must have felt a special affinity given his own similar line of work[419]. Basil's own scholarly work was met with formal recognition when, at the age of ninety, in the centenary year of the founding of the Broad Street firm, the University of Oxford admitted Sir Basil to degree of Doctor of Civil Law. He was described by the Public Orator, John Griffith of Jesus College, as 'the doyen of the book trade'. . . . who always had 'at heart the interests of the bookselling world as a whole, by vigorously campaigning for the fairest possible conditions of trade'. And he was, appropriately, in the company of one of his own distinguished authors: flanking him in the procession was Graham Greene who had first been published by Basil Blackwell. From the Tower of Merton College, a peal of bells rang out the news across Oxford City[420]. The sentiments of the assembly were summed up by Sir Arthur Norrington: 'Nobody better deserves to be pointed out to the citizens' children, as he goes on his way about our city, as a shining example of an Oxford man, in the full sense of that expression'[421].

Many in Oxford were drawn into Blackwell's centenary celebrations, and Sir Basil wined and dined his friends from the shop, the University, the town and from his home in Appleton. He stood as a reminder of an era that had passed: when his grandfather had offered tired workmen tea in the Temperance Rooms and frowned on their newspaper reading, in the 'new' public library; when his father had given the 'sons of Belial' a lucky break, and looked up to Matthew Arnold, a Newdigate prize-winner with a poem on Cromwell, who despised tyranny and advocated the benefits of education for all. At a time when the divide between 'gentlemen' and 'worker', and 'Town' and 'Gown' seemed fixed, the early Blackwells admonished them all alike: the government, the City Council and even those 'clever men of Oxford', if they didn't mind their ways. Basil had been summoned by Betjeman's bells to remember his childhood, and the long walk to church in uncomfortable, formal, dress. And they tolled for his friends, who never survived the war to move on from Merton. He was already thirty-one when the first woman officially received an Oxford degree, and Oxford bags made undergraduates into peacocks again, as his grandmother's waistcoats had fifty years before. No fewer than five generations of undergraduates knew something of Basil, either as a child, boy or man. And he could tell them of a time when there was no such thing as the Cowley Car Works, and no such thing as a Morris Minor. At the age of ninety Sir Basil Blackwell was older than ten of the Oxford colleges, and only twenty years younger than Keble College's quadrangle[422].

He had even outlived the Sheldonian's emperors. Those old despots on their pedestals, opposite Blackwell's, were made of less resilient stuff than the infant of 1889. These emperors, Jan Morris wrote, 'sank from the comic to the grotesque and finally the macabre, until, in Basil's eighty-third year, they were replaced by younger and less leprous incumbents'[423]. Oxford's Knight had outlived the emperors! Sir Basil could well have recalled the Psalmist's words 'The lines are fallen unto me in pleasant places: yea I have a goodly heritage'[424].

Sir Gaffer

... honours for ordinary folk in ordinary jobs[425]

Oxford was not the only source of honour for Basil Blackwell; a knighthood had already been conferred on this 'Jupiter of booksellers' in 1956, when he was in his sixty-seventh year. It was a first for the book trade: Basil Blackwell was 'the only bookseller in England ever to receive a knighthood from the monarch[426]. His Trinity neighbours wrote immediately with their congratulations, as did the City Librarian and the Library Committee, who in earlier years had spurned his father. With the announcement of this honour, recognition came to Basil, not only from his City, his University, his work colleagues and local friends, but from across many worlds. Most aptly, writers acknowledged his role in their world; many of whom had relied on Basil in the days when they had been 'unknown to fame'. T S Eliot, having first heard the news in America, wrote of this 'well-merited knighthood', but added that he was not sure 'how to address a knight before he has been knighted'[427]. Further afield, *The Auckland Star*, a leading daily voice of New Zealand, paid tribute to the man who developed 'a real bookman's shop'. An article in an American newspaper, the *St Louis Post-Dispatch*[428], saw the significance of 'this high honour bestowed on a vendor of books' as being 'symbolic of the considerable place in the national culture that books still occupy in England, despite the inroads of television and other competitors for time and money and the big rise in book prices'.

More importantly, the honour was symbolic of the post-war social changes taking place in England; 'People's Peers' would have been unthinkable still in the Fifties, but manifestly not 'People's Knights'. Post war Britain had woken up to the fact that there should be '. . . honours for ordinary folk in ordinary jobs'. Back at the office Basil's secretary teasingly tried to bring him down to earth, remarking 'apparently you have some friends!' Her Gaffer forbore to respond to what he hoped must be an understatement. And friends there were, none more important than those in the ranks of his own staff. They subsequently delivered an illuminated address, bound in the form of a book, signed by over 250 employees. It was headed simply, in beautiful Gothic lettering: 'Sir Gaffer'. The Rector of Exeter College penned a salutation from the university, which was framed and hung in the stairwell of the Oxford shop:

> *Reinae natalis adest: vos plaudite, docti;*
> > *Ecce Niger Puteus rite creatus eques!*
> *Profuit hic multos studiosis omnibus annos;*
> > *Haud umquam melior bibliopola fuit.*
> *Nam, quaecumque veils, librum tibi praebet emendum,*
> > *Teque libens gratis perlegere usque sinit.*
> *Hic etiam prelis edenda volumina curat*
> > *Ipse suis, lepida nota typographia.*
> *Ergo, quem Regina novo decoravit honore,*
> > *Granatur cives, grator et ipse, viro.*

It was also intended to honour Blackwell's itself; as a generous place and one where people could browse freely among the shelves. This was a tradition that the Knight of the Black Wells properly attributed to his father. For Blackwellians, the honour was all the more welcome because it came via trade, and service, not political patronage.

An independent spirit

Liberty to know, to utter, to argue freely

Basil Blackwell, for all that he had the reputation as a negotiator, had his run-ins with the authorities: with the government (he loathed the taxation system), and the local council (he hated the one-way traffic system), with the University, with authors, publishers and, occasionally, his customers. Some of these 'conflicts' even made the headlines of the day. Basil had the independence of his forebears, albeit tempered by the forbearance of his father, who preferred silence if in any doubt, and he possessed his mother's spiritedness; she was never artful or obsequious, sometimes to the embarrassment of her husband. Basil did not court favour: 'preferring to speak out forcibly without fear nor favour'. Political correctness was anathema to him. His early political education, influenced by such rare and diverse spirits as Fred Hanks, G D H Cole, Bertie Russell, Bernard Shaw, and William Morris, had made him an enthusiastic supporter, in more than token ways, of the social transformation set in train by Beveridge; yet, later, he hated the rigidities of state provision. He disliked the dissembling, and the machinations, of the Wilson and Heath days in equal measure. He loathed, for example, the watering down of the grammar school education system, which deprived secondary schools of a curriculum that emphasized book learning and the classics and literature, as well as single subject, specialist, science. This system had, after all, given politicians, from both sides of the House their start on the ladder, as it had helped Basil's many friends and their children, and his workplace colleagues and their children.

Basil particularly regretted 'the removal of opportunity for academically inclined children from financially poorer backgrounds'[429]. The wealthy could still opt to send their children to academic schools; the poor had Hobson's Choice! What the politicians dressed up as equal opportunity was, for Basil Blackwell, its negation. Schools, like Magdalen, had prospered in the post war period, admitting scholarship boys. When his old school, Magdalen, was in trouble, Basil was fast into the fray for its financial rescue. He pushed the idea of continuing with scholarships, flying in the face of the government's attempts to unravel the selective system. It was an old Blackwell family trait to cock a snook at politicians, and Basil did not prove to be the exception. When an injustice riled him, he exercised little restraint, except that of good manners. And riled he was by much, not only in wider society, but also in his own back yard, in the bookselling world. Here, he suggested, two issues, the dishonesty of the Ring, and the publication of obscene material, called for more than fine words. The issues demanded action. He took on the Ring, and weathered a fine old storm when he challenged the new orthodoxy of soft-pornography. The Blackwells, by tradition, had adopted a position of high moral rectitude: they had sought to put worthy books into worthy hands.

By the same token, Basil now saw it as his duty (he was still at heart a Victorian) to keep unworthy books out of unworthy hands. With the publication of DH Lawrence's *Lady Chatterley's Lover*, he had felt called upon to practise what he preached. Although he condemned the content of the book, he had, nonetheless, some sympathy for Lawrence, as a man. Basil famously described Lawrence's writing of this particular book as an understandable attempt, by the 'gutter born Lawrence', to extract 'social vengeance'[430]. Basil explained that, to his way of thinking, the book was much misunderstood; its theme was not sexual; rather, Lawrence was taking a vicarious revenge on an aristocratic society. 'Lady Chatterley, you notice', he emphasized, 'not Mrs Chatterley'. 'Lady C starts by having casual carnal connection with a weekend guest, and then she becomes the mistress of a gamekeeper, and then at the end she palms off her bastard on another man'[431]. With Basil on the offensive, it was downhill all the way for hypocrisy: in this sense, at least, the book had its place. 'There was, however, to be no such dispensation for *Last Exit to Brooklyn*. The row over the latter saw Basil at his most determined. It was not, however, Basil who had noticed the book; it was his son Richard who had instigated the trial, by drawing Sir Cyril Black's attention to the book. 'What have you been up to?', Basil asked his son, when a reply from Sir Cyril crossed his desk. Richard, a more retiring man, sent his father to the witness box, when the subsequent obscene publications trial got underway in 1967. Cross-questioned, Sir Basil railed against, what he described as, the 'pornographic content of the book'. He swore, to a hushed courtroom, that not only would the book corrupt others, but also that it had depraved and corrupted him.

Basil's stand, over *Last Exit*, attracted widespread criticism, as well as support. Terry Coleman, of the Arts Guardian, asked Sir Basil how it had corrupted him. Basil explained 'that the book had done him harm: phrases in it, and descriptions of sexual deviations, were new to me really. It was so horrid, just like stepping in a dog's turd . . . It haunts my memory. I am still trying to forget it'. That Basil did not like the book could be respected, but, the journalist questioned, was it any part of a bookseller's business to censor books, to determine what his customers should read?'[432]. But Basil was a man of contradiction. On the one hand he condemned obscenity in literature, but, on the other, he upheld the individual's freedom of choice. Despite his opposition, the book was still sold in other shops in which he had a large interest, in Parker's, where he was on the Board, for example[433]. In his defence of this softening, he recalled Milton who, in the English Civil War, had claimed the 'liberty to know, to utter, to argue freely according to conscience'[434]. Basil, understanding that he was between Scylla and Charybdis, came down on the side of freedom. Nonetheless, he had his own personal let-out clause: 'these days I am very much a novel-reader emeritus'. Added to this, the reputation of his family firm had been founded not on exclusion, but on inclusion, although its proprietors were the arbiters in any dispute. But did this reputation for independence bring fame or infamy? On another, less well-known, occasion, Blackwell's 'liberalism' was used as a benchmark, not to uphold 'good taste', but against which the narrow-minded practices of a London sex bookshop were judged. The story goes that an elderly aristocratic man asked to see a volume that was stored in a heat-sealed pack. The assistant regretted that the book could not be 'viewed' as the seals could not be broken, unless of course the gentleman wanted to pay for the book first. At this, the customer haughtily responded 'I do not have this trouble at Blackwell's'.

Whatever the level, Blackwell's was willy-nilly caught up in the changes affecting the entire publishing world. Modern publishing was a hybrid affair: 'If it was to be successful', Basil explained, 'it demanded policies and decisions that would cater to a market that, in this post war era, must reflect the very different social, political and economic imperatives of modern man, whether the individual publisher, or bookseller, liked it or not'. Attending a forum of young publishers in 1968, Sir Basil Blackwell mused on the inequities of success in the publishing world, which were clearly not predicated on literary merit. Thoughtfully he lamented that 'the judgement of contemporaries is seldom good. Look at Martin Tupper. In his day there could have been found ten thousand to speak of his literary merit: while for Blake, it would have been difficult to find ten'. It is not on record what Basil thought of Robert Maxwell's purchase of the girlie magazine *Mayfair*, which he paid over a £1m for, to provide books for the boys who were off to the Falklands. But then Maxwell was a 'modern man!'[435] Basil Blackwell was not modern man, but he was true to the traditions of his breed. 'Booksellers', Samuel Johnson had written, 'are generous liberal-minded people'. And they were individualists. In his Dent Memorial lecture, Basil expressed his fears 'that for the individual it was all too often a matter of "Heads I win, tails you lose"'. It was this injustice against the individual which prompted him to leave his desk at Broad Street and play an active part in the wider community.

And Basil's interpretation of wider was very wide. Just before the Second World War, he was lying in the bath reflecting on the ascendancy of Nazism and Fascism. Never one for the conventional cant of politics, he was deeply suspicious of the rhetoric of appeasement, 'I got the idea that Hitler and Mussolini were not only telling lies but also drawing false conclusions'. Basil recounted how his own brand of spiritual appeasement recommended itself as a way to combat them by appealing to the essence of Christianity. His strategy was to have the Pope or some other Christian leader take charge of the broadcasting stations throughout the world and recite the Lord's Prayer to the worldwide audience.

Unfortunately, Basil's peaceful strategy was pre-empted: 'Before I could put this idea to the Vatican or to Canterbury, Germany had invaded Poland'[436]. He was not surprised that, as an individual, he had no chance to play a part in the greater scheme of things. But Basil went on finding opportunities to assert his independence in any number of smaller ways. In ripe old age, when his eyesight was all but gone, he ignored the traffic cadres, and used the white lines, in the middle of roads, as a walking guide. When he could be persuaded not to walk, Cuthbert would drive him to lunch at Merton. This involved negotiating Oxford's one-way system, but no such petty inconvenience was to be allowed to keep him from his lunch. Cuthbert would take the direct route, and ignore the restrictions. At the age of 89, when offered a lift to church, he broke into a trot and ran fifty yards just to prove the point that he didn't want a lift! This was exactly the brand of individualism that his wife thought she had tamed. In reality it was only ever channelled—but to very good account. These puckish, irrepressible and insouciant characteristics had struck the wife of Graham Greene, when she had met Sir Basil some forty years before his death. 'I am encouraged', she wrote, 'to make public a theory that there was something about the light-hearted, high-spirited and what could be called "debonair" personality which, when combined with a pointed nose, fair flat hair and a tendency to quote from Edward Lear's verses (never the limericks) and particularly from the *Hunting of the Snark*, convinced me that here was the original of Lord Peter Wimsey'[437].

News from everywhere

Men live by trade, but not by their trade alone

A man of Basil Blackwell's freethinking disposition, reading and thinking at will, took in views, as well as news, from everywhere. His catholic tastes were represented in all the different aspects of his life. Although he was an opportunist of the best kind, and accepted, often reluctantly, changes within his own organization, he was also a self-confessed iconoclast. Never fully convinced by the dominant zeitgeist; that capitalist organization, mass-production and state-of-art technology was the only way forward, he attempted to uphold the traditions of service, design and craftsmanship, reminiscent of an earlier, slower, age. After all, the skill of the people engaged in trade and the crafts had made the industrial revolution, just as much as the new machines and the risk-taking of Victorian entrepreneurs. Depending on each other for success, some workers had 'done very nicely', and some of their masters 'had become very rich indeed'. Basil's own father had been rescued from the ignominy of poverty by trade, his mother's as well as his own. By stint of hard work and an unfaltering belief in self-education, people like his father, many fellow Blackwellians, and countless others like them, had provided the next generation of thinkers, writers and artists: people who did not live by trade alone. His thinking, on these lines, had much to do with his admiration for William Morris. As Virgil had escorted Dante to the gates of Paradise, so Basil adopted Morris as his own guide. His introduction to William Morris had been serendipitous: 'I do not know how I came to choose (Morris's) *Earthly Paradise* as part of a school prize. It was a happy choice, for the idle singer enchanted me for many an empty day and led me on to explore his prose romances (good reading in youth!) and so to an event of cardinal importance in my life—the reading of one of the best biographies in our literature, Mackail's *Life of William Morris*. It turned my head to fine printing, and so brought me friends who have enriched my life and bequeathed gracious memories. Among them I treasure most highly May Morris and Bernard Newdigate, whose friendship I wove into the pattern of my life until I stood at their graves'[438]. Basil wrote and published short accounts of these two seminal friendships, and they kindled his interest in the Kelmscott Press.

William Morris, combining, as his writing did, literary and political idealism with manual work, 'was the embodiment of things intellectual, spiritual and physical'; a union the young aesthete, Basil, aspired to. 'In an age', Basil wrote, 'which regarded the pre-Raphaelite as a Victorian episode, his faith was to be preached entire, his crusade to be carried on'. And to carry on the practices and ideas of William Morris was just what Basil Blackwell intended. Morris's philosophy, and his writings, had transported Basil as a young romantic, but his practical skills in craftsmanship were as big a draw. Morris, for example, 'had done much to stir up public enthusiasm for fine printing'. His Kelmscott *Chaucer*, published in 1896, a copy of which remains in Sir Basil Blackwell's library at his old home, served as a model when Basil set up the Shakespeare Head Press, in 1920. Basil regarded the *Chaucer* as Morris's

37 Basil at Osse Field.

'noblest memorial: that masterpiece of typography whose artistic glories are so strangely alien from the robust spirit of the author'. Feeding on this inspiration, Basil set out to encourage, and advance, the fine art of printing. Deep admiration for Morris's craftsmanship was not just a workaday passion. Basil brought its flavour into the construction and design of his, then, new house in Appleton, not so far distant from Morris's own 'Kelmscott House'. Basil's deep admiration for all of William Morris's work gave him one of his 'ideas'. Early in 1934, Basil wrote to Morris's daughter, May, enquiring: 'that if any scrap of her father's writing should still be unpublished, we might help to commemorate his centenary by printing it handsomely at the Shakespeare Head Press on the very same hand-press which once had been part of the equipment of the Kelmscott (Press)'. May Morris, who Basil esteemed as one whose 'aesthetic and mental equipment and her excellent prose style fitted her for creative work in her own right', responded almost immediately with a beautifully scripted letter. She thanked Basil, and explained that she would send all that remained.

Bearing in mind that the whole of May Morris's life 'was devoted to keeping her father's memory not only green but dynamic', it should not have come as a surprise when, some days later, a huge parcel arrived from Kelmscott House. It included a mass of type-scripts, pamphlets, periodicals and off prints; upwards of half a million words. Sir Basil recorded this memorable day: 'My first thoughts were of Alf Button', the apocryphal Alf Button had been a solider in the '14–18' War, and had come across a button that was made from a fragment of Aladdin's cave. 'When he polished it', Sir Basil recounted, 'an overwhelmingly obliging genie appeared whose ministrations proved to be, in the authors words "too bloomin 'olesale" for him'[439]. Thrown by May Morris's wholesale response, Basil looked to his publishing colleagues for assistance. His first port of call was Longman's, who had already published twenty-four volumes of Morris's work. Longman's, however, regretted that twenty-four volumes 'were quite enough for them'. May Morris had herself asked Longman's in 1932, and had been bitterly disappointed by their refusal. Basil then sought to engage the interest of Allen and Unwin, having in mind their 'Ruskin', an edition, according to Basil, 'which had made the firm'. His dear friend Stanley Unwin 'had a unique ability in finding markets for difficult books'. 'But Sir Stanley's generous heart was controlled by a strong and clear head, and his answer was the 'Pie man's'. 'For over a year', Basil was haunted by the 'silent reproaches' of May Morris's 'thumping parcel', which 'would not let me alone', he wrote. But, unlike those of his publishing friends, Basil's heart was more susceptible. Soft-heartedness won the day; in the house of B H Blackwell, father and son, sentiment had so often prevailed over commercial dictate when it came to the writers, or books.

Anxious to relieve himself of a burden, Basil set off for Kelmscott House. Ever the optimist, he hoped to persuade May to make 'a selection', adding a written account of 'the unchosen pieces in her own admirable words'. The House was museum-like; nothing had changed since William Morris's death. Upstairs, in his tapestried bedroom, lay abundant evidence of his 'versatile genius' and 'the silent poetry' of *La Belle Iseult* 'a further reminder of his unbounded talent[440]. May was the 'chatelaine' of this shrine, and received only 'those whom she deemed to be true pilgrims with gentleness and noble courtesy'. Anyone who gave off the merest whiff of patronage, or of cultural voyeurism, 'was frozen our by her hauteur and dismissed with a cutting phrase'. Basil had always been one of these 'true pilgrims', as well as a friend, and she accepted him as such. Would this advantage, however, guarantee his success in persuading her to make a selection? Ever the optimist, he had hoped that it would. Things did not go well with May. The look on May's face, 'one of noble and austere beauty, somewhat haggard, with eyebrows set at an angle reminiscent of a Greek tragedy', spoke legions. Escaping from the grim and chilling 'interview' room, Basil attempted to make his way to the car park, but he found his progress blocked by the family's 'land-girl'. Unlike May Morris, this androgynous figure was anything but Pre-Raphaelite. The ubiquitous Miss Lobb: 'large, hearty, crop-headed and always dressed in an old knickerbockers suit', was as strong as any male farm worker.

Using her own special charms, Miss Lobb managed to retain Basil until she had extracted a promise from him 'to publish all'. 'Don't think I care a scrap for the writings', she bellowed. 'I hate old William Morris—dreadful old bore—but I'll not have May worried'. She then proceeded to offer her life savings as an inducement to the bemused Basil. 'I've no money', she told him, 'I've only £50 in the world, but you shall have that and welcome if you do as I tell you. Basil was no match for May Morris's minder. Drawing a veil over her views on William Morris, he did as she had bidden: all 500,000 words were saved. And Miss Lobb was never called upon to relinquish her life's savings. May Morris saw two volumes of her father's remaining, unpublished, works roll off the press of Basil's 'Shakespeare Head', in 1936, 'appropriately under the direction of Bernard Newdigate, who had designed and printed the twenty-four volumes of *The Collected Works* during his time at the Arden Press at Letchworth'[441]. The work was entitled *William Morris: Artist, Writer, Socialist*, and the index was prepared by Basil's wife, Christine. Bernard Shaw, who must have overcome his confrontation with Basil, wrote an introduction. Basil wrote of this introduction, 'which revealed, with rare tenderness, his (Bernard Shaw's) youthful love for May Morris, disappointed by her surprising—and unhappy—marriage'.

Basil's persistence, and Shaw's introduction, reminded the onlooker of the importance of minor, a well as major, figures on the artistic scene that spanned Victorian and Georgian times. May Morris's own face is immortalized in a chalk drawing of Rosetti's, which shows 'May in girlhood . . . with the serene curved eyebrows of her lovely mother'. May's mother, Jane Burden, was herself one of the most painted of the Pre-Raphelite women. Why did her beautiful daughter's eyebrows 'begin to assume their tragic slant?' Basil asked. Her unhappiness was buried in her tireless efforts to promulgate her father's ideas, and to preserve his work. She was, Basil supposed, more than compensated by seeing her father's memory perpetuated in print. Such became her life's work. The Shakespeare Head book was a triumph for her, and it sealed a lifelong friendship with the Blackwells. But Basil's effort was just one among a number of memorials. Along with other bookish people, he helped raise funds for the building of a village hall in memory of William Morris, although the bulk of the money was raised by May Morris, from her writings and lectures. She had set her heart on this project, which she wanted to see completed by the centenary of her father's birth, in 1934. 'The hall was completed', Basil wrote, and 'her friends were invited to the opening'. They may have been invited, but they couldn't get in: 'for they found the hall thronged to the limit by an unexpected multitude of unknown disciples. With difficulty, and by way of the coal cellar, an entrance was contrived for Ramsay MacDonald; the rest of us stood outside listening to Bernard Shaw's elocution relayed by an intermittent microphone. It was good to see May's concern for her guests over-borne by her delight in the spontaneous cloud of witnesses to her father's fame'[442].

Later, Basil wrote an extended article about May Morris, for the William Morris Society, and he collaborated with the Society to produce an account of 'William Morris's Printing Press', contributing a lively memoir, autographing copies of a special edition only weeks before his death[443]. Sir Basil Blackwell had been President of the William Morris Society, and when he resigned the office, in 1978, the only President to resign before dying, he was accorded an honorary life membership of the Society. And divulging himself of all these extra-curricular activities was necessary, if he was to make time for his own reading. But, first, he wanted to see the Society in a safe pair of hands, while he still had any influence: 'I have resigned', as you know, the office of President, ... I fancy—and it is clear that in a short time I shall depart this life', he wrote to Alan Thomas, the Kings Road bookseller, which means 'that the William Morris Society will need to choose a Trustee in my place. Would you be willing to act?' His old friend wrote back expressing an interest in the Society, but also surprise at some of Morris's reading material: 'I have never understood how Morris, the kindest of men, let alone the ethereal Burne-Jones, could enjoy the 'company' of those blood-stained thugs, cleaving enemies in twain with their great axes'. (He had been referring to Beowulf.) Was it that Morris had, after all, led a rather protected life? Whereas Basil Blackwell and his friends 'had supped full of horrors', the horrors of the Great War, 'were the Victorian Middle classes so sheltered from the brutal side of life that it had a quaint fascination for them?'[444]

It was the beauty of Morris's work and writing, and the skill of his craftsmanship, that Basil preferred to carry with him. Serendipitously, the walls of his office, where he worked for over seventy years, were found to be covered in an early William Morris wallpaper. There are some discrepancies in the story of the wallpaper, and there may have been several different papers. Basil thought he had seen the pretty flowered paper on the walls of his mother's sitting room, the room which became his own office, but another record suggests that the Curator of the Ashmoleam Museum, C F Bell, hung several of the original stencilled Morris wallpapers in all the rooms of the three stories he occupied above the shop, the Blackwell family having migrated to Linton Road, in North Oxford, in 1896. The paper in question, however it got on the wall, had come off the Morris printing block in 1874: 'a gentle floral delicacy on a cool blue-green background, called *Powdered*'[445]. The Blackwell inhabitants of the room, which became their office, were far from 'powdered', but they may have appreciated the meadow-like calm that the paper gave off. A fragment of this wallpaper was preserved, on the wall, by Julian Blackwell, and 'it has been matched to the original and restored to its former glory'[446]. This example of old craftsmanship, still, at a cost, alive and well, symbolizes what Basil Blackwell believed in, or what he didn't believe in.

If Basil Blackwell's paradise was good workmanship, then his pet hate was 'industrial shoddy'. Sir Basil took on Morris's mantle, whenever he could get away with it, by rehearsing his favourite mantra: 'the pleasure of work itself'. Quaint it may have seemed, but most people, perforce, had to learn to serve the trade they lived by. But those who lived for their work, as well as their leisure, were rewarded with more than just their wages. Sir Basil's adventures, like those of William Morris, enabled him to his labour, 'and it's fruits'. Enjoying the fruits of Blackwellian labour, Basil came to understand why his father, by example, had sought to engrave this maxim on his mind, as well as his heart. In the conduct of their business, this independent-minded band of Blackwells tried, as Morris had done, to create a unity between philosophical belief and running a business. They had tried, and in many ways succeeded, to create a working environment where individuals thrived, where they learned, and improved their skills, and where creative, and artistic, considerations were, at least, as important as the commercial realities. Booksellers, after all, were not in business to make money first and foremost; they loved the trade and they loved the books. William Morris, in his essay *News from Nowhere*, had 'travelled' around England looking for answers to the great political and economic questions; Basil Blackwell looked to books, themselves, for answers.

'The best read man in Britain'

For him was have at his beddes head
Twenty bokes, glad in blac or reed
Of Aristotle and his philosophye[447]

Books did more than just provide answers for Basil Blackwell, they were not only his venerable, constant, and much sought after, companions: 'a good book', he liked to quote, 'is the precious life-blood of a master-spirit embalmed, and treasured up on purpose to a life beyond life'. Towards the end of his life, he spent even more time among his precious books; any other aspect of his busy life, however pleasurable, was a diversion. Finally he could turn his attention from bookselling and publishing to pursue a rigorous daily programme of reading. And there were rich pickings to be had in his own library, at Osse Field. It was an eclectic collection, and one that illustrated his independence; he did not 'collect' the classics, he insisted, and he did not accept received wisdom on what constituted a 'classic'. The classics, for him, were 'those books that survived'. They were not ossified in time, 'because you and I and other folks from age to age are forever finding classics new'[448]. He liked nothing better than to escort visitors into his library: 'Come into my library . . . and glance round the shelves' . . . which are 'typical of any discursive reader, save that I have had the advantage of acquiring the books at somewhat less cost than my neighbours'. 'Here', in the 'Rumble and tumble, sleek and rough, Stinking and savoury, smug and gruff', were novelists, essayists, diarists, letter writers, biographers, poets and dramatists, satyrists, and critics, travellers and naturalists, historians (just a few), with here and there a theologian and a pietist, and, in honoured follies for the most part, the great translators who have made the classics of other countries equally our own, North and Philemon Holland of the inexhaustible quill, who made Plutarch and Pliny virtually English authors; Lodge Chapman and Thomas Hobbes, who did no less with Seneca, Homer and Thucydides; Urquhart, Florio and Berners, who made us forget that Rabelais, Montaigne and Froissart wrote in French. Here in the strange fellowship of the bookshelf, stands Jane Austen beside Fielding and Smollett, the sniggering Sterne with the great-hearted Dickens (arch-sentimentalists both), the forthright Brontes with the tortuous Conrad, sanguine Walter Scott with fatalist Hardy. Shoulder to shoulder they stand, Pepys with little Burney, the Browning *Love Letters* with Swift's *Journal to Stella*, Lamb delicate and whimsical beside the massive Rambler, the hearty Chaucer by the austere Milton, Burns rubbing sides with Bridges, Shakespeare with Shaw'[449].

'What has brought this diverse company together?' Sir Basil asked. They are the 'writings of men and women of various periods, of differing creeds, sometimes of far different ethics, and with characters so widely differing one from another that any bond of sympathy or common ground would seem to be beyond hope: some learned, others untutored: some expressing themselves in prose, others in verse, this man's prose elaborate and involved, that man's simple and swift, this poet using the magnificent measure of the epic, that poet expressing himself succinctly in the gemlike perfection of the lyric'. 'What common title have they all to literature,' he asked? They are, he suggested, 'all recording or interpreting some portion of human experience' in a myriad of different ways. 'But in common', he explained, 'they are all able to impart a "truth".' It is this 'truth', in books, 'that is ageless, and above all fashion, which is to be found in the imaginative writer; the truth which we find in the Parables and in Aesop's *Fables*, the truth which, to generation after generation, unfailingly makes its appeal'. If the piece of writing 'rings true', then it will stand the test of time. It will live on, according to Sir Basil, just as the 'evil that man doeth liveth after him':

'The unrighteous deed of old doth bear
The unrighteous deed of later year,
Issuing in sorrows on the earth
When dawns the fated day of birth:
And that resistless, tameless spirit
Of godless pride: lo, these inherit
The likeness of their parents fell,
Blackening the house with gloom of hell.'

But all was not lost for 'the unrighteous', dead or alive. For the 'truth', which lived on in good books, could restore these unfortunate souls to Paradise. Basil, writing at the age of eighty-two, evoked his father's favourite poet, Milton; 'man was a burden to the earth' but he could, none the less, be transported by a good book. Basil's inheritance had been a happier one; he had been the son of 'a good man who did good things', and because of his good fortune, and the love of books his parents had fostered, he had lived in an 'earthly paradise'. Whenever this paradise fell into the shadow, especially after the death of his wife and his eldest son, Richard, his passion for reading redeemed him.

After a lifetime of dedication to his books, as much at home as at work, he was rewarded by the judgement of an institution no less than *The Times*, which gave Sir Basil the awesome reputation of being 'one of the best-read men in England'[450]. But for Basil it was the 'books that were awesome', not the reader. In his library at Osse Field, so full of books, he always had two, 'awesome' ones, open on the lectern. The first: Dante's *Il Purgatorio*, was his constant companion on the up-hill journey to Paradise. But the second tome, Barbara Tuchmann's (recent) account of the Fourteenth Century, was eventually banished for containing 'too much of man's inhumanity to man'[451]. Basil was, none the less, adventurous; his declared favourites were the sort of books 'we might find in the hands of an athletic reader in that still hour before breakfast, when the mind is most receptive—a reader say of riper years, reared in the disciplines of Greece and Rome but happiest in exploring discursively the fields of our own literature. He reads vigilantly, weighing the merits, but not overlooking the faults of his author. He may read a book twice, first to learn what the author has to tell him, and then to judge how he tells it'[452]. Basil's judgement of books, as in other aspects of his life, had nothing to do with fashion or style. He had scant regard for the critics, preferring to be guided by his own assessments and instincts. Basil described his collection as 'not that of a savant, for your discursive reader has essentially a flitting mind'. These books had been 'gathered casually down the years as one has led on to another or has been introduced by some praising reference in print or talk, and they are kept for the grateful memories they evoke'[453].

Books were also Basil's 'training circuit'. He wanted to qualify as Francis Bacon's 'full man'. Not all reading, however, according to Basil, fell into this category. In Basil's view, reading fell under one of two heads: 'sometimes we read for Relaxation; sometimes for Recreation. You will see an elderly clubman pick up his newspaper, sink into a comfortable chair, and a few minutes later fall asleep; many of us as we grow older keep books at our bedside to soothe us to sleep at the day's end; most of us occasionally read thrillers or detective stories, or glance over the pages of a magazine to take our minds off more serious matters, or just to pass the time. This "pastime" reading taxes neither our attention, nor our judgment nor our memory. It is the casual employment of a resting space'. To Basil's mind, Bacon's 'full man' was 'not concerned with such a "flashy thing", as reading for Recreation'. Paradise did not lie that way;

> 'Who to his reading brings not
> A spirit and a judgment equal or superior
> Uncertain and unsettled remains,
> Deep versed in books, but shallow in himself
> Crude or intoxicate, collecting toys
> And trifles for choice matters, worth a sponge
> As children gathering pebbles on the shore'

What Basil advocated was 'athletic reading': 'and when we read in this spirit we regard a book as a challenge to us to brace our minds to understand, appreciate, and judge our author. It is a kind of intellectual mountaineering. I may extend the metaphor and say that in this intellectual mountaineering we can choose to follow the beaten track, or to find our own way. If we do that, our Recreation becomes an adventure—an adventure which lasts all our lives and makes us full men'. And 'full men', of yore, as everyone knows, Basil reminded, 'were adventurers'. Basil's adventures had, perforce, been mostly in the mind. He had been debarred from National Service because of his eyesight, although he had been an oarsman to be reckoned with, and the demands of the family business had kept him mostly in Oxford. He had, from time to time, 'longed to go on pilgrimages', like Chaucer's adventurers, who were near to Basil's heart: they were a diverse and colourful crew, much prone to imaginings and hyperbole, with many a tale to tell.

Basil's adventures were not limited to April in Canterbury; his books could take him anywhere at any time. And he devoted a great deal of time to writing about his adventures in book land. Anyone could go on these adventures, rich or poor; the only qualification needed was an 'athletic mind'. Basil urged his colleagues, his friends, and his customers, to set off on these adventures. But he stopped short at dictating the type of adventure, the type of book. In his view, adventurers did not need that sort of advice: 'Thank the critics and writers of literary textbooks for their views; but make your own judgment'. His adventurers should, none the less, 'read with a pencil in your hand, and very lightly in the margin put a mark against any passage, line, or phrase, which you think good or bad (always provided it is your own book that you are marking!). But without experience, and advice, how were his fellow travellers to *know* a good book? Basil, as ever, had his answer at the ready: 'Well I believe we may know a good book in the same way as we know a good man. There can be few of us, I fancy, who cannot recognize truthfulness and kindliness in the men and women we meet. To that extent, at any rate, the critical faculty is in all of us; and truthfulness and kindliness I suggest are the essential qualities of a good book, and a good journey. Again, as there are few of us who cannot recognize failings and frailties in our friends, so we must be prepared for such imperfections in any book; for authors are men with passions like ourselves. The poet, Martial, in the dedication of his book of *Epigrams* fairly admits this frailty in books, and we shall do well to remember his words, which I may roughly render as follows: "good things, some not so good, more frankly bad, this book contains, that's how all books are made". And we should remember what Ben Jonson saw in Shakespeare. Protesting that he 'loved the man and did honour his memory, on this side idolatry as much as any,' he writes, 'I remember the players have often mentioned it as an honour to Shakespeare that in his writing (whatsoever he penned) he never blotted out a line. My answer hath been "would he had blotted a thousand. Which they thought a malevolent speech." His wit was in his own power, would the rule of it had been so too, but he redeemed his vices with his virtues, there was ever more in him to be praised than to be pardoned'. And that perhaps is as much as we can say of the work of most authors. Ben Jonson by refusing to 'go with the crowd' of uncritical admirers did Shakespeare a notable service.

If a writer did not go with the crowd, then how, Basil asked, did he gain enough support to be remembered? Shakespeare, not always popular, was remembered for his attempts to get at the soul: 'Truth is the very soul of Literature, and in all these diverse authors who survive, and throughout their works, that immortal spark is manifest. By Truth I mean not the mere record of historical facts, nor the proven conclusions of logic and mathematics. The historian, as opposed to the creative and imaginative writer, gives us the facts. Take St Joan of Arc as an example', Basil suggested, 'she triumphed, was captured, tried, condemned, and burnt. But now for the greater Truth—the genius of Bernard Shaw has grasped it and shows it forth in his *Saint Joan*. Every one of those who bring her to her death acts from the highest motives according to his lights. There is the tragedy. You are full of pity for the Saint, but there is no villain to blame for her piteous end. "The time cometh, that whosoever killeth you will think that he doeth God service." "So persecuted they the prophets before you." That Truth, which is as old as the history of Man, is presented to us dispassionately, convincingly and forever, by the genius of a writer recording and interpreting human experience'. Another of his favourites, Aeschylus, is said to have written ninety plays, of which only seven survive. 'Two thousand years hence of all the plays that Shaw has written I doubt if more than *Saint Joan* will survice. So hard a thing it is to enter into the Kingdom of Literature—to this "Life beyond life."'

But truth alone, Basil cautioned, would not guarantee the survival of a book. 'The second quality', he explained, 'is the ability, in whatever form, in prose or poetry, drama, epic, essay or novel, to express and interpret that Truth clearly and in language that delights us: as things delightful commonly abide in our memory when dull or displeasing things are forgotten (what a God sent gift that is!). It is a common experience that the same story told by two men may make two very different impressions. The one man gives us the facts in a dull and muddled way, using trite phrases, and the story is forgotten almost as soon as it is told: the other, by virtue of the genius that is in him, will so martial his facts and will express them in such living phrases, that the story remains in our memory for years. This second man sees further than the first—he glimpses the larger truth, and in his method of telling interprets that truth and, through the pleasure he gives us in the telling, permanently impresses it upon us. For example—if I tell you that I once heard tell that someone once shut up two insects (a louse and a flea to be precise) in a box with a glass lid and observed them under a microscope and saw them fight, and one of them—which do you think?—came off best; if I told you now, you wouldn't remember this time next week which insect was victorious. Yet you would have had the facts. But listen to this . . . here, seen through the veridical lens of literature are the same heroic passions which throb in the jousting of Sir Tristram with Sir Palomedes; here in essence are Percy and Douglas, Chandos and du Guesclin. A man's work in literature, like water, for all the machinery of man, eventually finds its own level, and that level is the verdict, not of professors of literature, not of writers of literary handbooks, nor of expert librarians, but of the folk—that is the ever-recurring verdict of athletic readers like you and me and the thousands who pass in the street, athletic readers of—yesterday—today—tomorrow—from generation to generation'. Posterity is the only sure judge of a man's work in literature. Unconsciously, unerringly, succeeding generations sift and garner the best. Again and again, from age to age, you and I and they discover with delight this book and that, this writer and that, and in our enthusiasm we become evangelists of the truth we find in him.

Survival, of books, then, according to Basil Blackwell, comes via 'Folks' infallible instinct, from age to age'. 'This instinct', he wrote, 'is one of the most satisfying facts in human nature, and I think we may draw two conclusions from it: first, when scholars lament that the Greek and Latin classics have come down to us in such fragmentary form, when for instance they observe regretfully that of all the plays Aeschylus wrote, a bare seven have survived, I think they would rather rejoice that the unerring instinct of men throughout the ages has preserved for us the quintessential best of a great dramatist. If there were other books of Homer, perhaps they were well lost. In the classics we have the very core of the wisdom and the gems of composition of the Ancient World—why fret about the second best?' His second conclusion, was that literature survives because it has turned out to be one of the least perishable of human things. Two thousand years ago a Roman poet, Horace, wrote '*Litera scripta manet*'—and see how the written word has abided!'

In Basil's opinion, 'the word would be made flesh, and survive, but flesh would wither away': 'Let me illustrate this immortal element in literature', he implored. 'as against the evanescent fame of kings and conquerors and the mighty ones of the earth who have sought to win abiding remembrance in materials vastly more durable than ink and paper'. Consider, he asked, some lines of Shelley:

> 'I met a traveller from an antique land
> who said . . . :
> My name is Ozymandias King of Kings
> Look on my works ye Mighty and despair!'
> Nothing beside remains. Round the decay
> Of that colossal wreck, boundless and bare
> The lone and level sands stretch far away

And that, wrote Basil, is all we know about this King of Kings—but for Shelley most of us would not have even heard the name. For Basil, it was the poets, not the historians, who captured people in their time, and immortalized them. Who, for example, has ever heard of Ergoteles? Ergoteles, the son of Philanor, was a native of Crete. He was an exile—a man of broken fortune. He had competed in the Olympic games in 472 BC and won the long foot-race. How is it that this obscure man has won fame? The poet Pindar, Basil explained, wrote an ode in honour of his victory. If Basil was looking for answers, he had arrived at one: 'Literature is the common ground on which diverse minds may meet and find themselves in sympathy; and on that common ground the athletic reader becomes the Full Man'[454]. And he got this answer from reading books. Such full flood of thought, and words, was typical of Basil Blackwell, as a man and as a writer. His father, a man of fewer words, had also penned the odd work, in Latin as well as the vernacular. Benjamin Henry never claimed to be a scholar, although a scholar *manqué* he certainly was, to say the least. Basil, for his part, claimed he was merely a 'gypsy scholar'.

The Gypsy Scholar

> *But once, years after, in the country lanes,*
> *Two scholars, whom at college erst he knew,*
> *Met him, and of his way inquired;*
> *Wherat he answered, that the gypsies crew,*
> *His mates, had arts to rule as they desired*
> *The workings of men's brains,*
> *And they can bind them to what thoughts they will.*
> *'And I,' he said, 'the secret of their art,*
> *When fully-learned, will to the world impart;*
> *But it needs heaven-sent moments for this skill'*[455]

Matthew Arnold 'wistfully imagines that the spirit of this scholar is still to be encountered in the countryside near Oxford, having achieved immortality by a serene pursuit of the secret of human existence'[456]. Like Keats' nightingale, and the gypsy scholar, Basil escaped the 'weariness, the fever, and the fret' of his modern life. His idea of a gypsy scholar was of someone travelling through life and acquiring an education, through books, and not necessarily in formal surroundings. Basil did not regard himself as a scholar: 'I may best be likened', he wrote, 'to a dog following exciting scents haphazard across an illimitable terrain. If I should chance to flush any ideas which may excite you to pursue them, that will be my reward'[457]. He always delighted in inciting others to study and learn, but not necessarily in the hallowed halls of academia. The narrow concept of a scholar: someone eminent in one small field and holed up in academic institutions, was something he never subscribed to, any more than his father had. Rather, while they both acknowledged the scholarly life of the cloister, they up-held the freedom of the 'Gypsy Scholar'. Many among the staff of Blackwell's would have stood as fine examples of the self-educated, but their wanderings had been solely through books; of necessity they had combined the practice of their trade with a 'quiet pursuit of scholarship'[458]. Basil's father had taught himself to be scholarly, and he inherited from his father the idea that scholarship was 'a means of the communication of minds, as well as the appreciation of books as beautiful things in themselves'. And Basil was far from the vagrant that, his friend, John Masefield had had in mind. Henry Schollick recorded how he used to find his old friend Basil every wintry Sunday, for over forty years, pouring over his books. 'I was invariably greeted with the question "What have you been reading?" and on the day he asked me "What shall I read?" I knew I was out of my apprenticeship'.

But Basil never left his apprenticeship as far as reading literature was concerned; he was always a student and a scholarly adventurer. If he wanted for new pastures, further afield than even Blackwell's could offer, then he had only to make his way down the road to the University and its libraries. There had always been an osmotic relationship between the Bodleian and Blackwell's. Books were ferried back and forth between the two 'institutions' until they found a fitting home. Basil greatly admired the Keeper of Western Manuscripts at the Bodleian, Richard Hunt. Hunt was in the tradition of great librarian-scholars through the ages, back to Cassiodorus at Vivarium, and for Basil Blackwell, his domain was the hub and focus of Oxford's intellectual life as well as the starting point for the humblest enquiry. If Hunt was elsewhere, Basil could always draw on the expertise of the Fellows at lunch.

Nothing would tempt Basil away from his daily diet of study. 'The fact of it being a workday', and the consequent need to be at his desk in Broad Street by 7.15am, 'or of it being a Sunday', attendance at church notwithstanding, was not allowed to intervene. It was sacrosanct. Basil saw no conflict: 'there is no division between our work and our enjoyment'. 'Joy in work was the essence of (his) life', he claimed. Whether in the study or the office, or at leisure, he always had a pencil near to hand, ready to note any new expression or phrase that may inform his mind and his work. The reader, as Basil himself explained, 'has a pencil in his hand with which to make a slight marginal mark (unless he finds one already made earlier by himself) against a sentence, a line, or a phrase that strikes him as excellent, or to record on the fly leaf the reference to some passage enlightening in fact or opinion to which at some time he may wish to refer'. Rich pickings were gleaned from these excursions, and Basil used these reservoirs to enliven his conversations with his customers, staff, family and friends or to illuminate a public address. He was never at a loss for words. But his researches were also the backbone of his many writings. Being a good student enabled Basil to be a good educator, and an informal teacher. The headmaster of his former school, writing in 1984 at the time of his death, described how he always sat next to Sir Basil at Governors' lunches 'not just to enjoy entertaining company but to be, in the most civilized and civilizing way, educated'[459].

Henry Schollick agreed that Basil was, in addition to his other activities, both a tutor and teacher. 'With him', Schollick wrote, 'I had a free lifelong tutorial with a superb teacher'[460]. Basil relished nothing better than an invitation to teach. He would move into his didactic mode at the drop of a hat. Basil was always on the look out for intelligent and inquisitive young minds to form. His own children had to embrace the disciplines of scholarship, even if it did not come naturally to them, and he was always on the look out for 'suitable minds' on which to impress the Blackwell stamp. From these extensive contacts, over the years, some did present themselves to train in the art of bookselling and publishing. Glimpsing an interested student in the bookshop, the Gaffer would capture the attention of a politely surprised youngster who would then be steered towards his inner sanctum. Drawing attention to the books and catalogues that lined the shelves of his room, representing different shades of 'Blackwellian' life, he would suggest that bookselling was a great career. Almost as an afterthought he would pause before finishing to present a copy of his own *Beginning in Bookselling*, and then depart without waiting for any thanks. Many generations of Blackwell's authors, some of whom had worked on either the bookselling or publishing side, had been on the receiving end of Sir Basil at his pedagogical best, holding their tongues as he explained to them the need for discipline and construction in their written work.

This close relationship between Basil and his 'writers', in the days when a publisher could personally oversee his lists, may mistakenly leave behind the impression that his chief role was that of a midwife. His was the responsibility to deliver the literary offspring of others. Yet Basil Blackwell was a prodigious and scholarly writer on his own account. Scholarship and writing were not, for Basil, public activities, they were an end in themselves. Despite his modesty, diffidence even, in this area of his life, Basil's work did not go unrecognized. His role as a bookseller/scholar was acknowledged when, in 1970, he was appointed as the President of the English Association. At the inaugural ceremony, he regaled his colleagues with a lecture modestly entitled 'The Origins of the Classics'. The ideas he presented were far from modest! Appropriately, as a classical scholar of repute, he had already served a term, in 1964, as President of the Classical Association[461]. But his greater, scholarly activities, were reserved for making the works of others accessible. Frequently they were semi-private celebrations of the lives of others: of other adventurers whose life, or work, would otherwise remain unknown. In this way, unconsciously perhaps, he added to the now well-established scholarly tradition of recording the life and work of 'ordinary' people. In 1956 Basil made the acquaintance of Edith Barfoot. Then in her sixties, she had been bed-ridden and in constant pain with rheumatoid arthritis since her 'teens. She told Basil how she had triumphed over her pain under the spiritual guidance of the Cowley Fathers. Encouraged by one of their number, she wrote down her thoughts on suffering, producing a short paper entitled 'The Discovery of Joy in the Vocation of Suffering'. Basil was much moved and impressed by both Edith Barfoot and her paper.

The following year Basil published Edith Barfoot's study, with a brief foreword. He drew on his own explorations into the idea of the Holy Spirit, but claimed nothing except 'to speak as a child'[462]. This small buff-coloured book was simply, although beautifully, produced and it points up another aspect of Basil Blackwell's work. Not only did he want to encourage people to find their muse, and to publish the results, but he wanted the 'product of their labours to be things of beauty in themselves'. He recalled Keats *Grecian Urn*, that 'sylvan historian' conveying the eternal truth that is 'all ye need to know'. This, he extended to the maxim that 'the form of the book itself was as important as the content'; he wanted books to be beautiful things. A current Blackwellian, Ken New, who had started work at Blackwell's in the Gaffer's days, explained this feeling: you need to feel a book, and see the layout and the print, before you decide to buy, or even read[463]. The Gaffer passed on his concern for the 'look of books'. In his time, he pursued a scholarly course to discover the art of fine printing, and to find a way to make fine books affordable. In this he was a friend to readers, writers, printers, publishers and scholars everywhere. At the end of Basil's life, his dear friend and colleague, Christopher Francis, claimed him as the 'Aldus Manutius of our time'. Many examples of books from his own publishing houses, the earlier ones displaying the typographical traditions of Bullen and Newdigate, lined his shelves at Osse Field and his room at Broad Street. But looking at fine books, like fine words, was not enough. Nearing the end of his life, this friend of scholars continued to set himself scholarly tasks, to be completed before he 'got off the bus'.

Quiet, beneficent things

Quiet beneficent things making a sheltering world within the world[464]

Scholarly pursuits were a way of learning to keep in touch with the spiritual side of life. And they provided much-needed comfort for Basil Blackwell, after the death of his devoted wife, in April 1977. If Christine Blackwell had lived three more years, they would have celebrated their diamond wedding anniversary. Basil had already had to adjust to the death of his eldest son, Richard, and this further loss made him determined to 'find a whole new way of living' if he was to conquer despair. He had told his old friend Henry Schollick that 'the penalty of extreme old age is to stand at the grave of one's children'. This sentiment may have seemed very bleak, but it was a measure of the grief he felt[465]. With the death of Christine, Basil drew on the support of his extended family, the new generation of grandchildren and great grandchildren and old friends and colleagues. But he looked inwards too. Help came in the form of books, what he called his 'soul-food'. In old age he was more than ever thankful for their company, and he gained a new lease of life from organizing a daily routine of reading and study: an exacting programme which was to include new and old works. To ease himself in, he set himself the task of re-reading the whole of Shakespeare. 'It will take me two years', he confided to a friend. It took him six months! Each time he read a book he had new adventures, and made new discoveries; these odysseys formed the subject matter of a lively correspondence, kept up with those bookseller/publisher friends, from his generation, who still survived. At the age of ninety, he had confided to (Lord) Asa Briggs, he only had time for great books. A letter to Alan Thomas, the Kings Road bookseller, gave an insight into his preferences: 'I went on from Boewulf to Dasent's *Burnt Njal*, a most remarkable book. Since then I have read Bede's *Ecclesiastical History*, in our SHP edition, Dottin's *Life of Defoe*, and I am now deep in *Robinson Crusoe* again'[466]. Basil commended Thomas for an account of a re-reading of his old friend Rieu's *Odyssey*, and his own book: *Great Books and Book Collections*, which featured Basil's favourites: on Aldus and Morris[467]. Thomas, for his part, who had asked Basil to send him Martin Lowry's *Aldus Manutius*, apologized for his 'impudence' in taking up Basil's time, when he should be reading *Beowulf*.

When he wasn't reading, Basil found further consolation at the shop in the minutiae of its daily routines, habits still surviving that he, and his father, had established over a lifetime. On arriving at the shop, he went straight on post-duty. The letters often included requests for his urgent attention. Such requests would be sent down the line with a note, in his own writing: 'please send at once—Gaffer'. His old friends were surprised at his efficiency, and then they had to return the compliment with another letter, a vote of thanks[468]. This coming and going kept him at it; as did daily visits to all departments at Broad Street, which Basil enjoyed up to the Thursday before he died. 'Never one to openly wear his heart on his sleeve', Gaffer would sit cheerfully in his office most mornings. In an interview given in 1981, four years after his wife's death, he described himself as merely part of the furniture, someone who 'just came in and then went to lunch'. 'In the afternoon', he added mischievously, 'I take time to reflect on the moral grandeur of man—then I wake up!' Insouciant to the last, he revelled in this teasing. But if he intended to convey an impression of contingency, he failed. He was, still, anything but. As the journalist observed: 'his workers bustle about answering telephones and unpacking books'. . . . but the eyes in the back of Sir Basil's head are very firmly at work and it is obvious that here sits one very active and perceptive piece of furniture'[469]. And active he stayed till the last, and very disconcerting it was too for those who had to care for him. He carried on, metaphorically, standing on his head like the apocryphal Old Father William, deaf to any rebuke. Whatever the nature of his infirmities and his inward anxieties, he was not letting on. In public he extolled the merits of old age. 'It isn't exactly that all passion is spent', he confided in an interview, 'but that all passion may be ridden. You can ride on a lighter rein'. 'Given that time becomes short', he added, 'I find that one prefers to devote it to lovely . . . beautiful things'.

Basil had talked of 'the end of life and the prospect of the world to come', with his old intimate, Austin Longland. Basil voiced his fears that he as 'one who weighs his own demerits, was in doubt how to regard the prospect. Was it a promise or a threat?' He asked Austin, 'How is it with you?' 'Oh, a promise! Only I wish I had done more for others,' he replied. Asked what he thought of the soul's adventures after death, he suggested *'Tam bona quam nostra est tua conjectura futuri!'*: 'your guess is as good as mine'. Basil, nonetheless, would not admit to being frightened. 'Death', he asserted, 'is like getting off a bus. You have to get off to make room for others'[470]. However upbeat his public persona may have seemed, his private and inner life was in a more reflective mode. Aware perhaps of the nearing the end of his own life, and complaining because he did nothing but go to funerals, Basil revived his interest in the work of the Holy Spirit. Under the prompting of his revered friend, Henry Chadwick, Sir Basil re-discovered Boethius' *Consolation of Philosophy*[471]. He found refuge in the study of his faith, which he both believed and practised. He had been a practising Anglican all his life, with, he always modestly remarked 'varying degrees of enthusiasm'. His devout parents had both ensured that he had a good grounding, and that he knew his Prayer Book and Bible, and especially the Collects and Psalms. As a young man, Basil's pleasure from these stemmed chiefly from the examples and usage of language, which he added to his store. Later in life they were put to good use, reappearing in Basil's allusive speech and writing. He was renowned for what he called his 'periodic encyclicals', which always harked back to the things he had learnt from these early studies. Across the flyleaf of the bible given him as a young man by his mother, she had written the text: 'What shall it profit a man if he gain the whole world and suffer the loss of his own soul'.

But, for Basil, the problems of the material world always remained a puzzle. In his view the (Roman) Catholics were best at dealing with this dilemma. Living a life of virtue out in the world, with all its temptations, was, according to Basil, 'more difficult than behind the gates of a monastery'. 'The Trappists and Carthusians', he suggested, 'have it very easy'. How could a man in the world love virtue, Basil asked, 'with the temptations of the world all around —temptations to be proud, to be greedy, to be avaricious?'[472] If the rich could not enter the Kingdom of Heaven and the poor, in the here and now, had to struggle to survive, and often didn't, then which situation was preferable? This question became all the more pressing for Basil, in the frailty of old age. If he resolved it, within himself, then he did so by keeping the simple faith he had been brought up in. For him religion was not an opiate, it was a chance to 'best bear his mild yoke', and to seek forgiveness. Like Bunyan's Shepherd Boy: he was content with what he had, but equally, he knew he, still, had much to be contented about. But even in matters of religion, his independence of mind and judgment did not desert him. His religion was a personal one, rather than one bounded by the dictates of the Church of England and its ineluctable Sunday rituals.

The final chapter

I am just a book-worm—with the emphasis on worm!

At the age of ninety, when even the most well preserved of mortals would have accepted, if not welcomed help, Basil refused to be 'minded'. He had warned the world on his eightieth birthday that at the age of ninety 'he would please himself'[473]. His own lack of awareness of any 'intimations of mortality' was such that he continued to defy his old enemy, the Oxford traffic. But he could not defy death. Sir Basil died in April 1984, in his ninety-fifth year, and shock waves reverberated around the world. Even those, close by, who had seen it coming, found the fact 'unthinkable and unacceptable'. His old friend and colleague, C N Francis, conveyed the stunned senselessness he felt when greeted by the news. 'Those of us', he wrote, 'who had seen him nearly every day on his pilgrimage to the shop had feared, in these last few weeks, that the end might be in sight'. 'Yet', he recorded disbelievingly, 'this seemed quite unthinkable for he had always been here, always the same, the very soul of Blackwell's for as long as anyone can remember'[474]. Death, always surprising, was even more so 'when it was visited on a man blessed with an iron constitution and scarce a day's illness in his life'.

What was the secret of Basil Blackwell's long life? Sir Arthur Norrington thought it was due to the daily dips in the freezing pool at the end of his wife's beloved garden, and to the mental faculties that had been laid down when he studied Greats in his youth at Merton[475]. Basil himself said it was his perpetual state of puzzlement. Or was it, perhaps, his love of risk? Even in extreme old age he had insisted on walking to church every Sunday. His legs being rather unsteady, he adopted the dangerous practice—all the more dangerous because he was very hard of hearing—of walking down the middle of the road rather than take the prescribed footpath. 'Thank God it's my legs' he would remark, when at last they proved inadequate; 'They tell me it's either your legs or your mind!' Yet, for all his cantankerousness, and his infuriating independence, he retained his capacity for 'simple content' in the moment. This is perhaps as good an explanation as any for his longevity. Good fortune had allowed him to spend his days in the pursuit of what he loved most and, apart from the sad bereavements of his old age, 'he had lived under a cloudless sky'[476]:

I have lain in the sun
I have toiled as I might
I have thought as I would
And now it is night.

My bed full of sleep
My heart of content
For friends that I met
The way that I went[477].

    The way that Sir Basil went, and he deliberately hadn't chosen to go Robert Bridges way, had been determined by his early commitment 'to serve the trade by which he lived'. In his early days, as Gaffer, he was continually reminded of his father's virtuous and noble deeds: 'For in them, it is not for lacke of commendable virtues, that they report others praise and glorie: but in joining their owne vertues, to the vertues of their ancestors, they do increase their glorie, as inheriting their virtuous life'[478]. By the time he was middle-aged, those who remembered his father had gone. Like his father, he would have wanted to be remembered by the world of books he had inhabited for nearly a century. A friend once asked Sir Basil for a book he wanted, and was given the clear instruction 'Downstairs to theology'. This may serve as a fitting motto for a man who was many things to many people, but never forgot to bring himself down to earth. Those who knew him most commonly described him as very funny, modest and deeply loyal, as someone who never deliberately sought the limelight but was happy to put you in the spotlight, if he could[479]. He had no time for secrecy or duplicity of action, and his puckishness was over-laid with twinkling goodness[480].

    For his last walk, legally down the middle of the road, Basil Blackwell had insisted on a simple service at his local church, St Lawrence, Appleton, where he had worshipped for over fifty years. The village church was packed out and the congregation all joined in a rousing 'For all the Saints who from their labours rest'. Among them were bookmen and ploughmen side by side; they had all come to hear his final 'grace before going'[481]. His son Julian helped to carry the coffin, to be buried under the open sky:

Under the wide and starry sky
Dig the grave and let me lie:
Glad did I live and gladly die,
And I will lay me down with a will[482].

As is the proper way of things, a memorial service followed, appropriately at the University Church of St Mary the Virgin. Here he was proclaimed as a merchant-scholar, a tag that had suited his father even better. The Blackwell Singers, a tradition still going strong from his father's day, sang Christopher Tye's: *O Come Ye Servants of The Lord*. The lesson was read by his old friend, Sir Rex Richards, Warden of Merton, and Henry Schollick, his esteemed fellow-Blackwellian, 'spoke the right words in the right and proper place'.

> St Mary's was the right and proper place
> For his memorial—the ancient forum
> Where Oxford luminaries sold across
> Their pulpit-counters Aristotle and God,
> Duns and Scotus, Adam Brome, Newman and Cranmer,
> Presences still, and with them Townsman Nixon,
> Good decent man planning his school, and Amy Robsart,
> Dead and inscrutable before the altar—
> All these, a cloud of witness compassing
> Basil about, making him one of them,
> For he, the merchant-scholar, dealt in books
> And life, and short changed neither; judging his fellows
> Shrewdly; with sure touch he gathered flowers
> For other men and took his private pleasure
> In their delight. Now from St Mary's pulpit
> He hears no grand encomium, but what pleases
> Far more this gentle man, this bookseller, this freeman,
> The simple praise of an old friend, who spoke
> The right words in the right and proper place[483].

If he had been among the congregation, he would have cheered, on hearing the names of some of his 'Oxford heroes'. As things were, he would have had to be content with 'his private pleasure in their delight'. Hereafter, his 'delight', would come from a new fellowship: the imaginary world of stories and books. During his long life he had passed on the romance, mystery, magic and irrepressible inspiration of many of these stories; ancient and modern. His own stories, too, are perennial. They are tangible in the written records, he left behind, but they are also in the air of the Broad Street shop. 'It matters not that Blackwell's is riddled with computer-gadgetry these days, that it has interests . . . all over the place. Still to book buyers everywhere it remains in essence the jumbled old shop in the Broad which Masefield loved, among whose shelves the golden generations of youth loitered on their way, between the river and the Union, through classical text or lyrical poet'[484].

The Gaffer

And the older members of Blackwell's staff, and many visitors and customers, still 'see' the Gaffer amongst them. But he was never one to 'palely loiter'. His old friend and colleague Christopher Francis had sped him on his way, wishing him: *Et lux perpetua luceat ei*[485]. In this perpetual light, Basil had set off, nearly twenty years ago, like *Adventurers All*, 'to sail beyond the sky'[486]. 'Our friend, the Scholar-Gypsy, was not dead'; his stories remain, and they are not beyond our imaginings.

Epilogue

Blackwell's of the 'Broad': into the new century

All books are divisible into two classes, the books of the hour, and the books of all time

Academic booksellers are a rare breed, as much now as they must have been in Benjamin Henry's time. Their main attribute, which in part they share with their academic customers, is an education to a scholarly level on what is often a single facet of a subject. Sometimes a lifetime's experience can be focused on the attainment of detail down to the minutest level on what might be just a single element of the printed works about that subject, and where those works can be found. For the best of them there is nothing of note in this; their skills are ordinary and can be picked up by anyone with only twenty or thirty years to spare in pursuit of this tiny excellence, and of course, a love of books.

I have worked, and count myself lucky to have had the chance to do so, with booksellers who spend their working lives in pursuit of the 'un-findable' in order to satisfy the needs of the 'un-enlightened' to have put into their hands the 'un-obtainable'. I have set off to find that elusive volume that both customer and bookseller know exists, or at least did exist once, that one had bought and the other sold countless times in what now seems like the very dim and distant past. The bookseller's challenge and the customer's ongoing search for their particular holy grail is a game that Benjamin Henry and the Oxford booksellers of his day would have been very familiar with.

In the past, it was booksellers like the Blackwells who opened the doors to knowledge, just as surely as the academic institutions did. Now technology has opened the doors of information to all. And the rate of change proceeds within the blink of an eye. But will the learned continue to seek out the bookseller to obtain books? Why can't they go direct to the originator and have the raw data sent at lightning speed down the cap six cable to the laser printer, and so have their needs satisfied on demand? In the distant past, books were the preserve of a select few; they were obtained directly from the publisher, second-hand dealer—at a premium, or obtained on loan for a set

Epilogue

38 John Thwaites, the manager of the Broad Street shop: 'Booksellers are a rare breed'.

fee from commercial lending libraries. Bookshops like Blackwell's did not exist.

When the first B H Blackwell put his name above the door in St Clements, he participated in a 'revolution': a revolution that spearheaded the rise of mass communication. Bookshops, like Blackwell's, began to exist and continue to do so because there was, and still is, a need for an efficient professional personal service by experts. These experts have the knowledge of and access to an infinite variety of sources of information and are capable of using their skills, at no extra cost, to track down the unique and specific requirements of the customer. A good bookseller, and not an absurdly named screen and keyboard combo, is still the customer's best chance of obtaining the object of his or her bibliographic desire.

Blackwell's in Broad Street will continue to serve the people of Oxford, whoever they are. It continues to serve the world's academic communities, embracing change and shrewdly adapting it to its own ends. Making a virtue of necessity is as much a trait now as it was when Benjamin Harris set up shop in 1846, and his wife determined that the name would be revived in their son—the second B H Blackwell: the thread from that day to this continues unbroken.

Ruskin said 'All books are divisible into two classes, the books of the hour, and the books of all time' and I think the same is true of the booksellers. Sir Basil Blackwell wrote some notes on books and the function of bookshops in 1952 from which the following is extracted.

> The bookseller will be able to commend the flavour of his stock with authority to his customers. It is proper that a wine-and-spirit merchant should taste and test the precious liquids he supplies, though he is unwise if he devote his whole leisure to potation. But the more of his stock a bookseller can absorb, the better for him and for his customers. But, again, he must have leisure for discussion and the trading of opinions with the good bookmen who frequent the shop. So he grows in knowledge and wisdom in his craft.
>
> Such practice naturally prompts an interest in books no longer current, and it may be claimed that no bookshop should be without a secondhand department—that intellectual lucky-dip which is the delight of the book-collector. Here the bookseller must have the knowledge, with a difference—knowledge of author and title, of course, but also of the rarity of a book and of the interest it has maintained with readers or collectors. One might perhaps say that he must have a knowledge of the history of the book. Such knowledge guides the bookseller in buying and pricing his stock of secondhand or (as the Americans very sensibly say) 'used' books. There is a further advantage in the handling of 'used' books, which, if they be of sufficient rarity and interest, are graced with the epithet 'Antiquarian', in that in this business there is some latitude in the margin of profit, and the possibility of occasional windfalls, which in the case of new books the narrow and rigid terms of supply do not follow.
>
> Knowledge and reading develop personality, and it is the essence of a good bookshop that it should have character. However mechanically efficient a bookshop may be, its cultural value is nugatory unless it be informed by a personality enriched by reading and commerce with literate minds. A bookseller's personality will attract kindred minds, which in their turn will aid and enrich his mind; and so a bookshop may reflect in its stock and atmosphere a kind of corporate personality representing and fostering the cultural character of its locality. Such is the effect of 'friends'.

Epilogue

Bishop Stubbs ('Character Stubbs') once described a certain bookshop, my father's, as 'the literary man's public house'. It is a pleasant and apt phrase. In a well-ordered bookshop there is an air of good cheer as the public sample the books which they may or may not choose to buy; for though his stock is for 'consumption off the premises' a bookseller deems it right that his clients should taste, and sometimes absorb freely, before deciding what to take away. A happy murmur is heard as the customers discuss them or subjects prompted by them with friends they may meet there, or with the bookseller. Here is the freedom and good fellowship of the tavern, with perhaps the same likelihood of rebuke for wasting time and money on returning home.

JOHN THWAITES

Postscript

The Last Word

Preserving tradition is good for business

My father strongly advocated the preservation of tradition, but he was never adverse to change if it meant 'serving the trade by which he lived'. But if I could have summoned my grandfather, Benjamin Henry, from the Elysian fields, what thoughts would have passed through his mind as he climbed the familiar stairs? Would he not marvel, recalling the cramped premises in which Blackwell's had its beginnings, at the thousands upon thousands of books around him; at the vastness of the Norrington Room; at the wonders of computers, which translate his painstaking study of the Quaritch Catalogue onto screens on which any member of staff, with but a few hours of training, can call up instant information on almost any published title? Might he have halted in the room, where three times a day he said his prayers, and then go below to where he had worked so long into the evening, and find some things little changed? Blackwell's is at the forefront of modern bookselling, but it is also in touch with its past, with its roots. More importantly, its tradition of service hasn't changed. We are still striving after the 'most acceptable and humane way of putting the right book into the right hand'. And if, while Blackwell's weathers the storms of modernization and rationalization, the steep competition in this new age of .coms and instant access to non-book information, that ideal is harder to realize than it was in happier times, it is still the lodestar by which Blackwell's and its associated companies steer.

Even when I entered the firm, in 1952, so many of the old customs had gone. Unlike my grandfather, and the first directors of the Company, my brother and I were not 'bound apprentice' in any formal sense. But just as my father had been dispatched to learn something of publishing, I did a stint at Oxford University Press, and, when I joined the firm, I was sent to learn the business from Henry Schollick, acting occasionally as sales representative for Blackwell and Mott. As a true Blackwellian, I, too, smelt the printer's ink, and I was quickly 'promoted' to learn the packers' art, and I was nearly as dab a hand with string as my grandfather. And I tried to keep alive other Blackwell traditions; keeping the government, and the bureaucrats at bay. When the second Labour Government of the 1960s and its Chancellor, Roy Jenkins, insisted by law upon disclosure of every infinitesimal financial detail of a company's working pattern, I encouraged the Board, and my father and brother, to circumnavigate them. Jubilantly, we formed U P Jenkins Ltd. The Memorandum of Association of U P was 'To erect, construct, lay down, enlarge, alter and maintain any roads, railways, tramways, sidings, bridges, reservoirs, shops, stores, factories, buildings, works, plant and machinery necessary or convenient for the Company's business . . .'

Back in 1956, I took over responsibility for the completion of the building of the top floor at Broad Street. From that time, I had a hand in every major building project—including the most ambitious, the Norrington room. The *Architectural Review* described the Norrington Room as 'a real triumph—one of the finest internal spaces of recent years'. When it opened, it contained 160,000 volumes arranged on two and a half miles of shelving, and it was for many years, according to the *Guinness Book of Records*, the largest open display of books within a single room in the world. Since then, there have been many other projects, ones which similarly satisfy my liking for the practical side of things. This was an interest that had always been with me, or at least ever since the happy times of my childhood and adolescence when I had been 'apprenticed' to the Gaffer's driver, Cuthbert White, as mechanic and general odd-job man. I have tried to keep my hand in with the restoration of my father's, and grandfather's, room. But this is not just, or even primarily, a commercial exercise. Among all the changes at Blackwell's, one tradition is still sacrosanct—the old Oxford custom, which was explained by a sign on the wall:

> *When you visit Blackwell's, no one will ask you what you want*
> *You are free to ramble where you will; to handle any book;*
> *In short to browse at leisure*
> *The assistants are at your service when you need them,*
> *But unless you look to them they will leave you undisturbed*
> *You are equally welcome whether you have come to buy or to browse*
> *Such has been the tradition at Blackwell's for fifty years*

And so continues this custom dating back a century and a quarter! The room is for everyone, 'you are welcome whether you come to buy or to browse', and it is a permanent memorial to my father, and the earlier founders of the firm. The restoration of 'Gaffer's Room' is a fitting tribute to my father's life and work, and it has, happily, re-kindled memories, not only mine, but also those of staff, past and present, and many friends of Blackwell's. Perhaps Blackwell's present customers and visitors will leave here having 'found out' something of the richness of the Gaffer's life, his contribution to education, to his beloved City of Oxford and to the world of scholarship, which he promoted, preserved and helped to disseminate. Times may have changed, but, as I hope this room will remind you, the Blackwell's 'brand' has not. B H Blackwell's, now in the fifth generation, is still 'in the family'.

JULIAN BLACKWELL

Appendices

1: Chronology

1808	Joshua Blackwell, father of the first B H Blackwell, was married in St Andrew's in Holborn.
1813	Birth of Benjamin Harris Blackwell, in London: the first B H Blackwell.
1823	Anne Nancy Stirling (Blackwell) was born in London.
1830s	Benjamin Harris, Isaac Blackwell and Nancy settle in Oxford.
1839	B H Blackwell writes an article on the importance of temperance, lamenting that his efforts in Oxford were largely unsupported 'by those who should know better'.
1845	Anne Nancy and Benjamin Harris are married.
1846	Benjamin Harris, at the age of thirty-three, rents a small ground floor property, for £18 per year at 46 High Street, St Clements, where he put the name of B H Blackwell above the door.
1849	Birth of Benjamin Henry Blackwell, the second B H Blackwell.
1850	The Public Libraries Act.
1854	Oxford City Library opens. Benjamin Harris becomes Oxford City's first librarian. The library had first opened in this year.
1854	The family moves to 3 Turl Street, which was later known as the Turl Cash Bookshop.
1855	Benjamin Harris Blackwell died, aged forty-one, a victim of overwork (angina pectoris). Buried in the public graveyard, beside the Church of St Cross, Holywell.
1855	Nancy fends for the family of three, dress-making and embroidering, and determines to see the name of B H Blackwell re-established. The Blackwell family leave Turl Street, and move to cheaper rented quarters at 1 Jews Mount, subsequently called Bulwarks Lane, looking down on the terminus of the Oxford and Birmingham Canal; now the site of Nuffield College.
1862	Benjamin Henry Blackwell, aged 13, leaves Price's School and begins an apprenticeship with his father's old friend, Charles Richards.

1870	Benjamin Henry Blackwell manages a branch of Richards' shop in the High Street, from where he rose in the ranks by getting himself appointed as an assistant at the more flourishing firm of Slaughter and Rose.
1874	The family moves into the more spacious quarters at 46 Holywell Street, with a boarder-apprentice and a servant; 'a house large enough to let lodgings in term time'.
1878	Benjamin Henry's brother, Fred, was married.
1878 (17 October)	B H Blackwell formally agreed to take 50 Broad Street.
1878 (24 December)	Stock valued at £126 with a nominal sale price of £190.
1879	Benjamin Henry Blackwell opened his bookshop at 50 Broad Street, in a room 12ft × 12ft with a loan of £150.
1879	Turnover was £1,267 2s 11d.
1880	Benjamin Henry took on his first apprentice, Master F W Chaundy.
1880	Benjamin Henry moves in over the shop with his mother.
1883	Parcel post was introduced.
1883	Sales were running at £3,000 a year.
1886 (26 August)	B H Blackwell married Lydia Taylor, daughter of a Norfolk farmer, at the Parish Church of SS Philip and James.
1887 (4 June)	Anne Nancy Stirling Blackwell died and was buried in Holywell Cemetary.
1887	Dorothy was born.
1888	Asked to supply books to the Oxford Union.
1889 (29 May)	Basil Henry Blackwell born in room over bookshop.
1896	Benjamin Henry and his family moved from their crowded quarters at 51 Broad Street to 1 Linton Road, North Oxford.
1899	Benjamin Blackwell becomes a founding member of the Oxford and District branch of the Associated Booksellers of Great Britain and Northern Ireland.
1900/1	Net Book Agreement.
1886	Basil to Madgalen College School.
1906	Basil Blackwell goes to Merton College, Oxford.
1911	Basil Blackwell goes to Amen Corner—Oxford University Press—'for an insight into publishing'.
1913	Basil Blackwell joins the family business.
1913	Basil Blackwell starts his adventures in publishing: *Wheels*, *Adventurers All*, *Oxford Poetry*, *Oxford Outlook* etc.
1914	Basil marries Marion Christine Soans.
1919	Basil Blackwell commences publishing independently—B H Blackwell becomes Basil Blackwell.
1920	'The firm was incorporated as a private limited company, and the first director's meeting was held on 22 March. The founder was chairman and his five fellow-directors were his son, the three 'pillars of the house' Hanks, Hunt and

Charles Field, and H S Critchley, who was appointed secretary of the company. Father and son held the majority of the ordinary shares, 2,200 were allocated in various proportions to the other four directors, and 100 each to the other founding members of the company, H Steele, W Bates, H S Rowles, H Cook, B Presley and C W F Bishop.' A L P Norrington *The History of a Family Firm: 1879–1979*.

1920	Formed the Shakespeare Head Press, producing scholarly reprints in luxury bindings of English classic authors, and the beginning of a famous partnership with Bernard Newdigate, typographer.
1921	Chevrolet van was purchased for £281.
1922	Basil Blackwell and Adrian Mott found the publishing house of Basil Blackwell & Mott Ltd.
1924 (26 October)	The second B H Blackwell, at the age of 75, died peacefully at his home in Linton Road. The third B H Blackwell succeeded his father as chairman of B H Blackwell Ltd.
1925/1926	President of the International Association of Antiquarian Booksellers.
1927	Lilla Blackwell's death.
1934/1935	Basil becomes President of the Associated Booksellers of Great Britain and Ireland.
1935	*Complete Works of Shakespeare* produced in one volume and sold for 6 shillings
1938	48 and 49 Broad Street rebuilt and merged with 50 and 51 to more than double bookshelf space.
1939	Blackwell's four binderies are incorporated into the Kemp Hall Bindery.
1939	Launched Blackwell Scientific Publications.
1946 (31 August)	First profit-sharing scheme for staff, based on points for amount of weekly salary and years of service. All staff with more than a year's service to share in scheme.
1947 (November)	Somerville and Ross start to build up a Blackwell's Music Section.
1948 (July)	University of Adelaide transferred their periodicals subscriptions to Blackwell's (£600).
1948 (September)	Blackwell's given licence to import foreign and American periodicals without limit. Expected soon to be able to trade directly with German publishers.
	Orders from Manchester University for German periodicals. First order from University of the Gold Coast—a new University.
1949 (May)	University of Iowa—first periodicals order (£550). Also begin to see technical libraries ordering—Paint Industries Research Institution, Durban (c. £100).

1949 (August)	Librarian of the new University at Ibadan visited Blackwell's and began to subscribe through Blackwell's. Economic crisis, and buying from America was restricted.
1949 (November)	New periodical customers—Benares Hindu University; University of Notre Dame, Indiana; Pietermaritzburg Technical College; Potchefstroom University College.
1950 (February)	The opinion expressed in BSP's annual report, that the introduction of the National Health Service had caused a reduction in the buying of medical books, was endorsed.
1951 (May)	The University of Queensland returned to subscribing their periodicals through Blackwell's. Blackwell's had retained their pre-war continuation orders, but new orders had been given for the intervening period to the University Bookshop.
1953 (January)	Kumasi College of Technology, Gold Coast—a new periodical customer
1956 (June)	A list of the totals of the subscriptions of a number of universities were made—Birmingham much the highest at £3,400.
1956	Led successful crusade against antiquarian booksellers auction ring.
1956	The third B H Blackwell created knight for services to bookselling and publishing. (The first knighthood to be bestowed on a bookseller).
1958	Campaign to reach the industrial and scientific libraries.
1958	£1,000,000 turnover reached.
1959 (November)	ASLIB Conference—the Blackwell's advertisements in *ASLIB Proceedings* were mentioned as having brought Blackwell's to the attention of the industrial libraries.
1960 (April)	Staff to get every other Saturday off.
1960 (May)	48% of all statements go to the USA. Two National Accounting Machine computers programmed to convert the total of each statement automatically.
1960 (June)	First periodical orders from York University, Toronto.
1960 (December)	Sir Basil Blackwell went to South Africa—possibly the first trip round foreign libraries? 3 January—17 February 1961.
1961 (February)	First periodical order from University of Western Australia.
1961 (April)	*Philobiblon* published.
1961 (October)	The *Patristic Greek Lexicon* was published after 54 years—Blackwell's had collected 440 standing orders.
1961	£1,000,000 export turnover reached.
1962 (April)	Blackwell's now hold 90,000 active accounts with book buyers.
1962 (September)	Letter from Macmillan Co, NY, said that an account with Blackwell's was very much a status symbol in universities and colleges there.

1963 (June)	It was reported 'In April for the first time in the history of the Periodical Department our sales touched six figures'.
1963 (July)	Richard Blackwell went to American Library Association in Chicago, for the first time.
1963 (November)	Periodicals passed £1/2 million in sales.
1963	Blackwell's take over leading Danish academic publishers and booksellers Einar Munksgaard of Copenhagen.
1964 (June)	A 5-day week was introduced on 29 June.
1964/1965	Basil Blackwell became President of the Classical Association.
1965 (June)	A breakdown appeared of Exports' annual reminders to publishers—6297 items from 581 publishers.
1965	Basil Blackwell given *Officer l'Academie*.
1965	Basil Blackwell elected an Honorary Fellow, Merton College, Oxford.
1965	Basil Blackwell awarded an Hon. LL.D. degree Manchester University.
1966 (January)	Richard Blackwell was appointed Managing Director.
1966 (June)	Blackwell's opened the Norrington Room, the world's largest single display of books in one room. (160,000 volumes on 2½ miles of shelving.) *Architects' Review* November 1966 hailed it as 'a real triumph—one of the finest internal spaces of recent years'.
1966 (August)	Julian Blackwell became Chairman of ASLIB Council.
1967 (March)	Munksgaard's 50th Anniversary with festivities in Copenhagen.
1967 (June)	Jack Wolsdorf's appointment as Blackwell's first overseas Libraries Service Adviser. Was joined by James Galbraith in February 1971.
1968 (January)	The announcement that a decision had been made to install a computer for Accounts, Publicity and Periodicals work.
1968 (October)	Blackwell's Art Bookshop opens at 53 Broad Street.
1968	Turnover tops £5,000,000 of which 66% is from export orders.
1969 (29 May)	Gaffer becomes President and Richard Blackwell Chairman of the firm.
1969	Sir Basil elected President of the English Association.
1969	NCR Century all disk computer to be installed.
1969	Plans for new £1,000,000 purpose-built distribution centre.
1970 (January)	Gaffer received Freedom of City of Oxford.
1971 (early)	The postal strike—ingenious arrangements devised for overcoming the effects of the strike.
1977	Death of Marion Christine Soans Blackwell.
1979	The Gaffer celebrates his ninetieth birthday: He was still coming to the office everyday, though he had given up, but only very recently, his habit of taking stairs two at a time.

1979 (27 June)	The University paid its homage at the Encaenia in the Sheldonian Theatre to this 'Jupiter of Booksellers', when the Gaffer received an Honorary Doctorate of Civil Law, and walked in the procession in the company of Graham Greene, whose first publisher he had been.
1979	Centenary Celebrations at Merton College Chapel. Harold Macmillan spoke of his belief in private companies 'doing our best for country, Church and people, if we work honestly and well'.
1979	Benefaction of £350,000 to St Cross College, one of the new Graduate Societies established by the University in 1965.
1984	Death of Basil Henry Blackwell.

2: The Gaffer's room

The very soul of Blackwell's for as long as anyone can remember[487]

The Gaffer, or Gaffer Basil as he was to his close associates, began his life above this room. It has now been restored in honour of this 'Jupiter of Booksellers' [488]. The room recreates the world of the first Blackwell's, alongside the modern coffee shop set among the thousands of new books; together, they 'Live not for today and yesterday, but for ever'[489]. Blackwell's as it is now, in the twenty-first century, remains much as it was when Jan Morris described it twenty years ago. It matters not that Blackwell's is riddled with computer-gadgetry these days, that it has interests all over the place—still to book buyers everywhere it remains in essence the jumbled old shop in the Broad which Masefield loved, among whose shelves the golden generations of youth loitered on their way, between the river and the Union, through classical text or lyrical poet'[490]. The Blackwell's of today is still instantly recognizable from the, earlier, nineteenth century lithographs, which show passers-by in top hats and crinolines and the still-shuttered windows of the rooms where the Blackwells first lived and worked. The main doors in the eighteenth century façade are still narrow and the modest threshold belies the huge and sprawling interior, running under the quad of Trinity College. It is still busiest at the beginning of the academic year, after finals when the students sell-on their textbooks, and at Christmastide. It is still the backdrop for many an unfinished argument, and an alternative to, and perhaps a refuge from, 'the timeless green gardens in the drizzle, the bells and the fragrant libraries'.

Above the shop, in this room, the Gaffer would meet with his 'seniors' and hatch the latest plans over tea and Chelsea buns. Reading between the lines, in the laboriously hand-written minute books, he clearly had to be brought down from his imaginative flights of fancy: first by his father's 'guardians', Mr Blackwell's former apprentices, and subsequently by his sons. Yet he also had his feet on the ground; he would not be surprised, if he sauntered into the modern shop, to find himself addressing his staff, some of whom remain from his day, over the head of a computer's mechanical monitor. He had seen it all coming long ago.

Nor would the sight of reclining figures surprise him. As a young student he had taken time out, from Merton's 'whispering towers of the Middle Ages', to visit his father in the shop, and he would have seen people so accommodated. The Firm's Minute Book of 1907, and the catalogue that was sent out to customers, recorded that 'A room has been opened upstairs, which may be found convenient by visitors wishing to examine books, write a note, or look through the literary papers; and may in some way supply that lack of seating accommodation which, it is feared, ladies have sometimes found noticeable'[491]. This tradition, along with many others, has been upheld.

If the Gaffer should venture now from the Elysian Fields, and seek the solace of his room, he could not only watch the world pass by in the Broad, below, but right in front of him he would be able to see students of all ages: in deep conversation, in deep thought, or lounging on a leather sofa lost in time or a Blackwell's book, probably as yet unpaid for. Manifestly, they still observe the old Blackwellian code: 'When you visit Blackwell's no one will ask you what you want. You are free to ramble where you will; to handle any books; in short, to browse at leisure. The assistants are at your service when you need them; but unless you look to them, they will leave you undisturbed. You are welcome whether you come to buy or to browse. Such has been the tradition of Blackwell's for seventy years' [492]. Here, right under his nose, the scholar-gypsies still take refuge, and their offspring doze, or not, in their buggies, just as he had slept in his perambulator at the back of the shop.

His father's old shop that the bank was loath to support, and Frederick Macmillan thought was on the wrong side of the street, is now home to the latest generation of book-lovers: locals, students, academics, authors, would-be writers and, dear to the heart of the Gaffer and his father, Mr Blackwell, unpublished poets rub shoulders with the more established. Today's established poets are of a genre Basil hardly knew, except as a very old man: Heaney, Paulin, Motion, the present poet laureate, to namedrop just a few, at the top of the lists. They walk unobtrusively, and usually unnoticed, in the footsteps of those who would have greeted aloud the Gaffer in his time. Among the famous of his father's day were: Beeching, Housman, Rennell Rodd, J St Loe Strachey, Mackail, L A G Strong, Sir Alan Gilbert, C M Bowra, and other professors of poetry[493]. Others claimed that they were 'launched' by Basil Blackwell; the likes of J R Tolkein, the Huxleys, the Sitwells, Sir Alan Herbert, Geoffrey Faber, G D H Cole, John Betjeman and Christopher Morley, whose *Eighth Sin* was published at 1 shilling, and fetched at auction some $60, and Stephen Spender. Spender, the Gaffer recalled, had from the start 'intimations of immortality'[494].

It is in this room, that such poets, and many more since forgotten, would have solicited the Gaffer's endorsement, and where his father had first suggested that he help to publish 'young poets unknown to fame'. It is not so difficult to imagine the physical surroundings for these encounters; surprisingly little physical change has occurred to the room itself, certainly nothing that diminishes the ethos of the Blackwell men. And there are many from the Gaffer's time who still come into the shop, such as his old friend the former librarian of Merton, and look up, involuntarily, as they pass the gaffer's door. It's location at the top of the first flight of stairs still invokes the Gaffer, and if you ask for the Gaffer's Room not even the newest employee, in 2001, will be in any doubt as to its whereabouts. In 1979 Jan Morris had interviewed Sir Basil, then aged ninety, in this room. She observed that 'there was nothing ingenuous, or even nostalgic, to its ambiance. From it, Sir Basil has created one of the most dynamic and progressive outfits in the entire book industry. Yet just as great restaurateurs often prefer to keep their check tablecloths, and their grandmother's fish-kettles, so he likes to preserve at the apes of this forceful entity, a savour of past times'[495]. Blackwell's Gaffer obviously liked his office that way, and he was equally convinced that preserving tradition was good for business.

Arriving each morning long before the shop opened to the public, the Gaffer liked to sit at his desk looking over his right shoulder at the street scenes below. He would emerge, when he had dispatched the contents of the post to be attended to urgently, to waylay, and escort, visitors. They would be treated to a full tour, ending up in his office, this inner sanctum. Sir Basil—he would not introduce himself in this style—'call me Gaffer', would start to pull down catalogues from the shelf, and draw their attention to his 'little volume' about bookselling, they would be taken on a quick detour to see the ornate Victorian bathroom, 'still in full working order', and the room above, where he had been born. Having toured the estate, he would sit his visitors down for a talk: more of a mini lecture—a tutorial from the 'unofficial college of the University'. Mischievously, he would point to a picture of his father, hung over his fireplace: 'This picture makes him better looking than I remember him'. The bookshelves in his room were lined with books bearing the Blackwell's imprint; proudly, Sir Basil would identify a recent publication seen through the press under his aegis, an edition of Boethius: *De Consolatione Philosophiae*, for example, written by a Christian theologian in prison[496]. Camouflaged by the glories of English literature, that helped to shape the work of Chaucer and Shakespeare, he was in his element; they were his natural habitat which never failed to overawe his visitors.

The room also provided clues to the Gaffer's other interests and preoccupations. 'He had around him, the rariora culled from a lifetime of communion with the learned: *La Vénus sans bras* cast in plaster, holding shadowy court in a corner behind the bookcase with.... an original block of a William Morris textile design (that had been presented to Sir Basil by Sandersons) still stained with woad and vermaille...; drawings of the half-timbered home of the Shakespeare Head Press, and a plaster bust of A H Bullen, its first begetter; on the desk a little commemorative silver pin-tray and a copy of a Conan Doyle historical novel'[497]. The bookshelves and furnishings in the Gaffer's room remain as they were first made, and fitted, by a local craftsman—ordinary, utility, furniture, but 'crafted'. On the wall the William Morris wallpaper had been restored; a fragment of the original had been preserved under a panel of glass, by Julian Blackwell, and it has now been replaced, having been matched with the original block, which was first cut in 1874. The room has been restored as near as possible to resemble how it was, in spirit, when Sir Basil Blackwell worked there, first as

Chairman, and then President, of Blackwell's[498]. Many of Sir Basil's treasured possessions formerly displayed in his workroom have, however, thanks to his impetuous generosity, found new homes.

In the Gaffer's heyday this room was the centre of the universe, and his secretary was at his beck and call just outside the door. In his later years, it was more peaceful. It is now opening as a Visitors' Centre, destined to be busy again: a source for researchers, a place for would-be writers to find their muse, and for the casual traveller or adventurer to seek respite, conveniently next door to the café. It is now a working room, as it was in earlier times, dedicated not only to the memory of Sir Basil Blackwell, but to all Blackwell's staff, customers and friends: past and present, old and new, without whom the bookshop would never have flourished. As you come up what was a Queen Anne staircase, the atmosphere and smell of bookselling still greets you, as it did the Gaffer, and his father, Benjamin Henry Blackwell. Come through the door, leaving behind the infamous Oxford traffic, the wind and rain, or the sun's brightness, and stand by the old fireplace. You may find yourself going back over a century to the time when the Blackwell children, Basil and Dorothy, played in this room, then their mother's sitting room. The view from the windows is not so different from the one they first knew. If you are young at heart, you might, in your mind's eye, see the circus procession coming down 'The Broad', a sight Basil loved as a child.

Looking now at this room there is little to remind you that the man who worked here every day for three quarters of a century presided over an empire, with a turnover of over £29 million a year, by the centenary year of 1979. The room is disarmingly old school. The switchboard looks as though it were installed in the thirties or forties, and could be loaned out as the perfect prop for an operations room in a wartime film. And the telephone is one of those heavy-duty affairs made redundant by the Post Office, and only ever seen now as an ornament. On the wall is another poignant memento of a bygone age—a speaking tube through which Sir Basil used to communicate the day's orders to the counter staff, some distance away. The Gaffer, not to be forgotten, is sitting, on his metaphorical bough, among his books. Like the Cheshire Cat, from *Alice in Wonderland*, he is watching what is happening[499]. Writing in 1971, this is how Sir Basil described himself. But he also had the wisdom to suggest that even the Cheshire Cat, in his elevated position, begins to fade out 'starting with the tail and ending with the grin'[500]. Yet Sir Basil's memory is a reality still for generations of the reading public, and this room will re-introduce him to generations more to come. Basil Blackwell would doubtless be pleased at all this effort to preserve some of the history of his beloved firm. But he would give his vote to the books. Books, the lifeblood of his trade, his ideas and his dreams, provide the best chance of survival 'they reveal the wisdom and the follies of ages past, to be our guides in years to come'.

Yet the books also invoke the soul of the man, the Gaffer. And it is the hope of Julian Blackwell, now life President of Blackwell's, as his father was before him, that visitors may not only enjoy the books, and learn something of his father, and his work, writings and ideas, but also of a bygone age, an age which is not without its resonance for today. It is to Julian Blackwell that we owe the restoration of this room; a room he remembers from his earliest childhood. As a director of the firm, in the eighties, he recalls his aging father, in full flood with Cuthbert—the man Julian calls his 'surrogate father'—ranting about the Oxford traffic, a topic that has become his own bugbear. Out of the window he sees the same procession of visitors, customers, academics and lifetime students come and go. Undergraduates still appear much as they did to an American journalist before the Second World War: 'they seldom carry books, and many of them have a vacant and unintelligent look, particularly when pedalling at high speed around corners and in front of automobiles on their antiquated bicycles'[501]. Appearances, however, remain deceptive; some things, thank goodness, never change.

Julian Blackwell dedicates this room to the memory of his father and to all Blackwell's staff and customers, past and present, for their repose and continuing education. At the time that the Gaffer oversaw the extension and renovation of the shop, in 1939, the *Oxford Chronicle* observed 'We have all grown up in the habit of taking Blackwell's bookshop, like other good things in life, very much as a matter of course. But I still remember the impression made on me when I first knew Oxford. In its strange capacity for making you fell as though you were at home in a vast library, of which some generous patron of letters had given you free run, it seemed like a book shop from a happy dream...'. Julian Blackwell hopes that you will continue to dream, and to buy books, in Blackwell's. It is, after all, the books that provide the real timelessness in his family firm. If you should now chance on this room, you can pause awhile and reflect, as his father so often did, that it is not just this room that is preserved but 'All the glory of the world would be buried in oblivion unless God had provided mortals with the remedy of books'[502]. And who knows, on some serendipitous adventure, in this room, you may draw your muses from the black wells:

> Sumite castalios nigris de fontibus haustus[503].

3: Selected sources from the Blackwell archive and from Basil Blackwell's private papers

This list is arranged alphabetically by author, with Anon as the final group, and in date order within the author listing. Undated items are at the end of each author's list.

Author	*Date*	*Title or subject*
G. Bettridge	June 1969	Shakespeare Head Press
C F Bell (curator of the Ashmolean Museum)	Undated	51 Broad Street occupants and William Morris wallpaper
Basil Blackwell	1898–1982	Diary (fragments)
Basil Blackwell	March 1906	*The Mosquito*; sonnet *On a Dead Cat* in Magdalen College School magazine, page 4

Appendices

Basil Blackwell	October 1929	Bookselling – Careers for Boys No 154, reprinted from *The Journal of Careers*
Basil Blackwell	1930s	A dog's ramble in the *Aeneid*
Basil Blackwell	9 April 1934	School books – why not net? An address to the Society of Bookmen
Basil Blackwell	13 February 1935	Unwin's departure from the the Booksellers' Association
Basil Blackwell	September 1935	Bookmen and books
Basil Blackwell	22 April 1936	Presidency speech for the Publishers' Association
Basil Blackwell	27 May 1938	Children's bookselling speech (2 drafts)
Basil Blackwell	30 May 1938	Children's bookselling speech at Miss Carey's dinner for the trade
Basil Blackwell	12 January 1939	William Hunt of Blackwell's: In Memoriam
Basil Blackwell	19 May 1939	Words, Words, Words
Basil Blackwell	23 October 1939	Gun-powder speech
Basil Blackwell (Ltd)	1 January 1941	Mailing list deposited with Barclays Bank
Basil Blackwell	8 March 1945	Bernard Newdigate Typographer: an address delivered to the Double Crown Club. London: Privately printed
Basil Blackwell	19 October 1945	The Good Bookman
Basil Blackwell	July 1946	Bernard Newdigate Typographer: an extract. *Signature*, page 19, London
Basil Blackwell	November 1946	Evolution of Books (Harold Raymond—Red Cross)
Basil Blackwell	23 July 1948	Literature Today (Exploring Literature)
Basil Blackwell	1948–	Origins of the classics (various drafts)
Basil Blackwell	August 1949	The Publisher in Literature (speech to the British Council)
Basil Blackwell	1949	On Books
Basil Blackwell	30 September 1952	The Function of the Bookshop
Basil Blackwell	2 February 1954	Juvenile Crime (address to the Dragon School)
Basil Blackwell	January 1956	Juvenile Justice System
Basil Blackwell	24 January 1958	May Morris – *The Earthly Paradise*
Basil Blackwell	January 1958	May Morris (background)
Basil Blackwell	27 October 1962	More about Miss Lobb (plus draft)

Basil Blackwell	5 June 1963	Basil Blackwell & Mott (why and how Basil Blackwell acquired the firm)
Basil Blackwell	April 1965	Retreat from Grammar: an address to The Classical Association on the bookselling success of classical books; with notes
Basil Blackwell	8 March 1968	Letters in the New Age, the first Jackson Knight Memorial Lecture, University of Exeter, The Abbey Press, 1969
Basil Blackwell	6 November 1970	Allen Lane's description (on request from Hans Schmoller of Penguin)
Basil Blackwell	11 July 1972	Austin Longland's Memorial Service
Basil Blackwell	25 September 1972	*Oxford Poetry* (description of collection of *Oxford Poetry*)
Basil Blackwell	18 May 1977	*Oxford Outlook* (some of the editors are listed)
Basil Blackwell	6 September 1979	Sir Basil's speech and history of Blackwell's at the Basil Blackwell Publisher party to celebrate 100 years of bookselling and publishing – 3 drafts
Basil Blackwell	Undated	Basil Blackwell & Mott (description of sales and success)
Basil Blackwell	Undated	Basil Blackwell Publisher (exploring Sir Basil's publishing life briefly)
Basil Blackwell	Undated	Definition of reading
Basil Blackwell	Undated	Dorothy (Blackwell)
Basil Blackwell	Undated	EWP (Ernest Wilfred Parker and his position of director of Blackwell's)
Basil Blackwell	Undated	Kay (a tribute to a good employee of Blackwell's)
Basil Blackwell	Undated	Ozymandias (moral story about King Leonidas and his selflessness)
Basil Blackwell	Undated	Publishing (the events introducing Sir Basil to publishing – 2 drafts)
Basil Blackwell	Undated	Refusing work kindly (as reported years ago by the Hong Kong correspondent of the *Central News*)

Appendices

Basil Blackwell	Undated	The Ring (Basil Blackwell's understanding of The Ring)
Richard Blackwell	17 September 1963	Article on the history of the firm printed for John Roughton Simpson CB
Richard Blackwell	18 August 1976	Notes on ALP Nottington *Blackwell's 1879–1979*, Blackwell's, Oxford 1983
Samuel Butler	30 January 1892	*The Humour of Homer*
Samuel Butler	1893	On the Trapanese Origins of *The Odyssey*, Metcalfe & Co, Cambridge
R. Chichester Clark	27 July 1956	Adjournment Debate [Col. 882]
gathered with the following 2 items		
Hugh Delaney	27 July 1956	Autiquarian Booksellers (Buyers Ring)
WF Deedes	27 July 1956	Parliamentary Debate (*Hansard*) All London, HMSO
AD Cope	1905	On a Recently Discovered Fragment of Housman (exploring the allusions behind Latin texts)
HFE	24 March 1948	Very Old Blues – the significance of the Boat Race, *Punch*
TF Highman	November 1967	*Dr Blakiston Recalled: Memoirs of an Oxford Character*, Basil Blackwell, Oxford, 1967
Robert Lusty	20 October 1962	My Literary Education (more on Miss Lobb), *The Bookseller*
David Martin	13 February 1981	History of Blackwell's Part II, Connell's version
Munby & Norrie	1974	Extracts from *Publishing and Bookselling*, 5th edition
Bernard Quaritch	10 January 1880	Letter to General Starring (about The Ring)
F Quiller Couch	31 May 1964	Mr Wardell (childhood memories of father's punishment)
Henry Schollick	31 May 1984	Address at the Thanksgiving Service for the life of Basil Blackwell, University Press, Oxford
David Vaisey	August 1984	Bequest to the Bodleian Library (the archive of William Beckford's literary manuscripts)
Anon	29 July 1927	Auctions (Bidding Agreements) Act, Parliament
Anon	19 November 1955	Cuttings on The Ring, *Oxford Mail*

Anon	20 January 1960	William Morris Society
Anon	January 1964	Service in general (of Blackwell's), *Broad Sheet*
Anon	8 February 1979	Archival material: partial inventory of additional archives, 5th meeting
Anon	6 July 1979	Blackwell's catalogues including the centenary catalogue
Anon	12 April 1984	Basil Blackwell's Funeral Service sheet
Anon	31 May 1984	Basil Blackwell's Thanksgiving Service sheet
Anon	Undated	Blackwell's archives listings
Anon	Undated	List of Blackwell's rare books on the move of the Antiquarian and Rare Books Department to Fyfield Manor
Anon	Undated	Notes on the Works of William Morris
Anon	Undated	Basil Blackwell & Mott Ltd Blackwell's report
Anon	Various dates	Blackwell's ledgers and minute books

4: Dramatis personae

The Blackwell family

Joshua Blackwell
Benjamin Harris Blackwell
Anne Stirling Austin (Nancy) Blackwell *Benjamin Harris' wife*
Benjamin Henry (Harry) Blackwell
Fred Blackwell *Benjamin Henry's brother*
Matilda Blackwell *Benjamin Henry's sister*
Lydia (Taylor) Blackwell *Benjamin Henry's wife*
John Taylor *Lydia's father*
Jack Taylor *Lydia's brother*
Charlotte Taylor *Lydia's sister*
Dorothy (Blackwell) Austin *Benjamin Henry's first child*
Sumner Austin *Dorothy's husband*
Basil Henry Blackwell
Marion Christine (Soans) Blackwell *Basil Henry's wife*
Richard Blackwell
Julian Blackwell
Corrina (Blackwell) Wiltshire
Dame Penelope (Blackwell) Jessell
Philip Blackwell
Nigel Blackwell

Blackwellians and other characters

Geoffrey Barfoot *Benjamin Henry's apprentice, an office boy in 1912*
W Bates *founding member of the company*
H C Beeching *the moving spirit in* Mensae Secundae, *the first book of the B H Blackwell imprint*
R J Beedham *illustrator for Shakespeare Head Press*
C W F Bishop *founding member of the company*

Appendices

W W Blair-Fish *secretary of Shakespeare Head Press*
Sir Adrian Boult *bumped by him in the Christ Church Crew*
Jim Broadbent *Blackwell's pensioner*
Phil Brown *from present antiquarian Department*
C E Brownrigg *Master of Magdalen College School*
A H Bullen *founder of Shakespeare Head Press*
George Bunting *a Director of Blackwell's*
Edward Burney *another of Basil's contemporaries*
Fred W Chaundy *Benjamin Henry's first apprentice*
Veve Collins *of OUP*
H Cook *founding member of the company*
Harry S Critchley *secretary of the private limited company and acting chairman of Shakespeare Head Press*
Lionel Curtis
Arundell del Re *co-director of Shakespeare Head Press*
Miss Carey *of Dents*
Frederick Dymond *directed Music Department*
Geoffrey Faber *Basil instructed him at OUP for a few months*
L R Farnell *Rector of Exeter*
Jim Feather *managing director of Blackwell and Mott*
S T Fenemore *Blackwell's employee, worked during the war*
Charles Field *Benjamin Henry's second chief cashier and a director of Blackwell's Limited*
Christopher Francis *Theology Department*
Miss E Joyce Francis *illustrator for Shakespeare Head Press*
Sir Henry Frowde *friend of Benjamin Henry and advisor that Basil go to OUP*
Robert Gandall *the late Laudian Professor of Arabic who donated a collection to Blackwell's*
David Ben Gurion *first Prime Minister of Israel*
Eleanor Halliday *Basil's secretary*
Fred Hanks *Benjamin Henry's second apprentice and also to be one of the directors of Blackwell's Ltd*
Ewart (Edgar) Hine *Benjamin Henry's apprentice from 1917—later to be a member of the board of Blackwell's (1952)*
Gerry Hopkins *former colleague of Basil Blackwell*
A E Housman of St John's *wrote a poem in* Primavera
William Hunt *apprentice and one of the directors of Blackwell's Ltd*
Mr Kendrick *the head 'comp' at the Shakespeare Head Press*
Will (Rex) King *Benjamin Henry's apprentice*
Allen Lane
Miss Lobb *the helper of May Morris*
Austin Longland *Basil's friend*
Frederick Macmillian *publisher*
Miss Sarah Mardon *Basil's first school*
C H K Marten *Lower Master of Eton, wrote educational history books*
David Martin *managing director of Blackwell and Mott*
Angela Melvin *worked for Basil Blackwell*
John Merryman
Lady Ottoline Morell *of the Garsington set*
Jan Morris
May Morris
William Morris
Adrian S Mott *director of Basil Blackwell & Mott and Shakespeare Head Press*
Ken New *Blackwell's employee*
Bernard Newdigate *of the Shakespeare Head Press*
John Newsom *a close student friend of Basil's*

Bowyer Nicholas *accessory to H C Beeching*
Sir Arthur Norrington *master of Trinity College, Oxford*
Messrs Parker *rival on Broad Street during Benjamin Henry's time*
Ernest Parker *Blackwell's*
B Presley *founding member of the company*
Bernard Quaritch *bookseller*
Charles Richards *Benjamin Henry's apprentice*
Charles Richards *Benjamin Harris' executor*
H S Rowles *founding member of the company*
Sir Michael Sadler *Benjamin Henry's friend who enlisted Basil's help*
Henry L Schollick *managing director of Basil Blackwell & Mott*
Bernard Shaw
Jo Shelton *Blackwell employee*
H Steele *founding member of the company*
Fred Stevens *Benjamin Henry's employee 1920; instrumental in founding the firm's famous Periodicals Department—was member of the board of Blackwell's (1952)*
Tom Templeton *employee of Blackwell's, started 1926*
Mrs Teressa Messer of Thame *Benjamin Henry's money lender*
Alan Thomas *the Kings Road Bookseller who took over William Morris presidency from Basil*
Mr John Thompson *chairman of Barclay's Bank*
Sir Fisher Unwin
Stanley Unwin
Emery Walker
Cuthbert White *Basil's gardener and driver*
Miss Wilhemia *Basil's first school teacher*
Charlie Williams *former colleague of Basil Blackwell*
Hugh Williamson *publisher, printer and author*

Blackwellian writers

Harold Acton
Edith Barfoot (*The Discovery of Joy in the Vocation of Suffering*)
Maurice Baring
Hilaire Belloc
John Betjeman
Laurence Binyon
Enid Blyton
Robert Bridges
John Buchan
Roy Campbell
G K Chesterton
Richard Crossman
Walter de la Mare
T S Eliot
Eleanor Farjeon
Graham Greene
Roy Harrod
L P Hartley
Gilbert Highet
Aldous Huxley
Cecil Day Lewis
J W Mackail
Compton Mackenzie
Louis MacNeice
Dudley Medley
A A Milne
Christopher Morley
Gilbert Murray
Beverley Nichols
Wilfred Owen
Dorothy L Sayers
Edith Sitwell
John Sparrow
Stephen Spender
Ronald Tolkien
Vaughan Williams
H E Wooldridge

Some members of the Inklings

Neville Coghill *produced* OUDS
Hugo Dyson *best friend of Lewis*
Humphrey Havard *Lewis' doctor*

C S Lewis John Wain
J R R Tolkien Charlie Williams

5: Gifts and bequests

A: Sir Basil Blackwell's gifts of rare books to Merton College Library

1 Apollonius Rhodius (1496)
2 Aristophanes, *Comoediae* (1498)
3 Aristotle, *Opera Omnia* (1495–98) 5 vols. in 6
4 Aulus Gellius, *Noctes Atticae* (Venice, 1509)
5 Boethius, *Opera Omnia* (Basle, 1570)
6 Catullus, Tibullus, Propertius (1502)
7 Cicero, *De Officiis* (1541)
8 Dante, *Le Terze Rime* (1502)
9 Dufour, S, *The Manner of Making Coffee, Tea and Chocolate* (1685)
10 Duns Scotus, *Quaestiones in Universam Aristotelis Logicam* (Venice, 1586)
11 Duns Scotus, *In Primum et Secundum Sententiarum Quaestiones* (Antwerp, 1620)
12 Earle, John, *Microcosmography* (1732)
13 Euripides, *Tragoediae* (1503)
14 Herodotus, *Historiae* (1502)
15 Iamblichus, *De Mysteriis* (1497)
16 Martial, *Epigrammata* (1501)
17 Martial, *Epigrammata*, ed. W M Lindsay (Oxford, 1902), A E Housman's copy
18 Overbury, Sir Thomas, *His Wife* (1638)
19 Ovid, *Opera* (1503)
20 Plato, *Opera Omnia* (1513) 2 vols. in 1
21 Pliny, *Epistolae* (Milan, 1478)
22 Plutarch, *Vitae Illustrium Virorum* (1519)
23 Richard of Bury, *Philobiblon* (1599)
24 Seneca, *Opera Philosophica; Epistolae* (Naples, 1475)
25 Seneca, *Works*, translated T Lodge (1624)
26 Sophocles, *Tragaediae* (1502)
27 Theocritus, *Eclogae* (1495)
28 Xenophon, *Opera* (1525)

In addition to his gift of books Sir Basil gave various papers of Professor Garrod in April 1961. They include a letter from Sir Winston Churchill and another from Sir Max Beerbolm.

From *Postmaster* 1996 (pp 51–52)

B: A bequest to the Bodleian Library

The Oxford bookselling firm, B H Blackwell Ltd, has presented to the Bodleian Library at Oxford, the archive of William Beckford's literary manuscripts, correspondence and personal papers which the firm bought at

Sotheby's in 1977. The gift is made in memory of Sir Basil Blackwell, the head of the firm, who died on 9 April 1984 at the age of 94. The presentation commerorates as well his father Benjamin, the founder of the firm, and his elder son Richard, who died in 1980. In this way the company seeks to honour its first three chairmen, who brought it to its centenary in 1979.

William Beckford, 1760–1844, was not only a gifted, learned, and artistic collector and connoisseur, he was also reputedly England's wealthiest son. His accounts of his travels, as well as his plays and novels (including the celebrated *Vathek*), brought him immediate fame. He was, in addition, a distinguished musician, architect and arbiter of taste. His enormous collections were housed in Fonthill Abbey, rebuilt to his extraordinary and extravagant designs, a residence (now vanished) which the late Lord Clark described as 'by far the most exciting building of its time'. The collections were sold in 1822 in a sale lasting 37 days. His library was dispersed by auction in 1822, and at that time the Beckford archive passed to his daughter, the Duchess of Hamilton. The papers reflect all his wide-ranging interests; architectural drawings, literary manuscripts, journals and diaries, music and biographical papers are preserved alongside over 2,500 lectures.

David Vaisey
Keeper of Western MSS
Bodleian Library

6: Play hours with Pegasus

It is hoped that this further, more detailed, study now in progress, will provide help to draw out the themes touched on in this book of tales. It will focus on the literary and other writings of Basil Blackwell, and the work of those associated with him. A P Herbert used the allusion to Pegasus in his poetry volume for B H Blackwell's. The Blackwells were very much among those who, allusively, bore poets on their poetic flights; they were steeds, and often the favourites, of the muses. Neither Sir Basil Blackwell, nor his father, nor his grandfather (B H Blackwell first and second) thought of bookselling as an end, or trade, in itself. It was a means to free people: physically, mentally, spiritually, and financially too, if they were lucky. For these Blackwells, 'work was play'.

Working on *Adventurers All* opened up the doors that had been closed for practical reasons (archives missing, not sorted, no time to do the research etc.). One of the earliest themes that suggested itself, while doing the research, was to make an inventory, and an analysis, of the poetry published during Benjamin Henry's time at Blackwell's, and his son's 'apprenticeship', the years 1879–1924. Benjamin Henry was a scholar in his own right, but never in his lifetime had any academic recognition. He was the first, however, to recognize, and promote others: 'to remove from the work of young poets the reproach of insolvency' (B H Blackwell). The B H Blackwell imprint started with *Mensae Secundae*, ed. H C Beeching, 1879 and then *Primavera* the next year. The publications ranged from A Huxley's first published work, *The Burning Wheel*, published poems of Wilfred Owen, Dorothy L Sayers, essays, and Newdigate prize-winning poems, to poetry series, *Oxford Poetry, Initiatives, Adventurers All, Waifs and Strays*, and *Wheels*. Many of the poets who first made their appearance in these poetry anthologies are now household names, but just as many are obscure. The later poetry, particularly, may be of interest to those studying Victorian and early twentieth century literature. Later, Basil Blackwell wrote of his disapproval of, although still published, 'the modernists'; he was incensed at Eliot's idea that it was a 'waste to educate the masses'.

The book will resemble, albeit with modern production techniques, original B H Blackwell imprints, as this has tried to do. It will provide an opportunity to include some of the photographic archive and other illustrations and prints, and to reproduce some of the fine book designs and typography of the period, especially Bernard Newdigate's, as exemplified in Blackwell's publications. The proposed book will contain edited versions of Basil Blackwell's writings, and specialist essays calling on experts for particular subjects: fine printing and the craft tradition, Victorian and Edwardian writing, a specialist examination of the Blackwell collections in Merton, especially the rare books, the classical writing and editing of the Blackwells, editing Housman for ex-ample, Basil Blackwell's 'Classical' collection of essays (he preferred Greek, his father Latin), other literary writings of Basil Blackwell and his father including some extracts from diaries etc, as well as extending the references of this present book and building on those in Norrington's.

Importantly, the book also includes a section on education. The success of Blackwell's, and the expansion of publishing for mass consumption, runs parallel with the development and growth of universal education, the university extension movement: informal, self, education. This was a key and constantly underlying theme of Basil Blackwell's, and his father's and grandfather's (the first Oxford City Librarian). They were pioneers in the development of modern educational publishing (B H Blackwell, Shakespeare Head Press, Basil Blackwell, Blackwell Scientific etc) and an adjunct to OUP—where Basil Blackwell trained. The imprint contains a very wide selection: academic, educational (school books—Marten's histories) and the Blackwells interventions to introduce and improve general books for children (*Joy Street*, for example), classics for the general reader and the English classics: a ground breaking innovation with a 'cheap' version of *The Complete Works of Shakespeare*! No study would be complete without a thorough examination of the Blackwell's catalogues, and the firm's ledgers, which tell much about second-hand and antiquarian books as well as providing an insight into the reading preferences of 'reading and writing folk'. Basil Blackwell always maintained that he did not approve of telling people what to read, *ma non troppo*, anyway! You can be your own synod.

If you should happen to read this book, and you can help on this new project, we would be very happy if you would get in touch with Rita Ricketts, Julian Blackwell, staff in Blackwell's or the publishers. Thank you.

References

ABBREVIATIONS
BB   Basil Blackwell
Fasnacht   Ruth Fasnacht, *A History of the City of Oxford*, Basil Blackwell, Oxford, 1952
Norrington   ALP Norrington, *Blackwell's 1879-1979: the history of a family firm*, Blackwell, Oxford, 1983

1 Literally all over the world—this quote comes from the *Auckland Star* 9 June 1956
2 Conclusion of *Pilgrim's Progress*
3 Philip Larkin, *Annus Mirabilis*, 1974
4 Ian Norrie, *The Bookseller*, 26 May 1979
5 This plea had been recorded in the diaries of Rex King, written between July and August 1920, and later recorded in Blackwell's *Broadsheet*, May 1948
6 See Michael Alexander, *A History of English Literature: Late Victorian Literature 1880-1900*, p 306
7 James Elroy Flecker, Oxford Canal
8 Vita Sackville West, in G S Thomas, *The Old Shrub Roses*, Phoenix House, London, 1955, p 5
9 Richard Blackwell, notes on his father, 18 August 1976 and in a letter to Sir Arthur Norrington, 13 September 1976
10 BB notes September 1955
11 BB Origins of the Classics
12 BB Origins of the Classics
13 BB from notes on Origins of the Classics
14 BB from notes on Origins of the Classics
15 BB notes, *World of Books*, 1955
16 The *Daily News*, 12 November 1924
17 *Morning Post* 1906
18 *Philadelphia Evening Post*, 4 April 1934
19 H Laski, *Turnstile One*, ed V S Pritchett, Turnstile Press
20 From Basil Blackwell's notes 'Words, words, words'. He attributes it to *The Fairie Queene*
21 Ved Mehta, Quiet Beneficent Things, *New Yorker*, 31 October 1964
22 A Letter to Corinna Wiltshire, 29 February 1984
23 The *Daily News*, 12 November 1924
24 *English Illustrated Magazine*, September 1902
25 John Masefield, *Shopping in Oxford*, William Heinemann Ltd, London, 1941, p 4
26 Laurence Clark Powell, *Books in my Baggage*, Constable, London
27 Jan Morris, Interview with Basil Blackwell 'Oxford man of all times', *Daily Telegraph*

28 *The Bookseller*, 2 June 1956
29 See, for example, the *Auckland Star* and the *St Louis Dispatch*, July 1956
30 Adam Fox, October 1966
31 This poem is reproduced with the very kind help, and permission of Lou Levitas, who I first saw in earnest conversation with a friend in the Blackwell's coffee bar, another Blackwell's addition! See letter BB to Lou Levitas, 9 November 1966, and Adam Fox to Lou Levitas, 5 November 1966
32 John Masefield, *Land Workers*
33 Notes, BB 22 April 1936
34 BB's notes on 'Words, words, words', 19 May 1939
35 ibid, reference to the Loeb translation of Livy
36 Norrington, p 18
37 ibid
38 Anne Stevenson, *Dreaming of (More) Spires*, in *Oxford in Verse*, ed G Pursglove and A Ricketts, The Perpetua Press, Oxford, 1999
39 Margaret Forster, *Rich Desserts and Captains Thin: A Family and Their Times 1831–1931*, Vintage, 1998, p xvii
40 Benjamin Harris Blackwell, *Oxford Teetotal Society Journal*, 1839
41 BB cites his grandfather as the founder and his father as the 're-founder'. See *British Books To Come*, No 45, 1948, pp 13–15
42 Taken from the title of a book written and published by Sir Basil to initiate the newcomer
43 Anon
44 Gilda O'Neill, *My East End*, Penguin, London, 1999, pp 20–31
45 *The Book as a Commodity*, L'Apparition du Livre, Albin Michel, 1958
46 See, for example, Adrian Desmond, *Huxley: the Devil's Disciple*, Michael Joseph, London, 1994
47 The Founder of the Salvation Army, General Booth, thus described the conditions in England
48 Fasnacht, pp 202–3
49 *Oxford Directory*, 1846, taken from the description of Oxford, pp 2–3
50 Fasnacht, p 203
51 Fasnacht, p 202
52 Fasnacht, p 200
53 Fasnacht, pp 198–202
54 Fasnacht, p 140
55 The *Oxford Directory*, 1846
56 The City Council became increasingly aware of the need to relax the 'Freeman' regulations: allowing more people to open up in trade and create employment opportunities, even if this meant sacrificing the preservation of Oxford's beauty: see Fasnacht, p 203
57 Thoughts on early beginnings— Basil Blackwell
58 In one case at least, Fred Trash, also a publisher
59 Fasnacht, p 193
60 Basil Blackwell, notes on the *Functions of a Good Bookshop*, September 30 1952
61 Scrapbook, Oxford City Library, 1855–1954, p 5
62 The Public Library Act, 14 August 1850. Joseph Taylor, Oxford City Library, 1855–1954, pp 4–7
63 Dutton, Allen and Co's *Directory and Gazetteer* for 1863
64 ibid, p 4
65 A story handed down to Basil by his father, Benjamin Henry
66 From an undated account of his life by his granddaughter, Dorothy Austin. Dorothy and Basil Blackwell's mother, Lilla, must

have had a chance to listen to the memories of Anne Stirling Blackwell, before she died in 1887, and must have passed on these memories
67 Letter from Sir Basil to J P Wells, the Oxford City Librarian, 17 February 1973
68 *Sunday Journal* 6 December 1981. But both Sir Basil and Lady Blackwell were 'secret' teetotallers and took at the very most a small glass of claret
69 Norman Franklin, Routledge, Kegan and Paul, to BB, 28 Febraury 1975
70 Marvell, *To His Coy Mistress*
71 BB's notes
72 BB, commemorative speech, Blackwell's 1979–1954 (1946), Christ Church 7 January 1954
73 Scrapbook of Oxford City Library, 1854–1954, p 7, in Oxford City Library: Oxfordshire records section
74 *Broad Sheet*, January 1979, p 3
75 BB spoke of copious love-letters written by his grandfather to Nancy Stirling, but their whereabouts is now unknown
76 Letter, BB to M Maclagan (Oxford Library) 7 January 1954, including some of the notes and material he used for his Christ Church speech
77 In the *Oxford Directory* of 1880, Nancy is described as a dress-maker, even though she was now living with her son at the Broad Street shop
78 Christ Church speech notes 1954
79 BB, Christ Church speech 1954
80 The 1871 Census records Ann Blackwell living at 1 Bulwarks Alley, formerly Jews Walk, with her three children, an apprentice and a servant. The 1874 *Oxford Directory* records the dress-maker living at 46 Holywell
81 BB's notes January 1979
82 BB's letter to Sir Arthur Norrington 2 March 1979
83 Christ Church speech 1954
84 Christ Church speech 1954
85 The conclusion of *Paradise Lost*, Book XII
86 Christ Church speech 1954
87 A description applied to BB, but one just as appropriate for Benjamin Henry Blackwell. See *The Lily*, Michaelmas 1984, p 5 (the magazine of Magdalen College School), in a poem by Maida Stainer
88 Polonius's dictum, which, according to Fred 'Father' Hanks, summed up the life of Benjamin Henry Blackwell, recorded in 'Rex' King's diaries
89 BB's allusion to Wordsworth's Newton
90 Dorothy Austin's account of her grandfather's life, undated
91 ibid
92 The *Publishers' Circular and Booksellers' Record*, 8 November 1924, p 666
93 ibid
94 From the diaries of 'Rex' King dated 3 August 1920
95 Dr Johnson
96 BB's notes
97 BB's notes
98 *Publishers' Circular and Booksellers' Record*, 8 November 1924, p 666
99 ibid
100 Douglas Bush's editorial note on *Paradise Lost*, quoted in A Thwaite, *Six Centuries of Verse*, Methuen, 1984
101 Benjamin Henry's diaries 1877
102 Lord Rosebery's words
103 *Oxford Magazine*, 1939

References

104 *Oxford Magazine*, 1939
105 *Oxford Magazine*, 1939
106 Notes for BB's Christ Church speech, 1954
107 From a speech by Fred Hanks made at BB's home 'Osse Field' 29 June 1933
108 BB's notes, probably taken from his father's diaries. See also Norrington p 119
109 ibid
110 ibid
111 Norrington, p 7
112 Norrington, p 22
113 Norrington, p 40
114 Norrington, p 41
115 Browsing in Bookshops, Orlo Williams, *World*, October 18 1910
116 *Oxford Magazine*, January 1939
117 *Oxford Magazine*, January 1939
118 Norrington, p 16
119 *Publishers' Circular and Booksellers' Record* 8 November 1924, p 667
120 BB's Christ Church speech, 1954
121 BB's notes: see also Norrington, p 18
122 BB's account, see Norrington, p 18
123 Bishop Stubbs's phrase
124 *Morning Post*, 26 December 1906
125 The shop was described in the *Oxford Magazine*, 4 June 1902
126 *Barbara Goes to Oxford*, Methuen, 1902
127 From a proof of Oxford University Press dated 9 December 1907
128 Dr Folliott's *Crotchet Castle*
129 Orlo Williams, Browsing in Bookshops, *World*, 18 October 1910
130 Norrington, p 18
131 Norrington, p 18
132 Carlisle's epigram
133 Norrington, p 19
134 'Father' Hanks's oral account in Rex King's diaries
135 Rex King's diaries. The 'shanty' was on the site of Gee's Market Garden and helped to make up for the lack of room at Broad Street. Similarly a small premises was used at the Octagon—a building at the junction of The Indian Institute and Hertford College, now incorporated into the latter as an entrance hall/porter's lodge
136 Rex King's diaries
137 Fred Hanks speech in Appleton, 1933. This can be found in BB's papers, also Norrington, p 28
138 BB's account, also Norrington p 32
139 ibid
140 The *London Daily News*, Wednesday 12 November 1924, p 6. Ironically the paper had been established in 1846 by Charles Dickens, a writer Benjamin Henry Blackwell disliked
141 BB's notes, 5 June 1963
142 Letter to Sir Arthur Norrington, 18 April 1975
143 ibid
144 BB's own notes on his father's life and work
145 BB, from his own notes on the firm's centenary, dated 6 September 1979
146 *Books To Come*, April 1948
147 *Daily News*, 12 November 1924 which mentions other minor poets such as Philip Guedalla, Robert Nichols, Ronald Knox and a famous poem by Roy Campbell, entitled 'The Flaming Terrapin.'
148 Basil Blackwell's notes, 5 June 1963. See also *Such a Strange Lady, An Introduction to Dorothy L Sayers 1893–1957*, Janet Hitchman, New English Library, p 48
149 BB's notes
150 Letter, BB to Christine Zwart, 9 December 1974

151 Letter, Professor J R R Tolkien, signed Ronald Tolkien, to 'My dear Blackwell', 5 July 1973
152 ibid
153 *Books To Come*, April 1948
154 BB's speech to celebrate 100 years of Blackwell's publishing, 6 September 1979
155 Christopher Morley's description of Benjamin Henry Blackwell
156 An extract sent by Jack Wolsdorf from an essay 'Concerning the first edition of *The Eighth Sin* by Christopher Morley' published by *Colophon* 1934. See Blackwell's *Broad Sheet* March 1985
157 Frank Sidgwick's diaries and other material relating to the Shakespeare Head Press are in BB's notes and his 1975 essay on Bullen and Newdigate. Sidgwick left Bullen and founded his own firm of Sidgwick and Jackson
158 BB in *Books To Come* April 1948
159 Hilaire Belloc's term
160 Benjamin Henry's own sentiments as recorded by his son, Basil
161 Sir Michael Sadler had gone to Trinity, Oxford, the year after Blackwell's opened its doors. He shared Benjamin Henry Blackwell's passion for education: he was a renowned educational pioneer—Vice-Chancellor of Leeds University (1911–1923) and Master of University College, Oxford (1923–34)
162 Dorothy Austin's account of her grandfather's life, undated
163 Norrington, p 25
164 *Oxford Magazine*, 1939
165 BB's notes, 6 June 1975
166 *The Bookseller*, July 1979
167 Basil Blackwell's own notes 1975
168 From a set of notes left by BB, dated 13 June 1975
169 Oxford Society 1880–81, December 1881 Vol. XXXIII No. 2, pp 27–28
170 Many who have left oral and written accounts of working class life in the late nineteenth and early twentieth century rest their case, for their own educational and social promotion, on the role of the church of all denominations with the support of Sunday Schools and church social clubs, in addition to the services offered by the WEA and working men's and other clubs. See, for example, the account of John Murray's youth (in preparation)
171 BB's notes, 6 June 1975
172 Dorothy Austin Blackwell's notes.
173 From the diaries of 'Rex' King who drew on the oral accounts of 'Father Hanks', published in the *Broad Sheet*, May 1948 nearly twenty years after Benjamin Henry's death
174 op cit Fred Hanks
175 BB to Sir Arthur Norrington, 5 December, 1975
176 'Rex' King's diaries
177 BB's noted account, also Norrington
178 BB's notes, also Norrington
179 BB's notes, also in Norrington, p 55
180 From an article by BB in *Broad Sheet*, January 1979 p 3
181 Bernard Quaritich (1819–99), born in Saxony, became a London bookseller in 1847 where he developed the most extensive trade in old books to be found anywhere in the world
182 Benjamin Henry, diary 1877
183 *Morning Post* 1906
184 Norrington, p 11
185 T P's and *Cassell's Weekly*

References

186 BB, 100 years of publishing 1979
187 Sir Maurice Bowra's sentiments, Norrington, p 14
188 Kipling's description of Auckland, New Zealand
189 Dante's *Divine Comedy* was a favourite of Benjamin Henry's, and his son, Basil's
190 Norrington, p 42
191 The *Publishers' Circular* 14 July 1906
192 It was under the 1911 Shops and Offices Act that the cause of a shorter working week was begun, with the closure of shops on Thursdays at 1 pm
193 See for example the account of the Carr family in M Forster, *Rich Desserts and the Captain's Thin*, Vintage, 1998, p 52
194 Annual General Meeting, 13 December 1920
195 Norrington, Basil Blackwell's Foreword
196 BB's definition of a good bookseller, in his article 'Bookselling', *The Journal of Careers*, October 1929
197 BB attributed to Dorothy L Sayers
198 Matthew Arnold, *The Scholar-Gypsy*
199 BB draft 1971
200 The *Daily News*, 12 November 1924
201 See *Isis* No 1710, 13 November 1980 pp 22–23
202 *The Life of Aratus*
203 BB's undated notes
204 BB's notes refer in this way to his mother
205 BB's notes on his mother
206 BB's notes
207 John Masefield, *Land Workers*
208 Dorothy Blackwell's notes
209 From the notes of Dorothy Blackwell
210 Notes on his sister, Dorothy, by BB, also used by BB for her funeral address
211 Interview Julian Blackwell, 20 April 2001
212 Interview Julian Blackwell, 20 April 2001
213 Fred Hanks, op cit
214 Henry Schollick
215 Interview with BB, John Owen, *Oxford Times*, Friday 25 May 1979
216 Op cit *Broad Sheet* 1979
217 W Tuckwell, Reminiscences of Oxford, p 245, in Fasnacht, pp 204–5
218 BB's first published poem, in the sonnet form he so much admired, *The Lily* (Magdalen College School magazine), March 1906
219 Schollick joined forces with Basil Blackwell in 1932—Schollick's address took place on Ascension Day, 31 May 1984. Schollick, together with BB, had set up the world wide Book Token system
220 Interview Julian Blackwell, 20 April 2001
221 Interview Julian Blackwell, 20 April 2001
222 Notes for *Postmaster*, not the final version
223 This account of his life at Merton was written by BB for *Postmaster* (Merton) in 1971 and reprinted in *Broad Sheet* in 1984
224 BB to Sir Arthur Norrington, 3 December 1975
225 Richard Blackwell to Thomas Norrington, notes 1976
226 see *Georgics* III, 105, at the start of Charioleus—BB's notes, *A Dog's Ramble* . . .
227 Draft for *Postmaster* 1971
228 Interview Julian Blackwell

229 The title of a poem by J Masefield, used by BB in an address given near the end of his life entitled: *Grace before Going*
230 Reference to Ecclesiasticus 38 and 39: 1–11
231 *Book World*, No 25, Vol 3, No 1, February 1984, Julian Bingley, p 4
232 Schollick p 18
233 Dent Memorial Lecture: Basil Blackwell; *The World of Books*, J M Dent.
234 BB's words from undated notes written around his eightieth birthday
235 BB's notes, May 1956
236 BB commemorated the work of Dent in the first Dent Memorial Lecture [233]
237 Ibid. BB attributed this story to R M Leonard, who edited *The Periodical* and undertook sundry duties at Amen Corner.
238 Ibid
239 Ibid
240 Interview, *Oxford Times*, Friday 25 May 1979
241 BB's notes for a speech to the Publisher's Association, 22 April 1937
242 BB's notes
243 *Joy Street* was the invention of Ernest Parket
244 Adrian Mott's notes for his retirement speech, 5 October 1954
245 Ibid
246 BB
247 His son was later very successful in the firm, as was Henry Critchley's
248 Adrian Mott's notes 1954
249 C N Francis, *In Memoriam, Sir Basil Blackwell 1879–1984*
250 BB's own notes—undated
251 Notes, BB, 25 September, 1972
252 Letter, BB to L F Herbert, 21 August 1974
253 Previous letter L F Herbert to BB, 17 August 1974
254 Notable, Sir Compton Mackenzie who vowed that he was indebted to B H Blackwell, quoted in notes dictated by BB 5 June 1963
255 Sir Basil Blackwell, dictated memoir, 6 June 1963
256 Phyllis Hartnoll (Editor of *The Oxford Companion to the Theatre*) to Sir Arthur Norrington, 1 August 1977
257 Margiad Evans, who had some success with a book entitled 'The Wooden Doctor'
258 Letter to Arthur Norrington from Ithaca NY, USA, 4 September 1977 from a scholar working on a collected poems of Wilfred Owen
259 This list was compiled by BB, 18 May 1977, mostly from memory as most of the records were lost
260 A L Rowse, 'The Good-Natured Man', in *Oxford, China and Italy, Writings in honour of Sir Harold Acton*, Edited by Edward Chaney and Neil Ritchie, p 64
261 Peter Quennell, ibid, pp 57–58
262 Harold Acton, 'When Frigates from Long Voyages. . . .', quoted in *The Good-Natured Man*, op cit, p 29
263 Aldous Huxley, *Out of the Window*, Selected Poems, Basil Blackwell, 1925
264 Ibid
265 Ibid
266 Ibid
267 Stephen Spender to Basil Blackwell, from Hamburg, undated but probably in the summer of 1930
268 Letter, BB to Nicholas Jenkins, Magdalen College, 19 June 1985

References

269 BB's notes, 22 April 1936
270 BB's notes
271 Ibid p 21
272 G Betteridge, *Scholastic Studies in Printing*, Advisory Council for Further Education, Manchester, June 1969
273 Adrian Mott's notes 1954
274 A proof, pre-publication copy, sent by BB, can be seen in the Bodleian.
275 *London Mercury* Book Notes, October 1933
276 Basil Blackwell, June 63
277 T S Eliot to BB, undated
278 Double Crown Club Address, see [281]
279 Letter, BB to J Cryer, October 28 1977
280 BB's own notes
281 Bernard Newdigate, Typographer, an Address delivered by Basil Blackwell at the seventy-ninth meeting of the Double Crown Club, March 8, 1945.
282 Basil Blackwell's own notes on Bullen and Newdigate.
283 Newdigate's life and work is commemorated in Joseph Thorp's book: *B H Newdigate, Scholar-Printer 1869-1944*: Blackwell 1950, and in an article by B B, in *Signature*, July 1946
284 BB, Bernard Newdigate, Typographer, *Signature, A Quadrimestrial of Typography and Graphic Arts*, ed. Oliver Simon, New Series, London, July 1946, pp 19-36
285 Notes, Sir Adrian Mott, 5 October 1954
286 Notes, Sir Adrian Mott, 5 October 1954
287 Philip Unwin, draft speech for the Society of Bookmen, 1971
288 *Oxford Times*, 6 September 1985
289 Blackwell's centenary issue
290 See BB's own notes, May 1956 and 6 September 1979
291 BB's notes, May 1956, 1963 and 1979
292 Sir Adrian Mott, hand-written notes, found by his wife after his death, in preparation for a speech on the history of B & M, 5 October 1954; he was then sixty-five.
293 Notes on publishing, BB
294 BB's own notes
295 Ibid
296 Notes by BB on publishing
297 The words are those of David Roy, who used them to describe W H Smith
298 From the minutes of the Board 1924
299 Basil Blackwell's own notes on his publishing adventures
300 Blackwell's Minute Book, 22 March 1920-16 December 1946, Minute of 12 December 1920. Similarly the minute for 26 November 1926 explained that none of Blackwell's activities had not been affected by the General Strike
301 BB's notes at the front of the firms Minute Book, 1920-1946. He must have looked back over the Minutes when gathering material for one or other of his writings or talks
302 Ian Norrie, *The Bookseller*, 26 May 1979
303 BB's own notes—undated (written after his eightieth birthday)
304 Ibid
305 Ibid
306 Letter to Sir Arthur Norrington, 7 July 1976
307 Christ Church speech, 1954
308 Note on the new buildings, BB 30 September 1938

309 BB writing in *Books and Bookmen*, January 1992, p 16
310 Mudra (Bombay) December 1973, p 13
311 These were BB's own dicta. See also C N Francis, *In Memoriam, Sir Basil Blackwell*
312 Ibid
313 From a personal account written by Gladys Roby, called 'Fuzzy', probably written in 1978.
314 *Broad Sheet* centenary issue 1979
315 Ved Mehta, Oxford and the Gaffer, *Books and Bookmen*, January 1972, p 14
316 *Oxford Times* May 25 1979
317 Hugh Williamson writing in the *Oxford Times*, 13 April 1984
318 Ved Mehta *Books and Bookmen*, January 1972 p 12
319 The letters remain amoung BB's papers, and are printed in full in *The Publishers' Circular* and *The Publisher and Bookseller*, November 3, 1934
320 Interview Julian Blackwell, 9 May 2001
321 See article by Ved Mehta, 'Quiet Beneficent things', *The New Yorker*, 31 October 1964, pp 63–126
322 The *Sunday Telegraph* article stressed the two faces of Sir Basil, the modern face excited by change and the looking back to pre-war days when bookselling was almost a 'sacred art', 13 May 1979
323 BB's notes, also in Norrington, p 143
324 *Oxford Mail* 11 April 1984
325 C N Francis *In Memoriam, Sir Basil Blackwell 1879–1984*
326 *The Guardian*, 29 May 1969
327 Telegram from BB re Dulau and Co Ltd
328 BB's collection of papers on Parker's
329 Text and list written by BB for Barclay's Bank Ltd, January 1941
330 *St Louis Despatch*, 25 July 1956.
331 Norrington, p 113
332 BB's notes
333 J Betjeman to BB, 43 Cloth Fair London, E C 1 (undated)
334 Term coined by Norrington, in Norrington
335 Conversation, Christchurch, August 1998
336 BB notes. These must have been for Thomas Norrington—see also Norrington, p 127
337 Adrian Mott's notes
338 BB's notes on Kaye
339 Interview Angela Melvin, Oxford 11 June 2001
340 Interview Angela Melvin and Phil Brown, Oxford 11 June 2001
341 Angela Melvin
342 Angela Melvin
343 Phil Brown
344 Phil Brown
345 BB, speech at the Banquet of the Booksellers Association, Isle of Man, 1–4 May 1971
346 Interview with the Gaffer by the editor of *Broad Sheet*, Centenary Issue, 1979
347 Ibid
348 Public Oration, University of Oxford, 27 June 1979
349 Interview Steven Tomlinson, Western Manuscripts, The Bodleian, May 2001
350 Interview, Ken New, 14 July 2001
351 Letter, Andrew Witwer, New York, to Corrina Wiltshire, 29 February 1984
352 Basil Blackwell, 'Bookselling' reprinted from *The Journal of Careers*, October 1929
353 Review by BB, 27 August 1974, of *Essays in the History of Publishing*, in celebration of 250th Anniversary

References

of Longman 1724–1974, edited by Asa Briggs
354 Ibid
355 See, for example, his notes on the *Functions of a Bookshop*, September 1952
356 From a speech by BB at the Banquet of the Booksellers Association, Isle of Man, May 1971
357 Interview BB and Ved Metha, *Books and Bookmen*, January 1972, p 14
358 BB, notes, 30 September 1952
359 See Margaret Drabble, ed, *The Concise Oxford Companion to English Literature*, OUP, 1987, p 187
360 Interview Roger Highfield, 19 July 2001
361 Richard Blackwell, interviewed in 1964 by Ved Mehta
362 As of July 2001
363 Letters Christine Blackwell to Basil, September 1919, Ramsgate
364 Ved Metha, interview with BB, *Books and Bookman*, January 1972, p 14
365 Letters, Christine Blackwell to Basil Blackwell, September 1919, Ramsgate
366 *Oxford Mail*, 13 January 1970
367 BB's Notes for his life of May Morris, 26 September 1919
368 Ibid
369 Scraps of drafts, mostly in pencil, are in BB's archives
370 Oral account, Julian Blackwell, January 2001
371 Oral interview with Julian Blackwell
372 One of BB's favourite quotes: '"Water inspires", Virgil's most brilliant simile,' he wrote. BB, *A Dog's Ramble in the Aeneid*
373 *The Wind in the Willows* was already, less than thirty years after its publication, a children's classic.
374 *Oxford Times* 28 May 1979
375 Euphemism for a tipple or drink
376 Robert Browning
377 Henry Schollick, Address at the Service of Thanksgiving for Basil Blackwell, 31 May 1984
378 Letter from The Gaffer to Angela Melvin, undated but after the death of his wife
379 Letter from The Gaffer to Angela Melvin
380 Edmund Blunden, a Blackwell's poet, 'Shells by a Stream,' quoted in G S Thomas, *The Old Shrub Roses*, Phoenix House, London, 1955, p 15
381 Wordsworth
382 Such a man, to BB's mind, was Austin Longland. See draft for *Postmaster* 1971
383 Draft for *Postmaster*, 1971
384 *Evading a Revolution*, Lionel Curtis, All Soul's, Oxford, published by Basil Blackwell, Oxford. The copy is inscribed 'to Basil Blackwell from Lionel Curtis in deep gratitude, 29 June 1953'
385 Notes on the Justice System, Basil Blackwell, January 1956
386 BB to Frank Pickstock, 19 March 1975
387 Letter from Lord Lloyd of Kilgerran, Joint Treasurer of the Liberal Party, to BB 28 July 1981
388 Letter from BB to Lord Lloyd of Kilgerran CBE QC JP, 4 August 1981
389 Notes for a speech to the Booksellers Association, 22 April 1936
390 The Secretary of the Association very kindly allowed me to go through all the old minute books, which included Benjamin Henry's own hand-written accounts, and subsequently, BB's
391 Will King
392 *The Times*, 31 July 1956

393 *The Times*, 1 August 1956
394 Letter to Sir Arthur Norrington, 11 October 1976
395 *Book World*, February 1984, p 4
396 Letter to Sir Arthur Norrington, 11 October, 1976
397 *The Times Saturday Review*, 24 May 1969
398 Dedication at the front of Fasnacht, selected by Basil Blackwell
399 BB's notes, 5 June 1963
400 Matthew Arnold, from *Thysis*
401 BB's notes for his essay on May Morris
402 Ibid
403 Henry Schollick, *The Bookseller*, 21 April 1984, p 16
404 BB's words and account; see also Norrington p 87
405 *Book World*, February 1984, p 2
406 Interview Roger Highfield, July 18 2001
407 *The Times Saturday Review*, 24 May 1969
408 Notes, Sir Adrian Mott, 5 October 1954
409 Notes, BB, 1956
410 Ibid
411 Dame Edith Sitwell to BB, 26 May 1964
412 Later in life, BB deplored government attempts to end the system of grammar school education, which resulted in less 'social mingling'
413 Letter to Sir Arthur Norrington, 3 December 1975
414 Mary Maddock writing a tribute for the *Oxford Times* 20 April 1984
415 Letter, The Town Clerk, A T Brown, to BB, November 20 1969
416 *Oxford Times* 13 January 1970
417 Letter, AT Brown to BB, Gosfield Hall, Essex, 13 January 1970
418 *Oxford Mail*, 13 January 1970
419 Henry Schollick, Address, in *Postmaster*, 1985
420 *Oxford Mail*, 28 June 1979
421 Henry Schollick
422 Jan Morris
423 Jan Morris
424 C N Francis, *In Memoriam, Sir Basil Blackwell 1879–1984*
425 *News Chronicle*, 31 May 1956
426 *Book World*, February 1984, p 4
427 Letter T S Eliot to 'Blackwell', 10 July 1956
428 29 July 1956
429 Henry Schollick, Thanksgiving Address, 31 May 1984
430 *The Times Saturday Review*, 24 May 1969
431 *The Guardian*, 29 May 1969
432 *The Guardian*, 29 May 1969
433 *Oxford Mail* 11 April 1984
434 *The Bookseller*, 21 April 1984
435 *The Bookseller*, 17 April 1982
436 Interview Basil Blackwell with Ved Metha, *Books and Bookmen*, January 1972, p 15
437 Letter from Mrs Graham Greene to the *Oxford Times* 18 February 1983
438 BB's essay on May Morris
439 Ibid; Alf Button is the character in a book of the same name by W A Darlington
440 Ibid
441 BB, *The Bookseller*, 27 October 1962, p 109
442 'Memoirs of May Morris', presented in an address to the William Morris Society, 1958
443 Obituary in the *Newsletter of the William Morris Society*, July 1984. Interestingly, Sir Basil's obituary took up three times the space of that of John Betjeman who died a month after Sir Basil!
444 Letter, Alan Thomas to BB, 20 October 1979

References
313

445 This is still available from Sanderson's
446 The restoration is due to Julian Blackwell, and this is his description. It took some searching to find the pattern, Sanderson's, at first, not being able to recall it. It was found, serendipitously, when my son had to 'do' a project on Henry Moore and we trailed around art galleries and libraries. Eventually, we found a little book on William Morris wallpapers in Woolworth's, a store Sir Basil had a great admiration for; it had done much to promulgate the cause of books for the 'general reading public,' and it still does
447 A clerk there was of Oxenford ... from the Prologue of the *Canterbury Tales*, Geoffrey Chaucer
448 BB's own notes on 'Origins of the Classics', for his speech, and paper, for the Classical Association
449 BB's notes on 'origins of the Classics'
450 *The Times*, London, 11 April, 1984
451 Ian Norrie, *The Bookseller*, 26 May 1979
452 Schollick, *The Bookseller*, 21 April 1984, p 18
453 Schollick, *The Bookseller*, 21 April 1984, p 18
454 BB's notes, undated
455 Matthew Arnold, 'The Scholar-Gypsy', *The Norton Anthology of English Literature*, Seventh Edition, Volume 2, W W Norton, 2000, p 1487
456 *The Norton Anthology*, Seventh Edition, Volume 2, p 1485
457 BB, *A Dog's Ramblings in the Aeneid*
458 This is still the case. Students at various universities around the country work part time in the various Blackwell outlets, many would-be writers, like the present Manager of the Broad Street shop, combine a hard day's work to earn their living, with study and composition. Blackwell's continues to attract such characters, as it has always done
459 *The Lily*, March 1906, p 4
460 Schollick, *The Bookseller*, 21 April 1984, p 18
461 *Newsletter of the English Association*, No 15, May 1984
462 Notes from the Rector of Appleton, Peter Wyld. Parts of these notes were published in the *Oxford Diocesan Magazine*, July 1984
463 Interview, Ken New, 14 July 2001
464 Phrase used by BB and adopted by Ved Metha for the title of his article for the *New Yorker*
465 Schollick, *The Bookseller*, 21 April 1984, p 19
466 BB to Alan Thomas, 24 October 1979
467 Correspondence between BB and Alan Thomas, March 75-October 1979
468 Letter, BB to Alan Thomas, 8 October 1979
469 *The Sunday Journal*, 6 December 1981
470 *Sun*, 9 January 1965
471 Boethius was the fitting subject for a symposium edited by Dr Margaret Gibson to mark BB's ninetieth birthday
472 Interview with Ved Metha, *Books and Bookmen*, January 1974, p 15
473 Norrie, *The Bookseller* 26 May 1979
474 C N Francis, *In Memoriam: Sir Basil Blackwell 1879–1984*
475 Ibid
476 Ibid

477 Henry Schollick summing up Basil in the words of Robert Bridges, *The Bookseller*, 21 April 1984
478 A text BB loved, from the opening page of vol. VII of Thomas North's *Plutarch's Lives of the Greeks and Romans*
479 Interviews with current Blackwell staff, who were recruited in the Gaffer's day
480 Henry Schollick's account of BB's life, *The Bookseller*, 21 April 1984
481 BB's own allusion to the Masefield poem, *Grace Before Ploughing*, 1966
482 The words of Robert Louis Stevenson, used as a requiem for Sir Basil, Thanksgiving Service, 31 May 1984
483 *The Lily*, March 1906, p 4
484 Jan Morris
485 C N Francis, *In Memoriam: Sir Basil Blackwell 1879–1984*
486 BB's own notes, written around the time of his eightieth birthday
487 C N Francis, *In Memoriam: Sir Basil Blackwell 1879–1984*
488 The term coined by Sir Arthur Norrington to describe Sir Basil Blackwell on the occasion of the conferment of the degree of Doctor of Civil Law, University of Oxford, 27 June 1979—one hundred years from the founding of the present business!
489 Richard Blackwell's description of the book trade, taken from Antigone
490 Jan Morris
491 From a page of a proof of an article for Oxford University Press dated 9 December 1907
492 *Books to Come*, BB, April 1948 p 14
493 *Vogue* July 1950
494 BB, dictated memoir 5 June 1963
495 Jan Morris, Daily *Telegraph* 1989
496 Op cit *Book World*, February 1984, p 2
497 Op cit *Book World*, February 1984, pp 2–3
498 The restoration of the Gaffer's Room was lovingly planned by his son Julian and his daughter Corinna. Julian Blackwell's generosity made the room, Blackwell's new Visitors' Centre, possible as did the work of John Thwaites (the current manager of Blackwell's Broad Street), Owen Dobbs, Rita Ricketts and Dudley Lincoln (architect)
499 Interview with the *Columbus Dispatch*, Tuesday, 7 September 1971
500 Ved Mehta, Oxford and the Gaffer, *Books and Bookmen*, January 1972, p 16
501 *Saturday Evening Post*, 7 April 1934
502 Richard de Bury
503 Op cit, Hilaire Belloc

Index

Note: BB in the index refers to Sir Basil Henry Blackwell; BHB refers to B H Blackwell's; BHB I refers to Benjamin Harris Blackwell (grandfather of Sir Basil); BHB II refers to Benjamin Henry Blackwell (father of Sir Basil).

Page references *in italics* indicate illustrations.

Acton, Harold 148, 150, 152
  'When Frigates from Long Voyages' 151
Adelaide University 285
adoption 242
Adventurers All 4, 20, 84, 152, 275, 300
Aeschylus 227, 263, 264
Aldus Manutius xii, 162, 246, 270
Alington, Cyril 169
Allen and Unwin 255
allotments 89
antiquarian book trade 210, 231–5, 286
Antiquarian Booksellers Association 107, 108, 231, 232–3, 234, 285
Antwerp 38–9
appeasement 252
Appleton, E R 154, 168
Appleton, Oxfordshire 65, 122, 198–9, 216, 217, 221, 244, 254
  church of St Lawrence 244, 273
  see also Osse Field
apprentices 64–7, 80–1, 97–9, 194
Arden Press 159, 256
Aristotle 10, 138
Arnold, Matthew 30, 224, 247, 265
  The Scholar-Gypsy 114, 265–6
  Thysis 235
Arts and Craft movement 160, 223
Ashbee, Edward 31
Ashcroft, Bertie 147
Asquith, H H, 1st Earl of Oxford 90, 192
Asterix 16, 145

Auckland Star 248
Auction and Bidding Agreements Acts 234
auction sales 232, 233
Auden, W H 152, 193
Austin, Dorothy *see* Blackwell
Austin, Sumner 120–1
authors 16, 173–4, 263
  rejecting 177–8
  women 150, 195
  see also poetry and poets *and names*

B H Blackwell imprint xi, 83, 84–8
B H Blackwell's
  bookshop 20–9
  opened in St Clements, High Street 29, 30, 40–4, 46, 61–2, 277–8, 283
  run by BH I 30
  after death of BH I 48–9
  opened in Broad Street 29, 37, 52–3, 60–1, 115, 284
  run by BH II 20–1, 24–5, 29, 32, 60–82, *61*, 92, 103, 115, 124, 137–8, 203, 207, 231, 281, 284
  1913 115
  on death of BH II 29, 115, 179, 285
  run by BB 1–2, 24, 25–9, 115, 121, 138, 179–207, 209, 212–13, 288–91, 124
  incorporated 100, 109, 192, 284–5
  shareholders 24, 109, 285

315

Index

centenary xi, 4, 246, 288, 314
today 13, 62, 115–16, 274–5,
  277–8, 280, 281–2, 288, 289
archive xiii–xvi, 2–3
Art Bookshop 287
binderies 183, 285
Board of Directors 67, 101, 109,
  179–80, 182, 281
customer lists 52
  1879 63
  mailing list, *1941* 190
as family home 52, 77, 91–2,
  123–4, 257–8, 284, 291
'Gaffer's Room' 2, 115, 123–4,
  181–2, 288–92, 314
innovations 24, 77
Norrington room 277–9, *28*, 183,
  280, 281, 287
overseas trade 24, 45–6, 71–2,
  172–3, 285–6, 287
stationery and publicity *113*
Visitors' Centre 291, 314
see also catalogues; computers; staff,
  BHB's
publishing xi, 6–7, 83, 88, 144–5
  academic 172–3
  by BHB II 82–8, 147–8, 150, 289,
    300–1
  by BB 144–78, 179, 236–7, 254–7,
    268, 269, 284
  Blackwell Scientific Publications
    173, 238, 285
Bacon, Sir Francis 261
Balliol, Oxford 17, 63, 83
Barclay's Bank, Oxford 76, 183,
  189–90, 227
Barfoot, Edith 174, 268
Barfoot, Geoffrey 66, 100, 172, 192,
  214
Baring, Maurice 85, 90
Basil Blackwell and Mott Ltd 145–7,
  150–7, 169–72, 179, 280,
  285
Basil Blackwell imprint 144, 179, 284
Bax, Clifford 152
Beacon, The 154
Beckford, William 299–300
Beeching, H C 17, 63, 73, 83, 84, 85–6,
  90
  ed. *Mensae Secundae* 83, 300

Beedham, R J 162
Bell, C F 257–8
bell-ringing 199, 221, 244
Belloc, Hilaire 85, 90, 98, 145, 306
  rebus design 90, 98
Ben Gurion, David 194
Berlin, Isaiah 152
Betjeman, Sir John 150, 151, 163, 193,
  247, 289, 312
Bibles 80, 141
Billings, printers 165, 171
binderies 16, 183, 285
Binyon, Laurence 85, 90, 148
Black, Sir Cyril 250
Blackwell, Anne (Nancy; *née* Stirling
  Lambert; grandmother of
  Basil) 37, 283, 304
  birth 50, 283
  early life 38, 50–4
  marriage 40, 50, 51, 283
  widowed and later life 48, 50–4, 55,
    56, 64, 77, 116–17, 283
  death 53, 284
Blackwell, Sir Basil Henry 25–6, *99*,
  107, *134*, *137*, *164*, *204*, *219*,
  220, *245*
  birth 26, 91, 123, 284
  childhood 10–11, 22, 55–6, 91–5,
    119–20, 123–4, 135, 191, 235,
    291
  education 124–37, 284
  university student xii, 126, 128–36,
    225, 289
  at OUP 141–3
  works in bookshop 100–1, 104, 115,
    137, 143
  marriage and family life 213, 214,
    215–25, 244, 267, 284
  on death of father 101, 114, 115,
    121, 138, 143, 179, 285
  runs bookshop 1–2, 24, 25–9, 115,
    121, 138, 179–207, 209,
    212–13, 288–91
  'Gaffer's Room' 2, 115, 123–4,
    181–2, 288–92, 314
  publishing 27, 144–78, 236–7,
    254–7, 268, 269, 284
  moves to Appleton 121–2, 216
  old age 1–2, 144, 198, 206, 243–7,
    269–71, 287, 290

death 272, 273
funeral 273
memorial service 274
appearance 127, 128
health 124, 225–6, 272
honours 115, 203, 244–6, 247–8, 287
  hon. Doctorate 3, 27, 203, 246, 288, 314
  Freedom of the City 217, 245
  knighthood 26, 115, 247–8, 286
and Oxford 25, 235–9, 243–7
papers and writing xi, 2–3, 4, 5–7, 10, 14, 32, 33, 53, 208, 268, 292–6
personality 115, 188–9, 198–9, 213, 249–52, 273
political views 31, 139–40
public duty 225–35, 238–44, 251
reading 213, 258–65, 266, 269–70
Beginning in Bookselling 2, 267
'Oh loyal heart farewell!' 192
'On a Dead Cat' 125–6, 307
Blackwell, Benjamin Harris (grandfather of Basil; BH I) 11, 37–50, 283
  birth 37, 283
  early life 37–40
  marriage 40, 50, 51, 283
  opens and runs shop 29, 30, 40–4, 46, 48, 277–8, 283
    catalogues 17, 46
  Oxford Librarian 44–5, 47
  death 46, 48–9, 283
  grave 49–50, *49*
  papers 4
  personality 47, 48
Blackwell, Benjamin Henry (Harry; father of Basil; BH II) 3–4, 55–116, 235, 300
  birth 55, 283
  childhood 8, 48, 51, 55, 56–7, 102, 116
  education 11, 33–4, 56, 58, 82, 102, 126–7
  apprenticeship 52, 56, 57–60, 102, 283, 284
  opens bookshop 52–3, 60–4, *61*, 115, 284

running shop 20, 24–5, 29, 32, 80, 92, 100–1, 103, 115, 137–8, 203, 207, 231, 281, 284, 289
  catalogues 17, 34, 64, 68, 77, 79, 80
  and publishing 82–8, 147–8, 150, 289, 300–1
  on Library Committee 66
marriage 53, 90–1, 103, 284
moves to Linton Road 91–2, 284
old age 96, 100–1
death 8, 20, 86, 101, 114, 179, 285
will 112
as father 92, 94–5, 123, 124, 127, 128, 143
hobbies 56–7, 66, 88–90
life-style 88–90
papers 4
personality 55–6, 92, 94, 102–4, 108, 112, 114, 116, 128, 137–8
photograph 115, 290
public offices 89
reading 58, 81–2
  book collection, *1878* 60–1
religion 55–6, 96
Blackwell, Christine, Lady (*née* Marion Soans; wife of Basil) 199, 213–25, *215*, 244, 256
  early life 213–14
  courtship 214
  at Appleton 199, 216–23, 244
  gardening 216, 217, 221, 225
  indexing 218, 256
  death 225, 269
Blackwell, Corinna (later Wiltshire; daughter of Basil) 13, 206, 220, 314
Blackwell, Dorothy (later Austin; sister of Basil) 3, 120–1
  birth 55, 91
  childhood 55–6, 91–2, 94–5, 117, 119–20, 123–4, 291
  career 96, 120–1
  accounts of family 3, 4, 48, 50, 55, 56, 64, 81–2, 97, 112, 116, 117, 118–19, 121, 303
Blackwell, Fred (uncle of Basil) 48, 52, 59, 284
Blackwell, Isaac (great-uncle of Basil) 37, 47, 283

Blackwell, Joshua (great-grandfather of
    Basil) 37–8, 39, 40, 283
Blackwell, Julian (son of Basil) xiv, 8,
    29, 121, 127, 128, 183, 187,
    214, 216, 221, 222, 223, 224,
    258, 273, 287, 290, 291–2,
    313, 314
  childhood 216–17, 221–2
  training 280–1
  Mott writes of xiv
  and father's memorials xiii, xv, xvi,
    2–3
  postscript by 280–2
Blackwell, Lilla (Lydia; *née* Taylor;
    mother of Basil) 91, 91–2, 94,
    116–20, 121–2, 128
  early life 8, 117–19
  marriage 90–1, 117
  personality 3, 117, 119
  widowed 116, 121
  death 119, 121
Blackwell, Matilda (aunt of Basil) 48,
    50
Blackwell, Nigel 29
Blackwell, Penelope (later Dame
    Penelope Jessell; daughter of
    Basil) 32, 216, 228
  childhood 216–17
Blackwell, Philip (grandson of Basil)
    29, 116
Blackwell, Richard (son of Basil) 7, 96,
    133, 145, 182, 188, 216, 250,
    260, 269, 287
  childhood 216–17
Blackwell (Basil) and Mott Ltd 145–7,
    150–7, 169–72, 179, 280, 285
'Blackwell Crawl' 25
Blackwell Scientific Publications 173,
    238, 285
Blackwell's Singers 90, 199, 200, 274
Blake, William 251
Bliss Court, Oxford 76
Blunden, Edmund 151, 193
  'Shells by a Stream' 225, 311
Blyton, Enid 145, 166
Bodleian Library 13, 67, 81, 203, 266
  BHB's bequest to 299–300
Bodley, Sir Thomas 44, 209
Boethius 271, 313, 290
Bohn, Henry 60

Book Clubs 98, 186
Book of English Essays, A 141
bookkeeping 188
books
  children's 70, 105, 145, 301
  classics 14, 154, 163, 164–5, 259
  good 14–16, 154, 213, 258–64, 291,
    292
  second-hand 46, 103, 210, 231–2
  survival 263–5
Bookseller, The 21, 192, 195
Booksellers Association 100, 108, 143,
    167–8, 170, 202, 231, 284,
    285, 311
  1906 Ripon Hall conference 74, 75,
    168
  1935 dinner 182
  Oxford and District Branch 108
booksellers, bookselling and bookshops
    16–18, 26, 31, 143, 179, 202,
    207–12
  in 19th-cent. 103
    Oxford 16–17, 44
  academic 22, 31, 204–6, 276–9
  antiquarian 231–5, 286
  customers 212
  see also B H Blackwell's
Boswell, James 189, 211
Boult, Sir Adrian 132
Bowra, Sir Maurice 50, 88, 238
Boynton, Sir Henry 157
Bradley, A C 73, 129
Bridges, Robert 85, 148, 192–3
  Nimium Fortunatus 273
Briggs, Asa 269
British Empire 23, 106
British Medical Association 234
British Museum 141
Broadbent, Jim 199
Broome (printer) 202
Brown, Phil 196, 199, 201
Brownrigg, C E 125
Buchan, John 85, 90, 148, 193
Bullen, A H 87, 138, 155–6, 159, 162,
    290
Bunting, George 192
Bunyan, John
  Pilgrim's Progress 44, 61
Burden, Jane 256
bureaucracy 12, 140, 244

Burne-Jones, Sir Edward 257
Burns, Robert 211
Burney, Edward 136
Burton, J H 80
Bywater, Ingram 64

Cambridge Poetry 85
Campbell, Roy
   The Flying Terrapin 84, 305
Carlyle, Thomas 15, 53
Carter, E H 168
Case, Mr (Corpus Christi don) 89
catalogues 17, 34, 57, 68, 79
   BHB's 17, 34, 46, 64, 80
   No 1 34, 64, 68–70, 69
   1879 69
   1884 79
   1886 70
   1888 34, 79, 107
   1894 70
   1895 70
   1907 77, 289
   1912 71
   covers 98
   'A Roll of English Writers' 17
cataloguing 98
censorship 250–1
Central News 178
Chadwick, Henry 194, 271
Chapman, R W 142
charity 89
Charles, Matthew 62
Chaucer, Geoffrey, works of 12, 14, 259
   Canterbury Tales 149, 262
      Shakespeare Head edition *156, 158*, 160–1
      quoted 258
      Kelmscott edition 161, 253–4
Chaundy, Fred W 64–5, 67–8, 73, 188–9, 284
Chaundy, Harry 65
Chaundy, Theodore 22
Cherwell, The 151
Chesterton, G K 145
children
   adoption 242
   crime 238–43
Children's Act 241
children's books 70, 105, 145, 301

Christianity 95, 252
church
   attendance 10–11, 57, 80, 88, 94–5, 266
   and education 11, 95, 306
   music 52, 95
   and Oxford University 23, 39–40
   see also churches; religion and faith
Church, Richard 152
church of St Lawrence, Appleton 244, 273
Church of St Cross, Holywell 49, 283
Church of St Mary the Virgin (University Church), Oxford 94–5, 274
Church of SS Philip and James, Oxford 59, 88, 91, 94, 97
   school 66
Churchill, Sir Winston 227
Churchman's Union 57, 62, 76
Classical Association 13, 268, 287
Clough, A H
   Dipsychus 102
Cole, G D H 148, 249, 289
Coleman, Terry 250
Collins, Clifford 72
Collins, Harry 45
Collins, Veve 141–2
Commonwealth 71–2
computers 13, 24, 209, 274, 276, 277, 280, 287, 288
Constable and Co. 186
Conventual Sisters of St Thomas 51
Crane, Walter 31
credit 78, 185
Cresset Press 161
crime 238–43
Crimean war 45
Critchley, Henry 109, 163, 167, 169, 191, 285
Critchley, John 191
Crossman, Richard 150
Cunard, Nancy
   'Wheels' 7–8, 84
Curtis (OUP secretary) 142
Curtis, Lionel 226–7, 311
Cutforth, John 199

Daily Herald 186
Daily Mail 86

Daily News 84
Dante, Alighieri
   Il Purgatorio 260
Darlington, W A
   Alf's Button 255, 312
Darwin, Charles 15, 39
Dasent, Sir George Webbe
   Burnt Njal 269
Davies, Mervyn 190
Davies, Tom 211
Day, Ann 197
de Bury, Richard 213
de la Mare, Walter 145, 193
death 271
Dent, J M 108, *139*, 141, 169
Dent Memorial Lectures 139–40, 177, 251, 308
Devine, Matt xvii
Dickens, Charles 82, 156, 259, 305
   The Old Curiosity Shop 240
   Oliver Twist 240
D'Israeli, Isaac 58, 79
Dodgson, Charles (Lewis Carroll) 67–8, 108
Doves Press 159
Drake a Day 182
Drayton, Michael 162
Duckworth, Gerald 108
Dulau and Co. 188–9
Dymond, Frederick 193–4
Dyson, Hugh 11, 193

Eagleston, Henry 43
East, Edward 193, 196
education 11, 15, 24, 104–6, 126–7, 243, 249, 301
   19th cent. 65–6, 80, 81, 95, 105, 306
   and church 11, 95, 306
   and crime 241–2
   further / adult 39, 89, 104
   for girls 105–6
   legislation 168
   in printing 159
   publishing for 127, 168–9, 301
   scholarships 105, 243, 249
   in wartime 171, 172–3
   see also universities
electronic publishing 116
Eliot, George
   Middlemarch 14
Eliot, T S 149, 163, 165, 193, 248, 301
embroidery 51
Empson, William 193
English Association 35–6, 81, 268
Ergoteles 265
Euripides 214
Europe 12, 31, 129, 227, 228
Evans, Margiad 150, 308
Evening Standard 103
Everyman's Library 71, 141
Ewart, William 44
Exeter College, Oxford 237, 248

Faber, Geoffrey 84, 141, 152, 289
Falcon Boat Club 59
Falkner, Meade 90
Farjeon, Eleanor 145
Farleigh, John 161
Farnell, L R 237
Feather, Jim 172, 198
Fenemore, S T 145, 147, 172
Field, Charles 78, 81, 109, 182, 192
First Edition Club 155
Flecker, James Elroy
   'Oxford Canal' 6
flowers 223–4
Fogden, Frank 145
Forster, Margaret
   Rich Desserts and Captains Thin 35
Fox, Adam 27
   poem by 27–9
Francis, Christopher 194, 269, 272, 275
Franklin, Colin 159, 161
Fraser, George 193
Froissart, Jean 259
   Chronicles 60, 160, 218
Frowde, Sir Henry 108, 141, 142, 143
Fyfe, W H 136

Gandell, Robert 107
Garrod, H W 136, 193
Garsington, near Oxford 12, 138–9
George, William 189
Georgeades, Petra xvii
Germany 285
   19th-cent. 23, 45–6
Gibb, James 70
Godley, A D 90
Gold Coast University 285

Golden Cockerel Press 161
Golding, Louis 151
Goldwater, Walter 23
Gooch, John 46
Goodman, Richard 152
Graham, Kenneth
    The Wind in the Willows 222, 311
Graves, Robert 193
Great Western Railway 42
Greene, Graham 148, 150, 246, 288
Greene, Vivien 244, 252
Griffith, John (Public Orator) 3, 27, 203, 246
Guedalla, Philip 84, 86, 148, 151

Hall (tailor) 238
Hall, Frederick 142
Hall, Sir Hugh 237
Hall, Thomas
    The Loathesomeness of Long Haire 70
Halliday, Eleanor 195-6, *196*, 197, 198
Hanks, Fred 24, 138, 191
    early life 65-6, 80, 97
    apprentice 66, 76, 80, 81, 97
    charge of infant Basil 123, 124, 191, 221, 249
    director of BHB 109, 182, 192
    honorary degree 81, 191
    memories *quoted* 123
    On the Handling of Classical Books 191, 200
Harcourt, Sir William 241
Hardy, Thomas 188, 259
Hardy, W R 90
Harraden, Beatrice 188
Harrod, Roy 150
Hart, Horace 142
Hartley, L P 150
Hartnoll, Phyllis 150, 308
Hebel, John William 162
Heffer's 194
Heinemann, William 108
Henty, G A 70
Herbert, George 85
Herbert, L F 149
Herbert, Sir Alan P 86, 148, 289, 300
    Play Hours with Pegasus 86
Higley, Vera 145

Hine, Ewart (Edgar) 67, 192-3
Hobbes, Thomas 38
Holmes, Oliver Wendell 73
Holywell cemetery 49-50, *49*, 283, 284
Home Guard 244
Homer 264
Hopkins, Gerry 141, 143
Horace xii, 5, 90, 149-50, 244, 246, 264
    Horace Society 90
House of Commons 44, 234
Housman, A E 14, 83, 84, 136, 149-50
    The Welsh Marches 5-6
Howard, Brian 151
Howe, Walter 136
Hunt, Richard 266
Hunt, Will 81, 109, 169, 182, 191-2
Hutchinson, Lucy 60
Hutton, W H 73
Huxley, Aldous 84, 85
    The Burning Wheel 300
    Out of the Window 152
Huxley, Julian 85, 152
Huxley, Thomas 39
hymnals 85-6

Indian Institute 71
industrial revolution 104
Initiatives 84, 152
Isherwood, Christopher 193

Jay, Douglas 152
Jeffs, Mother 125
Jenkins, Prof. 22
Jessell, Dame Penelope *see* Blackwell
Joachim, H H 136
Joan, St 263
Johnson, John 243
Johnson, Samuel
    on booksellers 17, 208, 251
    meets Boswell 211
Jonson, Ben 262-3
Jowett, Benjamin 78
Joy Street 145, *146*, 169, 301
Juvenile Courts 238-9, 240, 241-3

Keats, John 2, 265-6, 268
Kelmscott House 254, 255-6
Kelmscott Manor 6

Kelmscott Press 160, 253, 254
  Chaucer 161, 253–4
Kemp Hall Bindery 183, 285
Kendrick (compositor) 163
Kilpeck church 223
King, William (Rex) 3, 187–8, 193
  meets BHB II through City Library 66–7
  diaries 98, 193, 302
Knight, Wilson 224
Knox, Ronald 84, 148

Labour Party 228, 229, 281
Lackington, James 34, 79
Lamb, Lynton 160
Lambert (BHB cashier) 81
Lane, Allen 155, 168
language 33, 271
Larkin, Philip
  Annus Mirabilis 1
Laski, Harold 22
Laver, James 151
law, criminal 238–43
Lawrence, D H
  Lady Chatterley's Lover 250
Lawrence, H W 155
Lawrence, T E 130
Leonard, R M 308
Levitas, Lou 27, 303
Lewis, Cecil Day 150, 152, 193
Lewis, Clive S. 10
Lewis, Wyndham 153
Liberal Party 140, 227–8, 229
librarians 16, 209
libraries 44–5, 104, 212
  see also Bodleian Library; Oxford City Library
Lincoln, Dudley xvi, 314
Lloyd of Kilgerran, Baron 228, 311
Lobb, Miss 256
Lockwood, Henry 62, 73
Loggan, David
  Oxonia Illustrata 68
London 121, 171
  19th-cent. 37–8, 42
  OUP in 141–3
London County Council 171
London Daily News 20, 25
London Library 141
London Mercury 160

Longland, Austin 135–6, *135*, 270–1
Longman's 255
Lovelace, Gladys 145
Lucas, St John 90

Macaulay, Thomas Babington 58
MacDonald, James Ramsay 257
Mackail, J W 84, 85
  Life of William Morris 253
Mackenzie, Sir Compton 83, 85, 308
Macmillan, Alexander 103
Macmillan, Frederick 29, 108, 115
Macmillan, Sir Harold 203, 288
MacNeice, Louis 152, 153, 193
Magdalen College School 243–4, 249, 267
  BB a pupil at 124–6
  library, 195
  The Lily (school magazine) 125, 304, 307, 313, 314
Magistrates' Bench 238–43
Makower, Stanley 141
Man the World Over 147
Manchester Guardian 77–8
Mardon, Sarah 124
Marsh, Edward 84
Marten, C H K 169
Martial 262
Martin, David 172
Masefield, John 266, 274, 288
  Grace before Going 308
  Land Workers 29, 118
  Shopping in Oxford 25
materialism 10, 31, 271
Mathers, Powys 84, 151
Maxwell, Robert 251
Mayfair 251
Medley, Dudley 86
Melvin, Angela 197–9, *198*
Mensae Secundae 83, 300
Merton chapel 52
Merton College, Oxford xii–xiii, 3, 137, 216, 239
  BB undergraduate at 126–36, *127*, *129*
  burial ground 49–50
  Chapel 288
  Honorary Fellowship xii, 246
  Library xii–xiii, xvi, 3
    BB's gifts to xii, 299

Messer, Teressa 64, 65, 76
Meyerstein, E H W 84, 151
Milford, Humphrey 142
Mill, John Stuart 15
Milne, A A 145
Milton, John 2, 10, 58–9, 83, 89, 251, 259, 260
  Against Censorship 116, 181
  Lycidas 58
  Paradise Lost 53, 58–9
  Paradise Regained 19, 261
  Speech for the Liberty of Unlicensed Printing 15
Monkhouse, Patrick 152
Morell, Lady Ottoline 139
Morison, Stanley 159–60
Morley, Christopher 85, 86–7, 151, 289
  The Eighth Sin 151, 289
Morris, Jan 20, 26, 121, 237, 247, 290, 302
Morris, May 218, 253, 254–7
Morris, William 2, 31, 138, 140, 148, 154–5, 159, 160, 189, 216, 223, 249, 253–4, 255, 256–7, 258
  memorial hall for 256–7
  textiles and wallpapers 2, 123, 257–8, 290, 313
  La Belle Iseult 255
  Collected Works 218, 256
  Earthly Paradise 253
  News from Nowhere 258
  William Morris: Artist, Writer, Socialist 256
  William Morris Society 257, 312
Morris, William Richard, 1st Viscount Nuffield 106, 112, 237–8
Mott, Sir Adrian 144–5, 246
  Basil Blackwell and Mott Ltd 145–7, 150–7, 169–72, 179, 280, 285
  notes *quoted* xiv, 160, 167, 170, 220, 239, 309
Munksgaard, Copenhagen 4, 287
Murray, Gilbert 85, 148, 214
Murray, Sir James 94
music 199
  BHB Music Dept. 194, 285
  Dorothy Blackwell 120
  church 52, 95

Nation, The 150
National Book Council 171, 181
Net Book Agreement 103, 108, 202
New, Ken 196–7, 209, 268
New College, Oxford 216
New Oxford Outlook 151, 152
New Statesman 194
New York bookshops 23–4
New Yorker, quoted 23, 187
New Zealand 2, 72, 248
Newdigate, Bernard 87, 88, 138, 155, 156–63, 165, 166–7, 253, 256, 285, 301, 309
Newdigate, Sir Roger 157
Newdigate Prize 84, 150, 157, 195
Newsom, John 181–2
Nichols, Beverly 21, 150, 168
Nichols, Robert 84
Nicols, Bowyer 83
Nonesuch Press 155
Norfolk 117–20
Norrington, Sir Arthur 4, 224, 272, 314
  Blackwell's 1879–1979: The History of a Family Firm xi, 4, 34, 68, 70, 79, 90, 102, 204, 246, 285
Norton, Lord 240
Nuffield, William R Morris, 1st Viscount 106, 112, 237–8

Ode to our only Customer 18–19
Ode to Scholarship 21
Oman, C W C 84
O'Neill, Gilda 5
Oriel College, Oxford 170
Osse Dyke Brook 222
Osse Field, Appleton 122, 168, 199, 218, 220–1, 226
  garden 199, 215, 221, 223, 225
  library 217, 259–60, 269
Owen, Wilfred 12, 148, 150, 300
Oxford xiii, 13, 21–2, 30, 121, 235–8, 292
  19th-cent. 38, 39–44, 41, 57, 105, 106–7, 117
  early 20th-cent. 71–2, 109, 125, 244
  mid 20th-cent. 189
  Bliss Court 76
  bookmaking in, early 43

Broad Street 20, 62, 76–7, 183, 189, 235, 285
  19th-cent. 20, 52–3, 60, 61–4, 61, 73, 76, 91–2, 189, 284, 291
canal 6
Freedom of the City 43, 217, 245
High Street 52, 57
  St Clements 30, 40, 43, 61, 283
Holywell cemetery 49–50, *49*, 283, 284
Holywell Street 52, 77, 283, 184
Jews Mount (Bulwarks Lane) 51, 283, 304
Linton Road, Summertown 92, *93*, 216, 284
Magdalen Bridge xiii, *41*, 43
Post Office 187
tour guides 90
'Town and Gown' 12, 42–3, 106–7, 117, 128, 237, 238, 247
trade 40–3
traffic 24, 221, 252, 292
Turl Street 47–8, 51, 283
Oxford Chronicle 21, 46, 106, 114, 292
Oxford City 30, 40, 43, 66, 107, 244
Oxford City Council 4, 89, 96, 100, 101
Oxford City Library 30, 44–5, 46, 48, 103, 247, 283
  Committee 66, 96
Oxford English Dictionary 171
Oxford High School 105, 120–243
Oxford Journal 46
Oxford Magazine 63, 92
Oxford Movement 51, 62, 189
Oxford Outlook 150, 151, 152
Oxford Poetry 85, 148, 151, 153
Oxford Preservation Trust 238
Oxford Prison 238
Oxford Society for the Blind 89
Oxford Teetotal Society 47, 48
Oxford Times 4
Oxford Union 70, 107–8, 284
Oxford University xiii, 21–2, 30, 81, 105–6, 107
  19th-cent. 23, 39–43
  Church 94–5, 274
  Drama Society 132

Honorary Doctorate 3, 27, 203, 246, 314
Medical School 238
Officers Training Corps 130, *130*, *131*, 225
scouts 131
Sheldonian Theatre 25, 26, 62, 115, 247
Town and Gown 12, 42–3, 106–7, 117, 128, 237, 238, 247
women 105
see also names of colleges; students
Oxford University Press 143, 280
  in London 141–3, 144, 173, 284
  in WW II 171

Palmer, C A 191
paper 159, 171, 172
Parker, Charles *107*, 108, 189
Parker, Ernest 167, 169–70
Parker, Samuel 189
Parker's bookshop, Broad Street 43, 44, 189, 251
Parsons, Mr (banker) 76
paternalism 8, 185
Pelican 155, 168
Penguin Books 155, 168
People's Palace, The 84
Philadelphia Evening Post, quoted 21–2
Pindar 265
Plantin of Antwerp 38–9
Plantin type 7
Play Hours with Pegasus (proposed volume) 300–1
Plutarch's Lives of the Greeks and Romans 273
poetry and poets
  published by BHB 4, 83–5, 86–7, 147, 148–54, 289, 300–1
  'Wheels' 7–8, *9*
  women 195
  typesetting 162
  war 12, 171
politics 8–10, 40, 89, 128, 140, 227–9, 249
pornography 250–1
Post Office 187, 287
Pound, Ezra 149
Powell, Laurence Clark 25–6
Priestley, J B 193

Primavera 83
printing, 16
　fine 31–2, 87, 154–6, 157–67, 254, 268–9
Prison 238, 239–40, 241
Private Press Movement 32, 154
Public Libraries Act 44–5, 283
publishers 16
Publishers Association 143, 144, 230
publishing 143–4, 177–8, 207, 230–1, 251
　after WW I 154
　by BHB xi, 6–7, 83, 88, 144
　　academic 173
　by BHB II 82–8, 103–5, 147–8, 150, 289, 300–1
　by BB 144–78, 179, 236–7, 254–7, 268, 269, 284
　educational 127, 168–9, 171, 172, 301
　see also names of presses
Punch 42
Pynson, Richard
　Ship of Fools edition 34, 79

Quakers 46–7
Quaritch, Bernard 34, 57, 68, 79, 102, 232, 306
Queen's College Choir School 56
Quenell, Peter 151

Radcliffe, John 70
railway 42, 171
Rawson, Jessica 3
reading 258–65, 266, 267
　women 214
religion and faith 39–40, 55–6, 95–6, 252, 271–2
　see also church
retail price maintenance 108
Rhodes Scholars 71–2, 173
Rhodes University 72
Richards, Charles 48, 57, 283
Richards, Grant 141
Richards, Sir Rex 274
Richard's shop, High Street 52, 57, 58, 284
Rieu, E V 141
'Ring', the (book dealers) 6, 231–5, 249–50

Ripon Hall Conference, *1906–74* 75, 168
Robertson, Ian 172
Roby, Gladys 310
Rodd, James Rennell 84
Rogers, Bruce 161
Rose, Mr (of Slatter & Rose) 59, 60
Rosebery, Archibald Primrose, 5th Earl 20
Routledge, George 48
Routledge and Co. 48–9
rowing 57, 59, 126, 132–4, *133, 134, 135,* 218, 236, 243
Rowse, A L 151, 152, 308
Roy, David 179
Royal Academy 192
Ruskin, John 31, 154, 278
Russell, Bertrand 12, 139, 249

Sackville West, Vita, *quoted* 6
Sadler, Sir Michael 88, 148, 237, 306
Sanderson, Cobden 159
Sanderson's 290, 313
Sanskrit 174, 176–7
Sassoon, Siegfried 151
Sayers, Dorothy L 3, 84, 151, 194, 195, 300
　as editor for BHB 144
　Peter Wimsey 244, 252
Scarrott, Charlie 131
scholars 103, 173, 265–7
Schollick, Henry L 126, 160, 162, 167, 170, 172, 173, 182, 224, 235, 266, 267, 269, 274, 280, 307
Scott, Sir Walter 211, 259
Seaman, Owen 90
Selby, H
　Last Exit to Brooklyn 250–1
Shakespeare, William 262–3, 269
Shakespeare Head Press 87–8, 138, 145, 155–67, 254, 256, 285, 290
　Chaucer 156, *158,* 160–1
　Complete Works of Shakespeare 165–6, 285, 301
Shaw, George Bernard 249, 256, 257
　letters exchanged with BB 186–7
　Saint Joan 263
Sheldonian Theatre, Oxford 25, 26, 62, 115, 247

Shelley, P B
  Ozymandias 264–5
Shelton, Jo 34
Sherbourn, James 145, 147
Shops and Offices Act 307
Sibbald, James 211
Sidgwick, Frank 87, 155, 306
Sitwell, Edith 7, 84, 242–3
  The Mother 147
Sitwell, Osbert 84
Sitwell, Sacheverell 84
Slatter & Rose 52, 58, 59, 60, 284
Smith, Frederick Edwin 78
Smith, W H 159
Soans, Marion Christine, *see* Blackwell, Christine
socialism 8, 10, 139–40
Society of Bookmen 171, 181
Solomon
  Proverbs 213
Song of Songs 150
South Africa 286
Sparrow, John 150
Spencer, Herbert 39
Spender, Stephen 85, 151, 152, 153, 193, 289
Spenser, Edmund
  Faerie Queene 82
St Cross College, Oxford 288
St Gregory's Press 157
St John's College, Oxford 3
St Louis Post-Dispatch 248
staff BHB's 8–10, 12, 180, 266, 313
  and BHB II 97–100, 108–12
  1921 24
  1922 145, 146
  and BB 184–5, 192–203, 205–6
  profit-sharing 24, 285
  recruitment 196, 197, 198, 218
  students 194–5, 313
  women 195–6, 197–9, 218, 223–4
Stafford Prison 239–40
Stainer, John 50
Steel, David 228, 229
Steele, Bert 109, 112
Sterne, Laurence 259
Stevens, Fred 67
Stevenson, Anne
  Dreaming of (More) Spires 34–5
Stevenson, Robert Louis, *quoted* 273

Stirling Lambert, Anne *see* Blackwell, Anne (Nancy)
Stirling Lambert, John Thomas 53
Stonyhurst school 157
Strachey, J St Loe 73, 84
Strong, L A G 151
Stroud, George Edmund 59
Stubbs, William 20, 279
students 25, 103, 105, 173, 267, 288, 289
  BHB staff 194–5, 313
Suckling, John 79
Swift, Jonathan 38
Swing, Charlie xvii

taxation 31, 172
Taylor, Charlotte (aunt of Basil) 90–1, 119
Taylor, Jack (uncle of Basil) 118, 119–20
Taylor, John (grandfather of Basil) 118–19
Taylor, Lydia, *see* Blackwell, Lilla
teetotalism (temperance) 11, 40, 44, 47, 48, 92, 283
Templeton, Tom 201
theology 194
Thomas, Alan 257, 269, 270
Thompson, John 76, 183
Thornton (Joseph) and Son 189
Thucydides 126, 129
  quoted 101
Thwaites, John xvi, 277, 314
  epilogue by 276–9
Tillotson, Kathleen 162
Times, The 42, 108, 166, 260
  BB writes to 233–4
Times Book Club 98
Tolkien, J R Ronald 85, 148, 193, 289
Tomlinson, Steven xvi, 203, 310
Toynbee, Arnold 31, 227
transportation 239, 240
Trollope, Anthony 70, 162, 163, 191
Tschichold, Jan 155
Tuchmann, Barbara 260
Tuckwell, William 125
Tupper, Martin 251
Turl Cash Bookshop 47, 48
typography 7, 142, 156–67

United States of America 23–4, 45–6, 71, 72, 173, 286
universities 23, 105–6, 243
  overseas 23, 72, 285–6
  see also names
University Extension Movement 81, 89
Unwin, Sir Fisher 82
Unwin, Sir Stanley 167–8, 170–1, 181, 255

Vaisey, David 300
Verlaine, Paul 76
Victoria, Queen 241
Vincent, Mr (church warden) 10–11, 95
Vincent Press 84
Vines, Sherrard 148
Virgil, *quoted* 133–4, 222

Waifs and Strays 83
Walker, Emery 155, 157, 160, 163
Walker, Ernest 120
Walpole, Hugh 171, 181
war 12, 129–30, 171
  see also World War I; World War II
War Office 160, 225
Ward, Arnold 90
Wareham, George 191
Warner, Maggie 195
Warren, T H 90
Waugh, Evelyn
  Brideshead Revisited 21, 137
Weaver's Guild 42
West, Rebecca 17
Wheels poetry series 7–8, 9, 84, 150
White, Cuthbert 203, 221, 252, 281, 292

William Morris Society 257, 312
Williams, Alfred 174–6, 177
Williams, Charlie 50, 143
Williams, Emlyn 152
Williams, Mary 174, 175–7
Williamson, Hugh 185
Wilson, Angus 193
Wiltshire, Corinna *see* Blackwell
Witner, Andrew 206
Wittgenstein, Ludwig 16, 173
women
  authors 150, 195
  of Blackwell family 32, 119, 120
  BHB staff 195–6, 218, 223–4
  education 105, 131–2, 247
  as readers 214
  Victorian 53
Wooldridge, H E 85
Woolworth's stores 313
Wordsworth, William, *quoted* 14, 101, 181
Workers Educational Association 104
World War I 129–30, 136, 225–6
  and publishing 154
World War II 140, 143, 148, 226, 244
  BB's plan to avert 252
  Dorothy Blackwell in 120–1
  publishing in, 160, 171–3, 189–91
World's Classics 71, 141
Worthen, John 5
Wynkyn de Worde 33, 161

Yattendon Hymnal 85–6
Yeats, W B 87, 193
Your Career at Blackwell's 200

Zimmern, A E 90

Tailpiece The 1920 *Adventurers All* title page opening.

THE RED DRAGON

BY

LLWELYN SLINGSBY BETHELL

OXFORD
BASIL BLACKWELL, BROAD STREET,
1920